# Milan Systemic Family Therapy

# Milan Systemic Family Therapy

*Conversations in Theory and Practice*

LUIGI BOSCOLO
GIANFRANCO CECCHIN
LYNN HOFFMAN
PEGGY PENN

*Basic Books, Inc., Publishers*          *New York*

*To our trainees*

Library of Congress Cataloging-in-Publication Data

Milan systemic family therapy.

   Bibliographic references: p. 331.
   Includes index.
   1. Contextual therapy—Case studies.   2. Family
psychotherapy—Case studies.   I. Boscolo, Luigi.
RC488.55.M55   1987          616.89'156          86–71985
ISBN 0–465–04596–0

Copyright © 1987 by Basic Books, Inc.
Printed in the United States of America
Designed by Vincent Torre
with Barbara DuPree Knowles
87 88 89 90 RRD 9 8 7 6 5 4 3 2 1

# CONTENTS

# ACKNOWLEDGMENTS

T HE AUTHORS would like to acknowledge first of all the inspiring work of Dr. Mara Selvini Palazzoli and Dr. Guiliana Prata; it was part of the matrix within which this book evolved. We are also greatly indebted to Dr. Karl Tomm, Dr. Esther Gelcer, and Dr. Helm Stierlin for their help. Last but not least, our thanks go to Jo Ann Miller, whose patience and intelligence as an editor were crucial in getting the book into its final form.

# HOW THIS BOOK WAS MADE

T HIS IS A BOOK that evolved the way ancient cities did. It started with a happy confluence of features and proceeded by a mixture of hopeful planning and serendipitous design. Luigi Boscolo and Gianfranco Cecchin came to Peggy Penn and myself in 1982 and asked if we would help them write a book. We thought of an interview book along the lines of the one Jay Haley and I did in 1969 (*Techniques of Family Therapy*); they readily agreed. We felt that the collaboration would have an informal usefulness in extending the relationship we had already established with Boscolo and Cecchin.

In addition, the work of Boscolo and Cecchin was becoming more and more influential. They were presenting their evolving model at workshops here and abroad. However, they had produced almost no written explications of their newer ideas. As a result, there seemed to us to be a hole in the field, and we were anxious to see that hole filled.

Peggy and I had been working together on the systemic model at the Ackerman Institute for Family Therapy in New York and adding to it our own innovations. Peggy was interested in extending the scope of interviewing techniques, using a circular format to explore future and hypothetical questions. I had been studying the constellation of new ideas that linked cybernetics to the life sciences in my search for a conceptual framework for systemic therapy.

In addition, we had been deeply impressed by Gregory Bateson's thinking in reference to the development of the family systems movement. We had been looking for a therapeutic approach that would fit with Bateson's ethic of ecological carefulness and his distrust of technologies too grounded in purposiveness. Boscolo and Cecchin's attention to the systemic context of therapy and their use of techniques that are non-strategic and somewhat non-instrumental—like circular questioning—seemed to bring the field more closely in line with Bateson's general stance. This was another reason why we wished to make Boscolo and Cecchin's own account of their work available in written form.

A preface on origins would not be complete without a comment on Peggy's and my work marriage. We had been colleagues at the Ackerman Institute for Family Therapy since 1976. We decided to form our own team to experiment with the newly evolving Milan method and this led us to develop our own material which we presented at workshops. When I left Ackerman to relocate to Amherst, I cast about for some way to keep Peggy and me connected; and the opportunity to work together on a book with Boscolo and Cecchin seemed like a wonderful solution.

Four persons, then, are the authors of this book. At the beginning, we all sat down together and watched the videotaped family interviews that Boscolo and Cecchin had selected as representative of their work. During this process, we audiotaped both the family sessions and the conversations the four of us had about those sessions. Text was thus interspersed with commentary. Peggy and I edited the conversations and wrote the introductions. Boscolo and Cecchin furnished the family sessions and shared the ideas that had gone into them.

In general, Peggy and I confined ourselves to eliciting ideas from Boscolo and Cecchin about what they thought they were doing step by step through each case and what generalities of theory and practice could be drawn from the specifics. To have used the conversations as a means of putting forward our own theories and techniques would have made this more a book on comparative practice, so we were fairly ruthless in cutting out extraneous comments. We kept our opinions for the introductory sections that we wrote ourselves.

The initial transcripts of our discussions, which comprised more than twenty-five hours of audiotape, created a mass of material to be boiled down and revised. That alone took nearly two years.

The need to choose sessions that were conducted in English was another constraint. All the cases used were families interviewed at workshops in English-speaking settings, and the interviews consequently all had the imprint of teaching consultations. However, Boscolo and Cecchin do not differentiate greatly between family interviews, consultations with "stuck" therapists, and interviews with professionals from larger systems outside the family. All are varieties of consultations. In addition, each single interview is seen in some sense as standing alone rather than embedded in a course of treatment, as traditionally perceived. As Boscolo and Cecchin view their work, each time they see a family they engage with a different system than the one they saw before. Thus, the fact that all these cases were consultations did not seem to make as much difference as it might have with therapists who work in a less episodic way.

The first three cases were the ones we initially used as a basis for our discussions. As the rough draft of the manuscript was being furnished, Peggy saw a tape of a session Boscolo and Cecchin had done with a family in Germany. She felt that it gave an extraordinarily clear impression of the Milan Associates' use of circular questioning. The first three cases had been done between 1978 (when the original Milan team, including Mara Selvini and Guiliana Prata, was still together) and the early 1980s (after the two men had started their teaching institute). By 1984, when the fourth interview was done, the technique of circular questioning had been greatly simplified and refined. Here, due to time constraints, Boscolo and Cecchin did their own interviewing, which is why the case differs in format from the other conversations in the book.

These conversations evolved spontaneously, according to what was suggested by the videotaped material; there was no thought of following a preordained schedule. Our hope was that sooner or later all aspects of Boscolo and Cecchin's work would be attended to, given enough criss-crossing by the participants. This process would bear a resemblance to the circular questioning in the family sessions. No one "move" is important; what is important is the building up of information as many perspectives on many levels are layered and contrasted and brought into play.

This free-handedness, however, called for an introduction to each case that would highlight the major issues covered. Peggy took on this task, and I took on the task of writing a historical introduction that would place the work of the two men within the larger context of the Milan method. In these sections, we tried to keep our voices clear and personal. We felt throughout that a work that took a "scientific" or "objective" stance, even with the quotation marks left in, would not be true to the larger philosophical context the four of us subscribe to. According to this context, there is no truth "out there" about which any of us can be objective or scientific.

Unlike many schools of therapy, the Milan method has been the product of an international collaboration between Boscolo and Cecchin and many other teams in different countries. Because the therapeutic concept involved teams from the start, the learning could take place in settings other than that of the originators. However, for there to be some coherence, it was important that Boscolo and Cecchin visit the daughter teams now and again. The incessant looping between the two men and these newer groups has meant continual movement and change. As soon as one feature had been codified, a new wrinkle would be added and the procession would move on. Between the time Boscolo and Cecchin first conducted the interviews in this book and the time they commented on them together with Peggy and me, their ideas had changed. So had our own. The commentary reflects the evolution of the ideas of all four of us as well as an exegesis of the material commented on.

By the time the reader has finished the book, yet another chapter of the conversation will have evolved. One could say that the predicament of the reader of this book is like the time confusion experienced by a student of the heavens. The student knows that the light from any star represents events that for the star are now light-years in the past. But the student uses these past events to shed light on processes going on in the present. In this way, the four of us hope that this book will shed light on the mysterious processes that go on in families and in their conversations with the professionals who are struggling with them to understand these processes.

LYNN HOFFMAN

# Milan Systemic Family Therapy

All names, locations, and other identifying characteristics of the family members mentioned and/or quoted in this book have been changed.

# INTRODUCTION

# *From Psychoanalysis to Systems*

THIS BOOK deals with the therapy and teaching of Luigi Boscolo and Gianfranco Cecchin. Their work, profoundly contextual in every respect, must itself be seen in the context of ongoing development in the field of family systems therapy. In 1967 Boscolo and Cecchin joined a group of eight psychiatrists organized by Mara Selvini Palazzoli, a child analyst in Milan. The group's intention was to treat severely disturbed children together with their families. Their orientation was psychoanalytic, however, and at first they struggled with the problem of how to apply analytic concepts to families. This effort proved exciting but discouraging. Therapy seemed to take a very long time, and the therapists were frustrated by what they felt was a lack of results. Only the families were satisfied. They continued to come despite the lack of improvement.

In 1972, the group became fascinated by accounts of family therapy and research that had been done under the aegis of anthropologist Gregory Bateson in the United States. During the 1950s, Bateson was involved in a project on communication in Palo Alto, California, which, in the 1960s, became the Mental Research Institute directed by psychiatrist Don D.

Jackson. The Milan group was greatly influenced by the work of the Mental Research Institute (MRI), in particular the book *Pragmatics of Human Communication* by Paul Watzlawick, Don Jackson, and Janet Beavin (1967).

These writers felt that the psychodynamic approach was incorrect in focusing on the individual as the "container" of pathology. They felt that this view ignored the contributions of the relationship context in which the problem behaviors took place. Chief among such contexts was the family. If interaction patterns in the family could change, these pioneers argued, the problem behavior would also change.

This debate between the psychoanalytic model and the family systems model was transferred to Milan, where a serious consideration as to whether these two models were compatible took place. Deciding that they were not compatible, Selvini, Boscolo, Giuliana Prata, and Cecchin split off in 1971 from the original group with the aim of working exclusively within a family systems—or, as they later called it, a *systemic*—framework. The new group formed the *Centro per il Studio della Famiglia*—Center for the Study of the Family—in Milan. Watzlawick of the MRI consulted to the group in its early days.

During most of the 1970s, the group acted as a therapeutic team that met for two days a week and saw an average of two families a day. The interview format was divided into five parts: the presession, the session, the intersession, the intervention, and the postsession discussion. During the presession, the team came up with an initial hypothesis about the family's presenting problem. Only two members would meet with the family. During the session itself, the team members would validate, modify, or change the hypothesis. After about forty minutes, the entire team would meet alone to discuss the hypothesis and arrive at an intervention. The treating therapists would then go back to deliver the intervention to the family, either by positively connoting the problem situation or by a ritual to be done by the family that commented on the problem situation and was designed to introduce a change. (A *positive connotation* is a message to the family from the therapist[s] that the problem is logical and meaningful in its context. A *ritual* is an ordering of behavior in the family either on certain days [odd days, even days] or at certain times [after dinner, in the morning]). Finally, the team would meet for a postsession discussion to analyze the family's reactions and to plan for the next session.

The team was divided into two male-female couples, one couple interviewing the family while the other couple stayed behind a one-way mirror and acted as observers. This method was later changed so that only one therapist sat in the room with the family. At first, based on the Palo Alto practice of time-limited therapy, the families were told that they would be seen for ten sessions; later this rule was abandoned in favor of following the timing of each particular case. The period between sessions was lengthened from a week to a month when it was found that this interval (initially proposed to accommodate families that traveled long distances) respected the longer time period needed for a family system to show evidence of change.

When they first started working together, the group agreed on a number of ideas. Their theory of pathology derived in great part from the Bateson project's focus on double-bind communication, exemplified by self-contractory messages from a parent to a child like: "Stay away closer." Following Bateson, the central issue in families with a schizophrenic was described in terms of a "mistaken epistemology," for example, that any one person can unilaterally control relationships. Since this notion is linear—that is, implies a one-way causality—and interaction is circular, or reciprocal, it is incorrect and leads to a vicious cycle. One person's attempt to establish control leads to another person feeling threatened and trying in turn to establish control. An endless game ensues where no one can clearly win or lose. The "paradox" lies in the oscillation that is set up between "win" and "lose" positions. (One must remember that Bateson's original interest in the way such double-bind sequences worked was sparked by hearing that when early computers were confronted by a logical paradox, such as the assertion "All statements within this box are lies," they would go into an endless "pathological" oscillation from yes to no.)

## The Influence of the Mental Research Institute

Although many of the ideas proposed by the Bateson project flowed into the work of the Mental Research Institute, the two projects had different basic philosophies. The therapy model that evolved during the early years of the Mental Research Institute took an essentially "strategic" stance. Bateson, on the other hand, had a profound distrust of the manipulative use of any kind of technology, physical, social, or psychological. He openly disagreed with researcher Jay Haley, who was brought in by Bateson during the early days of his project and who proposed that at the heart of the psychotherapeutic process was a struggle for control (Haley, 1976). This quarrel was never resolved, as subsequent attempts to review project history make plain.*

However, at the time the Milan group was formulating its ideas, the Bateson-Haley disagreement was only an underground rumbling of which few people knew. As a result of this hidden disagreement, there is in early writings of the Milan group, especially in *Paradox and Counterparadox* (Selvini Palazzoli, Boscolo, Cecchin, and Prata, 1978), an implicit contradiction between the influence coming from the Mental Research Institute's frankly manipulative approach to therapy and the Batesonian respect for "systemic wisdom," by which Bateson meant an understanding of the unintended consequences of the ways in which human conscious purpose tampered with the natural world.

Despite this confusion, the Milan group came up with their own formulations:

1. Families in schizophrenic transaction, as the group called their target population, are involved in unacknowledged family "games."
2. In these games, family members try unilaterally to control each other's behaviors.
3. The task of the therapist is to discover and interrupt these games.

In their therapeutic techniques, the group took some of the methods pioneered by the Mental Research Institute and expanded them. The therapeutic double bind (Watzlawick, Jackson, and Beavin, 1967), or, as the Milan group called it, "counterparadox," became the heart of their approach. The entire problem situation would be positively connoted, for instance, and the family warned against premature change. The strategic tasks that Mental Research Institute researchers suggested be performed at the end of an interview, such as telling a bed-wetter to deliberately wet the bed on specified days, found a counterpart in the Milan group's use of rituals. In addition, the Milan group formalized the practice of having therapists behind a one-way mirror, which was used at the Mental Research Institute for research purposes and by the Milan group as part of on-going therapy as well.

* Bateson later commented as follows on Haley's "Development of a Theory: A History of a Research Project" (Sluzki and Ransom, 1976, p. 106):

> . . . Haley slides too lightly over very real epistemological differences between himself and me. As I saw it, he believed in the validity of the metaphor of "power" in human relations. I believed then—and today believe even more strongly—that the *myth* of power always corrupts because it proposes such a false (though conventional) epistemology. I believe that all such metaphors . . . are . . . a groping in a wrong direction, and the direction is not less wrong or less socially pathogenic because the associated mythology is in part self-validating among those who believe it and act upon it.

The Milan group's pronounced adversarial stance could also be seen to evolve from the Palo Alto model. In line with the Milan group's initial focus on resistance, clients and therapists were described almost as if they were opponents. The therapeutic encounter was expressed in terms of "secret battles," "denied coalitions," "moves," "counterattacks," "escalations," "tactics," and "ploys." Much of this language may have been inherited from the influence of game and coalition theory on the Bateson project, which took place during the Cold War. Early Mental Research Institute writing, in fact, is full of Cold War terminology. It is possible that the Cold War furnished an unconscious analogy for descriptions of schizophrenic transactions and for transactions between therapists and families as well.

Whatever the source, original Milan team discussions sounded like councils of war. The therapists took care, however, not to challenge the family openly. They preferred to operate like guerrillas, using creative deceptions that would bypass clients' "resistance." Much time and thought was spent on ways to keep the family from rendering the team powerless. The paradoxical prescription was favored because, as Jay Haley often explained, there was no way a family could resist a therapist who told them to continue with the behaviors they were already engaged in unless they gave up those behaviors (Haley, 1963).

## The Positive Connotation

The most compelling invention of the Milan team, and the one that led to a new therapeutic gestalt, was the positive connotation. While this is often taken to be similar to the strategy of positive reframing (for example, suggesting a good motive for a negative behavior), actually it is much closer to a restructuring of the therapist's consciousness. The positive connotation evolved from the Palo Alto therapists' technique of prescribing the symptom: if a woman was phobic, they might "paradoxically" place that person under house arrest. But the Milan group perceived that by supporting the symptom, they negatively connoted family members' anti-symptom views. It was as if there had to be a cause to pin the blame on, and if one exonerated the symptomatic member, other family members would feel at fault. Such, they explained, was the tyranny of the linguistic conditioning of western linear causality.

This implicit division of the family into "good" and "bad" elements,

8INTRODUCTION

they further reasoned, not only perpetuated the symptomatic mythology but made it impossible to envision the family as a systemic unity. As a result, they decided to positively connote not only the behavior of the identified patient but the symptomatic behavior of the other family members as well. As the group states in *Paradox and Counterparadox* (Selvini Palazzoli, Boscolo, Cecchin, and Prata, 1980, p. 56): ". . . the primary function of the positive connotation of all the observable behaviors of the group is that of permitting the therapists access to the systemic mode."

A good example is the case of a family in which a little boy of eight had been brought in by the parents. Since his grandfather's death the boy had stopped doing well in school and was talking and acting like a caricature of a little old man. He insisted he saw his grandfather following him when he took walks with his father. The message the therapists gave to the boy went as follows:

MALE THERAPISTS: We are closing this first session with a message to you, Ernesto. You're doing a good thing. We understand that you considered your grandfather to be the central pillar of your family [the hand of the therapist moved in a vertical direction as if tracing an imaginary pillar]; he kept it together, maintaining a certain balance [the therapist extended both hands in front of him, palms down, both at the same level]. Without your grandfather's presence you were afraid something would change, so you thought of assuming his role, perhaps because of this fear that the balance in the family would change [the therapist slowly lowered his right hand, which corresponded to the side where the father was seated]. For now you should continue in this role that you've assumed spontaneously. You shouldn't change anything until the next session, which will be January 21, five weeks from now. (Selvini-Palazzoli, Boscolo, Cecchin, and Prata, 1979, p. 81)

At the end of the message, the boy jumped up and began to complain about the fact that he might be left back at school. He immediately started to do better at his studies and, over the next few sessions, the little-old-man behavior and the hallucinations stopped.

One can see that the positive connotation does not address itself to particular persons so much as to the self-maintaining tendencies of the system as a whole. The therapists prescribe the symptom not in a vacuum, or with a persuasive rationale, as a strategic therapist might do, but in relation to its social context—in the service of the family's "homeostasis" or some aspect thereof. In so doing, the family's need to protect its equilibrium is respected and the risk of increasing the family's resistance to change is thereby reduced.

The idea of positive connotation was a strong testimonial to the emerging nonlinear, systemic consciousness that was to distinguish the Milan method

from previous approaches in the family field. Formulations such
had enormous impact on *therapist* attitudes, let alone those of th
The positive connotation could not be seen simply as a trick to fool the
family system into accepting a change because the therapists began to
believe it too. A positive connotation is not, of course, the only possible
explanation of a symptom—after all, an equally plausible negative connotation would have already been made. But in a multivisioned view of
the problem, one could choose which of the "truths" one felt would be
most useful, since none was less "true" than the others.

During this period *Paradox and Counterparadox* became available. It was
published in English in 1978, although rough, pirated translations were
available as early as 1977. Through this book and also at international
meetings and workshops, the group began to disseminate their ideas.

## Bateson Revisited

The next stage in the development of the Milan method was the Milan
team's rediscovery of Bateson. During the late 1970s they read *Steps to an
Ecology of Mind* (Bateson, 1972) and found that the impact of Bateson in
the original was in some respects different from Bateson translated by others.
They were particularly struck by Bateson's notion of cybernetic circularity
as a model for living systems. Here is Bateson on the subject:

> The argument of purpose tends to take the form "D is desirable; B leads to C; C
> leads to D; so D can be achieved by way of B and C." But if the total mind and
> the outer world do not, in general, have this lineal structure, then by forcing this
> structure upon them, we become blind to the cybernetic circularities of the self
> and the external world. Our conscious sampling of data will not disclose whole
> circuits but only arcs of circuits, cut off from their matrix by our selective attention.
> Specifically, the attempt to achieve a change in a given variable, located either
> in self or environment, is likely to be undertaken without comprehension of the
> homeostatic network surrounding that variable. (Bateson, 1972, p. 445)

Although germs of Bateson's momentous and complex idea were present in much of the original Milan thinking, especially in the systemic notion
of the positive connotation, a new round of invention was now set off.
The model that Boscolo and Cecchin were beginning to teach as early as
1977 was becoming in some respects almost diametrically opposed to its

early "strategic" legacy. Chief among the influences that led to this shift was the development of circular questioning.

In the beginning, the group's interviewing technique was free-form and followed no particular guidelines. They simply used the session to arrive at a hypothesis that would describe the problem as having developed logically within that family context, as when the onset of a symptom coincides with a parent's death. Conversation with the family took a backseat to conversations among team members themselves. Toward the end of the 1970s, Boscolo and Cecchin found that their students were not interested in the elaborate paradoxical prescriptions the trainers would devise but asked instead "Why did you ask that question?" "Why did you address the mother instead of the daughter?" They wanted to know about the *therapists'* behavior.

The focus on therapist instead of family behavior clarified the development of a specific style of questioning which the team called circular questioning. After experimenting more deliberately with this technique, the Milan group published a sparse article crammed with important ideas: "Hypothesizing—Circularity—Neutrality: Three Guidelines for the Conductor of the Session" (Selvini-Palazzoli, Boscolo, Cecchin, and Prata, 1980). In addition to introducing three major therapeutic concepts, this article marked a step in the direction of a more clearly Batesonian world view. It also showed that the group was aware of the radical new positions in biology and physics that were coming to the attention of the family therapy field.

The three categories addressed by the article represent a brilliant attempt to translate the implications of Bateson's idea of cybernetic circularity into the day-to-day work of consulting with human beings and their families. "Hypothesizing" translated the concept into an assessment process; "circular questioning" translated it into an interviewing technique; and "neutrality" translated it into a basic therapeutic stance.

"Hypothesizing" is interesting because it implicitly proposes the idea of therapy as a research operation engaged in conjointly with the family. This research, however, is not traditional but more nearly resembles an experiment carried out along the lines of the New Physics. There would, in fact, be no such thing as truth, only an observer's attempt to construct together with the family a working hypothesis that sees the problem as making sense within its context. The hypothesis must thus be "systemic," that is, it must account for all the elements in a problem situation and how they link together. Since there is no attempt to see the hypothesis as true or false, what matters is that it proves to be *useful* in the sense of leading to new information that moves the family along.

In the article, the concept of circularity is applied to the technique of circular questioning. Bateson observed that the knowledge we have of external events is always apprehended by mechanisms that scan for difference. His example is the movement known as micronystagmus, vital to sight, by which the eye shifts quickly back and forth picking up differences in shape, color, and brightness. Following this insight, the Milan group created an interviewing technique that would also scan for difference: "By circularity we mean the capacity of the therapist to conduct his investigation on the basis of feedback from the family in response to the information he solicits about relationships and therefore about difference and change" (Selvini-Palazzoli, Boscolo, Cecchin, and Prata, 1980, p. 3).

Philosophically, this interviewing technique is based on the belief that living systems are characterized by loop formations rather than by linear sequences of cause and effect. Questions most commonly used fall into several categories: questions about differences in perception of relationships ("Who is closer to Father, your daughter or your son?"); questions about differences of degree ("On a scale of one to ten, how bad do you think the fighting is this week?"); now/then differences ("Did she start losing weight before or after her sister went off to college?"); and hypothetical and future differences ("If she had not been born, how would your marriage be different today? If you were to divorce, which parent would the children stay with?") Such questions comprise a series of mutually causal feedback chains creating a complex and nonlinear piece of circuitry.

As a context marker for how to proceed with circular questioning, the Milan Associates make use of the idea of "openings," clues dropped by the family in the course of the interview that indicate a fruitful avenue for developing a hypothesis. An example would be, in a family where there is a major doubt as to the security of any person's place, when someone brought up the theme of jealousy. Circular questions would explore the ramifications of that theme. A nonchronological and nonlinear decision tree thus informs the structure of this process. Two valuable descriptions of the circular questioning process can be found in Peggy Penn's "Feed Forward: Future Questions, Future Maps" (Penn, 1985) and in Karl Tomm's "Circular Interviewing: A Multifaceted Clinical Tool" (Tomm, 1985).

"Neutrality" is perhaps the least understood of all the Milan terms. At one level, it seems to be a way of translating into human terms Bateson's idea that all parts of a given system must, if the system is seen *systemically*, be given equal weight. You mean neutral like Switzerland? say outraged social activists who equate neutrality with condoning atrocities. Actually, the term's meaning is closer to multipositional than nonpositional. The Milan group states that if a therapist has achieved neutrality during a ses-

sion, no one in the family will be able to say that he or she has taken
anyone's side. This also rules out taking moral positions, since to do so
usually means to side with someone against someone else. The technique
of circular questioning is helpful since it allows the therapist to move in
an equivalent way from person to person. Whenever a problem is composed
of sticky sets of coalitions escalating against each other and jockeying for
place, "neutrality" means being able to move through these conflicting
claims like a charmed person without becoming ensnared by them and
worsening the situation. "Neutrality" becomes synonymous with the effort
to avoid induction by the family system and with the ability to move freely
in therapy. Perhaps, for the Milan group, "neutrality" does what keeping
the therapist in a hierarchically superior position does for therapists like
Haley and Minuchin, without the authoritarian implications.


## Including the Professional


Toward the end of the 1970s, the Milan group recognized that the therapeutic field included all the other professionals that might be attached to
a case. After several cases had failed to improve, the team investigated and
found that the family was primarily attached to the referring professional
and had no motivation to work with the new therapists they had been
sent to. Paramount was the question of loyalty: "Do we dare to do better
with these other therapists and thus show our old doctor that we think
her work has failed?" The family situation often improved when the family
saw the team honor "their" therapist. In some cases, when the attachment
to the referring person was intense, the team would warn the family that
should they give up their problem, this might also mean that the referring
person would have no cause to continue to see those family members who
were particularly close to him or her. This would be another version of
positively connoting the homeostasis of the family. Or the team would
positively connote the work of another professional, possibly an individual
therapist, as necessary in order to slow down the process of change.
    When the Milan team unleashed this type of message during consulta-
tions to other therapists, shock and surprise were common reactions. This
was particularly true when local therapists brought in families they were
having trouble with, only to be told that they were actually helping the
family by failing to produce a change. These therapists' discomfort was

often increased when the consultants conferred without them, leaving them to sit with the family. The rationale was that since the therapist had been "inducted" into the family system, they should be treated like a family member. In addition, if the consultants prescribed "no change," the therapist was thereby more free to disagree with them and the family more likely to side with the therapist to prove the consultants wrong.

One positive effect of this sort of move was to make therapists sharply aware of their contribution to an "impasse" situation. From then on, what we shall later call an "observing system" stance became part of the Milan group's repertory. Members of the therapy team themselves were not exempt from having team members from behind the screen positively connote their being stuck. This innovation, similar to the emphasis on countertransference in individual psychodynamic therapy, was an important step forward in family systems work, since it forced the therapist to include him- or herself in the total therapeutic field.

One final point to be made about Bateson's influence on the productions of the Milan team was the inclusion of Batesonian terms in their lexicon. "Moving to a meta-level" (moving to a level of higher Logical Type) meant something similar to being able to be "above the battle" and became a way to indicate therapeutic neutrality. A goal of therapy was to alter the family's "punctuation," meaning the way a situation or event was construed. And nonverbal behaviors of any kind became loosely defined as "analogics," in reference to Bateson's distinction between "digital" and "analogic" communication. As Boscolo and Cecchin became more and more involved with developing a teaching modality, these terms and others like them became almost a sort of shorthand for them in describing their work.

## Second-Order Cybernetics

Another far-reaching influence on the Milan group was their growing interest in what has been called "second-order cybernetics" by cybernetic researchers like Heinz von Foerster, Humberto Maturana, and Francisco Varela (Keeney, 1983). This position is foreshadowed in Bateson's later thinking, but the researchers mentioned above have expanded these ideas in their continuing exploration of the implications of the cybernetic revolution. Due in great part to Boscolo and Cecchin's seriousness in applying those ideas to clinical work, the systemic view is becoming more and more distinct from earlier models of family therapy and can fairly be called a second-order cybernetic systems approach (Hoffman, 1986).

In distinguishing between first- and second-order cybernetics, the single most important thought to keep in mind is that of the observing system. Von Foerster (1981) states that the observer enters into the description of that which is observed in such a way that objectivity is not at all possible. Furthermore, if the observer enters into that which is observed, there is no such thing as a separate observed system. Finally, since the way any observer perceives the world is through the lens of culture, family, and language, the resulting product represents not something private and self-contained but an "observer community."

Bateson contributes a more familiar piece of this argument; he obliterates the lines between units of creation like observer and observed, subject and object, by proposing that these units and their contexts represent a larger circularity called Mind. He is talking about nested circuits, never less than two: DNA-in-cell, cell-in-body, organism-in-environment. This vision argues against splits between parts or unilateral control of one part by another.

This second-order cybernetics describes a view that can be applied to any endeavor: social activism, ecology, religious work, education, and so on. Here we are interested in what such an approach to family systems work would look like. Perhaps the simplest way to describe this is to say that first-order cybernetics pictured a family system in trouble as a homeostatic machine. Jackson's model based on the concept of family homeostasis is such a case. According to Jackson, a symptom plays an important part in maintaining the homeostasis of the family.

This model was, perhaps, an advance over nineteenth-century models for psychopathology based on physical manifestations such as electricity or steam, but it still separated the therapist from the client. A second-order model conceptualizes the treatment unit as consisting of both the observer and the observed in one large bundle. This cannot be achieved easily as long as pathology is assumed to be in a container: as in a "weak ego," a "borderline personality," a "defective gene," or a "dysfunctional family system." The family system is itself an idea that may have taken us all off track. It is far better to do away with the concept of the family system entirely and think of the treatment unit as a meaning system to which the treating professional is as active a contributor as anyone else. We would then not say *the system creates the problem* but would reverse the sentence: *the problem creates the system.* In other words, the problem does not exist independently of the "observing systems" that are reciprocally and collectively defining the problem.

One corollary of this position is that psychiatric diagnoses exist only in the eye of the observer. Worse yet, diagnoses, because they carry attributions of causality and hence blame, act to reinforce the problems they are meant benevolently to explain. The Milan approach holds that no one can change, at least not easily, under a negative connotation. The dangers that follow in the wake of escalations of blame or guilt in families are well known: violence, scapegoating, somatizing, divorce. As soon as a treating professional agrees that something is wrong—as soon as he or she even agrees to let a family in the door—even more of the family's energies are apt to get sidetracked into forms of protection, often called resistance by the clinician.

From this point of view, the symptom is in part a way of blocking or containing the forces let loose by these negative escalations, and so it can be said to act at least partially for the benefit of the group as a whole. That is why therapists would always be wise to examine the effect of their own impact—yes, an impact report, in the ecological sense—before agreeing to help an individual or family change.

## Ongoing Modifications of the Milan Method

Over the years the demonstrations and teaching of Boscolo and Cecchin and those influenced by them have moved increasingly farther away from the instrumental models of the "strategic" days. The team's comment at the end of the session exemplifies this. In the early days, the family would be "paradoxed" with a prescription telling them to continue with the symptom or some related behavior because it benefited other people or was useful for the whole family. This was called the "sacrifice intervention." An example would be: "At a certain point your son decided to stay at home, not working, friendless, shut up in his room, because he believed that were he to go out and lead his own life like the friends of his own age, his parents would be left in a state of intolerable loneliness. Therefore, he said, 'I have to do something to help my parents,' " and so on. This kind of message acted as a negative connotation because the recipients of such generosity rebelled angrily and the giver of it ducked to avoid reprisals. The symptom often vanished, but the family often vanished from treatment too. In later versions of this intervention, instead of placing a child in the service of the parents' happiness, or a wife in the service of her husband's well being, it began to seem more "neutral" to place all the behaviors related to a problem in the service of a shared premise, value, or myth. For instance, to a family with countless crises one might say: "It is as though in this family there is a strong belief that family members will always come to the rescue when someone needs help. But now that the children are older, there is a fear that the family may break up, and this belief may become a thing of the past. And so people keep having problems, as though to test that they are still there for each other. The real problem in this family would be if there were no more problems." The usefulness of this formulation is not just that it leaves nobody feeling to blame but that it correctly elucidates the double-level bind: the "problem" is that people have to have "problems."

Another shift was to change the positive connotation, which implied the negative thought that the family "needed" a symptom, or even that the symptom was "good," into something closer to a "logical connotation." This involved therapists asking themselves such questions as "Let us see how this problem system works; what are the disruptions we might expect should it disappear? Should we even tamper with it before finding something to take its place?" There is no need to say that a problem is useful, beneficent, or functional—only that people have gotten used to it and that such habits are hard to break. In this way one avoids seeming to approve of some terrible symptom, which the family perceives as sarcasm, in favor of suggesting how meaningful it is in context, how understandable and by now perhaps necessary. A family that accepts such a consideration finds it much harder to keep its old ideas about the problem intact and is often freed up to search for an alternative for the symptom that answers the same dilemma but less destructively. There is no hint of "paradox" about such a suggestion. In fact, the entire vocabulary of "paradox" is being used less and less.

Another technique that is being used in a different way is the giving of rituals. These ceremonies usually address the double-binding communications people engage in together. One kind, thought of as "paradoxical" in the old vocabulary, amplifies a particular interaction to explode it. Another kind puts the interaction bind, consisting of simultaneous, conflicting directives, into a sequence. As Bateson said, if you put time into a paradox, it disappears.

An example of the first kind of ritual would be an effort to dramatize the positive connotation of a problem in the service of family members. For instance, each person, at dinner, would solemnly thank the symptomatic member for having his or her problem and cite the particular benefit accruing from this generosity for the speaker. This often produced strong and sudden changes, but people were apt to feel negatively connoted or blamed.

Boscolo and Cecchin now seem to prefer the second kind of ritual. They give a directive that on odd days, one of a set of contradictory messages or opinions will be considered to be true, and on even days the other will be. For instance, a mother might be asked simultaneously to be wife to her husband and mother to her daughter. The contradiction is undone if she is told that on odd days of the week she is to be a wife to the husband and on even days she can be a mother to the daughter. The directive for the seventh day would usually be to "act spontaneously."

The spirit in which the Milan team gives a ritual also has changed over the years. The ignoring of a directive is no longer taken as a "maneuver" to defeat the therapy team, but rather as new evidence about how the family system works (and how far off the therapists were in their attempts to understand it). The team then weaves this information into its ongoing, evolving hypothesis. In one case the Milan team treated, the mother was recently divorced and the children were out of control. The rituals and interventions addressed to issues in the family consistently failed. The mother reestablished control only when the team widened their hypothesis to include the impact of numerous court, school, and welfare-system officials who were attempting to coparent her. The mother could no longer be seen as a resistant client seeking to defeat the therapists once the larger context was taken into account.

The advent of circular questioning brought about another change. This technique challenged the need for a prescription or positive connotation at the end of the interview. With this type of questioning, it was possible to lay out the architecture of the problem system. The family contributed most of the separate parts; the questioner had only to juxtapose them in order that the connections between them could more readily be seen. A useful analogy for this process is doing a gravestone rubbing. Although many studies of circular questioning have treated different types of questions almost as separate interventions (Tomm, 1985), the questions must fit within the entire scanning process, with the hope that when the chalk has traced the rubbing enough times, the picture will finally show itself. An apocryphal example comes from an article by Hoffman (1983, p. 44):

Q: Who is most upset by the problem? A: Mother.
Q: What does mother do about it? A: She tries to motivate Johnny to go to school.
Q: Who agrees with mother? A: The school psychologist.
Q: Who disagrees? A: Father.

Q: Why do you think he disagrees? A: He thinks they are babying Johnny.
Q: Who feels the same as father? A: Grandmother.

Regarding the time of onset of a problem, one might find that the structure of relationships in the family changed suddenly, making the next sequence go as follows (Hoffman, 1983, p. 45):

Q: When did the problem begin? A: A year ago.
Q: Was anything else happening a year ago? A: Grandfather died.
Q: Who missed him the most? A: Grandmother, then father.
Q: Who was his death hardest on? A: Mother.
Q: Why do you think that? A: She and grandmother don't get along and grandmother is now living in our house.

It is clear that a new balance has been created around the boy's problem that brings everyone together in the wake of an important death. The information is embedded, however, in the questioning process. One can begin to see how plausible it might be for the team to consider letting the questioning itself be the intervention rather than spelling out the logic of the problem in a final comment.

In general, Boscolo and Cecchin agree with biologist Humberto Maturana that there can be no "instructive interaction," only a perturbation of a system that will then react in terms of its own structure. For this reason, interventions, whether in the form of rituals, final comments, or the interviewing process itself, are not directed toward any particular outcome but act to jog the system toward unpredictable outcomes. Cecchin has remarked that the paradise of first-order cybernetics is gone when it was thought possible to place a "bomb" into a system that would hit the precise target the therapists wished to hit. Instead, there are no bombs, no targets, no "out there" anythings, only a large evolving, observing system that is comprised of all the people who have become attached to the tar-baby-like original problem. The outcome is determined by the collaborative heaving about of this composite monster in ways that are usually surprising to all.

## From Behavior Systems to Meaning Systems

The Milan group has been in the forefront of another shift in the field of family therapy. The more "cybernetic" proponents of the family systems movement—represented mainly by Haley and the "Interactional" school founded on the work of the Mental Research Institute—differed from family therapists taking psychodynamic approaches in their emphasis on changing behavior (Fisch, Weakland, Segal, 1982; Haley, 1977). Although not behaviorists per se, they promote techniques that change behavior, believing that insight follows change rather than vice versa. Their slogan often seems to be "Down with Insight."

Over the past decade there has been a surge of interest in cognitive and perceptual processes, sparked perhaps by the cybernetic revolution and the fascinating analogy the computer offers for understanding what goes on in the brain. Bateson brought this focus to the family field through his concern with mental process and the central position he gave to the concept of "mind" (Bateson, 1979).

A more recent influence has been the above mentioned work of cognitive biologists like Maturana and von Foerster and the theories of "radical constructivists" like Ernst von Glasersfeld (Maturana, 1979; von Foerster, 1981; von Glasersfeld, 1984). The view that reality is a social construct and that our ideas about the world are observer-dependent and not necessarily matched by events and objects "out there" is not a new one, but it has gained new currency. As a result, ideas, beliefs, myths, values, perceptions, fantasies, and other such "internal" productions have come out of exile and are once more in fashion.

From the beginning the Milan group took mental artifacts as seriously as behaviors. Their philosophy of change was tied to the notion that families come in with "maps" of what is going on and that the therapist attempts to challenge or shift these "maps." The Milan group also makes therapeutic use of Bateson's emphasis on premises—reference values or guiding principles that are programmed in at the level of deep structure and out of the reach of conscious mind. They look for a "myth" or "premise" that seemingly holds the behaviors attached to a problem in place and try to enunciate this premise or myth in their messages to a family. Often the problem is commented on as being in the service of such a myth. If the premise, usually a collective one, shifts or changes, this will hopefully affect major areas of family behavior, producing what the Mental Research Institute researchers have called a second-order change (Watzlawick, Weakland, and Fisch, 1974), but what we might more simply call a change in premise.

This does not mean that Boscolo and Cecchin ignore behavior change. Instructions to change behavior directly, as in a ritual, may be given, but these are usually framed in reference to a hypothesis about a premise that family members appear to hold. In part 1, "The Crying Boy," the children are given the ritual of holding weekly meetings to decide whether they are (by their problem behavior) successfully helping their parents to maintain

the myth that they are perfect parents. A more obvious example of a behavior change that is attached to a premise comes from the annals of the
Mental Research Institute. In this case a perfectionist was to make one
deliberate mistake a day (Fisch, Weakland, and Segal, pp. 133–134). The
conclusion is, of course, that you cannot separate ideas from behaviors;
each is an aspect of the other. However, the Milan group takes the meaning
framework as primary, and in this sense their model is distinctive.

## The Influence of the Training Center

In 1980 the Milan Center underwent a change in organization. Splitting
off from Selvini and Prata and calling themselves the Milan Associates,
Boscolo and Cecchin continued to focus on training while the two women
focused on research. Like finches on the Galapagos Islands, the two pairs
still resembled each other more than they did other species, but they evolved
in different directions. The constraints of the training context deeply influenced the outlook of the two men, since trainees in their home agencies
were not always able to use the techniques they had learned at the Milan
Center but had to find some other way to apply systemic ideas.

Currently the center has ten trainers, several assistants, and about twelve
groups. But from 1977, when the program began, until 1982, Boscolo and
Cecchin did the training alone. Their first groups consisted of twelve persons
each. Several members of these first groups were strong supporters of the
antipsychiatry movement, which at that time was enormously influential
in Italy and had won a major battle, the closing of the psychiatric hospitals.
One group member stated his reason for applying to the center in the
following words: "Our struggle to close the psychiatric hospitals is meeting
with success. We will now have to treat clients outside the hospitals. We
wish to learn family therapy in the hope that this will prove more effective
than drugs and individual therapy."

The encounter between trainees who, like this one, were mostly employed
in public settings, and the trainers, whose model had been developed entirely within a small, private clinic, had an unpredictable, complex, and
interesting outcome. The emphasis of the work shifted dramatically from
the family to the larger institutions where the trainees were employed.
Instead of dealing with a family system, as they had been taught to do,
the trainees found themselves dealing with their own systems. Systemic

work became not family therapy per se but the enterprise of introducing new ideas about treatment into a milieu where the trainees themselves became the identified patients. The trainers, in turn, found their original identity as family therapists fading away in favor of an identity as therapists of larger systems. Because of the demands of this new context, new approaches to systemic work evolved and the training program tapped both trainers' and trainees' invention and imagination.

But this metamorphosis did not take place without confusion and growing pains. At the time the training program began, only a few private institutions in Italy practiced family therapy; it was unheard of in public institutions. The trainees had little knowledge of the family therapy tradition as it had developed elsewhere. Most of them had applied for the program after reading *Paradox and Counterparadox*.

At first, the trainees were very enthusiastic. A few months later, however, their enthusiasm had vanished and signs of increasing frustration appeared. The trainers tried to make some hypotheses about this state of affairs. The most obvious idea was that they were bad teachers, or confused. But increased efforts to be clear and to teach better only made matters worse. When confronted with the problem, the trainees explained that their unhappiness was more connected with their relationship to their colleagues at work than with their experience at the center. Their descriptions of the new things they were learning at the center evoked opposition, resentment, and fear in their colleagues. For instance, many trainees believed that difficult cases could be successfully treated in a few sessions with the Milan method. They thus implied that their colleagues' different therapeutic orientations were becoming obsolete. The verbal or non-verbal message— "Since I am doing family therapy, I am going to be more effective than you"—provoked an inevitable escalation of tension between the trainees and other agency staff. Milan-style trainees would also fail with clients who were connected simultaneously or at different times with other staff members in the public services.

Boscolo and Cecchin attempted to correct these errors. Trainees were instructed to behave modestly, to back down on any issue regarding therapeutic method, and even to cast doubt on the new teaching they were getting. Once this became instituted as a policy, trainees were able to establish from the start a more fruitful and cooperative rapport with their institutions.

A second reason for trainees' failures was the fact that in the settings they came from, family therapy was strange and new. During the first few months of the training program, the reported dropout for cases trainees were seeing in their agencies was an unheard-of 90 percent. Most of these families dropped out after the third session. The trainees' inexperience was not enough to explain such disastrous results. One reason, as a discussion at the center made clear, was the negative stigma of the treatment modality. Treating the family rather than the individual was threatening because it implied that the families were responsible for the symptoms of their "sick" members. Many families dropped out and went to other agency staff members who offered traditional individual therapy.

This problem was solved by doing family therapy without calling it that. The therapist would define the sessions with the family as "consultations" and not therapy, or would just offer a few "meetings" to the family in order to be able to decide what to do next. Now, of course, family therapy has become a much more widely accepted modality, and families often refuse individual therapy or dismiss a therapist who only sees the individual.

A third error came from neglecting the context in which the trainees operated. At first, the trainees quite naturally imitated their trainers; they would treat families in the public institutions where they worked as if they were at the Milan Center, and would often fail. The following example will illustrate this clearly.

A school psychologist suggested an intervention to a family referred to him by a teacher. The identified patient was an eight-year-old boy who had not attended school for the past six months. The psychologist positively connoted the boy's refusal to go to school as a task he took upon himself in order to stay close to his lonely mother. He had seen this exact intervention done with a similar family treated at the center, and the child returned to school almost immediately. The ill-fated psychologist was heavily criticized by the school principal, who was totally unable to understand the rationale behind the action. Moreover, after the story had spread around the school, the psychologist was ridiculed by the teachers, who would go to him and humorously ask if he would free them from an obnoxious child by seeing the child's family.

## The "Significant System"

This and many other such situations clarified the importance of contextual differences which therapists must consider in order to prevent the therapeutic solution from becoming the therapeutic problem. Mainly, they must take into account the effect their intervention may have on clients, on the other significant systems connected with clients, and also on themselves. The idea of the "significant system" thus came into being, since it was seen to be far more accurate in defining what was problematic than the classic idea of the "family system." The significant system includes all those units (persons or institutions) that are activated in the attempt to alleviate problems brought to professionals for a solution. Adding the professionals, including the Milan professionals, to the treatment picture was a major step in conceptualizing the problem in terms of "observing systems" rather than "observed systems." The concept of the "significant system" brings the model closer to a definition of the problem as an ecology of *ideas* about the problem (Bogdan, 1984) rather than behaviors located in individuals or families thought to be dysfunctional or sick.

For the therapeutic team at the center, the significant system usually includes the center itself, the family, and the referring person or agency. Occasionally other systems, such as schools and courts, that impinge upon the treatment are also taken into account. The cases referred to the center are often serious ones that have been treated unsuccessfully by others. Because these colleagues consider the Milan group to be experts, an immediate alliance is created between the referring person or agency and the therapeutic team. If the family in treatment returns to the referring person and complains about the work at the center, the response often is: "You do not need to understand what they say or what they do. They are the best. Go back." Families often endure frustrating experiences and accept strange interventions without dropping out of treatment.

But for the trainees, the situation is quite different. Most of them are young and occupy the lowest positions in their agencies. Therefore, the families do not easily connect with them and often abandon treatment to find other, more prestigious, therapists. But the trainees' "weak" position can become a challenge for them, as it forces them to find original solutions that then provide teaching material for other students and, more important, for the trainers.

For instance, in the public services, only some requests are purely for psychotherapy. Frequently clients ask for drugs, financial support, rehabilitation, pensions, or a combination of these. They are not looking for a "talking cure." One way to handle this situation and still be systemic is to reframe the use of requests for hospitalization or medication as Not-Therapy, giving the client the message "This will not change anything; in fact, it will slow down any possibility of change. However, this may be what you need right now. If you decide later you want therapy, let us know and we will be happy to work with you" (Fruggeri, Dotti, Ferrari, and Matteini, 1985).

Another dilemma is when the therapist is called upon to act as a social controller, rather than a therapist, in trying to keep someone from suicide or violence. In these cases, there is no problem as long as the therapist is clear about which hat she is wearing, a "therapist" hat or a "social control" one. She might say to a client "I wonder what happened to make me become your policeman instead of your therapist. Perhaps we should look at how that came about."

Overall, the focus in training has shifted from the family system to larger systems, with the individual and family seen within more complex contexts. As students become more skillful at analyzing the communication patterns of the networks they have to navigate, they are able to avoid some problems that originally created frustration and disappointment. They become skilled at detecting the effect of their actions on others and at calibrating the feedback coming from the systems to which they are connected. They remain coupled with those systems and viable, rather than discounted or dismissed.

As evidence of this new emphasis on the "larger system," including that in which the therapist works, there has been an increasing effort to apply this approach to public agencies, where it is difficult if not impossible to do Milan-style therapy. David Campbell and Rosalind Draper (1985), representing a team teaching the Milan method at the Tavistock Clinic in London, have recently edited an anthology that contains a wealth of ideas for intervening in wider systems without getting shot down or wiped out. Boscolo and Cecchin are fond of stating that although Bateson may have been the first major influence on their work, feedback from their students has been the second major influence. And it is true that their teaching has been radically changed by this input. As Boscolo has said, the coevolution between trainers and students has caused them to think of themselves not as family therapists but as "systems consultants."

## The Team Phenomenon

Although family therapists are almost always trained with a supervisor and one or more trainees behind a screen, therapeutic observation teams did not formally exist until the Milan group began to experiment with their four-person format. The therapists behind the screen balanced the two in the room with the family. The membership of the couples rotated from case to case, but a male and female therapist were always together, recalling the old role model idea of marital cotherapy.

Over time, as we saw, the Milan team broke down into pairs. After Boscolo and Cecchin separated from Selvini and Prata, the cross-sex component disappeared, as did the idea of having two persons sit in with the family. However, the demise of the four-person team did not seem to be necessarily bad; rather, it seemed more economical and less cumbersome. The one prerequisite for a therapeutic team seemed to be that it fulfill some version of Bateson's idea of binocular vision. As long as there was one person who could be immersed in the family and one person who could watch—one who leaned out the window and one who sat on that person's feet—a depth dimension could be achieved.

While most followers of the Milan method utilize the team format, some use more and some use fewer than four persons. "Teams" of one member can exist. The therapist in the room may go out to commune with him- or herself and then come back with a comment or an idea. Or a therapist may come to a session after having consulted with a colleague or group of colleagues and say that they have suggested the following opinion, message, or even letter. Sometimes, it must be admitted, the consultants are imaginary.

As Boscolo and Cecchin have traveled about giving workshops, daughter teams have sprung up in various countries. These teams tend to spend a lot of time together and can become intensely self-absorbed and cliquish. As a result, they often offend the host setting. It is not just that they feel themselves to be on a creative frontier, but they exude a sense of missionary zeal. As discussed, in their later teaching Boscolo and Cecchin have stressed the importance of keeping a low profile and a modest stance, but it is doubtful that such advice can ever be wholly successful. A group of four or more is ipso facto a political presence, no matter how low a profile it keeps. In this sense, the teams have a potential for radicalizing any setting where they appear, if they don't, through injudicious behavior, invite their own demise. Splitting and permutations are also common, as old teams branch out to make new ones.

One common fate of Milan-style teams, in the United States at least, is that they become grafted onto a strategic stem. People working in a Mental Research Institute fashion or using an Ericksonian approach may use teams to enhance the search for the miracle task or prescription that will break the symptomatic behavior in a single karate chop. This emphasis was admittedly embedded in the stance of the original Milan four.

The split between family and therapist implicit in the strategic model has also been amplified by the amount of time and conversation that can go into the search for a final intervention. Team breaks can be like secret cabals during which nervous hilarity at the family's expense or complaints against its "maneuvers" may take place. The team's isolation also seems to intensify the strategic ban against sharing the therapeutic rationale with the client. Many interventions, such as the "paradoxical" prescription, were originally designed to circumvent the family's so-called resistance. If family members knew that they were being restrained from change in order to induce them to change, it was felt that this tactic might not work.

Families have reacted in various ways to the team's presence. Some object to being watched by strangers, but most seem not to mind and even to become fond of these invisible others who keep sending in messages. Families are not prevented from meeting the team, if they so desire, but the tendency has been to keep the team's boundary (and its invisibility) intact. One hazard of Milan-style teams is that if they come too close to approving of a symptom in order to deliver a positive connotation, this has tended to upset and anger families. Reactions have ranged from dropping out of treatment to threatening the parent clinic with a lawsuit.

One major problem with therapeutic teams has been the handling of conflict and power issues. Because they are usually nonhierarchical, there is no easy way to resolve a deadlock or stop a divisive escalation. Teams of four or more are often plagued by inner dissension and turmoil. Burying differences and enforcing consensus is no solution, as this will merely drive discontent underground. Being on a team can be exciting and creative, but it can also be difficult and messy. At times, a research team will break down into twosomes, as the original Milan team did. For ongoing therapy, this seems to be a more stable form than the larger group, as well as being more economical.

However, the team of four or more has turned out to be a blessing in terms of training. It has avoided the "not economical" charge and has proved to be a way of giving beginning therapists an active experience both behind the screen and in front of it. Boscolo and Cecchin, in their training institute, will take groups of twelve at one time, dividing them in two. The "T-Team," or therapeutic team, consists of six persons: one in the room and the other five behind the screen. The "O-Team," or observing team, is comprised of the other six. Their job is to observe and comment on the relationship between the T-Team and the therapist in the room. Only the T-Team, however, can give the family a message. After the session, both teams can share observations and hypotheses both about the family and the therapeutic supra-system. The T-Team can utilize these ideas during the next session.

This use of the team has been a brilliant way to offer live supervision of ongoing family therapy to a larger group. Before the advent of the Milan-style team, only the therapist in the room would benefit from the interview with the family and from the supervisor's input, at least in any active sense. With the Milan team, the participation has been enlarged. As a result, more and more family therapists are being trained by a team behind a screen, and not just in the Milan method. The Milan method may transmogrify into other shapes and sizes (and is rapidly doing so as this is being written), but the Milan training team seems to be here to stay.

A curious feature of the Milan teams has been their spontaneous prolif-eration. New teams would often form after a group, or person, had seen the Milan team at a workshop or had them visit. These teams would then obtain sporadic teaching and supervision from Boscolo and Cecchin either by arranging to have them come to their place of work or by following them to whatever subsequent workshop they could find. Boscolo and Cec-chin are extraordinarily responsive to this type of enthusiasm and have returned several times even to some obscure clinic simply to help the fledg-ling team along.

In this way, a transatlantic network of Milan teams evolved very quickly. By now there are many self-styled Milan teams, or settings built around teams, in most of the countries of Europe, in Canada, in the United States, and in Australia and New Zealand. Milan teams have been slower to "take" in the United States, partly because the Italian group has had easy access to European countries, but also because by the time the method hit North American shores, American family therapy had already stabilized around native gurus. If anything, the Milan method has been defined in the United States as a category of "strategic" therapy and only recently has been seen as a point of view in its own right. The approach has taken root in North America only in the Department of Psychiatry directed by Karl Tomm at the University of Calgary, the Ackerman Institute for Family Therapy in New York, and a few small newcomer institutes.

An interesting aspect of this movement is the holding of spontaneous "team" conferences. Several have taken place under private sponsorship from 1980 to the present. These are by-invitation-only affairs, run not for profit but rather to allow Milan-style teams to get together and exchange ideas with Boscolo and Cecchin. The most recent one, held in Oxford in the summer of 1986, featured the Chilean biologist Humberto Maturana.

One final aspect of the Milan team network that deserves mention is its structure. Milan-style teams are laterally, not hierarchically, distributed. They are continually experimenting rather than dedicated to one set method. Frequent forming and reforming is another characteristic. The original Milan team has gone through at least three permutations since its inception, and the newer teams also shift about while still considering themselves part of the larger network.

There is a curious radical quality to these Milan teams. The Milan center does not act as the head of a movement but rather as collaborator in a horizontal process with other teams. These teams, a diffuse federation, are everywhere and nowhere—rather like crabgrass. The host agency often experiences them as noxious but they have learned to avoid extermination by going underground. And even when no new shoots appear in the host lawn, new roots may be working their way toward the yard of an unsuspecting neighbor.

## Conclusion

We believe that the Milan method is different from a set of procedures, to be passed along like recipes. It has programmed into it the ability to evolve into new and different forms. It is a "learning to learn" approach in Bateson's sense. The vehicle for this process is the network of teams, proliferating outward into many different contexts, and by their nature incapable of cloning.

In addition, this method embodies ideas about change that are easily adapted to other kinds of social systems, although in the process the method moves farther and farther away from family therapy as traditionally known. The notion of "therapy" has become too thin to bear the weight it is being asked to take, and the concept of the "family system" is inapplicable because we are no longer talking about units of treatment but "ecologies of mind."

One final observation is that this approach, identified as it is with Bateson's fascination with events on the frontiers of the scientific imagination, challenges its adherents to translate the emphasis on epistemology of the New Biology into the down-to-earth language of clinical work. Thus what intrigues the people who have been following and extending the work of Luigi Boscolo and Gianfranco Cecchin is not merely the chance to experiment with new ideas about therapy, but the chance to experiment with the new ideas researchers in the natural sciences are giving us about the world.

# PART 1

# *The Crying Boy*

## INTRODUCTION

T HIS CASE focuses on three important categories of Milan systemic therapy. First is the attention to the therapist's own context, which reflects a concern with replications between family dynamics and the dynamics of the team. The Milan group always looks at the ways in which they may be inducted by the family and how the family is able to clue into the organizational problems of the team to create paralysis. Here the team uses its own process to provide a healing solution. Second is the use of circular questioning to interrupt labeling in a family, turning it into an interactive process so that labels describe shared or potential behavior in the system and not the illness of any one member. Third is an exploration of family myths or premises which are developed by a family in response to a dilemma in the past but restrict the family's construction of a more flexible reality and impede the possibility of change. In this case, the behaviors of all the children, not just that of the problem child, were positively connoted in the service of a myth which seemed to fit this family's very particular history. This interview, unlike the other three in the book, was done just before the original group of four broke apart and Boscolo and Cecchin started their own training institute.

## The Double Context: Family and Team

There are several important features about the following consultation that make it different from the others in this book. First, it is an initial session with a family that is not yet in treatment. Second, the team consists of the original Milan team: Drs. Mara Selvini, Luigi Boscolo, Gianfranco Cecchin, and Guiliana Prata. Third, a male and a female therapist take part in the interview—Cecchin and Selvini—with Boscolo and Prata behind the mirror. The team itself is balanced on a crisis point, which turns out to have considerable impact on the case. Finally, the team is consulting to this family in order to demonstrate their work at a conference, and the interview is being viewed on closed-circuit television.

The case offers its own complexities. Mrs. Y called the clinic asking them to see her son John, age seventeen, who had just spent three weeks in the hospital for "an acute schizophrenic attack." John's mother had several concerns. The family was not certain whether or not John had been abusing drugs. Then, since the psychiatrist had refused to see the parents, Mrs. Y said "the family had no idea what to expect from John." Finally, Mrs. Y wanted to discuss whether John should continue to be medicated as he had been in the hospital. The purpose of the Milan team's consultation was to clarify the nature of John's problem and to discuss a treatment plan with the clinic.

The most outstanding feature of the Y family was its construction: it was a blended family and represented a second marriage for both Mr. Y and Mrs. Y. This "new" family had been together for five years. The Y's were in their mid-forties. Between them the Y's had five children: Harry, age eighteen; John, the identified patient, age seventeen; and Barbara, age sixteen, are Mrs. Y's children; Donna, age twelve, and Deborah, age ten, are Mr. Y's children. One piece of information from the intake interview was more noticeable than the rest: Mrs. Y's first husband had possibly been alcoholic and unpredictably violent.

The Milan team made an important mistake in the prehypothesis stage— they assumed that all the children belonged to Mrs. Y—and constructed a working hypothesis about the children's natural father. They speculated that one or more of these children might be identified with their father and/or still be loyal to him. Confirmation of this prehypothesis, which is a guess about the presenting problem's meaning within the relationship context, is the first piece of work done in the interview and consists of a process of feedback between the therapists and the family. This feedback is important because it indicates how successful the joining has been between these two discrete systems. The team's mistake skewed both the team process and the questioning in the first part of the interview. We will look closely at the team events and their similarity to the events in the Y family.

The diverse issues of blended families are highlighted when the Milan team discovers its first hypothesis to be an error and realizes the children are divided between the parents. The delicate repositioning that occurs among children in a blended family is examined. Questions abound: Who is still close to their natural sibling? Who is drawn away toward the new siblings? Can they remain together and yet be part of the new group? If an "old" sibling couple splits up, will one of the split siblings move closer to a parent? Which parent? and so on. These relationship variations that are possible to the children are of cardinal importance in understanding a blended family. Throughout this first interview, there are tangled reminders of significant and confusing changes in the sibling relationships. Additionally, blended families contain the memory of past failed marriages, and the children often take on or represent conflicts from the old family in loyalty to the old parents or to protect the unity of the new couple. In addition the new family, with its own unpredictable permutations, makes strong demands on each member.

The discussion that accompanies the case of the Y family frequently returns to the issue of team structure, its function and limitations. A team plays both an observing and a participatory role in the therapeutic process. What it lacks is the capacity to observe itself. Similar to a family system, it has its own rules, history, interests, assumptions, and lacunae. If the Milan team had been able to construct a metateam, or an O-(observer) Team, during their consultation to the Y family, perhaps that team would have noticed how the family was organizing the problem in the Milan team. Lacking that, the Milan team had to rely on their own rules and the completion of their own team process to rescue them from the problem that had developed between themselves and the Y family.

Isomorphism between a team and a family is always of significance, and the Milan team's experience here is particularly revealing, since the group was on the brink of a structural and theoretical change that was not yet complete. Soon after the interview began, it became apparent to the therapists behind the mirror that Selvini and Cecchin were developing two entirely different lines of questioning. Selvini was asking questions about the natural father of the mother's children, while Cecchin was tracking the current sequences in the family. When it was revealed that the children did not all belong to the mother, as the team had thought, Selvini became quiet and Cecchin suddenly took on her hypothesis. He asked if the mother's three children still had contact with their father: Do they visit him? Who visits him most? How far away is he? Is he remarried? and so on. It is at this moment that Boscolo knocked at the door and Selvini left the session to confer with him.

It had become clear to Boscolo and Prata that Selvini and Cecchin were working along divergent paths. According to Boscolo, Mara Selvini was the official leader of the team at the time of this consultation, but she and Prata were not as fluent in English as the two men. Consequently, Boscolo said, the women felt a bit paralyzed. Boscolo called in two or three times to share his ideas with Selvini, feeling that if he had called Cecchin he would have violated the hierarchy of the team. Understandably at the time, all these considerations were outside his awareness. He was reacting as a member of a family. Cecchin, too, felt paralyzed. He couldn't go on with his own questioning because he felt he had to follow Selvini's lead. Looking back, Cecchin remarked that their team was in the midst of an organizational shift that eventually led to the men separating from the women. These problems were unconsciously utilized by the family to protect their status quo. The family as a system calibrates itself to whatever information the team introduces into the session. This isomorphism, Cecchin feels, does not represent intentionality on the family's part.

In the training protocol that Boscolo and Cecchin designed after they began to work on their own, they decided against using a male and a female therapist. They felt that the "cotherapy" model was based on the rationale of providing the family with a corrective experience that depended on identification and role modeling. Instead they decided to have only one therapist in the room. This facilitated the use and development of circular questioning, which depends on the refinement of one hypothesis at a time and/or the construction of another. The new information that creates the new hypothesis is based on the openings the family presents. If they present ten openings, the therapist must choose which one to follow. It is impossible for two people to agree on which opening to choose. The process works best when one therapist is behind the mirror and the therapist in the room selects openings and develops a hypothesis. The therapist behind the mirror can then fall in step and work toward hypothesis refinement or ask for a conference to choose a new direction. Everyone, family and team, can become confused if more than one hypothesis is being developed at a time. In this case the group waited for the discussion at the end of the interview to "cure" their sense of confusion, trusting that the ritual of their own team process would restore clarity and coherence. That is exactly what happened.

## Labels Versus Process

Labeling plays an important part in this case. People give and accept labels in the hope that they will supply meaning to something poorly understood and frightening, such as mental illness. Unfortunately, labels are most often supplied by experts and then adopted by families who find increasing evidence for them. The Y family has already concluded that John's "jitters," his "hyper" quality, crying, hallucinating, and so on are the symptoms of "an acute schizophrenic episode," which was his hospital diagnosis. Once a label has been accepted, all subsequent behaviors become related to that label and every action becomes testimony to schizophrenia: he sleeps too much, he sleeps too little; he talks too much, he talks too little; and so on. The Milan Associates have used circular questioning as an antidote to labeling because the questions investigate and promote a different distribution of the labels, even when they are "good" labels. If the identified patient is described variously as "hyper" or "cooperative," the circular questions elicit information about the other children in the family who are, at times, "hyper" or "cooperative." This immediately challenges the problematic status of the identified patient and begins to put all the children on the same level. If John is considered "ill" and the other children are considered "healthy," this difference between John and the other children will be amplified in time, with John becoming more ill and the other children becoming, by contrast, healthier. If you ask "Who was the most 'hyper' or 'jittery' before John was?" or "Who will be most cooperative in the future if John stops?" then "hyper" becomes a description of shared or potential behaviors in the system and *not* testimony to the illness of one member. This approach to labeling changes the therapist's emphasis; instead of affixing labels, he or she may undo them by turning them back into an interactive process.

Formerly, Boscolo and Cecchin turned identified patients into saints or

sacrificers, positively connoting them as protectors of the family. In retrospect, they felt this often risked insulting the family, especially if the
patient was chronic. Saying that such a person was sacrificing his or her
life for the family often made the situation worse because it was a negative
connotation for the rest of the group. Thus they say: "You must look at
the individual histories to find a way to change the story so that people
can be united, leave each other, and fight, without tremendous danger and
without being labeled."

## Myth and Future Questions

The development of questioning techniques by the Milan Associates continues to be a unique feature of their systemic family therapy. Future questions represent an important variation on the technique of circular questioning. Circular questions collect information toward the construction of
a hypothesis and a problem premise, whereas future questions challenge
a family premise or advance a new one. Future questions evoke a different
map for the family and are usually employed at a later point in the interview,
after information is collected that describes the present sequences around
the problem and the coalitions in the family.

These questions—such as "When your daughter leaves for college, do
you believe your sex life with your wife will improve or grow worse?" or
"If your mother were to talk more to you in the evening than to your
brother, do you think your father would complain of being alone so
much?"—are transformative and can fit themselves to many family themes.
Survival questions, separation questions, punishment questions, existential
questions, can introduce an entirely new possibility for the family in the
future.

If a family is organized around a premise that is creating a problem,
future questions can also challenge the power of the premise to continue
into the future.

These questions often have an upsetting and arousing effect on the family.
The Milan Associates feel that future questions introduce so much information that they almost preclude using a prescription or comment at the
end of the session. They feel a ritual is a better ending because it can
monitor the rate of absorption of new information and restore the family

to calm. The future questions used in the interview with the Y family provided important feedback information from the children, pointing to the presence of a shared family myth according to which everyone had to perceive the parents' new marriage as perfect. Only John did not totally subscribe to this myth, but he then disqualified himself by acting crazy.

## The Myth in the Family

The premise or myth in this family—unconscious and therefore needing to be put into words by the consultants—was as follows: This second marriage for Mr. and Mrs. Y had to be "perfect" so that they might recoup the losses each had suffered in their former "bad" marriages. In particular, each spouse wanted his and her children to have a better parent than the one they had lost. For Mr. and Mrs. Y to be satisfied that their children were enjoying better parenting, the children had to participate by showing happy, normal behavior. Children who had perfect parents do not have problems!

This premise of perfection in the second marriage mythologized the family's past. It was important for each parent to demonstrate over and over how bad their former spouses had been, and for the children to believe this. A rigidly constructed myth thus restricts the options of all family members to conceive of a more complex reality. In this case, it gave the children no opportunity to have independent ideas about either of their natural parents, nor could they perceive their new parents independently. Boscolo comments that this kind of myth can be related to psychosis. The person who behaves in a psychotic manner is usually the one who cannot accept the myth and, through his or her behavior, challenges it.

The Milan Associates observe that if you talk in terms of myth you move to a more abstract level of explanation than, say, a triadic explanation, in which you are only making evaluations of coalitions, noting who is left out or included. The myth furnishes everyone with cues on how to act. But because it prescribes specific behavior, it becomes a straitjacket. It may even borrow from a higher level of logical type—the societal level, where Father is the ruler, Mother backs him up, and the children are cooperative. A myth like this is very hard to keep up; at a certain point, someone has to break and, if they do, that person can present behavior that looks psychotic. This case presents a good example of such a myth.

When Mrs. Y tells the story of "the bad husband and father," she weeps, and her husband says this experience was so hard on her that she was suicidal. Her tears become a powerful message to her husband, her children, and to the therapists. The stories of the old marriage are an important aspect of myth making, for they keep the mother from moving beyond it and supply a constant contrast between the old, bad marriage and the perfect, new marriage. Mr. Y also had a bad first marriage, but it seems he suffered less and, in this new family, enjoys considerable power.* He had taken charge of this family, demanding of the children that they listen to their mother or he will punish them! Though this appears to be a more benevolent solution, it is clear that in neither family has Mrs. Y been considered a full partner.

Each of the children supplies different variations on this theme of the "perfect marriage." Harry, about to leave home, is the one of Mother's children who is most attached to his natural father. A complication in his life is that he has been offered the last name of his new father; his acceptance of this name would please both his mother and his new father. He has separated from his brother John—they will not attend school together this year—and has drawn closer to his sister Barbara. How can he claim any attachment to his natural father and at the same time accept the name of his new father? What will he risk if he turns down his new father's name?

Barbara, now a prestigious member of the new family whose counsel everyone seeks, has been drawn into the new father's family as a surrogate mother to the youngest girls. From being the youngest sister of two older brothers, she is now the oldest sister of two younger sisters. This has removed her from John, but it allows her to assist her mother in a most positive way. If she helps Mother take good care of the little girls, Father will be impressed and pleased, and Mother will never again be accused of being crazy.

Donna, Father's oldest daughter, became obsessed with the possibility that disasters might befall the family. In her earlier family, before her mother left, she was the problem child, and she is still the one Father worries most about. Her sister Deborah seems least disturbed by all the new arrangements.

It is John's problem that has challenged the myth of the perfect marriage. The Milan Associates hypothesize that he has perceived the imbalance in the new marriage and worries that it may be particularly hard on his mother.

* This fact, that women suffer more financial and emotional adjustments than men do when marriages break up, is consistent with the most recent demographics on the different changes in men's and women's status after divorce (Goldner, 1985).

Once again, she is in a dependent and powerless position. She has handed over her children to another, albeit kinder, parent, but she remains vulnerable. In the old family, when his natural father was violent, John and Harry would team up to help their mother. Now that Harry is leaving, John cannot correct or modify the balance between his mother and his new father. He is faced with this myth that now contains an intensified premise: We must believe our former parents were bad or we endanger this marriage.

In the last section of the interview, Cecchin poses some future questions, asking "Who will leave home first?" and "Who will take Mother's place and take care of the children when Mother is out of the house?" Suddenly Donna volunteers that if this new mother were to die, Barbara would take her position! The family is stunned at this idea, cautioning her not to think that way. Cecchin takes this opening and asks, "If your father died, who would take his place?" Barbara responds "Harry would take his place." This unexpected response of the children—that they were prepared to be surrogate parents should a disaster occur—reveals the fragility of the new family. The idea of the children as surrogate parents is another challenge to the myth. This idea combined with John's problem positions the myth for some negotiation. John is no longer isolated in his perception and can rejoin his sibling group.

## Team Discussion and Intervention

The team has a number of subtle things to accomplish during this discussion. They must assist the host clinic in assessing the family in regard to therapy; they must attend to their own involvement with the family; and, since this is a consultation and first interview combined, they must personally respond to the family. The intervention the team chooses is particularly impressive because it offers an opportunity for the family to heal itself and blocks any further induction of John as the identified patient. Their intervention is a ritual that, if the family agrees to perform it, could obviate the need for future therapy. It is interesting to note that after Dr. Selvini delivers the intervention to the family, John puts his arms around her and hugs her. Follow-up shows that the family did not come back to the clinic.

# THE CASE: CONSULTATION AND CONVERSATION

PENN: What was the context of your seeing this family?

CECCHIN: This was a family our original team interviewed during a conference on closed-circuit TV. The mother had called the clinic two weeks before, saying that her seventeen-year-old son, John, had just been discharged from a hospital outside of the city after a two-week stay. He was hospitalized the first day of school for what the physician in the emergency room called an acute schizophrenic attack. The psychiatrist who was treating him had refused to talk with the family, and the mother said that they had no idea what kind of behaviors to expect from the son or how to deal with them. She knew he had had some sort of breakdown and that he had been on medication, but that was about it. So there was all this confusion about the nature of the problem.

PENN: What were the doctor's reasons for not communicating with the family?

CECCHIN: That was never clear. The intake indicated that there was a possibility of drug use—marijuana, maybe LSD. The parents may not have known about the drugs, and the boy may have asked the doctor not to tell them. There was also an indication that the doctor believed that the family was putting too much pressure on the boy to succeed, and he may have assumed that the family was making the situation worse.

PENN: How was the boy behaving since he got home?

CECCHIN: He was acting depressed and anxious. He would come home from school and sleep all afternoon. That kind of thing.

PENN: Who was in the family?

BOSCOLO: A mother and father in their forties and five children. This is the second marriage for both of them. The children are Harry, eighteen, out of high school and working; Barbara, sixteen, still in high school; John, seventeen, the patient; Donna, twelve; and Deborah, ten. When we first went in we were under the mistaken impression that all the children were the mother's. Actually, only the three oldest—Harry, Barbara, and John—were.

PENN: What did you know about the parents?

CECCHIN: Just that they were divorced from their previous spouses and had been married to each other for five years. On the intake sheet, there was a note that described the mother's former husband as possibly alcoholic and temperamental.

PENN: Were there any therapists attached to the case?

CECCHIN: Only the therapist who had brought the family in for the consultation. She asked us for help regarding the diagnosis and also the treatment plan. She said the mother had some questions in that regard, especially around medication. The boy had been on medication in the hospital but was not any longer.

HOFFMAN: When did you find out that the children didn't belong to the mother?

CECCHIN: Later in the session. We built our prehypothesis on a mistake.

HOFFMAN: Can you describe what you mean by prehypothesis?

CECCHIN: A guess about the meaning of the presenting problem in the relationship context. Also, since we were seeing an English-speaking family, it was useful to share our understanding of the circumstances of the case and to decide what aspects to attend to.

HOFFMAN: What aspects did you feel were important?

CECCHIN: For us, the natural father stood out. We gave him great importance because we assumed that all the children were his. There could be an identification of one or more children with this father, or a loyalty. In the presession, we had some ideas about questions to ask: which child looked most like the father, or who missed him most. Unfortunately, all this thinking had to be changed when we found out our error.

### FAMILY INTERVIEW

[Family is brought in by the female psychologist who asked for the consultation. They introduce themselves to Dr. Selvini and Dr. Cecchin, who are already seated.]

CECCHIN: We'd like to hear from you what is the problem in this family at this moment. Who wants to say something?

FATHER: I guess John is the main problem. But, you know, it's a problem that can be fixed.

CECCHIN: A problem that can be fixed?

FATHER: I think so. I hope so. He got quite hyper and ended up in the psychiatric ward of a hospital. And he was there for two weeks. He was released. He went back to the hospital for some of his schooling for a week or a little better.

CECCHIN: He had schooling in the hospital?

FATHER: Yes. They have a teacher right there.

CECCHIN: When did this happen?

MOTHER: Well, the first day of school is when he ended up in the psychiatric ward.

CECCHIN: Where was it?

MOTHER: In L——.

CECCHIN: *So this was the first day of school?*

MOTHER: *Tuesday, the first Tuesday in September. And then we took him down to our own hospital, first, to emergency, and then the doctor said if there were any problems to call him back. Because he sent us home with Valium and asked us to try to get him to take them. And, of course, he wouldn't take anything. Then, by midnight, we had to phone the doctor back, and he said to take him to the other hospital. So John was in for two weeks after that. And then he was out for a week. And then he was back in for a week just to go to school.*

CECCHIN: *What do you mean when you say he was hyper? Could you describe it?*

FATHER: *Well, he just couldn't sit still. He had to be on the move all the time. He couldn't keep a train of thought. He would jump from one thing to another. I guess you would call it hallucinating. He was hearing voices, and if the doctor would say something he didn't like, then he'd say he knew it was somebody else talking through the doctor.*

CECCHIN: *But these things started before he saw the doctor—right?*

MOTHER: *Right.*

CECCHIN: *Who noticed this kind of behavior first?*

MOTHER: *Well, we did—well, I did, I suppose, after—well, some of the kids. Harry, you noticed the night before John went in. . . .*

SELVINI: *Not in the school?*

FATHER: *No, this was just a couple of days before school.*

MOTHER: *The day before school, the night before, he kept Harry up to four in the morning talking to him about how he was going to save the world. [Girls laugh]*

JOHN: *No, I didn't say anything.*

MOTHER: *Okay. And then the next morning, John was getting ready to go to school and he lit up one cigarette after another. And I said, "Gee, you're smoking a lot." And he said, "Well, I'm kind of nervous, it's my first day back." And I said, "Well, after twelve years, you would think you're kind of getting used to it." And he said, "Yes, but Harry won't be coming back."*

CECCHIN: *Harry was not going back to school?*

MOTHER: *No, he finished grade 12 and he had gone to work.*

CECCHIN: *So it was the last year for him.*

MOTHER: *Right. And they are eleven months apart, these two. So then John started to cry, and I thought, well, maybe he has a real case of the jitters. So he got ready and went on to school. Well, that night, about five thirty, he called and asked if he could go to his friend's place for supper. And, like, we normally eat at five thirty, and the rule is if you're going to stay out, you notify me ahead of time so I don't prepare for extras. So he was kind of late, but I said, "You might as well stay there now." So he came home about seven thirty, and him and a friend of his were coming down the street and they were laughing and talking. We could see them coming. My husband and I were sitting and playing a game on the kitchen table, and he walked in and he said, "Where is Harry's jean jacket?" And I said, "Well, are you going to wear it or are you going to take it back to Harry?" And he just grabbed the jacket and started to cry. So then the* two of us took him upstairs, because we thought obviously there is a problem. And then he started saying, "Something is happening to me. I don't know what's happening. Maybe it's good. Maybe it's not." And then he would say, "I trust you. I don't trust you." So from that point on, he just kept going.

CECCHIN: Did this happen before?

MOTHER: No.

CECCHIN: John, do you agree with what they said about this behavior? Everything they said?

JOHN: No.

CECCHIN: Before you said "I didn't say that." You seemed to disagree with what they were saying.

FATHER: Oh, that was about keeping Harry up.

JOHN: I never said anything.

CECCHIN: So it was not true that he was saying these things? Who first noticed this kind of behavior? [to Donna] Did you notice it?

DONNA: Yes.

CECCHIN: The same time that others did?

DONNA: Well, like, I noticed it when my boyfriend drove me home from school one night after school, and John asked him to take him into town. So [my boyfriend] took him in, and then, I don't know, he said that John was saying things like "I understand and you don't understand," and all this, or something. So after he told me, I started noticing that he was acting different.

CECCHIN: [to Barbara] Did you notice?

BARBARA: Yes.

CECCHIN: Somebody said it was two or three days before school started—right? Do you think it was something to do with the school?

BARBARA: He was talking to me before school started. He was sitting on the back porch on the freezer and he was telling me he wanted to tell me something. And I said, "Well, go ahead and tell me." And he said, "Well, I can't," and he just started crying. He was trying to tell me something, but I didn't know what he was talking about. And he was just crying.

CECCHIN: He was crying?

BARBARA: He wanted to tell me something, but he just said he couldn't tell me. It was too hard for him.

CECCHIN: [to John] Everybody said that this was a problem. Do you agree?

JOHN: I don't know if it was really a problem.

CECCHIN: How do you see it? I asked "What's the problem?" They said "Oh, it's John." So they say you're a problem. Do you see it differently?

JOHN: Not really.

CECCHIN: How do you see it? As a problem, or is it something else?

JOHN: Well, I don't know.

CECCHIN: It's interesting. The family already defines the boy's behavior as crazy. For example, the mother said that he had a case of the jitters. The father said he was hyper. The sister said he was crying and couldn't talk. The father said he was hallucinating. So they talk in terms of symptoms. And every time I ask him "Do you agree with what they're saying?" he says "Well, I don't know; perhaps."

HOFFMAN: He told the mother that he was upset because Harry wasn't going back to school. Then he began to cry.

CECCHIN: He was crying and he was smoking a lot. Then he went to school, and he called up that afternoon to ask "Can I stay with a friend?" And Mother says "You should tell me if you're not coming home so I don't prepare an extra place." Obviously he was trying to say something that nobody understood. And they classify all these behaviors as symptoms. One says he was talking crazy, the other says he's acting "different," the other that he's hyper.

HOFFMAN: First he says "I wasn't doing these things," and then he says "Maybe I was."

CECCHIN: What is interesting is that when I keep asking "Do you agree or not agree?" he's totally blank. He has already entered into this system in which he's crazy, in which he cannot speak. He can't talk to me either. He gave up.

PENN: At this point in the interview, what information—according to your definition of information—do you feel you have about the family?

CECCHIN: The important information seems to be that Harry wasn't going back to school. Maybe he upset the family by deciding not to go on to college. We know that father works as a laborer. It's interesting that the father says that when John was in the hospital he attended some kind of school program. Maybe John felt he had to carry out some ideal in the family that at least one of the boys has to get a good education. So he reacts by saying he wants to save the world. In reality, he elects not to go back to school.

### FAMILY INTERVIEW

MOTHER: *Well, we were asked before if we had noticed anything previous to this, and the only thing, looking back, that we find now that was different in his past years was that he's got a bad temper. And when you ask him to do something, he just flies off the handle. And, you know, he was very high-strung. So this summer, when we would ask him to do something, he would either say "Yes,"*

*and go ahead and do it, or he would say "Do you mind waiting? I have something*
*else to do." He became very cooperative.*

FATHER: *But he'd come back and do it later.*

CECCHIN: *This was during the summer?*

MOTHER: *Yes.*

FATHER: *How do you go to a doctor and say "There is something wrong with my*
*son, he's doing what he's asked"?*

MOTHER: *We just thought he was maturing.*

FATHER: *Which was something new—right? Just during the summer, not before.*

CECCHIN: *After school finished?*

FATHER: *Yes. But then, since he's left the hospital and started back to high school,*
*he's off all medication and we started him on these multiple vitamins, and that*
*kind of fell off. He stopped taking them. And then he seemed to take a complete*
*reversal. He starts to sleep all the time. Comes home from school and he sleeps*
*until suppertime. Get him up for supper, and then by seven thirty he's back in*
*bed again.*

CECCHIN: *Who was cooperative before he became cooperative?*

---

HOFFMAN: What are you trying to do here?

CECCHIN: We often go after some word or phrase used by the family. Here
I ask "Who else was cooperative?" For instance, the father said John was
hyper. We would ask "What do you mean by hyper?" We never accept
any description like that at face value. We will ask "Who notices it? Who
is most upset about it?" They say he's a problem. "In what way is he a
problem for you?" In this way, we try to make these issues of his sickness
into relational issues.

PENN: It's as if you try to define what coalition exists around that theme.

CECCHIN: We're not as interested in the question of the coalition as in the
question of message. What kind of message is sickness? Who picks up
the message? How do they react to it? Why do they use the term hyper?
What do they mean by that? How do they define "cooperative"? All
these statements look like knives.

HOFFMAN: Everything they say defines him as "sick."

CECCHIN: Yes. "Cooperative" is sick. "Hyper" is sick. The boy is being
attacked by all these people who are trying to give him labels. You get
to the point where even if you're a good child, it's a label. So you're not
a human being any more, you're just a label.

PENN: He ends up by accepting these labels.

CECCHIN: He's lost. He doesn't know what to do. He's almost crying. Even being cooperative is a label.

BOSCOLO: So this is why the therapist asks who else is cooperative.

HOFFMAN: To take the label and spread it around.

BOSCOLO: Yes. So you ask all the other children, and in this way you put them all on the same level.

PENN: You also take the patient out of the position of being different from the others.

CECCHIN: Notice that when they talk about John being cooperative, they all laugh. He should never be cooperative—right?

HOFFMAN: It's a kind of joke. You must be sick, you're acting so good.

CECCHIN: You get the idea that this family is kind of strange. The parents say you must rebel against your parents if you want to be good. They give the prescription to be spontaneously rebellious.

BOSCOLO: They do something else here. The parents laugh when they talk about John being cooperative, but they don't laugh when the other children are cooperative. This is a difference that, in time, can become more and more amplified.

HOFFMAN: It ends with John becoming more and more cooperative. He wants to be more and more helpful until, finally, he starts to talk about saving the world.

BOSCOLO: Once labeling has been accepted by the family, then all behaviors are related to the labeling. John, for instance, is seen under a label of illness. He can be cooperative or not cooperative; he can be anything you like. Illness becomes the context marker for his behavior. The other children, although they are on the same level hierarchically, have a different context marker: they are healthy, and all their behavior is judged accordingly. In time, there will be an amplification of difference, so in this sense I think that the therapist does an important thing. He cuts into this amplification between John and the other siblings by picking up one behavior—cooperating—and placing the other children in the same class: "You say that John is cooperating. How are the others doing? Are they cooperating more or less?"

CECCHIN: I am always impressed by the power of labeling: "You are cooperative"; "You are good"; "You are bad." It is like being cast in a role in a play and never being able to get out of it. If you say "I get along with my son, we have fun together," that's relational. But if you say "My daughter is intelligent," you use words to kill the relationship. To unstick that kind of system, you must bring in a process that helps people get away from labels—not only negative ones, but positive ones too.

PENN: It's true that a label in the early learning situations of a child—

where you say "This child is smart" or "This child is dumb"—becomes amplified over time. The label is a context for understanding all the behaviors of the child.

CECCHIN: For example, if the child who is labeled "stupid" does something intelligent, you say he guessed it, it was by chance. So there's no way he can be intelligent. If he is thought to be intelligent and he does something stupid, he was trying not to show his intelligence because he's too shy or something. The child can't get out.

BOSCOLO: But there's another point: that when a difference starts to be amplified, as in this case, then the expert who comes in tends to amplify it even further—by psychiatric labels, by medication, and by other messages that perpetuate the amplification. This is why therapeutic intervention, instead of solving problems, so often aggravates them. There is a theory that says it takes three generations to produce a schizophrenic. Well, you have to extend this theory by saying three generations and a psychiatrist who provides the label.

PENN: And also an institution to back up the psychiatrist.

CECCHIN: But you can't blame the psychiatrist. He's part of a system that is looking for someone to help it do what it is supposed to do.

HOFFMAN: You imply that a psychiatrist is a kind of systemic blamer.

CECCHIN: In a way, yes. But this is a serious thing, this business of dispensing labels. There are people who sell four, five diagnoses a day and make a living out of it. You cannot say they are bad. There are millions of other people who want to buy from them.

BOSCOLO: It's not only the psychiatrist who labels people. In this interview, you can see the family going on a binge of labeling.

PENN: People look for labels when they are confused. In the beginning of this illness, there is a great uncertainty about this boy on the part of the family. Is it because he has the jitters or because he's hyper? Is it drugs or smoking? The therapist who presented the case said that the mother wanted a diagnosis; she wanted to know if the boy was schizophrenic or not schizophrenic. If so, should they medicate him or not medicate him? There's an enormous necessity within the system to come out with labels, because it gives an orientation, a meaning, to something that is frightening because it is poorly understood.

CECCHIN: But you have to find a meaning that doesn't put people into a box or lock them up. Here, there was a big connection between the brothers. One idea would have been for the family to organize a ritual around the separation of the brothers.

BOSCOLO: Instead you had another kind of ritual, the ritual of the psychiatrist who enters and gives a label.

CECCHIN: The trouble with these labels is not the label itself; it's that they are timeless, they are forever. It would be interesting to have a kind of temporary labeling.

HOFFMAN: That's what giving the brothers a ritual to mark their separation would have done. The job of a ritual like that is to put time back in, and the brothers could eventually have gone their separate ways. Instead, the "healthy" one stays because he's preoccupied with the problems of the "unhealthy" one.

## FAMILY INTERVIEW

MOTHER: *Well, we've never had any problem.*

CECCHIN: *You said John was a very high-strung boy. . . .*

FATHER: *Well, I'd say "Cut the grass," but he wanted to go out with the boyfriends, so he would prefer to go with the other kids.*

MOTHER: *He would do it.*

FATHER: *He would do it, but he would do it under protest.*

SELVINI: *But you said during the summer he was more cooperative. What about Harry, was he cooperative?*

MOTHER: *Harry's always been good.*

FATHER: *He's always been pretty good.*

MOTHER: *I think they wouldn't be normal, if . . .*

FATHER: *They're normal kids.*

SELVINI: *Was he more cooperative than John?*

FATHER: *As a rule, yeah.*

SELVINI: *As a rule, he's more cooperative.*

MOTHER: *Also, as a rule, we've always sat down and had family discussions, and we would sit sometimes for hours talking about nothing. And John has never really been able to take any type of criticism, be it constructive or otherwise, and so he would just leave.*

CECCHIN: *What about the girls? Are they cooperative?*

MOTHER: *They have their moments, the same as I do. [laughter]*

CECCHIN: *Who's the less cooperative?*

FATHER: *I wouldn't say the less cooperative, but I'd say the most forgetful would be Donna. If she's going to do something upstairs, she's forgotten what she's supposed to do by the time she gets there.*

SELVINI: *[naming the girls] Barbara, Donna, and Deborah.*

MOTHER: *Barbara's the oldest, then Donna, and then Deborah.*

*[Selvini is called out.]*

CECCHIN: *Are they cooperative with their father in the same way they're cooperative with their mother?*

FATHER: *I'd say more so.*

CECCHIN: *Who? The girls, you say.*
FATHER: *I don't know.*
CECCHIN: *More so, more cooperative? More cooperative with you?*
FATHER: *Well, yeah. If I say do it, they usually do it.*
*[Family laughing and joking with Cecchin. Selvini comes back in.]*

---

HOFFMAN: Why did you ask Selvini out?
BOSCOLO: We wanted to discuss with her the idea of putting an explanatory question to the family, to ask them to give their hypotheses about John's behavior. With somebody this upset, especially when he is so heavily labeled, the family doesn't give much information. They tend either to be tangential or else they give the opinion of the experts, the doctors. This family gives us the feedback they got from the doctors, as you see. If you ask for a hypothesis, you introduce a possible connection between them and the one who is sick. There is the possibility that they will reveal themselves. This can make family members very anxious.

### FAMILY INTERVIEW

SELVINI: *I want to ask, when John began this behavior two days before school, what was the explanation you gave for this behavior? When you tried to find out . . .*
FATHER: *No, the kids knew, they didn't tell us. We didn't notice it until the day he went to school, but the kids are starting to tell us that these things happened a few days before, but they didn't tell us.*
BARBARA: *We didn't think nothing happened until [boyfriend] told us that John was having a nervous breakdown.*
SELVINI: *What was the explanation you gave for this behavior of John's?*
FATHER: *We didn't know. We took him right to the doctor. We talked to him and we knew, obviously, that he had a problem we couldn't cope with, so we took him down to emergency in the hospital and had the doctor check him.*
SELVINI: *But commonly in the family, they try to find out some explanation for this sort of behavior or strange behavior, why—*
FATHER: *What we first suspected was possibly drugs.*
MOTHER: *That was our first, you know . . .*
FATHER: *I mean, we didn't know; that's the first thing you think of. So the doctor checked him and he said there was no evidence of anything being taken.*

---

PENN: That feedback, where Dr. Selvini finally gets the father to say he suspects drugs, relates very strongly to your first hypothesis, the one that you made before you discovered that the children came from both parents. In other words, it must have confirmed your idea that maybe there was some relationship between the natural father, the aggressive, alcoholic man, and the symptoms of the boy. Is that what you were thinking at that point? That your hypothesis was confirmed?

CECCHIN: That's right.

BOSCOLO: He had to follow along in the tradition of the father.

PENN: To hold a place for the father or resolve a split that the family held about the father, or something like that.

CECCHIN: Yes.

## FAMILY INTERVIEW

MOTHER: But then later on he said that during the summertime, when he was on vacation for a week, that the boys had tried some acid, LSD, so we thought maybe he'd had a recurrence; and it was very confusing because the psychiatrist— we couldn't speak to him. And I was trying to figure out whether you could differentiate from an acid trip and a schizophrenic episode. And the doctor said, "Oh yes, definitely, he was having a schizophrenic episode." Later on he said he didn't think he was schizophrenic, and I said "Are there any tests to determine yes or no?" And he said "No, there aren't." So then my husband and I came to the clinic because we saw an ad in the paper, and then we asked one of the doctors here if it could be confirmed one way or the other. And he said yes. So then I went back to the doctor and I said "Could we take him up to the clinic to have him assessed?" and he said "Well, yes, but you won't find out anything more than you know now." And I said "I want to find out one way or the other," and he said "Oh, he's definitely schizophrenic." He said "You were there, you saw all the symptoms."

CECCHIN: Did you find out if he took LSD or not during the summer?

MOTHER: He says he didn't.

CECCHIN: Anybody else in the family try drugs? [Children laugh.] LSD? At the same time he took it?

HARRY: Yeah.

CECCHIN: [to John] Did you have some strange effects?

JOHN: No, didn't have any side effects.

CECCHIN: From what you understand, is there a relation between LSD and what happened to you?

JOHN: *No.*

CECCHIN: *There's no relation? What's your explanation of what happened to you?*

JOHN: *I don't know.*

CECCHIN: *You said to your sister "I have something to say, but I cannot say it," so you must have had something on your mind.*

JOHN: *I know, but . . .*

CECCHIN: *You forgot or you couldn't say?*

JOHN: *I don't know.*

CECCHIN: *Even now you don't know. Whom do you talk to in the family when you have some problems?*

JOHN: *Everybody.*

CECCHIN: *Anybody special?*

JOHN: *[starting to cry] No, just anybody—Barbara, Harry, Donna.*

---

HOFFMAN: What do you think the crying is related to?

CECCHIN: I think it was when I asked "Do you talk to anybody in the family?" He's totally isolated because nobody understands what he wants to say, so when I ask who he talks to, he says "everybody." Then he looks at the sister who is close to him but who couldn't understand him, and he starts to cry. I ask "Can you explain now?" and he says no. He's tried for a month to explain; how can he explain now? So he starts to cry while everybody's laughing.

BOSCOLO: One thing I find fascinating in families like this is that it's as though everybody in the family has to deal with negative definitions. You take the story of God and paradise. We were in heaven, with God, when God sent us out because of this badness we have, this original sin. So all the members of the family must accept some of this badness. But in some families, the badness concentrates in one member. This is often the start of a career of being sick or bad. When one member accepts the negative position in the system, all the others become healthier, they become united, they are all angels. When you get to this stage, you get a chronicity and it's very difficult to go back.

CECCHIN: That's the scapegoat position.

HOFFMAN: Often when there is a scapegoat, you also find division in the wider field. Here the parents are at a point where if the children start to leave, they will have to face their own problems, get angry at each other, maybe divorce. That's the danger, that the group will be split; and in order to counter that, everyone unites to attack one member who agrees to take all the sins on his shoulders.

BOSCOLO: The potential split is also related to what all the systems around the family will do, what the experts will do. The experts keep the family in a position of unity at the expense of one.

CECCHIN: But now we understand that when we make a positive connotation of the scapegoat, saying to the patient "You are the Jesus guy helping everybody," you probably create a worse situation. This labeling is not doing a very good job, but at least it's helping the family to stabilize. If you go in the opposite direction, making the scapegoat into the saint, you throw everything into turmoil. So you have to find a third solution. Systemic therapy tries to find a solution where you don't need either a scapegoat or a saint. You must look at the individual histories to find a way to change the story so that people can be united, leave each other, fight, without tremendous danger.

HOFFMAN: Yes. The old way was to say that the child is protecting the parents from a split. You would make the parents into scapegoats.

CECCHIN: What we did in one case was to say that the families of the parents were both good, but they were like Russia and America. They believed that they couldn't get along, so they had to make war and kill each other. We said that was a myth, that they didn't have to.

BOSCOLO: We don't use the sacrifice intervention anymore.

HOFFMAN: Even though you now criticize this idea, didn't you find that it often was surprisingly effective?

BOSCOLO: For a few years we used it. I agree that it worked, but the cases where it worked were often not very serious cases. In cases where the patient was chronic, the sacrifice intervention was not successful.

CECCHIN: So it confirms what we are saying: that scapegoating is a serious thing. A mild case of scapegoating probably doesn't exist. If the sacrifice intervention works, it probably wasn't scapegoating.

HOFFMAN: And if you attack the mechanism that's protecting the family before they can find some other way to deal with the situation, the family will not change, or it will change for the worse.

CECCHIN: Yes. Changing from the scapegoat to the saint is just changing the punctuation; it doesn't change anything.

### FAMILY INTERVIEW

CECCHIN: [to John, who is crying] Who responds better to you when you talk to them?

JOHN: Nobody, really. They all respond about the same.

CECCHIN: *No one of them is able more to listen to you, to be useful to you?*

JOHN: *Not really.*

SELVINI: *Do you feel alone, very alone in the family?*

JOHN: *No.*

CECCHIN: *What about Harry? Which one are you closest to in the family?*

HARRY: *Probably Barbara.*

CECCHIN: *It's always been like that?*

BARBARA: *Used to be me and John. Then it was Harry and John. Then it was me and Harry.*

CECCHIN: *When was this change between you and John? Last month? Three months ago? Two years ago? When?*

BARBARA: *I don't know, really.*

JOHN: *It just happened gradually over a long period of time.*

MOTHER: *Well, when you went to public school, who were you closer to at that time? [No response. John blows his nose.]*

SELVINI: *For example, if this strange behavior had not been exhibited by John but by another child, in your opinion who would have been the other child? To present an episode like that presented by John? I ask this first of the father and then of the mother.*

FATHER: *I would expect it from John; he was the most high-strung. The others are about even.*

SELVINI: *If we exclude John, which one would be most apt to present an episode like that?*

FATHER: *I would think maybe Donna. She's the most emotional.*

SELVINI: *She was crying with John. They were crying together. [To Donna] You are close to John?*

DONNA: *We're not really close, but we're good brothers and sisters.*

BARBARA: *She's closer to him than Harry.*

CECCHIN: *Because it's very clear that you and Harry are closer, and Donna is closer to John than to Harry. And Deborah?*

BARBARA: *[indicating Donna] Till a month ago, she and Deborah wouldn't stop hanging around together.*

CECCHIN: *You stopped?*

BARBARA: *They wouldn't stop.*

FATHER: *The two girls were very, very close.*

CECCHIN: *Oh, you were very close. Not so much now?*

DONNA: *No, I switched over to these two [John and Barbara].*

MOTHER: *Well, you see, it made a difference, because it was quite obvious—you know, they [Donna and Deborah] were both in public school, and now this is her [Donna's] first year in high school.*

CECCHIN: *So there were many changes in school.*

MOTHER: *And she [Deborah] went from her school in our village, which only went to grade 6, to a senior public school.*

CECCHIN: *And the two of them [John and Harry] were in the same high school?*

*And then he [Harry] doesn't go back anymore. [To Barbara] What about your
position in school?*
BARBARA: *High school. Same high.*
SELVINI: *So you go together.*
MOTHER: *These three [Donna, John, and Barbara].*
CECCHIN: *Oh, the three of them. [To Donna] You took the place of Harry.*

---

CECCHIN: It looks as if the family divides into three couples. Father and
Mother present themselves as very close; Harry is attached to Barbara;
and the two youngest girls stick together. In fact, they are sitting on
either side of the couple.

PENN: Who is attached to John?

CECCHIN: Nobody. He used to be close to Barbara, and then he was close
to Harry, but now Harry and Barbara are close. So John is odd man out.

HOFFMAN: I notice that you are asking many circular questions here: Who
is closest to whom? Who would be a problem if John were not a problem?
and so forth. This might be a good time to ask about this technique.
How did you start developing it?

CECCHIN: When we first started to teach students, we were trying to explain
about the final intervention. They didn't care very much; they only
wanted to know what we were doing in the session. They would ask:
"Why did you ask that question? Why did you go out then?" They were
challenging us, so we were compelled to explain.

PENN: You mean they were trying to connect the intervention to what was
happening in the session?

CECCHIN: Yes. So we had to be more refined. We began to think about
what we were doing, so that if someone asked us about it we could tell
them.

BOSCOLO: I remember we were having a discussion in Zurich, in 1977,
about the question that we called "gossip in the presence of the family."
We asked ourselves: What is the difference between asking a question
of one person and asking a person about the relationship between two
others? We wondered why the second question, the triadic question,
seemed better than the dyadic one.

HOFFMAN: Why did you think it was better?

BOSCOLO: Because it's a metaquestion—you ask for information about a
communication instead of asking for it directly. You say "How do you
think these people get along? Why do you think they fight?" You talk
about fighting as a communication within a relationship.

HOFFMAN: "Why do you think these two behave like that?" is different from asking "Why do you behave like that?"

CECCHIN: Yes. Also, we are interested in the problem *as you define it*. How you communicate about your problem is more important than the problem itself.

BOSCOLO: The central idea, as Bateson says, is that information is a difference. You try to get more differences from the family, more meaningful relations from the data. So you ask about differences in time, differences in degree, differences in points of view.

HOFFMAN: So first you began asking relational questions, then you began to ask difference questions: "more or less," "before or after."

BOSCOLO: Yes, classification questions.

CECCHIN: Bateson believed that the world is a world of communication. So that's what we say to the student. If you see everything as information, you get away from a lot of trouble. A couple is information, disease is information; incest, cancer, death—it's all information.

HOFFMAN: In other words, nothing is negative or positive by its content.

CECCHIN: That's right.

HOFFMAN: So far the interview is organized very cleanly around the lead questions. You start by asking what they think the problem is and you then get a lot of data about labeling. All the boy's behaviors are seen as subexamples of his craziness. So you take one of his behaviors—his cooperativeness—and ask who else is cooperative. Next you ask an explanation question and go round the family. John can't answer this question, and you find out he hasn't been able to get across to anyone what he feels is wrong. You ask who in the family he is closest to. He starts to cry, and you get a confirmation that he is in an extremely isolated position. It's a lot of information in a very short time.

CECCHIN: Yes, we are doing a lot with these questions. And now we are moving in a more challenging direction, asking questions like "What criticism does your wife make of you?" "That I am very boring." "Is being boring something that is genetic, or did you decide to be boring?" "I don't understand." "You are born with the gene of being boring?" And he's laughing, and he says "Ask my wife." And the wife says "Oh, he was brilliant before I married him." "So marriage made you boring; it's not a genetic thing? According to you, what did your wife do to you to make you boring?" "I don't know—probably nothing." "So she didn't do anything purposefully." Later on I ask the same question about her. He says she's very nasty, very aggressive. "To be nasty, is it genetic?" He says "No, she became like that after I married her." "What does he do to make you so nasty?" It becomes like a game. He became boring, she became nasty. This is a circular intervention without making a big statement.

### FAMILY INTERVIEW

SELVINI: *[returning to the question of which other child in the family might be expected to have a symptom like John's]* How about the opinion of the mother? The same question, because for the father it was John and possibly Donna; and for you?

MOTHER: *Well, I'd have to agree with him because the thought hadn't entered my mind either, but Donna is the most easily upset emotionally. Her tear ducts are very close to the surface. If she's watching TV or anything and there's a sad show on, she always . . .*

SELVINI: *And John also was easily upset emotionally, also when he was a child, always very sensitive. . . .*

MOTHER: *Yes, yes.*

———————

HOFFMAN: This is a good example of a hypothetical question. I wondered if you'd talk about it, because these questions seem to have so much power to set off a process of systemic understanding in the family.

BOSCOLO: This question has two aims. One is to detect whether there is a self-fulfilling prophecy in the family about one member being the bad or sick one. For instance, members of the extended family sometimes pick (unconsciously, of course) one of the children who looks like a certain relative, and they will expect this child to act like the relative or to have the same problems. The second is to take the designated patient out of the isolated position, because you introduce the possibility that other people can have the same problem.

PENN: That kind of question also has an interventive aspect. It gets family members to think that the problem may not belong to John. You see how struck Mother is by the question; she says "The thought hadn't entered my mind."

## FAMILY INTERVIEW

CECCHIN: [to Donna] Why did you feel like crying when he was crying? Because he said he had something to say that he could not say; this was his problem. You feel the same way sometimes?

DONNA: Yeah, like if I have a problem and I want to tell someone but I can't, I usually just go upstairs and cry.

CECCHIN: There are so many people in this family, you must find someone to talk to you.

DONNA: Yeah, but I can't say it, like if I want to, if I call someone up, then I can't tell them—I just, they just go away and I go into . . . tears.

CECCHIN: [to Mother] Does this happen to you too? If you have some problems, who do you talk to in the family?

MOTHER: Well, I think basically my husband—

DONNA: Sometimes Barbara.

MOTHER: Oh, if I have a problem about what to wear.

CECCHIN: Do you think she's going to Barbara sometimes?

DONNA: Everybody goes to Barbara. She knows what to wear.

CECCHIN: Do you think she goes to Barbara more than she goes to her husband?

MOTHER: No.

CECCHIN: What about your father, who does he go to?

HARRY: Himself.

CECCHIN: Most of the time, it's your mother. Does he have any one of the children who takes care of him?

DEBORAH: I don't know, I can never cure him.

CECCHIN: You could never care?

DEBORAH: I could never cure him, make him better.

CECCHIN: Why not? He doesn't need it, or he's incurable?

DONNA: She just doesn't know how to do it.

CECCHIN: If the father needs some support, and she doesn't know how to do it, what about you?

DONNA: I can't either.

CECCHIN: Barbara is going to do it.

MOTHER: I think if ever we have problems . . . well, I can't think of an example right at the moment, but I think we talk about a problem first, and if it's something to do with the kids we automatically go to Barbara and then we find her opinion, and then we go to the rest of the family if it's something that concerns the whole family.

DONNA: [to Barbara] Gee, you take an awful load, don't you?

CECCHIN: [to Father] What about you, do you go to Barbara too?

FATHER: I have.

SELVINI: Because Barbara is such an authority for you, prestigious, giving you support, sensitive . . .

CECCHIN: *People go to Barbara for support. Once John was closest to Barbara. The mother goes to Barbara sometimes for advice about clothing.*
SELVINI: *Mrs. Y, you told us that the most sensitive and full of affective problems are John and Donna. They take after you or after their natural father for this particular sensitivity? [Mother laughs.]*

---

CECCHIN: It's interesting here. Selvini and I are following two totally different lines. Selvini is asking about the natural father, according to the hypothesis we came in with. She is probably looking to see who could be the alternate scapegoat, who John could be protecting or is identified with in the family. I feel it's better to find out what's going on in the system in the present. So I am asking this question: "Who do people go to in the family when they have a difficulty like John's?"
HOFFMAN: Why wouldn't you ask about the natural father here?
CECCHIN: Selvini is extending the context. She goes away from the present family to the family in the past. Usually we wouldn't do this so soon after the start of the session. The most correct way, from my point of view, is first to identify the sequences of the game—who helps who, how the relationships are organized around the themes they bring—and then to enlarge the system to other relatives, or to search for premises or other more general meanings.
PENN: This was very useful, however, because in asking about the natural father, Selvini finds out that the children come from two fathers, not one.

## FAMILY INTERVIEW

MOTHER: *But you see, my husband and I have both been married previously.*
CECCHIN: *No, no, she said the natural father.*
MOTHER: *Oh, the natural father. Oh, they definitely take after me.*
FATHER: *As far as emotions, but not as far as anything else is concerned.*
CECCHIN: *So you have been married before?*
FATHER: *Yes.*
CECCHIN: *You have children from the first marriage?*
FATHER: *Yes, these two. They [Donna and Deborah] are my two; her three [Harry, John, and Barbara]; and our five.*
CECCHIN: *The first three children are Harry, John, and Barbara—they are the children of the first marriage of the mother.*
SELVINI: *You are the stepmother....*

MOTHER: *Of these two, Donna and Deborah; I adopted them.*

FATHER: *It's very confusing in school, so I gave them their choice. I sat down with them, and they all wanted my name; so that's the way they wanted it. Harry's now eighteen, so he can change his name now.*

CECCHIN: *Do the three of you still have contact with your natural father?*

HARRY: *Sort of—not too often.*

JOHN: *Once in a while.*

CECCHIN: *Do you go to visit him? Do you still have contact, see him?*

BARBARA: *We used to go visit him.*

CECCHIN: *The three of you go together? Separate?*

HARRY: *If I'm in town, I drop in.*

CECCHIN: *How far is it from your place?*

HARRY: *Twenty-six miles.*

CECCHIN: *So it's up to you to take the initiative to visit him. If one of you feels like going to see him, you just go.*

HARRY: *Yes.*

CECCHIN: *Is he married?*

BARBARA: *No.*

CECCHIN: *He lives by himself?*

FATHER: *No, common-law marriage.*

MOTHER: *And she has two kids. She was married before too.*

CECCHIN: *Of the three of you, who goes to visit him more often? [Boscolo knocks and indicates that Selvini and Cecchin should come out.] I must explain that two colleagues are behind the mirror, and once in a while they call us to discuss what is happening here and to make some suggestions. Who is going more often to visit him?*

DONNA: *Like, if they go into town to go shopping, they'll just drop in for five minutes.*

JOHN: *Every once in a while we visit him.*

SELVINI: *[to Harry] When was the last time you saw your natural father?*

HARRY: *This summer. July.*

SELVINI: *Was it pleasant, the meeting?*

HARRY: *She [Barbara] went up two weeks before us to the summer house. Me and him [John] went up, but we weren't in the same house as him, so we didn't see that much of him.*

SELVINI: *Is he nice with you?*

HARRY: *He gives us money and stuff.*

BARBARA: *Sort of trying to buy our love.*

SELVINI: *[to Father] The same situation you have?*

FATHER: *I haven't seen their mother.*

DONNA: *Kind of the same thing; she gives us money—kind of forces us into taking stuff.*

CECCHIN: *You feel she'll get hurt if you don't take it?*

DONNA: *Right. I think it's phony.*

CECCHIN: *When did you stop seeing her?*

DONNA: *About two years ago. She stopped seeing us for two years, and then my mom decided to adopt us, and then she wanted to see us as soon as she found out.*

CECCHIN: *She decided to see you after you were adopted?*

DONNA: *No; as soon as she found out Mom wanted to adopt us, she started seeing us again, and then my mom couldn't.*

FATHER: *We maintained right from the start that even though they were my wife's children and these two are my children, that they were our children, and if they wanted to see their natural parents, we would not stop them. We didn't think it was fair to say No, you can't see them, and start a big fight over it. They're their children too; so if they wanted to see them, we said it was all right.*

CECCHIN: *But you said in the last two to three years, they haven't seen her. Because they decided not to see her?*

FATHER: *No, not in their mother's case. She didn't see the kids for . . . well, it was over two years that we were separated before I applied for a divorce. She hadn't seen them at all until I applied for a divorce, and then she wanted to see them.*

CECCHIN: *Then she became interested after you applied for the divorce.*

FATHER: *Because the courts had given me custody of them.*

MOTHER: *She told my husband that he could have custody of the children as long as she got the car.*

FATHER: *No, she gave me a signed affidavit, witnessed.*

SELVINI: *When you visit your father, who is it who decides?*

HARRY: *If we're shopping or visiting friends out near his house we may drop in. Nobody decides.*

BARBARA: *In the summertime, he asks us to go stay at his summer house.*

SELVINI: *He invites you.*

*[Selvini and Cecchin go out.]*

---

PENN: You obviously are going to have to put together a new hypothesis.

BOSCOLO: Certainly, we had to change the whole thing. The hypothesis we made before the session began was completely useless because the family was different from what we thought.

CECCHIN: One general feeling we had was that these two parents were disqualifying their previous marriages. Father's wife preferred a car to the children, the mother's husband is a phony. Somehow, these two people had bad marriages and now they have to make a good one. So they have to be close to each other, and rather than the two of them showing any disunity, it's the children who have to split. If the children got very close to each other, the two parents probably wouldn't know what to do.

HOFFMAN: You think that the reason John's sick is that he's excluded?

CECCHIN: No, that by itself doesn't make someone crazy. He probably is the one who has to make a ritual to keep everybody together.

BOSCOLO: We could also say that the mother, who had such a bad husband, is looking to this husband as a savior, and this may have alienated her from her own children. The children of the mother may feel more left out than the children of the father. The mother seems very attached to this man.

HOFFMAN: You go out here. What did your team want to tell you?

CECCHIN: They were noticing that the two older boys used to be very close and are now breaking up. So they suggested that we ask some questions about that, especially about the role the oldest girl may have played in that process.


### FAMILY INTERVIEW

*[Cecchin and Selvini come back into the room.]*

CECCHIN: *Our colleagues were thinking about one problem, that John and Harry somehow were very close to each other in high school—doing things together, spending the summer together—and that now, perhaps, you are not as close as in the past.*

HARRY: *No, not really. We're not as close now as we were before.*

CECCHIN: *So there was a period in which you were close to each other?*

HARRY: *Yeah.*

CECCHIN: *When was it?*

HARRY: *We've always been pretty close.*

*[Girls laugh.]*

CECCHIN: *You're the only two males, you must have been together for a long time. Who was the most prestigious of the two of you in the family? Was there a competition, as there often is between brothers?*

HARRY: *I suppose I am because I'm the oldest.*

CECCHIN: *Did the two of you ever make a kind of friendship together to keep out the sister? You have one natural sister? Did you try to keep her out? Barbara?*

HARRY: *I don't know, I'm not sure. I don't remember if we did or not.*

CECCHIN: *When did Barbara become so important?*

HARRY: *Maybe when she got in high school.*

CECCHIN: *[to John] Do you remember when she got so important?*

JOHN: *Around the time we were in high school.*

CECCHIN: *You were already in high school and she came in and she became very popular? Did she put herself between the two of you sometimes?*

JOHN: *I don't know.*

*[Girls laugh.]*

CECCHIN: *[to Donna and Deborah] What do you think? Barbara somehow [inaudible] between the two brothers?*

DEBORAH: *[laughing] Yes.*

SELVINI: *She separated the two brothers?*

DONNA: *No, I don't think so. She just hung out with them a lot. She didn't separate them or nothing.*

---

HOFFMAN: What was your thinking here?

CECCHIN: We are asking why, instead of sticking together and becoming more important, the two boys are separating. One is going to work and the other is staying in school.

BOSCOLO: Also, we see that a new man came into the family and he's sitting exactly in the middle here. There are three members on the left side and three members on the right. The mother is very attached to this man; he's the patriarch. After this patriarch came into the family, Barbara became very important and the boys were displaced.

CECCHIN: The new man became the alpha male, with the females all around him. The young males are outside, and they haven't much possibility to gain prestige.

HOFFMAN: But nobody has a breakdown until Harry leaves, so it was apparently all right as long as the young males stuck together.

CECCHIN: It's especially hard on John, because Harry not only leaves, he gets Barbara, who used to be attached to John. And Barbara is the most prestigious female in the family—even Mother and Father go to her for advice. So John lost both the important sister and the important brother.

HOFFMAN: If you want to look at it this way, he's lost everyone in his own family. His mother is sitting at the feet of this new father. His sister is like a second wife. Harry is leaving. And he can't connect with the little girls because they belong to the father. The father has given them all his name and refuses to let the two families even remember that they used to be separate. When he says "our five," that's a real message: Now you are all mine.

PENN: Yes. There's something in that joined system that's very hard on the young males, both of them. Harry's leaving has to be an indication that he isn't very comfortable there either. There seems to be an unspoken agreement between the parents that the three girls are going to be taken care of and the father is to be their father. The mother says "I tried very hard to be a good mother to Deborah and Donna," but the father doesn't say "I tried very hard to be a good father to John and Harry." So the men seem quite fragile. There's nothing in the family rules that protects them, so that they are at risk in a way the girls are not.

BOSCOLO: It's possible that this very strong relationship the older boys used to have was because the natural father was seen as so bad and so negative. So these two brothers had to get together to protect the mother, and now they're no longer needed.

## FAMILY INTERVIEW

CECCHIN: *There were three of you, and then the two girls joined your family. Being the only girl in your family, how did you feel about the addition of two more girls?*

BARBARA: *I wanted more sisters. I never thought I'd get them. [laughter]*

MOTHER: *We thought we were fortunate to be together as one family. In the past, my children didn't listen to me, didn't have any respect for me, because my ex-husband would tell them "Don't listen to her, she's crazy!" Consequently, if I taught them something, they'd ignore me. I remember one of the first times we had all five children together. These two boys were acting up, and I wanted them to settle down. My husband said "Listen to your mother!" They wouldn't, so he stopped the car and they got spanked. I didn't say anything, but he said if I had, that would have been the end of our relationship, because if they were going to be our children, they were going to be our children—not his children and my children. Consequently, they've always been treated as our children.*

CECCHIN: *Your first husband told them not to listen to you, and that disqualified you as a parent. Which of the children took advantage of your position?*

MOTHER: *Well, they were pretty young at the time.*

CECCHIN: *Your present husband tells them they have to listen to you?*

MOTHER: *Oh yes, he backs me up, definitely.*

FATHER: *If she disagrees with something I do, she won't say anything at the time, but take me off to the side later, away from the kids, and we discuss it. If I'm wrong, I go back and apologize to the child . . . if she gives me a legitimate reason why I was wrong.*

*[There is a short discussion between Cecchin and the father. Father is asked what the general discussions in the house are about. Father gives an example of how when the kids wanted a rec room, he sat down with them and explained in a reasonable manner how all the money they had was spent.]*

―――――――――――――――

CECCHIN: The first father, the real father, told the children that their mother was crazy and they shouldn't take her seriously. The new father says "Listen to your mother." This boy is probably confused about what position to take with his mother and who he should comply with. He's probably tried both positions.

HOFFMAN: Also, even though the mother's authority is protected, she's not allowed to treat her children as permissively as she used to.

PENN: I believe that "our" children means they must be raised Father's way. If that's true, the boys must feel their mother doesn't speak for them, that nobody is speaking for them.

HOFFMAN: Right. Remember, the mother said "If I had protested [the spanking], that would have been the end of the relationship."

CECCHIN: That's only her premise. Mother may be giving the discipline of her boys to this husband in order to keep the relationship. The boys may feel that rather than break up the relationship, she is giving them to this man who punishes them.

BOSCOLO: The matter of how to raise the children is totally defined by this new husband. The children must be sacrificed in order not to sacrifice the spouse relationship. If these boys are together, they can take it; but if they are separated, one of them must find it intolerable.

PENN: I think John perceives the confusion of these messages. The new father doesn't mean "Listen to your mother"; he means "You must listen to me and she must listen." To perceive that correctly again disqualifies his mother as a parent. Perhaps in protection of her, he acts crazy. Indeed, that was a label used against her in the past.

HOFFMAN: The boys must feel they should champion their mother against this man, as they did with the father who was bad to her. But if they're rebellious, she allows the new man to punish them.

BOSCOLO: Mother puts this father in a very powerful position. She may fear that this marriage may fail so she gives him a lot of power. It's possible that John would like to correct this situation, but it's too dangerous for him now that Harry has left.

HOFFMAN: He may be the secret agent of Mother, who in some way may also feel rebellious but can't express it.

CECCHIN: It's hard to fight anyone who is so serious, so reasonable, so willing to help everybody. John needs to defend himself against this man, but he doesn't know how. It was easy with the other father: he was bad, and you could fight him.

## FAMILY INTERVIEW

SELVINI: *Please explain to me why Barbara has so much prestige in this family. What qualities does she have that are so important? For instance, why does she have so much prestige and you have less or Donna has less?*

DONNA: *Barbara is the most responsible one in the family, and that's why I go to her for advice.*

SELVINI: *Give me an example of how she behaves responsibly.*

HARRY: *She always gets high marks in school.*

SELVINI: *Is that important in your family—doing well in school?*

HARRY: *Yes, it is.*

CECCHIN: *Who is watching your performance in school?*

MOTHER: *Barbara works; she has very good work habits. If she had a project three months in advance, she would start working on it immediately. She wouldn't leave it till the last night. Harry has also been very good in school, but he doesn't apply himself.*

FATHER: *He wants to be an accountant, and he's planning to work for a year and then go to college.*

---

CECCHIN: You can see here that all the drama is gone when they talk about school. The parents are united and real differences don't exist anymore. I am concerned that we missed a few openings, like when mother said "My ex-husband always told me I was crazy." We never used that, and it's a fantastic statement. The other opening was when she said "My husband said it would end the relationship." That too is an interesting statement. We missed a couple of beautiful opportunities. Now they're just talking about trivia.

PENN: Suppose you had not passed up those opportunities? What questions would you have asked?

CECCHIN: Questions like: "Your husband said you were crazy. Did you agree with him? Did your children agree with him? If a man tells you you're crazy for many years, it's hard to get rid of that idea. Do you feel your present husband perceives you as crazy?"

PENN: She may have a perception of herself as crazy in both families. After all, we're sitting here with a boy who's been diagnosed as schizophrenic; the label may have jumped to him.

CECCHIN: It also sounds as if the husband's first wife was crazy too. So I would ask the children if they think their mother is afraid of this condition. Then you bring out the whole thing. We would talk about the idea of craziness in the system.

HOFFMAN: That would have made John systemically crazy.

CECCHIN: Yes. But with two therapists in the room, you cannot use these openings. I would not know, if I suddenly started on this track, whether Selvini would agree. It's a major change to go in like that. In fact, Selvini is following another idea: Barbara's prestige in the family. One observation we have made is that every family, within the first five or ten minutes, gives you all the openings. Three months after the first interview, if you look at the first fifteen minutes, the openings are all there. The whole point is to learn to see them and learn how to use them immediately. To enter and develop those openings with your questioning.

### FAMILY INTERVIEW

FATHER: *I get mad when they make a lot of mistakes in school. I find it is just stupid. They go too fast and don't think.*

CECCHIN: *Who makes you most angry?*

FATHER: *John, definitely. Because I know he can do better. He doesn't apply himself.*

MOTHER: *In the third term last year, he didn't even take his English exam; he just went downtown. Consequently, he failed.*

CECCHIN: *That makes you angry?*

MOTHER: *It's his life he's playing with, not ours; because after he's a certain age, he's not our responsibility any more.*

FATHER: *Well, he is morally but not legally.*

MOTHER: *No, but I mean he isn't going to depend on us for a livelihood, so, consequently, he's the guy that's going to suffer.*

CECCHIN: *[to John] Do you agree with them? Do you think your mother is right? I know many kids who don't agree with this kind of talk.*

JOHN: *I agree.*

---

CECCHIN: I tried to attack this kind of talk so the boy won't accept it so easily. John says his parents are interested in his schoolwork, but then his mother says it's not her problem, it's his problem. They say it's his responsibility, but they are nagging him all the time. So I introduce the idea that he could disagree.

PENN: You introduce some doubt, to indicate that he doesn't have to accept the parents' confusing messages.

CECCHIN: John has this kind of doubt. If you say "I have doubts," you reassure him tremendously. In essence, you say "I don't understand this kind of message you are getting: 'You must apply yourself: but it's your life, so do what you want. But when you come home, you don't do anything,' " et cetera. Lots of double messages.

## FAMILY INTERVIEW

CECCHIN: [to Harry] Where do you plan to go to college?
HARRY: To the closest college to my home, so transportation costs won't be so much.
CECCHIN: How far is it from home?
HARRY: About twenty-five miles. I'd be living at home all the time.
CECCHIN: Why do you want to live at home?
HARRY: Expenses.
CECCHIN: If you had the money, would you go somewhere else? [To John] Would you, too, like to go to a college close to home?
JOHN: I would like to go to college, but I don't have the money.
CECCHIN: It's a question of money. Are you planning to do what Harry does, work for college?
JOHN: Yeah, probably.
CECCHIN: [to Barbara] What's your plan?
BARBARA: I don't know what I want to be, so I don't know what I'm going to do.
SELVINI: Are there other examples of Barbara's responsibility in the family or at school? Are any of you competitive with Barbara?
FATHER: Do you try to beat her, to try and be in the same position?
DONNA: No, not really. I don't think I could handle it.
MOTHER: Everyone seems quite happy in their position.

---

PENN: Your direction is unclear. Selvini is talking about Barbara's position in the family; you're talking about the school issue. I don't understand what you're doing.
BOSCOLO: It's more related to the context in which the interview is taking place. The context is that we are in an English-speaking country and Gianfranco and I understand English, while the women of our team, Selvini and Prata, don't understand as much. They are a bit paralyzed because of the language barrier. This may have been a problem. Cecchin

is doing most of the talking because he understands English and communicates with the family very well. I, as supervisor, call two or three times to talk to Selvini, to share some ideas.

HOFFMAN: Why did you only phone Selvini?

BOSCOLO: I think I felt if I had called Cecchin, Selvini could have felt left out. Every team is like a family. It is a group with a history, it develops its own rules, and a special sense of its own organization. For example, if I had called Gianfranco, the women might have felt displaced. You must remember that Selvini was the official leader of the team and she was the one who was in the session. So I think that for these reasons the team had become somewhat paralyzed. What is interesting is that at the time we were doing this interview, we were not aware of this.

PENN: That you were paralyzed?

BOSCOLO: Exactly. I called Selvini three times. I was not aware, not conscious of it. The things we're talking about now were not present in my mind at that time. But somehow I reacted as a member of a system, of a family.

PENN: You were rescuing Selvini.

BOSCOLO: Exactly. I wanted to rescue Selvini. At the same time, I think I felt that it would be too dangerous to get into an alliance with Cecchin. I would feel as if we were completely neglecting the women.

HOFFMAN: [to Cecchin] Did you feel paralyzed?

CECCHIN: Now that we're talking, I recognize the same feelings. I couldn't go on with my questioning, I had to follow Selvini's lead. She went out, she talked to the team, she made decisions. But now we get to an interesting point: when the team is paralyzed like that, we can say there are organizational problems. Every team has organizational problems which the family immediately utilizes, unconsciously, in order to make a paralyzed team. This is homeostatic and keeps the situation the same. That's why it's very useful when you have a team to have a metateam that is observing the interaction. This doesn't mean that you are disorganized or have problems; it means that the family is bringing out this problem in you. The family, as a system, calibrates itself to the information the team introduces into the session. It's a problem of calibration rather than intentionality on the family's part.

PENN: It's really quite mysterious how those events take place, how the dilemma of the team and the dilemma of the family reflect each other. For instance, all morning we've been talking about the lack of confirmation for the two young males in this family, while at the same time we see that the two men on the team feel they must restrain their effectiveness to keep in sync with the rules of their team.

BOSCOLO: For instance, in Milan, we are in a completely different context because all of us know the language equally well. Let me give you an example of how we can be conscious and corrective at the same time in our own context. Selvini, who is an expert on anorexia, and I were doing cotherapy with a family in which there was an anorectic. During the session, the mother in this family often looked at Selvini, listening carefully to her every word; they were very connected. The male therapist, myself, was completely neglected. It was also interesting that the father in the family, like me, was completely ignored. When I would try to talk, the women would both look at me as if to say: Who is that person? Why does he interrupt us? I found myself becoming quite aloof and withdrawn, and I saw that the father was doing the same. The women kept talking, and the father and I looked at each other or at the ceiling, and we were somewhat embarrassed. Suddenly I thought that if I had had some playing cards, I would have said to the father: Would you like to play? I'll get a small table, because we don't count. Then I looked at Selvini and said sternly, "Can you come out! I don't agree with what you are saying!" Selvini, who understood me immediately, became very submissive. The mother was shocked because I had given Selvini this command to follow me. I opened the door and said "Come out!" in a very loud voice. The man started to come alive at last. Behind the mirror, we were laughing with the team, and Selvini said: "I understand why you did that. It was good to do it." We made a hypothesis and decided that when we reentered the session I would make the intervention. Se we entered, and the family looked at us as if to say, What happened? Selvini assumed a very compliant attitude, and I said "I asked Dr. Selvini to come out because I didn't agree with what she was doing, and now I would like to explain why I don't agree with her." Then I delivered the intervention. From that point on, the session was completely different. I became important and the husband became important. But that was conscious, and in our own context in Milan. In that different context, we were not aware of this.

HOFFMAN: The other thing worth commenting on is that you were also developing the technique of circular questioning. Maybe your "missed opportunities" reflected the management of two people in the session doing circular questioning around a hypothesis. You get mixed up if there are two hypotheses being researched at the same time.

CECCHIN: Right. Circular questioning is connected to the refinement of a hypothesis or the discarding of one and the taking on of another. Before we go into a session we have a discussion and choose a simple hypothesis, but when we go into the room we keep changing. We make new hypotheses according to the openings the family offers. But if the family offers you ten openings, you have to choose one, and it's impossible for two people to agree on which opening to choose while you're working. Sometimes the questioning can be quite indirect, and your partner would find it hard to understand what you're doing.

BOSCOLO: It is possible to work this way in cotherapy. If one therapist is asking the questions, the other one must listen to see what kind of a hypothesis the cotherapist is getting at. When he thinks he understands his partner's hypothesis, then he can either step in or not. Or one therapist can conduct the session until he or she runs out of ideas, and then the other therapist steps in.

CECCHIN: When we do a simulated family with students, we say "If you run out of ideas, stop and say 'I have no ideas.' " Then we talk about what was happening in the family when the ideas ran out. We try to see what the family did to make the therapist's head feel empty. After that, we ask the therapist if he feels like continuing or if another student can take his place. When he runs out of ideas he stops, and another one starts. So you have five or six leads to follow, and each of the student-therapists tests their own hypotheses. But that's in the training setting. In fact, if you are in a session working with one hypothesis and suddenly the other therapist comes in with another, you or the family can go crazy.

BOSCOLO: It's possible to do this work using cotherapy, but it takes time. You have to get to know each other's style, the way you relate, et cetera. It's not always worth it. It's much better to have one therapist behind the mirror and one in the room. It's much more useful to leave the family when your head is empty and go out and discuss the session with your colleague.

HOFFMAN: When did you start to have only one therapist in the room with the family?

CECCHIN: It was around the time we started to work together on our own.

PENN: Did you think of it as an experiment? How did your team manage that idea? Did anyone object?

CECCHIN: It happened by itself because Luigi and I started to conduct training groups and the women started to do research. When we started the training groups, one of us was in the room and the other was behind the mirror. We had experimented and found that if two people were in the room, it was a waste of time. We also discarded the idea of a heterosexual couple as a "corrective" experience. That is an old belief from psychoanalysis based on ideas about role modeling, identification with the therapists, et cetera.

PENN: Can you expand on that?

CECCHIN: The idea is that you give the family an example of how to get along. If you look at other people fighting and getting along, then you can fight and get along. But since every organization is bound by its own special rules, that doesn't always work. They can watch you being fantastically healthy while they remain neurotic. So we believe that therapy does not consist of introducing yourself as a "person," it consists of introducing information and ideas.

HOFFMAN: Good-bye "use of self."

CECCHIN: You can use yourself by saying "I don't know what's going on." That's using your confusion. You can say "I don't know what I am doing." You cannot say "I will show you how I handle the situation, and that will help you." We noticed that every time we made a personal example—"this is what I would do with my wife"—immediately the faces become totally bored. They don't want to hear about you, they don't care; it's their system that is interesting to them.

BOSCOLO: Earlier, when we were doing cotherapy, we had the idea that learning was related to identification. If the woman in the family was too strong and the man too weak, we said that the therapists should behave in an opposite way, to provide the experience of a more successful couple.

CECCHIN: The trouble with that is it means you have a model of what a family should be like; a model that says the man should be more active, more involved than the woman.

PENN: Or they should be equal.

CECCHIN: Or they should be equal. But why? It's better to go to the family and say "Oh, I see in this family the women have tremendous energy and the men are very quiet. When did you decide to be quiet like that? Or energetic like that?" You try to find out why they've made this decision so that they come out doing something different from what society usually expects. You say "This arrangement probably works for you." You would never say "Look at this man. He doesn't take initiative, he's totally destroyed by his wife," because that implies they shouldn't be this way.

PENN: Do you also ask "What do you think of your husband's behavior?"

CECCHIN: Yes. And if she says "He's too compliant and doesn't take the initiative," then we discuss the problem as she sees it.

### FAMILY INTERVIEW

CECCHIN: *If Barbara decides to go to college or leave home, who will take her place in the family?*

MOTHER: *When my husband and I got married, Barbara became the big sister because*

*she had two little sisters. Before, she had been the youngest sister with two older brothers.*
CECCHIN: *So nobody would like to change positions now; but suppose she leaves home? Then what happens?*
FATHER: *Then you'd turn to your mother more.*

---

HOFFMAN: That's an interesting hypothetical question: Suppose Barbara leaves home. You suddenly see that everything would change.
CECCHIN: Yes. Now I confirm the hypothesis that when the new family was formed, Barbara gained importance because she became the big sister and the boys lost prestige.
HOFFMAN: There is an implication that Barbara is more important than Mother. They said if she left, the kids would turn to Mother. Obviously they don't now.
BOSCOLO: Selvini had tried two or three times to confirm a hypothesis about the importance of Barbara. She saw Barbara as the balance point. Barbara is the sister of Harry and John; and when Mother and Father got married, Barbara's response was "Oh, I wanted sisters." So she became very close to her new sisters, and they made a very connected group. That left the two boys out. The fact that Barbara switched positions left her brothers out. Also, Mother's position is less important than Barbara's. We felt Barbara's place was the most important in the entire family.
CECCHIN: Another idea is that Mother gives Barbara the task of being a substitute mother for the two girls because she doesn't want to make a mistake in Father's eyes.
PENN: Her daughter protects her from making a mistake, just as John protects her from the accusation of being crazy. They're loyal kids.
CECCHIN: Yes, she is afraid to be a mother because this man may criticize her. He has already told her: I'm going to be in charge, and you shut up. The mother is thoroughly confused here. If the mother were available, the girls would go to her now—they wouldn't have to wait for Barbara to leave.
BOSCOLO: We also learn that the first mother gave up these girls for a car. She neglected them. So the father gives a strong message: Here are my two girls, please take care of them; they had a terrible mother who sold them for a car.
CECCHIN: Here you can use hypothetical or future questions, like asking the father "Since your daughters had such a terrible mother, how long do you think it will take them with this new mother to get the mother

they're looking for? How long will it take the sons in the family, since they had such a terrible father, to finally have a good father? Who is better off here—the girls, who need a good mother, or the boys, who need a good father? How long will it take for your father to feel secure as a father? How long do you all have to remain children in order to make him feel secure as a father? How long do you have to remain at home in order for your parents to assure themselves they are good parents?"

PENN: This is an idea that particularly interests me: the use of future questions as interventions. By the end of the interview, these future questions often introduce so much new information that they preclude giving the family a task or prescribing the situation or using a positive connotation. The family is free to make what it will of these new ingredients that have been stirred into their system. They will organize themselves in some kind of relation to them, without any formal request from the therapist.

BOSCOLO: I agree. These questions are interventions and they can be very unsettling. The feedback can be very emotional. If it is, an intervention can be used to calm it down—for instance, a ritual where the daughters are to behave in a special way with mother, the sons with father. In that way, you give them some control.

PENN: You're saying that the ritual monitors the rate of absorption of the new information.

CECCHIN: Yes. The questions are unsettling, and you give a little hint about how the family can organize itself around this new information by saying: You do that on Monday; you do that on Tuesday.

BOSCOLO: The development of this approach in the future could be to use the circular questioning as the primary intervention and then give a small task just to reassure the family. It's like a prescription: every four hours, you take this pill. If you go to the doctor, you get a pill; otherwise, you think he's a poor doctor.

### FAMILY INTERVIEW

CECCHIN: *Do you think your children are planning to leave home or not?*
MOTHER: *I don't know.*
FATHER: *I have my doubts.*
HARRY: *I'm planning on leaving home, but I'm planning on going through college first so I will have something to go into, so I can make money.*
FATHER: *I would like to see them get an education before they leave home.*

MOTHER: *Sort of a foundation.*

CECCHIN: *Who would be the most likely to leave home first?*

MOTHER: *Harry, probably.*

CECCHIN: *[to Mother] Who takes care of the family when you're out of the house?*

MOTHER: *They're pretty independent now.*

CECCHIN: *Does Barbara take the mother's position?*

MOTHER: *I don't think so.*

FATHER: *Actually, I would say they would all be capable of that because there was an instance—a wedding—when all the kids were away and only Deborah was home with me, and Deborah worked out for me. She had all the meals ready, woke me up at suppertime. Nobody was there but Deborah and I. She carried on very well.*

CECCHIN: *She just needed a chance to do it?*

MOTHER: *They all know what to do when they have to.*

DONNA: *If Mom ever died or something, I think Barbara would probably take that position.*

DEBORAH: *Don't think that way!*

---

HOFFMAN: Did you hear that? "If Mom died, Barbara would take Mom's place." You've confirmed your hypothesis about Barbara.

BOSCOLO: Yes. The father gave the message "care for my family" both to his wife and to Barbara, so that if the wife were to die, Barbara would take her place. I think he has a tremendous need to be loved by these women.

### FAMILY INTERVIEW

CECCHIN: *If your father died, who would take his position?*

BARBARA: *Probably Harry. I think Harry and I have an obligation because we're the oldest—he's the oldest boy and I'm the oldest girl.*

CECCHIN: *[to children] So you have two parents; but if they go, you have two other parents; Harry and Barbara feel that obligation since they are the oldest.*

DONNA: *Maybe that's why we're so close.*

SELVINI: *[to Mother] When you were with your first husband, you had many difficulties with your children: they were disobedient, disrespectful, et cetera; but with your second husband, you received help with them, and they became obedient, good in school, et cetera. Maybe they are doing even better than the children of your husband. Can you make a classification, beginning with who is doing the best and ending with who is doing the worst?*

*CECCHIN: No one is actually the "best," but who behaves the best?*
*SELVINI: Exactly! Not the "best" in an absolute sense.*
*DEBORAH: Oh, dear! That's going to hurt one of us.*
*MOTHER: As far as I'm concerned, they all have their good qualities and they all have their bad times and their bad points.*

---

CECCHIN: When we ask family members to rate each other in terms of "better" and "worse," we get a negative reaction. It's much better to make comparisons with couples or threesomes. For example, you could say that when this new family got together, the children helped each other. You could then ask, were the two younger girls able to help the older children improve? Were the three older children able to be useful to the younger girls? You divide them into groups. You ask who got the best out of this union, the older group or the younger group. Instead of using a word like "best," you ask "Who improved most?"

BOSCOLO: It was also the wrong moment for that question. We had just been talking about the possibility of a parent's death and which children would take their place. It was probably the most important moment in the session, and John was left out.

CECCHIN: Yes. John is not a parent and not a child. Harry and Barbara would be parents and the younger girls are close to Father and Mother, but John is left out. We could have asked John, "If you could choose, would you choose to join the parents or the children?"

HOFFMAN: It's interesting, because the two who would be the surrogate parents are both the mother's children. So she has the stronger children but is the weaker marital partner.

CECCHIN: There's also the idea that when she was in the first marriage, she was helpless, causing Harry and Barbara to become more responsible. When they moved to this new family, the father said to Mother: "These children have to be obedient, compliant; your method is totally wrong." So they are confused as to how to position themselves.

## FAMILY INTERVIEW

*MOTHER: I just treat them as individuals, and sometimes I think, Oh, isn't this nice, or this; but sometimes I think they're all little rotters. I don't even think I could classify them.*

CECCHIN: *The older children have all improved with your marriage, but what about your girls? Did they improve with the new marriage?*

FATHER: *Donna was very time-conscious, she was a real worry-wart. I think this was a lot my fault. She was compulsive, because I'd get them up at five thirty in the morning and take them to a baby-sitter.*

CECCHIN: *You were alone for a while with your daughters?*

FATHER: *Yeah, over three years.*

CECCHIN: *So you were both mother and father to them?*

FATHER: *Right. And I would hurry them up, always looking at the time, to get to the baby-sitter's. Then Donna got obsessed with time. For years after that, if we were going someplace, she'd ask: "What time is it, Dad?"*

DONNA: *Anytime I got a new watch, I'd just sit there looking at it, asking "What time is it?" every five minutes.*

FATHER: *When I got married to Elizabeth and we were a unit, Donna didn't have these worries, and I think she was kind of lost for a while. Took her awhile to settle in. . . .*

———————

PENN: The relationship between Father and Donna was defined by the time obsession and Donna's being the wife of Father—she's the older daughter. Now she gets demoted by Barbara and is perceived as fragile, like John. She became a little girl in this family. Imagine all the role repositioning in any kind of restructured or recombined family. One must look at the differences between the old positions and the new ones to understand the nature of the new system.

## FAMILY INTERVIEW

MOTHER: *I can remember going for a ride, and Donna would say: "We are the only car on this road, and what if we break down? There will be no one to help us." Then she'd ask "Do you have enough gas, Dad?" It was constant worry.*

CECCHIN: *She doesn't do that anymore?*

DONNA: *I'm always afraid when someone's going away that something awful is going to happen to the house, like when I don't know where they are. Toilets are going to overflow or something. I always think something is going to happen, and we will really drown.*

FATHER: *Well, but you're not as bad as you were.*

CECCHIN: *Earlier you said that if Mother and Father didn't exist any more, you'd have two other parents. Suppose those two parents, Harry and Barbara, also disappeared?*

FATHER: *Then they would go to their aunt, Elizabeth's sister.*

MOTHER: *They are officially legal guardians if anything happened to us. Aunt Millie and Uncle Bob. But I think at the age they are, I'm sure they would never go there because they don't agree with the way my sister and her husband raise their children.*

---

PENN: Donna is responding to her father's injunction: Take care of me. But she does it through her symptom so she doesn't challenge his role.

CECCHIN: Yes. Probably the father is right. He sees her as the next one who is going to be crazy. The little one, Deborah, is taking care of father.

PENN: So now we have two first marriages that produced kids who have trouble; but as long as it's John who acts crazy, the father's first marriage looks better.

BOSCOLO: There are many divisions in this family between healthy and mad, good and bad. This couple thinks that they are the good ones and their former spouses are the bad ones. Also in the children's group some are healthy and some are crazy.

PENN: If you say the kids are compared to see who is crazier, and the two marriages are compared to see which is worse, we must then assume that the parents compete for who is a better parent.

BOSCOLO: My hypothesis is that there must be some that are good and some that are bad, and in this family the goodness and badness are too separated.

## FAMILY INTERVIEW

FATHER: *John, if he applies himself, can really do well. But he is usually thinking about football or out with the guys. This, I suppose, is normal.*

CECCHIN: *How about the other one—Deborah?*

FATHER: *I think if she was there and had to do it, Deborah might do it. I think they would all chip in together.*

HARRY: *I don't think any one person would take over a job.*

MOTHER: *I'm not sure about John. Dad asked him to bring the Rototiller in from the garden, and it took two weeks of constant reminders for him to get it in; so I think he'd remember to eat, but things like that are not too important to him at the moment. So I'm not too sure.*

DEBORAH: *I think all John would do is eat and sleep.*

SELVINI: *[to John] What do you think of this diagnosis that was made of you?*

JOHN: *What do I think of it? A diagnosis? That's what the doctors made of me. It's kind of stupid, really, what they did. I don't agree with the diagnosis, really.*

SELVINI: *How do you react emotionally to a diagnosis of schizophrenia?*

JOHN: *Well, I don't think I have a mental problem. I have a problem.*

SELVINI: *How did your father react to this diagnosis?*

JOHN: *I don't know. I can't remember.*

SELVINI: *Was he upset?*

JOHN: *Yeah.*

SELVINI: *More than you?*

JOHN: *I don't know. Was I upset?*

BARBARA: *He was too freaked out to be upset, too hyper to be upset. He was in his own little world, so what did he care.*

SELVINI: *Who was more preoccupied about this—your mother or your father?*

BARBARA: *Mom was more upset. I don't know, they both really . . . Mom was mostly trying to do everything, but that was just because Dad was at work. But they both really tried to get the doctors to do stuff with John—*

FATHER: *No, but I think she's referring to the night we took him to the hospital.*

BARBARA: *I think Mom was more upset. We've never really seen you upset with something like that, so we can't really tell. . . .*

FATHER: *No, I very seldom show it.*

BARBARA: *That's right. So how are we supposed to know how upset you are?*

---

HOFFMAN: I don't understand what Selvini is trying to get at with her question about the diagnosis.

CECCHIN: We wanted to talk about the therapeutic context—that was the main idea. "When the doctors made a diagnosis, what did you think of it? Did you agree or not? Your mother agreed, your father agreed. We know that they agreed, and they've come here to this consultation to get a further confirmation of the diagnosis."

### FAMILY INTERVIEW

CECCHIN: *[about Father] Does he cry sometimes?*

BARBARA: *No, we've never seen him cry.*

CECCHIN: *Does Mother cry sometimes?*

BARBARA: *Yes. You could tell Dad was upset because he's always close to Mom, and they sort of both think the same way: if one is upset, the other is upset.*

CECCHIN: *They think the same way because they have agreed to think the same* way, or do you think they really think that way?

BARBARA: They usually don't talk in front of us.

CECCHIN: They have their discussions in private, eh? They don't show their disagreement in front of you—right?

BARBARA: Well, sometimes they did.

MOTHER: My former husband spoiled Barbara.

SELVINI: How was he with John when John was a little boy?

MOTHER: I remember one time my cousin tore the shirt off my ex-husband's back because . . . I think he's an alcoholic. But he would put beer caps in John's hand and keep squeezing them until he would cry. My cousin said "Don't you do that again." And he says "Well, he's my kid, and if I want to do that, I can do that!" She said "Not while I'm around." So he did it again, and there went his shirt. And I can remember coming home at two in the morning, after a dance, and he'd be fighting with me, and I'd say "You're going to wake the kids up." And he'd say "I'll wake them up," and then he'd pull them all out of their beds and throw them on the floor. [starting to cry] And he did things, like torment the kids' pets. He tried to drown their kitten, and he just did terrible things.

FATHER: And tell the kids "This is your supper." Jeez.

MOTHER: Anyway, the doctor told me to leave because he said I was soft in the head if I didn't.

CECCHIN: A doctor told you to leave? For your own safety, to leave the house?

FATHER: She was becoming suicidal. Like, he'd have a cigarette and he'd tell her to have a puff; and she'd say "I don't want it," and he'd shove it in her face.

MOTHER: But we never really talked about what he did. From what Barbara tells me, I don't think he's really changed.

CECCHIN: [to Barbara] You say you were always close to your father and he to you?

BARBARA: That was because he used to spoil me. I used to really like him a lot, I guess. But this summer I haven't been too interested in seeing him or nothin' any more. I guess I really just found out what he's really like.

MOTHER: He was the kind of person . . . unless you knew him, you would probably never suspect, because he did magic tricks and he had a great sense of humor and he was always the life of the party. But then we'd come home and, like that [she snaps her fingers], he'd be a different person; so people outside didn't really know.

———

HOFFMAN: It's interesting the way she said "the doctor told me to leave," as if she has no responsibility. Her tears are a powerful message to the children that nobody can leave.

BOSCOLO: The tears mean she is still attached to this man. Even after all this time, she still thinks about him. She said he abused the children, so she had to leave. Perhaps she left because of the children—you don't know.

HOFFMAN: I think it's more a reminder to the children of what she's gone through. It triggers them into an emotional position where they are very angry at this father and very protective of their mother.

CECCHIN: But the tears are a message which you can see in three or four different ways, depending on the context you give it. One is that she misses this man, this brilliant pianist, who behaves this way only with her; and she cries because she feels guilty about what she did. Another message reminds the children: Look how much I have suffered; look how much I gave up for this man because of you, because I was afraid for you. Or perhaps she's crying now because she's not as happy in this marriage as she could be. Or her crying could be a message to her husband that he's not enough for her. Or it could be another message to the children: Don't leave me; I cannot solve my problems. Look how many possibilities there are.

*FAMILY INTERVIEW*

CECCHIN: *Barbara, you say you finally found out how he was? And then never saw him?*

BARBARA: *He came home when we were up at the summer house, and he was giving me heck for something just because I was saying something. I was getting mad because he was drunk, and he just came home and started giving me heck for something I never did.*

MOTHER: *When his mother was baby-sitting on the Fourth of July, we came home and she was sleeping on the chesterfield. And he just walked over and slapped her across the face and said "You get up out of there, you son of a bitch!" And that's the way he was. That was his mother, and he did that.*

CECCHIN: *You still think about that sometimes, just now as we talked about it?*

MOTHER: *[crying] Oh no, just if I have to.*

BARBARA: *Whenever we were up at the summer house, whenever he came home, he was saying something about this girl that he was with; and she was a stripper, and she wanted him to bring her back, and it just turned my mom right off. . . .*

BOSCOLO: I have the impression that this family is inventing its own history. We often talk about the creation of history—a myth that the family needs. You could see the family story differently if you wanted. The

mother said her first husband mistreated her, but she also said her children mistreated her, and Barbara, at least, was on the father's side. When
they separated, the children went with the mother. Now the mother is
telling us how terrible this father was and her husband is telling us how
terrible his first wife was. They paint the past in a certain way so as to
demonstrate something in the present.

HOFFMAN: But what about drowning the kitten?

BOSCOLO: Yes, that's a demonstration that the husband was cruel, crazy.
The mother tells this story to explain about her husband. But it's also a
way the family creates a myth. You can observe the children when they
talk about their father: they say he's crazy. And the father's children
agree that their mother was terrible. Once in a while the children give
us information that conflicts with the myth. But this myth is like a
straitjacket, it creates a rigid way of seeing the past and the present.

HOFFMAN: How do you see the way it influences the present?

BOSCOLO: First, there is no flexibility in the family for any of the children
to think positively about the other parents.

HOFFMAN: Or to think badly about the present ones.

BOSCOLO: Yes. That's why I think a myth of this sort can be related to
psychosis. Usually it's the psychotic who cannot accept this myth. I'm
making a hypothesis now, but the only way to express your disbelief in
a myth of this sort is to become crazy. It's like the case we describe in
*Paradox and Counterparadox*. In the Cassanti family, there was a powerful
myth, where all the men of the group had to share the same ideas. It
can be very bad if one goes against a myth. A powerful myth continually
reframes the past in a very rigid way. In this family, the mother gives
the example about the cat to prove that her husband is crazy and has
always been crazy. Where if you asked him for his perception, he would
probably say "My wife is crazy."

CECCHIN: Some of the information the mother gives about her husband
is probably true. Some of it may not be true. It's impossible that her
husband was completely one thing or another. But this new family needs
to believe he was totally bad and crazy and needs to believe that the
father's first wife was terrible. The myth restricts the options of family
members to conceive of a more complex reality. They always have to
think in terms of black and white; and the black—the bad—is always
outside, and the white is all inside.

PENN: That's the straightjacket; they can't grow up and leave in the presence of the myth. When the mother talks about the bad, crazy husband,
her tears remind the children to protect her because she is in danger. A
myth like this operates like a premise; it says: If you (the children) ever

stop believing that those other parents are crazy and terrible, you will endanger your current parents.

HOFFMAN: You could see the situation in terms of triangles. The mother is obviously in a very submissive position in this marriage—not so unlike what she was in before, except it's defined now as good. If she has any feelings that it isn't so good, she's not allowed to entertain or express them. By remembering the bad first husband, you could say she "projects" any negative feelings away from the second one.

BOSCOLO: If you talk in terms of myth, you move to a more abstract level than the triadic explanation. For instance, you can say that the mother is afraid that the father will feel she is not close enough to him, and so she leaves John outside. This kind of explanation is on one level. But if you go to a higher level, the level of myth, you see very differently the submissiveness of the mother or the patriarchal attitude of the father. The myth gives them the cues for how they should be in order not to be the family they were in the past. The myth is a straitjacket in the sense that it prescribes specific behaviors for all of them, and it borrows from an even higher level of logical type—the societal level, where the father is the ruler, the mother backs him up, and the children cooperate.

PENN: It's the boy who really challenges the myth.

BOSCOLO: When there is a myth like this, I think it's very difficult to keep it up. At a certain point, someone has to break; and if they do, we have a psychosis.

## FAMILY INTERVIEW

CECCHIN: *Now I want to ask John, how do you see your situation? How do you see this episode in September that scared everyone? You went to a hospital and a diagnosis was made. How do you understand that situation now?*

JOHN: *I don't know.*

CECCHIN: *You're not sure. Do you feel you're out of that situation?*

JOHN: *I don't know.*

SELVINI: *You're going to school and doing fairly well?*

JOHN: *Fairly well.*

SELVINI: *Do you still show a need to cry once in a while?*

JOHN: *I don't really need to, not really really really.*

CECCHIN: *Now we will discuss all this with our colleagues behind the mirror.*

*SELVINI: We have to discuss here.*
*CECCHIN: [to family] You can go out and get coffee.*
*[Selvini and Cecchin go out.]*

———————————

HOFFMAN: Two questions: First, why did you change the topic here? Second, what clued you to take the discussion break?

CECCHIN: In answer to your first question, my idea was to introduce a change in punctuation. It was like saying, "Your father scared everybody by trying to drown the kitten, but you are pretty good at scaring people too by getting yourself into the hospital." However, this attempt to introduce a different idea to the family failed and I felt also that my partner was not following my lead. For my part, I did not understand what Selvini had in mind when she questioned the boy about his crying. Therefore I decided to take a break. Taking a break is a good solution when the team becomes confused and disorganized.

## DISCUSSION BREAK

*SELVINI: At the beginning of the session we are very intimate, we talk. We made, for example, a sort of family meeting; we talk very much; but nobody's very intimate because I have the impression that in this family there is a sort of rule: We have to be a united family. Everybody's very careful to have an apparently good relationship, but I am not sure at all that the relationships are so good and so normal and so clear as they say. The two girls, who apparently had a horrible mother, have found this woman and apparently they have a good relationship with this woman, but in my opinion—I did not understand everything—they have a very superficial relationship with this woman. More important is the relationship with the father, because the father is very seductive. When the mother began to cry, thinking about this horrible husband, the father was a real god in this moment. A savior arrived in this family, saving everybody.*

*BOSCOLO: I see it slightly differently. I see a pathological myth in this family, and the myth is this: these two parents each had a very bad partner. He says his wife was crazy, and she says her husband was crazy. So when they met each other they made this myth, and the myth is, from the mother: If you are good to my children, then you will make me have a good husband; and the father: If you are good to my children, you will make me have a good wife. The children are in the situation that all their behaviors have to fulfill this myth, because if they are rebellious they break the myth. So each one of the parents keeps saying about the other parent, in a reciprocal fashion: You must be the best. The couple presents itself as close to each other and as having each found the ideal partner. But in order for the partner to be ideal, the children must show behavior that fulfills this myth; so it's a very pathological situation.*

SELVINI: *Very pathological.*

CECCHIN: *It's not just a myth; it's a kind of project, an expectation. For example, the father said "I had a terrible wife." So he's compelling this wife to be a good mother to the children. But the children are in a difficult situation because they have to show she's a good mother. And Mother had a terrible husband who was also terrible to the children. So now the mother is saying to the husband, "You have to be a perfect father." How can you be a perfect father? Only if the children are perfect. So the children have to do everything they can to keep this expectation of the parents alive—to confirm it. And who is most successful in doing this? Barbara is successful, Harry is successful. All are successful except this boy here, John. No matter what he does he's not able to succeed, because if he obeys, he obeys too much; if he disobeys, he's high-strung, some kind of nervous character. He can never do anything good.*

SELVINI: *So we have the intervention now. He's the only sane point in the family; he's only acting crazy because he's the only one who is free not to be perfect.*

CECCHIN: *He's the only one who can destroy the myth.*

BOSCOLO: *It's a terrible myth. The children have to be perfect. They cannot have a relationship between them and they can't leave the field; they must be perfect so that the parents can believe they have the ideal partner.*

SELVINI: *This is the truth, and you can positively connote the behavior of John because he's caught in a trap—a terrible myth that each partner is a perfect parent.*

CECCHIN: *Also, the father talks to the boy for six hours to show that he is a good parent. The moment John becomes sick, the father has to go there: for six hours he's talking.*

SELVINI: *And Barbara, two hours.*

BOSCOLO: *They said that for six months before he had the breakdown he was too obedient. Maybe the obedience he showed was not the obedience they wanted; which tells you that these parents expect only one kind of behavior from all the children—the behavior that fulfills the myth they have that she's the best mother and he's the best father. Then the system—*

SELVINI: *—has the problem: Is this behavior the ideal behavior for the best, best mother? Is this behavior the ideal behavior for the best, best father?*

BOSCOLO: *As a matter of fact, analogically, I was very impressed when we talked about his problem; the siblings cried, but the parents didn't cry.*

SELVINI: *The mother cried at the end.*

BOSCOLO: *But she cried because her first husband was so cruel. When they talked about John's behavior, first one sister, then the other began to cry.*

CECCHIN: *Funny, the mother said: "The doctor told me I had to leave."*
SELVINI: *Because he's a sort of killer [former husband].*
CECCHIN: *But he was very fascinating too. So he is very important still.*
SELVINI: *Very seductive, very sympatico, and so on.*
CECCHIN: *She was becoming very suicidal.*
BOSCOLO: *He's a stimulus, that man, to make this father look better and better.*
CECCHIN: *To be the savior.*
BOSCOLO: *I had the feeling of a kind of slipping of contexts. For instance, these two parents, having had crazy partners, have given their children the message that they have to confirm that now they have the best partners. Also, the father says at one point [deleted in transcript] "My house is full of all the boys and girls in the neighborhood." They have become social workers, the parents.*
SELVINI: *They are becoming the fundamental parents for all the youth in the city.*
BOSCOLO: *We should prescribe the myth.*
CECCHIN: *The myth is that they have to be perfect.*
SELVINI: *I am against prescribing the myth because it's paradoxical. In my opinion, this is not the situation for a paradoxical prescription.*
CECCHIN: *First, we have to decide something about therapy, that's what is most important. Because there is the problem of assessment. The doctor made a diagnosis, then somebody else said "Probably it's LSD."*
SELVINI: *In the first session we are asked for a diagnosis, prognosis, and so on.*
CECCHIN: *If we prescribe therapy now, we have to motivate them.*
BOSCOLO: *I would not prescribe therapy.*
SELVINI: *Because the therapist is John.*
BOSCOLO: *I would prescribe a ritual in which I would put all the five children together.*
SELVINI: *Reading a prayer to John: "John, we thank you so much because you are freeing us from the terrible obligation to be the perfect father, the perfect mother." Because the two children had the horrible mother, the other three the horrible father. And this perfect father is now a disaster because he has a schizophrenic child.*

---

HOFFMAN: Here is another example of putting the therapeutic context first. You're going after a detailed hypothesis about the family; you've almost got the intervention, and you suddenly pull back.
CECCHIN: We have to remember the therapeutic context because the family is just here for a consultation; they aren't in therapy with anybody yet.
HOFFMAN: It was such a quick shift.
CECCHIN: We have to focus on the main context, which is the relationship between them and us.

## DISCUSSION BREAK

CECCHIN: *Let's turn this around for a moment. We can say that Barbara and Harry succeeded in giving a lot of satisfaction to the parents. Somehow the job of the parents was finished. But if they finish the job, they have no reason to stay together. So we can say that John and Donna somehow are keeping up the job for the parents. Because it's very clear that all Donna's problems come from the natural mother. And since these parents somehow need to do a social work job, the two "sick" ones are keeping up their activity. I'm trying to look for a possible prescription. John and Donna help the parents to continue to be good parents.*
BOSCOLO: *I think it's impossible to put Donna and John on the same level.*
CECCHIN: *They've been defined as the sick ones.*
BOSCOLO: *I wouldn't designate anybody. I would say this: This family had much suffering in the past, and they have this big task—I will explain the myth—that the kids from each of the former families, they try to— [Tape runs out.]*
SELVINI: *They are two people, each of whom needed a perfect parent for their children.*
PRATA: *But don't you think that's very strange? In saying that he's the best father for the children, she's the best mother for the children, it's a way of underlining . . .*
SELVINI: *Yes, this is another idea we can use for a conclusion. I don't know if it is a conclusion for the family or a conclusion for future therapy. But what is our problem? What is the epistemology of John? Why did John have this crisis? This epistemology I describe as vengeance, because he's so furious at the father? This father is in love with Barbara, he's in love with Harry, but he's not in love with John because John is not bright enough and he doesn't give satisfaction enough, and so on. John feels himself very inferior to Harry and Barbara. But Harry and Barbara did nothing to free the parents from the terrible duty to be good parents. Only John is doing this, because he's breaking the myth that they had to be perfect parents.*
BOSCOLO: *I think there could be a higher-level intervention which puts the children on one side and the parents on the other. I talk about the myth now. Mother had a difficult husband, Father had a difficult wife; they got together and the children cooperated so that the parents were helped to arrive at a good relationship. However, at a certain point this solution stopped working, and the reason we know it isn't working is because of John. John is the sign. Of course, it could have been any of the five. The message we got today from the family is that there is something not working. So at this point we could give a ritual to the children to talk together and to decide how they can operate to keep the husband feeling that he found the best wife and the wife feeling that she found the best husband. We could prescribe the myth in this way.*
CECCHIN: *Why not say that the parents have had a problem because they had no*

time to be married to each other, and John is helping them to realize that because he keeps telling them: *Don't try to help me; forget about helping me.* Barbara and Harry are the ones who are not helping the parents because they are too much of a success. The parents have had a bad myth, which is bad for them. . . .

BOSCOLO: *Because if they go on, they may never become husband and wife, only parents.*

SELVINI: *What I can't understand, Gianfranco, is Donna, because I didn't understand what Donna is doing that is not perfect.*

CECCHIN: *She's very emotional and she's scatterbrained; you cannot trust her because she changes her mind. The father said if you put Donna and John together, they couldn't run the house because they're too confused. They don't have any sense of responsibility. Father keeps saying that only Barbara is responsible. Donna was obsessive, because she was talking about time all the time, she was worrying about being alone in the car—all these kinds of stories. Even now he says he wouldn't trust her; he didn't say so clearly, but he won't trust John and Donna together, he doesn't think they could make it. So they're still children to be cured in some way.*

SELVINI: *They can disqualify us in some way—saying that they are a very happy couple.*

BOSCOLO: *Why don't you think in terms of putting all the children together? Once a month, for instance, they meet for a few minutes; they talk together and they discuss how to continue to keep the myth going in order for the mother to feel she is a good mother and for the father to be a good father, because the children's own mother and father were no good. Then the parents don't have to ask what were the conclusions.*

SELVINI: *Explain a little more about the details.*

BOSCOLO: *Because from the beginning of the session, it came out that one of the members is perceived as no good. John, in order to make him not a schizophrenic (because in this family the labeling of schizophrenia makes the family stick together to help the schizophrenic), has to be taken out of the position of being the sick and different one. He has to be put together with the other children in helping the parents.*

SELVINI: *Yes. I am with you. [Everyone talks.]*

BOSCOLO: *But using different styles. They have to make this meeting to maintain this myth in their different styles. Harry and Barbara are assuring the parents that they are perfect parents. John and Donna, and maybe Deborah, give them something to be preoccupied about, to fight against, and so on.*

PRATA: *Why don't you let them find out something for themselves? You are telling them what to do.*

BOSCOLO: *The children have been helping the parents to maintain this myth, so now we should prescribe this meeting for once a month until, in the future, they feel it is unnecessary. Until they get a message from the parents that they don't need this myth.*

SELVINI: *Exactly. Not to stay together, but to maintain the myth.*

BOSCOLO: *Because they had a really sad experience.*

PRATA: *So you say this in a very empathic way, and as long as it works, the children don't have to phone here. If it doesn't work, they can phone.*

BOSCOLO: *I would prefer to address the children.*

SELVINI: *Yes, because from John's point of view, it's necessary to be ill; he has some power in being crazy.*

CECCHIN: *What, for example, do Harry and Barbara do?*

SELVINI: *[as if addressing the family] I wish to tell a story. We see this family . . . we ask for the first consultation assessment of this family and we see a terribly sad story—you, Mr. Y, because you had a horrible wife, not a wife, but mother for your children; Mrs. Y, because you had that horrible father for your children. Now you marry and you built a very important myth, a myth very necessary: that you, Mrs. Y, you married a perfect father for your children; and you, Mr. Y, married a perfect mother for your children. And now we see that all your children are doing what they can, in different styles, to maintain this myth. Harry and Barbara are perfection, satisfaction. The others give you preoccupation, social work, therapy for hours, and so on. And you children should meet, for example, each fifteen days, meeting to decide in what way to continue this operation that you do to maintain this myth until [Everybody talks at once.]*

BOSCOLO: *When you said that, I would turn to the children, all five, and say "You should meet once a week, for half an hour."*

PRATA: *"Very precisely."*

BOSCOLO: *"And talk among you . . ."*

CECCHIN: *"Without the parents . . ."*

BOSCOLO: *Yes, and to say how they help their mother be the best mother for the . . .*

CECCHIN: *What about therapy? We forgot about therapy.*

PRATA: *No. If you succeed in maintaining this myth, therapy is not necessary. . . .*

CECCHIN: *That doesn't make sense.*

SELVINI: *This is a problem. Cut completely the relationship to this institute? No, that is not good.*

BOSCOLO: *I would start the intervention by saying something about their being here, and by communicating that it could have been John that brought them or it could have been anybody. "At a certain point we asked a question whether Donna or Harry or any other of your children might have some problems. We asked this question because of the fact that one of your children has a problem." There you put all the children on the same level. "John is a sign for us that at a certain point—" and then you start the comment about the myth.*

CECCHIN: *But this myth is not very stable. "If you see that you don't succeed, you must come back."*

PRATA: *"So once a month, for half an hour, on Monday—"*

SELVINI: *"—you can call someone personally." They have to have someone here that knows them.*

PRATA: *"If you succeed, your family will not need a John. If you don't succeed, call here."*

SELVINI: *Yes. [Team gets up to leave.]*

## INTERVENTION

*[Family now comes in. Boscolo and Prata have gone out, leaving Selvini and Cecchin in the room.]*

SELVINI: *[to family]* So I want to give you the conclusion of our team concerning the present situation of your family and what we have seen. What we have observed during the session are very sad, tragic things. Mother and Father have had disastrous experiences in previous marriages, and you, Mrs. Y, had a very terrible, sad experience with the father of your children. And you, Mr. Y, you had a very negative mother for your children. So you married with a very strong decision that you, Mrs. Y, should give a very good father to your children, and you, Mr. Y, with the strong decision to give a very good mother to your children. And you succeeded. And I am convinced, and also the team is convinced, that this is very important for your children. But it is more important for you due to the fact that you had very negative, very tragic, very dramatic experiences before this. So I think that you children, all of you five children, you are doing very much to maintain this conviction, this myth. This is a very important myth, a sort of myth for your parents. What you are doing to maintain this myth, to maintain this conviction, is in many different styles. For example, Harry and Barbara are maintaining this myth with perfect behavior; they are successful and very good in school. So Mother can think, "I have given a good father to my children, to Harry and Barbara"; and Father can think the same thing. But also Donna and John are doing a great deal in a different style: giving their parents preoccupation, giving them something more to do for their children, so as to be perfect parents, to be very good parents. Deborah is little now, but maybe in the future you can choose to be perfect or to be a problem. You are free to choose what you want, so it's very important this thing that you are doing for this need of your parents. So we think that therapy is not necessary for the time being. In our opinion, it's not necessary because the children are doing all these necessary things for your myth—to give this meaning to your life, this very important meaning and value to your life. We ask only one little thing. Have a meeting together, you siblings, once a week or every two weeks, at a time you choose, and stay together, you five children, and discuss how to continue this work you are doing. And it is good to do this until you succeed. But if in the future you *have the impression that you are not succeeding, in that case you have to phone here to ask for help, if you have the impression that you are not successful in maintaining this need your parents have, which is very understandable. I can understand it very well because I understand your previous tragic life. So I've finished, and this is our conclusion.*

[Murmurs from family. Someone says "Okay."]

CECCHIN: *Was it clear that the five children should meet together without the parents? The parents should be left out because it's a problem the five of you have: to assess if you are successful or not successful. So for the time being the parents should be left out. Probably you should not even tell them what happened. If you want to, you can; but we suggest that you don't. You should keep it to yourselves. John, you must take responsibility to call the meeting once in a while?*

JOHN: Yeah, okay.

SELVINI: Yes.

CECCHIN: *Okay, we are finished now.*

[Final leave-takings. John puts his arms around Selvini and hugs her.]

---

PENN: It occurred to me that even though one could see that many things were happening to the four of you, and that there were opportunities that you consequently passed up during the interview, it didn't affect your capacity to create a good intervention.

CECCHIN: I think that this confirms the value of the team; that in the moment when we were conferencing together, all four, we understood each other and we became very productive.

HOFFMAN: It's interesting. The process of working with a team means that if the therapists become paralyzed and can't reach a conclusion through the questioning process, then the team offers another format for reaching a conclusion. Here you became temporarily paralyzed and then you convened around the intervention, and that brought you out of the paralysis.

CECCHIN: Sometimes the family succeeds in confusing you. You get a lot of information, but you're not able to connect it. Then you need this kind of exercise or ritual, the ritual of team discussion, to become coherent again. That's how you cure yourself. You enter a team meeting with no ideas, but you don't care because you know that when you begin to talk something will come out. It's a kind of trust. We never say: Now what do we do? We say: Let's talk; something will come out. There's a confidence that through the team ritual you will come out with a solution.

BOSCOLO: There's also an example here of the engineering of an intervention. For instance, when the general hypothesis is accepted by all of the team members, you fine-grain it until it makes sense.

HOFFMAN: You seem to start with the most general classification: a description that can be on the level of a myth. Then you go to the level of the groups or units, and give a ritual to a couple or place one group in the service of another—children to help parents, as you did here.

CECCHIN: When we look for an intervention, we try to find a logic that will appeal to the family. The content of the intervention can be crazy, but formally it must have a logic. And we can speculate that the logic of the intervention will be directed to the left brain of the family (if you want to think like that) and the crazy part of the intervention will go to the right brain.

BOSCOLO: Another way to put it is that when you find a premise—like the crazy idea that people have to be perfect—you can build a logic on it so that everything the family does connects with that premise. Here we made a logic according to the premise of being perfect, which we incorporated into the myth of the perfect parents and perfect children. According to this premise, it's logical that the parents need the children; it's logical that the children should never leave home; it's logical that one of the children should be crazy; it's logical that therapy should be useless. You could say, of course, that this premise can be contradicted by commonsense logic: by the idea that children should be good, that therapy should help, and so on. But we only include the logic that explains the behaviors in terms of the premise.

CECCHIN: Now we can see that what people call paradoxical is really an effect of contradicting commonsense logic. The logic of the so-called paradoxical intervention is clear, orderly, precise—it behaves like a gene that organizes the structure of the cell in a coherent way.

BOSCOLO: If you look for the premise, then it's very easy to build a descriptive proposition that organizes the information you get about the problem. And the premise is always a statement that is relational, like "I have to be in control of myself." That idea controls a whole class of behavior.

PENN: Changing the premise starts a domino reaction: all the old behaviors fall down like a deposed regime.

HOFFMAN: Bateson, talking about the economics of flexibility in an adaptive system, says that you have to have rigid premises, automatic ones, laid down at a level below consciousness. When those change, it's like pulling a master switch.

CECCHIN: Yes. The biggest shifts in family therapy come when you succeed in operating at the level of deep premises.

BOSCOLO: That's exactly what Bateson says about the alcoholic's position. You have to change the basic premise. The premise is "I'm in control of myself." You have to help him to say "I'm not in control of anything." If he can accept that idea, then all his behavior changes meaning and he becomes a different person. A better intervention in this family would have been to change the premise and not accept it as we did. We should have said "We understand why the parents have created this myth of having to be perfect. They have this myth because they suffered too much. But now we see the myth is not necessary. It will take a lot of time, two or three years perhaps, for them to get over this myth and forget their old partners. And while they're waiting for this moment, the children should meet together to see what they can do to help their parents."

HOFFMAN: Did you do a follow-up on this family?

CECCHIN: They didn't come back to the clinic as far as we know, so we assumed the family had handled the crisis without further therapy.

HOFFMAN: If they had come back, would you have felt you hadn't done a good enough job?

CECCHIN: No. We set up a win-win situation, where if the family doesn't come back that is of course the best option. But if they do come back, this is still within the terms of the intervention. I think you are operating more like a strategic therapist if you reframe a behavior or event in the hope that they will resist you and go the opposite way.

PENN: It's not really a consultation, you know. The family didn't have a therapist when they came in, so this was more in the nature of an intake interview.

BOSCOLO: Yes. We became in this instance the "referring persons"—I am alluding to our article of that name (Selvini Palazzoli, Boscolo, Cecchin, and Prata, 1980)—in the sense that if the family had come back to see another therapist, they would have been a different family from the one we saw. They would have become the family-plus us. The referring person has often introduced a solution, or new information, whether on purpose or inadvertently, and the therapist would have had to take our presence into account.

HOFFMAN: It's interesting. You include in your formulations all the contaminations from the context.

CECCHIN: Yes, except that we don't think of them as contaminations, just part of the social field. A further contextualizing force was the fact that we were interviewing the family as part of a training conference in which we were trying to show how we work and think. The intervention is as much for the audience that is viewing the interview on closed-circuit TV as for the family. If we had not been demonstrating in front of a group of professionals, we might not have come up with the same intervention at all.

HOFFMAN: Since your clinical theory challenges many accepted ideas about psychotherapy, you are always intervening at the level of the professional context just by offering such a different treatment approach.

CECCHIN: That's true. More and more we feel that it's too narrow to remain a closet family therapist, seeing families in the protection of the private setting. We are trying to push out into the world, into the public sector, and apply our ideas to work in hospitals, homes, aftercare facilities, residences, and all the places where we used to feel they could not be put into effect. Now we feel that these are the frontiers and that family therapy per se is only a good, pioneering start. The private institute, the team format, and other hallmarks of our approach are useful for training, or for research, but we will have to continue innovating if we are to move systemic thinking out into the community, out into the streets.

# PART 2

# *The Family with a Secret*

## INTRODUCTION

T HE CARDINAL POINTS of the Milan Associates' approach to therapy and training—circularity, neutrality, and hypothesizing, as set forth in their article on these themes (Selvini Palazzoli, Boscolo, Cecchin, and Prata, 1980)—can be clearly viewed in the following case. Though these concepts are discussed throughout the text and are integral to all the consultations presented, the path of that discussion is carefully laid out here and will be the first focus of this introduction.

We will also examine how the case illuminates this methodology—that is, how the particular techniques of the Milan Associates fit the dynamics and the progress of the case. And we will discuss the team process and how the particular ritual given to the B family affected the problem through repositioning family relationships. A particular feature of this case is the injunction the consultants were given to respect a "secret" in the family.

Their method of continually addressing the effects of the secret without ever alluding to its content provides a new model for coping with this familiar dilemma of family work.

## Constructing a Hypothesis

The first act of any therapy and a nodal principle of the Milan team's methodology is hypothesizing, a process that produces many permutations as the treatment interview unfolds. The construction of hypotheses is a continuous process, coevolving with the family's movement. The act of hypothesizing is best described using the concepts of cybernetic feedback loops, for as the family's response to the questioning modifies or alters one hypothesis, another is formed based on the specifics of that new feedback. This continuous process of hypothesis construction requires the therapist to reconceptualize constantly, both as an interviewer and as a team member.

Regarding hypothesis construction, the Milan Associates have described a centrifugal design that guides their exploration of the various dimensions of the significant system—that is, the one organized by the problem. They begin the interview by asking for a description of the problem *now*; the family often responds by presenting a symptom bearer, one who "has" the problem. The team follows with "Who noticed the problem first?" This question accomplishes two things: it immediately gives an interpersonal definition to the problem, with the implication that a problem does not exist without a "noticer," and it defines the problem as an event that is outside any one person. The event, or the problem *now*, is seen as a communication between at least two (and doubtless more) people. At this point, the team's questions connect the problem bearer and the noticer to the wider family system. What remains is to connect the family system with the extended family and referring context. This process has a centrifugal motion; it reflects the idea of circularity exemplified by the connection of people who share a pattern through time.

At each centrifugal expansion, the Milan team makes a new hypothesis, or a new explanation of the pattern over time that resulted in a problem. For instance, they may begin with a father and a problem person, then move to father, the problem person and mother, then father, the problem person, mother, and father's brother. Finally they connect the whole family system with the referring person(s). It is the joining of all extended relationships and contexts that produces an overarching *systemic* hypothesis.

The entire system the "problem" has managed to organize is now accounted for in the construction of this systemic hypothesis.

When Hoffman and myself interviewed Boscolo and Cecchin, we paid special attention to the refinements of their hypothesis construction—that is, when they changed it, based on what information, and so on. In each consultation several hypotheses were tested using different varieties of circular questions. We observed two things: first, the team's hypotheses about the system and its dilemma shifted from session to session, and second, their hypotheses about constructing hypotheses have shifted over time. When we asked them about their model for hypothesis construction, Boscolo and Cecchin said: "It has not remained fixed, and this is why people say we don't have a theory. We don't have a theory because a theory means you have a fixed hypothesis on how a family should be. We don't know how it should be."

One of their most important contributions to the act of hypothesis construction has emerged from their training procedures. For example, they train therapists by using two teams behind the mirror who together generate different and complementary hypotheses. In this design, the T-Team consists of the supervisor and the treatment team. It is their job to construct hypotheses and interventions and suggest them to the therapist for use with the family. The O-Team does not communicate with the therapist or with the family but constructs hypotheses about the family *and* about the treatment context, or T-Team. These are reserved until the end of the interview, at which point both groups exchange their hypotheses and ideas for interventions. Each group has become a "systemic mind"—that is, they have created an overall explanation about the problem situation that satisfies themselves; it is idiosyncratic to them and different from all others. This exchange of thinking at the end of the session is a very important investigation of the case, and it stimulates new ideas and possibilities for both groups. Thus the act of hypothesis making by the teams is an ongoing structuring orientation. It is always the next step ahead of the one just taken by the therapist and the family.


## Circular Questioning


The technique of circular questioning, which is original to the Milan group as an interviewing method, has not only stayed central to their interviewing design but has, over time, produced its own variations.

Circularity is based on the idea that people are connected to each other in particular patterns through time, and it is these patterns that we identify as families.* Family members demonstrate their connection through the communication of information in the form of verbal and nonverbal language. This language describes the exchange of messages that, in problem systems, are often confused or unacceptable to the family. The circular questions define and clarify these confused ideas and questionable behaviors as well as introduce information back to the family in the form of new questions. In this manner the therapeutic system and the family system co-create multiple meanings through language which allow the consideration of more rather than fewer alternatives.

Circular questioning may also be described as a Socratic method of inquiry supported by Gregory Bateson's definition of information as "news of a difference." The Milan team has refined this to mean "news of a relationship difference." By using circular questions in a Socratic manner, they are able to elicit statements of difference about relationships from the family and, at the same time, introduce statements of difference about relationships back into the family system. If a consultant asks "Who agrees most with Grandmother that this is a problem?" a relationship between that person (the agreer) and Grandmother is being defined *by the question*. Using this method of questioning, information is separated from data—data being a compilation of facts that do not describe a relationship (such as: I am depressed, he is crazy, it was in the summer, and so on).

Circular questioning also respects the therapist's neutrality toward the family. Asking "What is the problem in the family now?" randomly, prevents the therapist from forming an alliance with family members, and therapeutic neutrality stays intact. Agreement and classification questions usually follow the "now" question: Who agrees most with Mother that son is too independent? Who agrees least? This type of questioning becomes another attempt to clarify coalition patterns in the system. It is important to note that the questions only ask for structural alignments, comparisons, and classifications from the family. They are in no way declarative in themselves.

A special comment must be offered about the Milan team's use of "openings" in questioning. An opening is a cue word, a theme, or an idea presented by the family and having meaning for them. The interviewer takes that idea as if it were an *indentation* in the system and fills it with circular questions. For example, if a family presents notions of independence, the

---

* The patterns may be biological, psychological, sociological, longstanding, temporary, and so on.

interviewer will follow that idea, making classifications, seeking agreements and explanations, until the indentation or opening is filled with relationship information about the varieties of independence in that family. It is through this give and take, the therapist questioning, the family answering, that the family's own notions of their "independence" amplify or change.

What is interesting to observe is that, though the therapist does not superimpose openings on the family, the ideas family members offer change as the questions introduce news of relationship differences. The questions become interventions in microcosm throughout the interview process.* This is the explanation Boscolo and Cecchin have given for tending more and more to give minimal interventions at the end of the session.

Any method must be examined to determine its validity. The manner in which the Milan Associates use circular questioning in their training procedures using the T-Team and the O-Team demonstrates the theory's ability to reproduce itself successfully in different contexts. Since the Milan group is able to train as well as treat within the parameters of its theory, this methodology is validated through its possibility of application.

## Neutrality

Neutrality, the traveling companion of circular questioning and hypothesizing, is pervasive throughout the Milan team's theory and methodology. It is best described by its results. If anyone in the treatment family were asked "Whose side is the therapist on?" everyone would agree he or she is on no one's side.

The concept of neutrality poses an important question: How can therapists intervene in a system and remain neutral? Isn't that a contradiction? Obviously, they cannot remain entirely neutral.† However, let us consider neutrality as the following therapeutic position: the therapist accepts the

* Openings are discussed in more detail in the introduction to part 4.

† It is important to note that a feminist critique of systemic family therapy states that a therapist's neutral stance still leaves women one down since their position in the larger social order, whether represented in their marriage, work, or other relationships, is given less value in a patriarchal society. Neutrality is used here to describe the rejection of a family's acceptance of labeling its members, a practice that tends to surface more often as a "psychiatric problem" rather than a social justice problem. In both cases, justice is an issue to be dealt with. But in labeling situations, the therapist's siding with the labeled person frequently leads to a worsening of his or her situation as others become activated against that person.

family's solutions as the only ones possible, logical, and congruent for the family at this moment. So far, that is not a contradiction. Since, according to the Milan team, the therapists can never know a priori how a family *should be*, the therapists must act as a stimulus, a perturbation that activates the family's capacity to generate its own solutions. In a sense, the neutral position presents a double message to the family. It says the solution they have found has been perfect until now, but from this moment on they have entered into another interaction (the therapy) that will allow the therapist and the family to invent together other possibilities from which new solutions may arise.

When the therapists maintain a neutral position, they are free from the family's labels of good and bad. It seems that every system has a sense of justice that is distributed among its members. For this reason, he or she is bad, good, sick, well, and so on. Every therapist confronts these labels when working with a family. If they can be converted into process, the therapist can be said to be neutral. Therapists must view these labels as family attributes to be curious about, interested in, but not as facts to be believed. In this sense, neutrality operates as the opposite of morality.

To free themselves from the general tendency to believe in these labels, the Milan group invented the following exercise. Early in their work they decided to reject the use of the verb *to be*. For example, they could not say "Mother *is* overprotective." Instead, they had to say "Mother behaves in such a way that *appears* overprotective." Or, instead of saying "Father *is* close to his son," they said "Father seems to be *showing* feelings of closeness with his son." This exercise altered their way of thinking and compelled them to think in a relational way. Ideologically, then, neutrality could be construed as the ability of the therapist to see, in a systemic manner, the whole thing.

## The B Case

In order to see how the Milan team's methodology can be applied to the interview with the B family, we shall look closely at a few critically important events in the first half of the beginning interview. The consultation spanned a year and a half and was comprised of three separate interviews, each offering unique considerations.

The first interview, done in 1980, was requested by Dr. S, who had seen the B family for three sessions. The family presented a problem with Diane, their sixteen-year-old daughter, who was having behavioral difficulties at school and was fighting with her father. The family found this fighting between Diane and Father unusual since, until six months ago, they had enjoyed a close relationship. Mr. and Mrs. B are in their early forties and have two other daughters: Lisa, age twenty-one, and Dori, age fourteen. Though the family presented Diane as the problem, Dr. S was more concerned with the oldest daughter, Lisa, who had made a serious suicide attempt—she had taken an overdose of tranquilizers and slit her wrists with a razor blade. She was the child of the mother's first marriage. In Dr. S's third session with the parents alone, the mother revealed that her husband had made several attempts to have sexual contact with Lisa, though it was unclear whether sexual intercourse had taken place. Mother said to Dr. S that Lisa complained that her father (in fact, her stepfather) had been sexually attracted to her since she was nine years old. By way of example, Mrs. B mentioned that her husband would watch Lisa through holes he made in her bedroom wall. The mother reported she had tried to prevent her other two daughters from knowing this about their father. Though the parents disagreed about most things (including the incest report/accusation), they did agree that Dr. S should not *talk* about this matter to Diane and Dori. The injunction from the parents to "keep the secret" from the youngest daughters blocked the progress of the therapy. Dr. S was also concerned that Lisa might make another suicide attempt, and she recommended a consultation for the family. The parents agreed to the consultation, but on one condition: both the consultant, Dr. Boscolo, and his team, Dr. Cecchin and Dr. S, must also accept their request not to talk about the father's incest behavior.

It is well known that secrets in families often have a pathogenic effect on the family and, when introduced into the therapy, can paralyze the therapeutic process. Secrets are a powerful way to control not just a relationship but the therapy as well. If one or more family members succeeds in binding the therapist with a secret, the therapist loses not just autonomy but his or her neutrality. In this case, the parents' request also put all three therapists on the same level, thereby nullifying the consultants' task which was to take an observer's position in relation to both the family and the therapeutic context.

The Milan Associates decided to treat the "effect" of the secret without touching its content. In other words, they assumed that at some point in the interview the family would offer an opening around "not talking," or a "secret," or some similar metaphor. They would accept this opening and turn it into process with the use of circular questions. At no time would the content of the secret be solicited or revealed. Instead, the secret would be discussed as a *boundary marker* for the entire family. Since the circular questions involve the entire system, the discussion of the secret as a boundary marker would involve everyone. This approach broke the bind that kept the consultants on the same level as Dr. S, and also allowed them the freedom to move therapeutically.

The beginning of the interview is organized around the idea of *communication*: it is the first opening presented by the family. The circular questions immediately sketch the current coalitions in the family, and the therapist and the family begin the work of evolving a new "map" of the problem together. Because of the injunction about the secret, it was anticipated in the presession that the family would present the premise of no talking. Indeed, the family immediately "talked about talking" and, in response to the questions, cited who talks more easily to whom, as well as who talked to whom with more difficulty.

However, early in the interview the family correctly perceived that they were talking about not talking and they began to block the questioning. The consultants responded to their silence by suggesting that perhaps some members of the family were being more cooperative with the consultants than others. They presented the possibility that the parents seemed to be, understandably, the most cooperative, and that perhaps the children did not understand why they were there and for that reason were less cooperative. The result of this "suggestion" was that the consultants were able to make distinctions among the daughters. Mother volunteered that Diane's relationship to her father had changed from what it was six months ago. This was a critical response that allowed the consultant to enlarge his map, include the past, and contrast the family's coalitions before and after the "problem" occurred. The family had given him the opportunity to make a bridge that connected present-day behavior with past behavior and the current explanations of that behavior with explanations of the past behavior. The circular questions not only introduced new connections for the family but they were presented as doubts, as possibilities, so that the family was in the position of making a choice, saying, in effect, "This is the explanation that fits us best."

After the opening that led into the family's past, Boscolo continued to ask who was closer to whom. The father responded that Lisa was closer to her mother in the past. A new theme emerged, *the theme of the two families*. Lisa and Mother belong to the first family. Diane, Dori, Father, and Mother belong to the second family. The consultants immediately began to hypothesize about how these two families were connected to the problem. Then they linked the two hypotheses: the one about not talking with the one about the two families. In fact, it could be asked whether the family was "not talking about" the fact of these two families.

At this early point in the interview, the family was on the verge of revealing another and perhaps more important "secret." Crucial ideas emerged. Mother felt her first marriage had been a failure, and now she was willing to put up with many difficulties to have this one succeed. This idea was dramatically stated later in the interview when Mother remarked, "I'm not a failure because it [the marriage] didn't work."

The consultants' response to this situation was unique to their methodology. Sensing a dilemma around "being" in the family, they switched to "existential" questioning. Boscolo asked Mother, "Do you think the situation would have been better if Lisa had not been born?" This question articulated the dilemma as *Lisa* has been perceiving it. There was a suggestion that her suicide attempts might be tied to this unspoken perception. This questioning was supported by a unique non-verbal behavior: as Boscolo spoke to Lisa, the mother's lips moved in sync with Lisa's responses. At this moment it was clear that the telling or the not telling, the being born or the not being born, was part of the confused relationship between Mother and Lisa. It was a description of the bond between Lisa and Mother, a paradoxical bond that was affirmed and denied at the same time.

With this question, the ambiguous messages around Lisa leaving home or staying became activated and Lisa, weeping, wanted to leave the session. However, her confusion about her relationship to her mother remained and could be dealt with by the question: Was she helping her mother's marriage more by staying or by leaving? An important premise in the family was strongly suggested: Mother must have a successful second marriage! Mother quoted herself, saying she wanted to keep things "even" in the family and, on behalf of that idea, instructed Lisa to listen to her stepfather: "If he says 'jump,' jump; if he says 'lay down,' lay down." It is clear that Lisa has been reading the unspoken subtext clearly. To stay means she must "listen" (sexually) to her stepfather; but, on the other hand, if she leaves, will she be assisting Mother's marriage or making it worse? This is why the existential dilemma formulated as "Things would have been better if I had *not* been born" appears to offer a solution to Lisa. The connection of the incestuous behavior to the hypothesis about talking and not talking and the connection of that idea to the organization of the two families is at last revealed. This is what the secret represents, and it has now been brought into open negotiation.

## The Intervention

The process of constructing an intervention is bound to reflect both specific techniques and a theoretical stance. The stance the Milan team takes in regard to intervening in human systems has been influenced most recently by second-order cybernetics and Humberto Maturana's formulation of structural autonomy in living systems. The rise of second-order cybernetics took away the notion of an "objective" observer who is out to influence a system in a predictable way. In addition, we are more and more compelled to take note of and respect the events in the system that represent the family's self-creative activity—this is what the Milan team means when they refer to the family's capacity to heal itself. This idea comes from Maturana, who claims that the response to any perturbation offered to a living system will be determined by that system's inherent structure. Therefore, the therapist can no longer search for specific interventions that will produce specific results; rather, he or she must try to achieve a structural coupling with the system—that is, the point where the interaction between the therapist and the family is in continual calibration, and that calibration is in the service of the self-organizing capacity of the system.

There are some unique features in the Milan group's use of the team in constructing an intervention. They wish the team to be noncompetitive and *not* to strive for agreement or consensus. In the process of working toward an intervention, each team member speaks in a linear manner, neither agreeing nor disagreeing with the last speaker about his or her thoughts concerning the family. After a round or two of linear observations, a team member may connect two of the thoughts, then another team member may add a third, and so forth. In this fashion, new connections are made in regard to the system that are no longer linear but circular. Soon a hypothesis or two emerges, and the team is able to select which one best fits their "systemic mind." Through this process, the team is able to jump levels, reaching a higher level of logical type. That is, by the end of their observations, more systemic formulations are evident than when they first began. Now the team not only constructs an explanatory hypothesis about the problem but a hypothesis about change, which turns into an intervention. In the B family, the Milan Associates concluded that Lisa and Mother had once had a strong bond between them that had been denied in order to protect the second family. The team felt that if Mother and Lisa had demonstrated their strong bond, it would have not only made them the strongest couple in the family but it would have challenged the dominance of the second family. In order to continue to protect the second family while reorganizing the bond between Lisa and her mother, they constructed a ritual: Mother and Lisa were to spend one day a week together in any way they chose and they were to tell no one what they did together. This day was to be a "secret" between them.

This ritual did two important things for the family: first, it gave Lisa an opportunity to find out if her mother *clearly* accepted her or not; and, second, it *clearly* gave Mother to Lisa's sisters on the remaining six days of the week. The ritual broke the ambiguity of the bond between Mother and Lisa; it both restrained and underlined their "strong" relationship, and it did not challenge the dominance of the second family. The "secret" of their day challenged the "secret" of the incestuous behavior between Father and Lisa. It was hoped that by reinstating the relationship between Lisa and Mother as an overt and strong one the incestuous behavior would stop because Mother would be able to clearly ally with Lisa without jeopardizing her second family.

The Milan team saw the family two more times. It could be said that the first consultation was too successful, for the family subsequently refused to bring their issues to their clinic therapist but agreed to be seen when a follow-up consultation was offered by the Milan team six months later. During this session, only the parents were present. Boscolo and Cecchin were careful to represent this interview not as a therapy session but as a research follow-up. They asked circular questions in a deliberately monotonous way, methodically tracking all the current moves in the family and the changes in the relationships. The most important piece of information was that Lisa had moved out of the home.

They saw the family again one year later. Most of the family attended the interview including Lisa who had married and had a baby. The father, however, was very angry. He insisted on closing the blind on the one-way screen and refused to let the other consultants watch the session. The family related the news that though Lisa had moved out, Diane had hospitalized herself because she wanted to go and live with her sister and her parents had opposed her. The Milan team had acted on the assumption that if the oldest girl's situation was solved, the family would settle down. It could be argued that the consultants should have followed up the plight of the middle girl, Diane, who continued to be unhappy at home to the point of going to a hospital. There are two possible explanations for this outcome. One is that the consultation model itself may not have tied the family securely to an ongoing therapy. The other is that the therapists' consultation hypothesis focused too exclusively on the idea of the first family versus the second family and did not regard all the girls as potential victims of the father's harassment.

The presentation of the B family ends with a discussion of the nature of consultations, their inherent problems, how they can best be used, and the ultimate place of consultations in our field.

# THE CASE: CONSULTATION AND CONVERSATION

HOFFMAN: What were the circumstances of this consultation?

CECCHIN: We did a workshop in 1980, and we were asked by Dr. S, the therapist of the B family, to see them. Dr. S had seen this family for three sessions; the whole family for the first two, and only the parents in the third. The family is composed of the two parents plus three daughters: Lisa, twenty-one; Dori, sixteen; and Diane, fourteen. Lisa came from a previous marriage of the mother's. The presenting problem at that time was that Diane for six months had been having behavioral problems in school and at home. The parents complained that she had become very hostile to her father and that she was fighting with him all the time, where before she had been very close to him. In addition, in the session with the parents, the mother accused the father of having been involved in an incestuous relationship with Lisa. He would make holes in the bedroom wall to watch her getting undressed, and although it was not clear that he had had sexual intercourse with her, he had made several attempts. During the past year, Lisa had made a suicide attempt and on one or two occasions had run away. The therapist felt that the mother was not very concerned about Lisa but gave this information as a way of accusing her husband. At the end of the session, Dr. S felt that she needed a consultation.

PENN: What reasons did she give?

CECCHIN: The situation was quite complicated. The family only complained about the problems they were having with Diane, while the therapist saw Lisa as needing more help than anyone else. In the first two sessions, the therapist saw her as very down, very depressed. But the parents did not want the therapist to talk about the incest in front of the children.

The therapist asked for a consultation because she could not extricate herself from this injunction.

PENN: The problem for you, then, was the fact that the therapist was silenced by the family.

CECCHIN: Yes. She said, "Can you help me?" But the injunction was also for us.

BOSCOLO: The other reason for the consultation was to have a family that we could interview. When Dr. S asked the parents if they were willing to have a consultation with the Milan team, they said they would agree on condition that the consultants, too, would agree not to talk about the incest. So it was a very good opportunity to demonstrate how we handle the problem of a secret.

HOFFMAN: Was that all you knew about the family?

BOSCOLO: Yes. Usually we don't ask too many questions of the therapist. We only want to know why the therapist is asking for a consultation.

HOFFMAN: How did you see the therapist's problem?

BOSCOLO: As we said, the therapist was in some kind of double bind. The family presents one problem: the younger girl, Diane, is fighting and not doing well at school. But what impresses the therapist is that the other girl, Lisa, has been suicidal and has been sexually harassed, and the parents talk about this incest problem by saying "Don't talk about it." That was all we wanted to know beforehand. Otherwise, we feel that our heads will become clogged with too much data and, above all, by the interpretation that the therapist makes of this data. For instance, if the therapist tells the consultants about a grandfather who died three years ago, they might begin to make connections which are not connections that the family is making.

PENN: You would put the idea that the therapist gave you into the system instead of generating your own.

BOSCOLO: Yes, instead of helping the family to come up with their own connections. We have to find out through the process of interviewing if the death of a grandparent was an important issue or not for this family. It could be totally unimportant, or it could be very important. But you find out only through the information provided in the interview, so it might be better if you didn't know this fact beforehand.

CECCHIN: For instance, when we see a family for a few sessions and we keep making interventions and the family doesn't move, we get into an impasse. In such circumstances, we very often give the family an appointment for six months or a year ahead. When we see them we try to see them as a new family. We don't watch the tapes, we don't read the notes, we try to get rid of all the constructions we had made during the therapy. In the same way, when someone presents a case to us, I usually listen only to the presenting problem and to the therapeutic relationship, and then I close my ears.

BOSCOLO: The family usually comes with a rigid map, that is, a fixed explanation of what is going on. Suppose the therapist also has a rigid map based on what he knows about the family. You have two systems with rigid maps that are going to collide: "My explanation is better than yours." Therapeutic teams can also get stuck with the same idea about a family, with consequent therapeutic impasse.

CECCHIN: For instance, in this family the therapist was impressed by the incest, and being impressed means that she began to make a map. She saw the incest as the most important problem in the family, while the map the parents had was quite different.

PENN: In describing your interview process, you often make a distinction between getting information and getting data. Can you elaborate on that?

CECCHIN: Yes. We base the idea of information on what Bateson said, that information is news of a difference. Information is a relationship between at least two elements, something that is connected to something else. If you say "I am depressed," it is pure data, but if you say "I am depressed when my wife looks at me with an angry face," then it becomes information. Charts that describe patients in hospitals are full of data but not much information.

PENN: How do you change data to information?

CECCHIN: It is an active process that can only be done while interviewing the family. You can't do it with the referring person because then you get a map that is prefabricated.

PENN: So the map you are talking about is a new one that you make together with the family; it's not your map or their map.

CECCHIN: Yes. And the process of interviewing can often change the way individuals in the family construct their maps.

PENN: I see a training problem. Trainees in the beginning often make a hypothesis and follow it blindly without responding to the feedback from the family. It never becomes shaped by the explanation that is evolving in the session. In the end, the picture that they get of the family will be dictated by that first hypothesis.

BOSCOLO: The problem is compounded when you think that the therapist, in making a hypothesis, is often being faithful to a hypothesis that a supervisor or a teacher gave him, in the same way that a family is faithful to its original hypothesis.

PENN: When you do a consultation, I assume that you are making hy-

potheses on several different levels: your relationship as consultants to
the therapist; the therapist's relationship to the family; and, finally, the
family dynamics.

BOSCOLO: Yes, all three levels are part of a larger loop that comprises what
we call the significant system—the complex of information and relationships that constitutes a problem and its social ecology.

CECCHIN: To get at the dimensions of the significant system, we proceed
in a centrifugal manner. First, we want to know what the problem is (or
rather what the family *thinks* the problem is) and how the problem is
connected with the other people in the family. Second, we ask how the
family is connected with the larger context, the relatives, the clan. Finally,
we look to see how the family system is connected with the therapeutic
system. You enlarge the context until you find an explanation that satisfies
you as the observer. You can never say what the actual limit of a system
is, so the decision is arbitrary. And when you make all these hypotheses,
at all three levels, then you connect them into a single explanation that
makes sense. That is what we call the systemic hypothesis.

BOSCOLO: In training, we utilize a supervisory group and also an observing
group. The observing group, independent from the supervisory group,
will make hypotheses. Then, when the supervisory group has delivered
its intervention, they meet with the observing group and share their
thinking. When they meet, the two sets of hypotheses and the two sets
of interventions are different. Yet each team comes up with a systemic
hypothesis and intervention that satisfies them, even though they are
different from each other.

HOFFMAN: How do you explain that?

BOSCOLO: This phenomenon is not related to the content of the hypothesis
but to whether the explanation satisfies the systemic mind. We try to
make the team into a systemic mind.

HOFFMAN: One can't know whether the second observer's hypothesis
would have been better or worse; there is no way to compare the two
of them. Experimentally, all one can know is whether the family comes
back and has changed in a meaningful way.

CECCHIN: We have begun to tell our students that the end of therapy is
when the family doesn't define itself as pathological and the therapeutic
context doesn't define itself as therapeutic. Somehow the family cures
itself of the idea of being sick and the team cures itself of the idea of
being useful. That's when you say "We have nothing to say, we have
run out of ideas," and they say "We don't need you anymore." You part
from each other, and then you become therapists again with another
family, because you have this need to be useful.

HOFFMAN: It's interesting. People are beginning to think in terms of the "identified therapist."

CECCHIN: Both of them have to be cured, because if a family gets better and the therapist remains the therapist, it becomes interminable therapy. And even if they do stop, the family will call the therapist once in a while to reassure him, saying "Look, I'm not doing very well," or the therapist will do a follow-up. Therapy can be a very addictive pursuit.

### FAMILY INTERVIEW

*[The family's therapist, Dr. S, enters with Dr. Boscolo
and presents him to the family: Mr. and Mrs. B,
Lisa, Dori, and Diane.]*

BOSCOLO: *I am Dr. Boscolo, from the Family Therapy Center in Milan, Italy. Behind the one-way mirror is Dr. Cecchin, who works with me in Milan. We have been asked to see you today, so I will have a conversation with you. I would like to start by asking, what is the problem now?*

———————————

HOFFMAN: I have a two-part question. First, why do you start with "What is the problem now?" Second, why do you open it out to anyone, rather than choosing someone?

CECCHIN: We ask "What is the problem now?" because we know that, at a certain point, the so-called healthy members will point to the identified patient, and we will then ask the identified patient whether he agrees to be a patient or not. Then we ask the different members of the family who most thinks that this person has problems and who least thinks it. We want to see how people line up around the behavior they want changed.

HOFFMAN: It immediately becomes a difference question.

CECCHIN: Yes. But as soon as they clarify the problem, we ask "How did you arrive at this definition? How did you decide that? Why did you decide that what you define as a problem is a problem?"

HOFFMAN: What importance does it have that you throw out this "What is the problem now?" question at random?

CECCHIN: It allows us to be neutral, in that we can't be seen as joining anybody. If we address one of the parents, for instance, we already have an alliance: parent/therapist against child. If we ask the child "What is the problem?" it's like accepting what people are saying about him. We leave the decision of who speaks first up to them.

HOFFMAN: So if Mother comes out and tells you what the problem is, that tells you something about them already.

CECCHIN: Exactly. Usually they come out with a very clear distinction between the sick member and the healthy ones. And we find out who is the I.P. [identified patient], who is the spokesman, who is the cotherapist, and so forth. Then we can go to the patient and ask "Who decided that you have a problem? Do you agree? Who made the decision that you shouldn't eat? When did you decide to commit suicide?" We change the problem as they define it into a decision.

BOSCOLO: But I think that one of the reasons why we throw out the question for anyone to answer is because in the beginning it is important not to be too directive. If you start right away to direct questions at particular people, then you cannot have an idea of how the family interacts without a therapist. So the first question is designed to detect how the family responds to a question that anybody can answer.

PENN: You are already communicating, in your very first question, something about your neutrality.

BOSCOLO: Yes. Also that we aren't going to base our ideas on what we have seen or been told by anyone beforehand. It would be easy to say "We have been told that John has been sick for a year. How is he doing now?" I think we would lose the whole session if we started like that.

PENN: By asking the family how they decided about the problem and who agreed with that decision, the *premise* that you're introducing into the family is the beginning of a change in terms of how the family thinks about itself. It implies that they can also decide not to have the problem. When you ask "When did you decide to stop eating? Who agrees with you?" you imply that they can also decide not to eat again or whatever. In the *future* they can decide not to have the problem. Essentially it is a premise about change.

HOFFMAN: Another thing. Why do you begin in the present? Why don't you begin in the past? Why don't you say "When did the problem start?"

CECCHIN: This is a question that relates to what we said before. From a spatial point of view, you start with the patient, then you enlarge your view to the close relatives, extended family, and the therapeutic context. And with time you do the same thing. You start with the present; then you say "When did the problem start? What do you think will happen in the future?" You go through a similar process in both space and time. But your starting place is the here and now.

PENN: The fact that you put in the word "now" gives the message that you are going to be interested in time. The other thing that the "now" means to me is that it's the time when you and the family come together.

CECCHIN: Yes, it's like saying "We don't care about what you did before. You and me, we're going to see what's going on now." It's from this point in the present that we go into the past and explore the future.

PENN: You said every question also introduces information. That is very different from the idea that you ask questions to get information. Your questions give information as well.

CECCHIN: Most of what we say takes the form of questions. When you ask a question you introduce a difference. It is the Socratic method of inquiry: What happened? How do you see it? The answer is secondary because you have already introduced something new.

BOSCOLO: Therapists who do genograms spend the first session by going into three generations, four generations of history. This type of operation implies that the therapist thinks that the problem is related to the extended family in the past.

CECCHIN: We are not interested in historical causality.

BOSCOLO: We tend to avoid talking about the extended family in the beginning of the first session. We start from the center and go out. If, in the beginning, we ask questions about the grandfather, the grandmother, these questions imply historical causality, that there is some connection between the problem and their grandmother and their grandfather.

*FAMILY INTERVIEW*

FATHER: *Everyone seems to want to fight with everyone else. We all want to fight with everyone.*

BOSCOLO: *That you see is the problem?*

FATHER: *Yes.*

BOSCOLO: *Do you see any other problem?*

FATHER: *Not really.*

———————————

HOFFMAN: Why do you ask for another problem?

BOSCOLO: The father said "Our problem is that we fight with one another." But the therapist had told us about "other problems." There's the specific problem of Diane and then there is the problem of Lisa. So the question is: Are there any other problems?

HOFFMAN: Certainly you know they're not going to mention incest. But you're putting in the idea that there might be more than one problem.

BOSCOLO: The most correct thing would be to start from what the father said: "We are fighting with each other." We should use only the things they bring to us. I could also have said "Do the children agree that the problem is that you are fighting with each other?" We don't want to be too influenced by the construct that was given to us in the beginning by the family's therapist.

### FAMILY INTERVIEW

BOSCOLO: *If I ask your wife this question, will she agree with you or will she think there are other problems?*

FATHER: *That's hard to say.*

BOSCOLO: *Do you agree with your husband?*

MOTHER: *No. There is a great deal of problems in our family. Some is the lack of communications, problems with the children, problems communicating, problems trying to get through to each other.*

BOSCOLO: *Between which of you is there a lack of communication?*

MOTHER: *There's no communication between me and my husband. Can't seem to talk to each other or try to understand each other or, you know, it's really . . .*

BOSCOLO: *How is the communication with your daughters?*

MOTHER: *Well, lately there is no communication.*

---

BOSCOLO: I asked the father a question that we call a "mind-reading" question. We know that excessive mind reading in families can be pathogenic. But in therapy, these mind-reading questions can be useful because they bring in a new perspective. The wife is listening to what the husband thinks she is thinking. Here I want to get the husband's hypothesis about his wife's hypothesis. But it doesn't always work. When we interviewed families in Edinburgh, every time we asked a mind-reading question, the answer was "Why don't you ask my wife?" They implied that I was very rude. Whereas in Italy, if we ask a member of the family "What do you think your wife or brother thinks?" they will be very glad to tell you.

HOFFMAN: In America, it was a great shock when this type of question was first introduced. The idea in family therapy was that you should always get people in the family to take what was called an "I" position— "What do you think?" "I think this"—rather than asking another person what that person thinks. So this was very radical for many people.

BOSCOLO: We don't try to be educational in the sense of teaching people to communicate correctly. If you tell a client "You have to talk for yourself; you are responsible for what you are thinking, for your thoughts," you are teaching people what you think is normal. We accept the system as it is. If you do otherwise, it's all right, but you then have to understand that you are now becoming an agent of social control.

CECCHIN: Another point is that, like many of our questions, this one puts information into the system. We might ask the children "How do you think your parents are getting along?" And they may say "I think they are getting along well," or "They are getting along badly." But we don't ask a wife "Are you getting along well with your husband?" Instead we bring out the idea that their behavior is such that their daughter sees them a certain way. You, as the couple, become information for somebody else. Your behavior creates ideas and fantasies for your children. So I ask the children "What fantasies do you have about your parents?"

PENN: It seems as though this process breaks up individual linear perceptions. The family members become detached from their habitual perceptions of each other and start to free-float for a while. They experience their own system in a different way than they have before.

CECCHIN: Some therapists are upset by this type of question. They feel a moral disgust, as if we are doing something wrong to the family.

HOFFMAN: Like your occasional practice of asking the children about their parents' sex life?

CECCHIN: Yes. I think that it's useful for parents to hear what other family members think about their relationship. They are protected in that we usually don't ask them to confirm or disconfirm these perceptions.

BOSCOLO: We ask a number of different types of questions. One kind is a question about behavior. For example: "What does your wife *do* when your daughter does that?" The other is a question about ideas: "What does your wife *think* about this event?" The first question has to do with phenomenology, the other with cognition; it's asking what hypothesis does a person have. The two levels—behavior and cognition—are related. Richard Rabkin, in his book *Strategic Psychotherapy* (Rabkin, 1977), divides therapy into prescriptive and insight therapies. That is a dichotomy we do not accept. We believe behavior and ideas are related. That's why some of our questions are aimed at thoughts and others are aimed at producing information about behavior.

CECCHIN: For example, I was once talking with a depressed woman and I asked her a question: "When you go in your room and stay in there and cry, how many hours does it take before your husband or children come knocking on the door? How many minutes? Sometimes it takes days before they come, right?" And then another question: "When you're there crying and they are having fun eating together, do you think that they think about you? What do you think they think about you?" Two questions. You never ask them if it's true or not true. You're interested in the effect of the depression. First, what effect it has on what these people do, and, second, what effect it has on their thinking, their fantasies.

BOSCOLO: The fantasy world is part of the whole system. Sometimes you have depressive thoughts; perhaps you think they are just intrapsychic, but they are part of the whole relationship system.

HOFFMAN: So what you're doing is to reintroduce perceptions, thoughts, and feelings into family therapy instead of focusing mainly on behavior.

CECCHIN: But we include thoughts and feelings as having an influence in the present, not just in the past. If you are paranoid, you have very good reasons to be paranoid. It's not only something that belongs to your past. Perhaps you had some learning situation in the past that made it easy for you to be paranoid, but you also have a situation in the present where it makes sense.

BOSCOLO: In the last few years we have been asking more and more of what we call explanatory questions. We ask members of the family to tell us what their hypotheses are about their own behaviors. At the beginning, years ago, we tended to ask descriptive questions about behaviors. We used to ask "What do you *do*?" Now we ask "What do you *think*?"

CECCHIN: An interesting point about the use of feelings is that therapists have been taught to connect on an emotional level with the patient, thinking that if this connection is made, the person will improve. But the person does not improve. He wants somebody else to connect with him—his wife, his children, his sister. If the therapist connects with him, he feels worse. He says "Look, the therapist connects with me and my family does not." Or, if somebody cries, instead of paying attention to what has made the person cry and what they are feeling now, and so forth, you ask somebody else "Why do you think this person is crying?" You always make it a relational event.

## FAMILY INTERVIEW

BOSCOLO: *How is the communication with your daughters?*
MOTHER: *Well, lately there is no communication.*
BOSCOLO: *Between you and them or between them?*

*MOTHER:* Well, mainly between us and the children.

*BOSCOLO:* How is the communication between them? How do they communicate?

*MOTHER:* Well, these two, they communicate okay, but Diane and Lisa fight a great deal.

*BOSCOLO:* And how about Dori?

*MOTHER:* Oh, they have their little sisterly fights, but it's nothing that serious. I think it's normal.

*BOSCOLO:* But would you say that the girls communicate between them better than you communicate with your husband?

*MOTHER:* Oh, definitely.

*BOSCOLO:* Who communicates better with the daughters, you or your husband?

*MOTHER:* I don't think . . . I can't communicate because they won't communicate and he doesn't talk to them, so I would say, if anything, I try, I try to get through to them.

---

HOFFMAN: You are getting information about the relationship structure here. The two younger girls are close, Lisa fights with Diane, and Mother and Father don't get along either.

BOSCOLO: Yes. We always start by getting information that you could put under the heading of "Who is with whom?" All these questions have this aim. But one thing I would like to underline is that in determining "who is with whom," the non-verbal or analogical behavior is more important for us than what they say. The way they sit down, the way they move. For instance, we see that Dori and Diane look alike physically. They are sitting close together, they exchange smiles as if they were exchanging secrets. In contrast, Lisa is looking at the floor. She looks sad, depressed; she is sitting apart from the other children.

HOFFMAN: What are you responding to in the way they present themselves?

BOSCOLO: It seems from the analogics that the only couple that is doing well is Dori and Diane. Lisa seems separated from them, and Mother and Father seem separated from each other. But I am not getting much information from the questions. All three girls have their coats on, they don't answer the questions, the only one who talks freely is the mother.

HOFFMAN: And she says "I can't communicate." But what are you looking for in these relationship patterns?

BOSCOLO: The therapeutic team has a map that we are constantly making, changing, revising. For instance, we might ask ourselves "What is the most important marriage in the family?"

PENN: By "marriage," what do you mean?

BOSCOLO: The primary relationship, the most connected one, perhaps denied, perhaps incestuous, the one that seems most central to everyone else. However, we have to remind ourselves that this is only an idea. If we get too fond of it, we will start to make mistakes. There can be a *folie à team*.

CECCHIN: Yes. The therapist can be too much in love with his idea. Four or five years ago we were convinced that everything that was going on in the family was the fault of the grandmother. She had this hidden power, and because of this, we were always looking for grandmothers to kill. Every team that uses our methods goes through such periods. There was one period where we looked for the most important marriage. Another period was spent determining who had the most authority in the system.

PENN: Most therapists who create a new or original approach, as you have done, eventually find a model they like and stick to it. What keeps you from doing that?

BOSCOLO: We are very impressed with the danger of becoming seduced by our own hypotheses and beginning to shape the families we see in relation to them. What we are looking for is a reality that the therapist and family create together. In this sense, I think the team is useful. First, it can correct the tendency of the therapist to confirm his own beliefs. Second, a team can watch the analogical responses of the family to the inquiry, something that is hard for a therapist in the room to see. The family will give cues that will tell a therapist whether to discard a given hypothesis or stick to it.

HOFFMAN: I want to put a little circle around one piece. Not only do you say that your hypothesis shifts and changes from one session to another, but you're also saying that, over time, your hypothesis *about* hypotheses has been shifting and changing.

CECCHIN: That's why people say we don't have a theory. We don't have a theory because a theory is to have a fixed hypothesis about how the family should be. We don't know how it should be.

BOSCOLO: There is another hypothesis, on a very general level, that we are entertaining now. We feel that many therapeutic interactions with families or patients are socially determined. This is what we are calling the sociological hypothesis. We think that in our consumer society, psychotherapy has become an object to consume. So therapy is made available to everybody, not because they really need therapy, but because it is a social good. A general concern we have now is how to decondition a family from having the idea that they need therapy.

CECCHIN: They might think they need it the way people need an education or a house.

## FAMILY INTERVIEW

BOSCOLO: *With whom does your husband communicate most?*
MOTHER: *Diane. He used to.*
BOSCOLO: *He used to? Something has changed recently?*
MOTHER: *Yes.*
BOSCOLO: *What exactly?*
MOTHER: *They don't get along anymore, and Diane seems to have taken a different stand, where she doesn't like him.*

---

PENN: That's the first time that the past has been mentioned. Why did you move to a question about the past rather than continuing to track relationships in the present?
BOSCOLO: The therapist, at the same time he asks questions, has to make choices. He silently records what is being said. He might put off going into a specific difference between past and present until he gets the relationship picture. Or he might go into it at that moment. Usually the family's response to a question guides the therapist to the next question. When the mother said "He *used* to," this gave a clue to why they think Diane is a problem.

## FAMILY INTERVIEW

BOSCOLO: *Since when?*
MOTHER: *Within the last six months to a year.*
BOSCOLO: *What explanation did you give? Do you have an explanation about that?*
MOTHER: *I just, I'm kind of at a loss, I don't know, I don't understand. I understand her change in a way that she has become hostile toward him because of his negative attitude. But I don't understand fully why, why such a drastic, hostile change.*
BOSCOLO: *Let me ask Dori. Do you agree with what your mother just said: that your father, up to six months ago, communicated better with Diane than with Lisa and you? Starting six months ago, there was not much communication between your father and Diane. What explanation do you give for that?*
DORI: *I don't know.*

BOSCOLO: *Lisa, do you have an idea? [No answer.] Do you think that if I ask this question of Diane, she will give me an explanation?*

LISA: *[softly] No.*

BOSCOLO: *Why not? Is it because she doesn't want to, or because she can't, or she doesn't know?*

LISA: *I don't know.*

BOSCOLO: *Diane, do you agree with Mommy that you were the only one who had some communication with your father? And then, six months ago, something changed?*

DIANE: *Yes.*

BOSCOLO: *What happened? [No answer.] Dori, if Diane were to answer now, what would she say?*

DORI: *I don't know.*

BOSCOLO: *Your father thinks that there is a problem of communication and everyone fights with everyone else. Your mother sees the problem as a lack of communication between her and her husband. Let's start with you, Dori: What problem do you see in the family now? [No answer.] Diane, what problem do you see? Do you agree with your father and mother?*

DIANE: *I guess so. There is too much fighting.*

BOSCOLO: *Too much fighting between who? [No answer.] Dori?*

DORI: *There is too much fighting between Mom and Dad and Diane and me.*

BOSCOLO: *Diane and you. How about Lisa? [No answer.]*

---

HOFFMAN: This seems like such an impasse. You use your usual techniques of asking one what the other would think, and it's as though the girls know they're not supposed to say anything. It's so oppressive in the room.

BOSCOLO: The therapist is stuck. He starts to make headway with these questions, but he doesn't make a breakthrough. If he persists, he creates an escalation of tensions and the situation gets worse. So he can do two things. One possibility is to change topics, talk about the past, for instance, or talk about other issues. Another way is for the supervisor to call the therapist out.

PENN: [*to Cecchin*] You were behind the screen. Do you remember what you were thinking about?

CECCHIN: Very soon I will call him and say that it looks like the therapist, no matter what he does, creates resistance.

PENN: You were noticing this?

CECCHIN: Yes. So then we ask What are we doing now to create resistance? It could be a problem of the referring context, or it could be this incestuous behavior. Everybody is afraid to talk, this seems to be a rule. We have already been told that the family has given us the injunction, "There are secrets in the family. We cannot talk." Now they seem to be saying the same thing by their behavior. So we have to deal with this problem of secrets. One intervention would be to say "I see that you cannot talk. It is probably very important for you not to say anything, so I will do the talking." You give a prescription not to talk.

BOSCOLO: Another way is for the therapist to talk about the unwillingness to talk. By asking questions about coming to therapy—who decided to come today? who came the most willingly? who didn't want to come? and so on—he can focus on the relationship between the family and the consultants. It is possible that only one person wanted to come. The others did not want to, and so they are silent, they are not cooperating.

PENN: It seems as if it's only Mother who wants to be there.

CECCHIN: The father and the daughters look angry. Perhaps they are angry at the mother. She brought them. "So why should I talk? You wanted to come here, right? You talk."

PENN: That's a real difficulty, when you start out in a therapeutic situation and you are told that the family is unwilling to talk about something important. In trying not to address that topic, it's almost impossible not to address it in another way and to create the kind of resistance we are seeing here.

BOSCOLO: Another possibility is that since the original therapist had seen the couple alone before bringing in the consultants, the daughters don't know whether the couple has disclosed the sexual behavior or not. They may be unsure about what will be expected of them.

CECCHIN: We thought that perhaps the mother was going to accuse the father of harming the children. We felt that the daughters might have believed that they would have to testify against him, as in cases where there is child abuse. Usually the children defend the parents in that situation. Here it could have been that the daughters were defending the father. The message was clear: "Protect the father by not speaking." And everybody is complying with that, including the consultants.

HOFFMAN: Let's see how you get out of that.

*FAMILY INTERVIEW*

BOSCOLO: *Was it always like this or has it been getting better or worse?*
MOTHER: *It's been getting worse.*
BOSCOLO: *Worse?*

MOTHER: *Yes.*

BOSCOLO: *Since when?*

MOTHER: *Since last year. A lot worse.*

BOSCOLO: *Do you refer to the fights you have been having with your husband?*

MOTHER: *The whole family has been getting along worse. I could talk to Diane and reason with her and get her to understand and reach a mutual understanding; but within the last year, I can't. Well, at times I can reach her very well, other times I can't. Lisa, we've had a certain amount of problems during the last year, and I can't talk to her. Dori is in a different situation; sometimes you can talk to her, sometimes not. And, between my husband and I, problems have got a great deal worse because I have changed. I am no longer willing to do all the giving. So the fights are a lot more . . . [Cecchin knocks.]*

*[Boscolo leaves the room.]*

DR. S: *[to the family] Drs. Cecchin and Boscolo will frequently confer with each other, sometimes for a few minutes, sometimes for a lengthier time. I think I'll join them. [Leaves]*

---

HOFFMAN: How often do you usually call each other from behind the screen?

BOSCOLO: Lately we have been calling each other much less. One explanation is that we have become more confident. Sometimes we go right through without calling. We have a discussion after the session.

HOFFMAN: You sometimes go through a whole session without having to connect?

CECCHIN: Yes. We have become less interested in the small details. If we see that the therapist is missing some very important opening, something very obvious, we call the therapist out. But you can get obsessive, phoning in questions, "Why don't you ask this . . . If I were there, I would have asked . . ." and so on. We don't do that so much anymore.

HOFFMAN: What do you do with trainees in the room?

BOSCOLO: Often we see that a trainee is overimpressed with the ideas of the supervisor. One way we can paralyze therapists is by calling in too often. In order to avoid that, we set aside a period of thirty minutes. We say to the trainee "For thirty minutes, you can do anything you want. We will call you only after that time."

CECCHIN: Occasionally we have called a trainee and said "You have to be more aggressive" or "Perhaps you should be kinder." In our experience, prescriptions of this type tend to fail. So instead we say "You are very aggressive. Let's see how we can use your aggressiveness." Or: "You are very soft, you don't alarm the family. Let's make use of that."

BOSCOLO: Training has to be isomorphic to, that is, be similar to, what the therapist does with the family. If you criticize the trainees, you connote them negatively. If you imply that they should have done something differently, you tend to communicate to the trainees that they should think the way you think. It is more helpful to connote positively each trainee's specific way of dealing with families.

PENN: Does that sometimes have a paradoxical effect? Does the shy trainee tend to get a little ruder?

CECCHIN: Sometimes. But then it is a change that comes by itself. We didn't engineer it and we didn't intend it.

HOFFMAN: Most trainers tend to direct their students quite specifically. They tell them what to say, give them assignments for the family, messages, and so forth.

CECCHIN: That's based on the prejudice that the supervisor or the team behind the mirror has better ideas than the therapist inside the room. If you believe this, then the therapist in the room always has to obey the team.

BOSCOLO: Instead we believe that it is the team's job to convince the therapist. If you approach them with a criticism, or if you say "You made a mistake, you should use another technique," you don't convince anybody. You usually don't convince a patient to change by telling him he is wrong. It's the same thing.

CECCHIN: Parents criticize their children because they don't like the way they are growing up. The fact is that they don't grow up if they are criticized.

BOSCOLO: The half hour period that protects the trainee from being called is also intended to keep the trainee from becoming enmeshed with the supervisor. The trainee who begins to wait for the supervisor to tell him what to do doesn't connect with the family. This is unfortunate, because the therapist is between two systems: the family and the team. He has to learn how to be connected with both of them.

HOFFMAN: Other models—in particular, the structural school—would call that joining. You usually don't have anything specific to say about joining, at least as a separate process.

BOSCOLO: We also believe in joining. The thirty-minute rule protects the relationship between the therapist and the family. If we don't have this rule, the trainees will only be able to join with the supervisor.

CECCHIN: Yes. We emphasize neutrality so as not to become part of the system. But this can become a problem, because a student can seem to the family to be very cold and indifferent. It may be better for him or her to become enmeshed with the system, manipulated by the system, part of the system, because in the process of coming out of this manipulation, that's therapy. You must go from being a therapist to being a nontherapist. Then the family gets cured.

HOFFMAN: To get back to this consultation, when you go out to talk to Cecchin, the family's therapist goes with you. Doesn't that go against your practice?

BOSCOLO: Yes. Usually we discourage this. In a consultation, if the therapist goes out with the consultant, the family will believe that every decision the consultant makes is shared with the therapist. The family can become confused. We believe that any statement the consultant makes should be perceived as totally independent from the relationship between the therapist and the consultant. In other words, the consultant should remain at a metalevel as Bateson puts it; that is, at a higher level of logical type, in relation to both the therapist and the family.

CECCHIN: However, we haven't yet learned how to avoid the embarrassment of leaving the therapist with the family when we go out of the room. It is very hard for the therapist to sit there doing nothing. This therapist decided to come out with us, which is not something we usually allow. It is important for the family to know that the therapist is not in collusion with the consultants.

### FAMILY INTERVIEW
[Boscolo and Dr. S reenter.]

BOSCOLO: *Dr. Cecchin called me out to ask me to tell you that he has the impression that Father and Mother are here to cooperate; but he has the feeling that the daughters don't understand why they are here, so it seems as if they don't want to cooperate. He asked me to ask Mother and Father if there is some explanation.*

MOTHER: *Well, they don't want to be here.*

BOSCOLO: *They don't want to be here?*

MOTHER: *No, and they don't want to answer the questions. I would say that mainly they don't want to be here.*

BOSCOLO: *They don't want to be here. Who did not want to come here the most?*

MOTHER: *All three. None of them wanted to come. [Dori laughs.] Mainly Lisa.*

BOSCOLO: *Mainly Lisa. And do you have an idea why they did not want to come today?*

MOTHER: *I don't know why she didn't really want to come. I guess it's because she doesn't feel that she would be of any use. I don't know. She hasn't really explained why she . . .*

BOSCOLO: *Did your husband want to come today?*

MOTHER: *I don't know.*

FATHER: *I didn't mind coming, but there's a lot of work to be done at the shop today.*

BOSCOLO: *Let me ask this question. You were saying that since a year ago things were getting worse, especially the lack of communication with your husband, fights, and so on. And six months ago, Diane started also to fight with her father. Do you think that this contributes to the fights between you and your husband? If Diane would get along with her father better, would you have more communication with your husband?*

MOTHER: *No, not really. The problem isn't the communication between Diane and her father. I think it's that he has favored her and babied her all her life and spoiled her. She could do no wrong. And this was extremely hostile, in my mind. Why should one child be singled out and favored when he has two others? And Lisa was the exact opposite. She was picked on her whole life. . . .*

BOSCOLO: *By whom?*

MOTHER: *By her father. And Diane was babied, and Lisa was picked on, and Dori was ignored. She was there, she was spoken to, and she was disciplined and all that, but she was never picked on or babied.*

BOSCOLO: *Did Diane like being preferred by your husband?*

MOTHER: *Oh, yes! She played on this all the time.*

BOSCOLO: *Up to six months ago?*

MOTHER: *Yes.*

BOSCOLO: *And then something changed. Do you have any idea what happened?*

---

BOSCOLO: I noticed something interesting. When the therapist reenters the room he doesn't usually say "The consultant asked me to tell you . . ." or "The consultant has this idea . . ." In this case I said "Dr. Cecchin called me to say he noticed that the children do not cooperate; that only the parents cooperate." I think I used this format to put Cecchin at a higher level in relation to the family and therapist. "My colleague thinks we are stuck. So he asked me to ask you these questions."

PENN: So the therapist is the target of the intervention?

BOSCOLO: Yes, because he's in an impasse.

PENN: It has an immediate effect on the family. Their participation becomes much more detailed and relevant. Do you think it works that way because there's a tendency for the family to want to rescue you?

BOSCOLO: It's possible. It's interesting that the family doesn't feel accused by the therapist.

PENN: He's just the transmitter of bad news.

BOSCOLO: My colleague observed that it looks as if the girls don't want to be here. Is it true? I don't know. I'm not accusing you of not wanting to be here.

PENN: So the therapist doesn't have to be seen as pejorative or blaming.

BOSCOLO: If the therapist had not done that, it could have been dangerous, because he would have connoted part of the system negatively from the beginning. It has to be somebody from outside who does that.

CECCHIN: As an association to this, I'm thinking that when we utilize the splitting of the team, especially when the family is not moving, the most negative statement usually comes from the supervisor, not the therapist. "My supervisor is of the opinion that nothing is going to change and that there is no hope. I'm the therapist, I still have hope. In time, if I don't see some change, maybe I will agree with the supervisor—right now, I don't." This is related to the question about joining. The therapist is at an interface of two systems—family and supervisor, as we said. It is important that the family has the feeling of having a person on their side.

HOFFMAN: What's interesting in your method is that there's always an ambiguity about the therapist. With more directive techniques, the therapist joins strategically with this one or that one. With you, the family is never sure whether the therapist will be on their side or not. Maybe they will lose the therapist, maybe not. There's an ambiguity that gives the therapist a certain freedom, even if you don't split the team.

CECCHIN: That's true. Usually we don't split the team, but people get the idea that it could happen.

PENN: One of the things I have noticed is that when a private therapist brings in a case for consultation, the family often gets very angry at the team. The consultation tends to jeopardize the relationship between the family and the therapist because the family perceives the therapist as more allied with the people behind the mirror.

BOSCOLO: If a therapist asks for a consultation, it is often because he feels the therapy is not moving. The family usually doesn't have the same idea as the therapist. Families in therapy tend to relate to the therapist as they would to an important member of the family. If they improve, they will lose the therapist. So the one who wants to change is the therapist. When the therapist calls for a consultation, the family often agrees in order to please the therapist, not because they feel they need it. The first question we usually ask would be this: "Dr. So-and-so asked me to see you because he thinks that the therapy is at an impasse. Do you agree?" Very often the family members look startled. "But we think the therapy is going very well." This answer impresses the therapist very much, because he did not expect such a reaction.

CECCHIN: Another point is that the consultant is introducing a new parameter into the relationship between the family and the therapist. One of the frequent responses of the family after the consultation is to disqualify the consultant. This puts the therapist in a bind. If the therapist accepts the disqualification, he shows himself to be inconsistent because he was the one who asked for the consultation. But if the therapist allies himself with the consultant, he is also wrong. The only possible thing the therapist can do is to take a metalevel position, above the battle, basing his verdict on what happens in the future. Any time that the family tries to test what the therapist thinks of the consultation, he can answer: "I don't know. They're the experts. Maybe they're right."

BOSCOLO: He can say "Time will show if they are right or wrong." Otherwise, the therapist would begin to feel crazy.

CECCHIN: An interesting point about an impasse consultation is that the family acts very comfortable, very content. The family seems to have dropped out of the struggle for change. Instead the therapist is in that position. So the family begins to feel better.

BOSCOLO: The therapist feels worse because he's part of the therapeutic community that makes him want to change people. So he begins to feel a malaise. Our students ask "What are the symptoms?" And the symptoms are always the same. When you are seeing a stuck family you begin to have fantasies about changing your job, fantasies of changing your wife. Fantasies of giving up this family and finding a new one. You start to have physical symptoms—you begin to be sleepy during sessions.

CECCHIN: And you think other therapists are better than you.

BOSCOLO: So the therapist will begin to have this kind of malaise. Perhaps you have chosen the wrong profession—you should have gone into business. All our students laugh at this, because all of them have had these symptoms.

CECCHIN: An important epistemological point is that we introduce this force stronger than yourself that Bateson talks about in his essay, "The Cybernetics of 'Self': A Theory of Alcoholism" (Bateson, 1972). If you say "Time will tell," you are introducing a factor from outside, so that nobody is really responsible. This idea takes the suffering away from the therapist and from the family. "Time," you say. "Time," with a big T.

HOFFMAN: So then the family has an incentive to show the consultants that they can change.

BOSCOLO: The impasse consultation often helps the therapist more than the family because the therapist is more the patient in this context. This move takes the therapist out of the impotent position, trying to change the family and creating a never-ending game.

CECCHIN: The impasse therapist is usually the one who gets into the position of being a chronic therapist. He's always there, suffering, because the family doesn't change. If you tell him that the fact that the family doesn't change is the most successful kind of therapy—that for them to change would be dangerous for many reasons—this can be helpful. When the therapist goes back in and says "Nothing is changing, but you're doing very well," his analogic message about change is totally different. What keeps people in the same place is the therapist who tries to change them, the therapist who becomes part of the problem.

### FAMILY INTERVIEW

BOSCOLO: *Do you have any idea what happened?*

MOTHER: *No, I don't know what changed Diane. It was a very sudden and a very drastic change. It wasn't a really slow process; it was like one month she was the best of friends and the next month she was an enemy.*

BOSCOLO: *I see. For years Diane was the one who was closer to the father.*

MOTHER: *Oh, yes.*

BOSCOLO: *Who was closer to you of the other two, Lisa or Dori?*

MOTHER: *Well, I would have to say Lisa because Dori isn't a person who gets close to anyone. She is more to herself and more, you know, she goes and hides and she doesn't really cause too terribly many problems; she goes away and hides.*

BOSCOLO: *[to Father] What was your impression? According to you, over the years, who was closer to your wife?*

FATHER: *Lisa was.*

BOSCOLO: *Lisa first. And second?*

FATHER: *Well, toss-up between Dori and Diane.*

BOSCOLO: *[to Mother] Now, from the information that I was given by the therapist, you were married twice.*

MOTHER: *Yes.*

BOSCOLO: *And from the first marriage, Lisa was born.*

MOTHER: *That's right.*

BOSCOLO: *I see. And then you separated.*

MOTHER: *Yes.*

BOSCOLO: *How old was Lisa when you separated?*

MOTHER: *Actually, my husband left me before Lisa was born, and, ah . . .*

BOSCOLO: *You were never married?*

MOTHER: *Oh, yes. But he left me before she was born—you know—he would come back and forth for a day every so often, but when we finally got our divorce, she was about two.*

BOSCOLO: *Why did you finally divorce your husband?*

MOTHER: *He had a girl friend.*

---

PENN: Why did you go into the mother's history now?

BOSCOLO: This was a decision. At a certain point in the interview, the therapist usually decides to enlarge the context. Since these daughters come from two different families, at some point I decided to go into the past to get information about the previous system that had an influence on these families.

PENN: Is it also because you now have a clearer idea about the couples in the family? The basic couple seems to be Lisa and Mother. This has twice been confirmed by Mother and once by Father. There had been a coalition between Father and Diane up until six months ago, but now the two younger girls have become close and Father is an outsider. It's as if you have to go back to the beginning to see how the first family got together.

BOSCOLO: I'm saying to Mother and Lisa "Not only are you very connected, but at one time you were a family alone, before these other people came into it."

PENN: What hypothesis were you following at that time?

BOSCOLO: One of the reasons I began exploring the mother's first marriage was related to the idea that since this is her second marriage, she may have had a fear of failing again.

PENN: Do you think she accepted the incestuous behaviors of her husband for fear that the second marriage would break up if she didn't?

BOSCOLO: Possibly. What is also important is the attitude of the mother's family toward her two marriages. If they were blaming her she would feel obliged to stick to this second marriage, no matter what her husband did, to show that she was not a failure.


### FAMILY INTERVIEW

BOSCOLO: *And when you divorced, did you meet your second husband soon after? Or were there some years in between?*

MOTHER: *There was about two and a half years from the time my husband left till the time I met Jack—about two years.*

BOSCOLO: *Two years. And in those two years you were alone with Lisa?*

MOTHER: *Yes.*

BOSCOLO: *Did you have some support from your family?*

MOTHER: *No.*

BOSCOLO: *Not at all?*

MOTHER: *No.*

BOSCOLO: *Did your family live in A——?*

MOTHER: *Yes.*

BOSCOLO: *. . . at the time you lived in A——?*

MOTHER: *Yes.*

BOSCOLO: *Is your family in A——?*

MOTHER: *Yes.*

BOSCOLO: *Do you have brothers and sisters?*

MOTHER: *Yes.*

BOSCOLO: *How many brothers and sisters do you have?*

MOTHER: *I have two brothers and one sister.*

BOSCOLO: *Married?*

MOTHER: *Yes.*

BOSCOLO: *How are their marriages?*

MOTHER: *Well, both my brothers have been divorced and remarried. My other brother will be getting remarried in a couple of weeks. My older brother has been remarried. My one sister is the only one who is still with her husband.*

BOSCOLO: *Your one sister?*

MOTHER: *She's still with her husband.*

BOSCOLO: *And your mother and father are still alive?*

MOTHER: *Yes.*

BOSCOLO: *Do they live alone?*

MOTHER: *Yes.*

BOSCOLO: *Do you have contact with them?*

MOTHER: *Not what you would call a really close contact. Our family life is very— well, they don't come and visit and if you want to visit them, you have to go and visit and it's not a really close relationship. My mother and I are closer, but not a really close relationship.*

BOSCOLO: *Your daughters are close to your mother? Which one of them is closest to your mother?*

MOTHER: *Not anyone really, because my mother is not the person who shows her emotions either. She don't favor anyone over anybody else, she don't make any fuss over any of them, she doesn't buy them anything, she doesn't really get close to anyone.*

BOSCOLO: *What did your family think when you decided to get remarried? Were they in favor of Jack or not?*

MOTHER: *Well, they weren't in favor of my getting married, but they didn't really know I was seeing Jack because I didn't tell them until I was already married. They have always objected to everything I have done in life. Everything was wrong. So I just never told them.*

BOSCOLO: *But were your father and mother hoping that you would not remarry?*

MOTHER: *Yes.*

BOSCOLO: *Did they tell you explicitly that you should not remarry?*

MOTHER: *They wouldn't even lend me any money for a divorce. They said no way.*

BOSCOLO: *Did they offer you support after you were divorced?*

MOTHER: No.

BOSCOLO: *So you got married, but they were not very happy about your second marriage.*

MOTHER: No. *They didn't really physically object to it; but they didn't say they were glad either.*

---

PENN: When Mother was talking about her family of origin, I realized that she, too, had a confusing relationship with her mother, where she was close but not too close. And she also had a father who disapproved of everything she did.

BOSCOLO: You mean Lisa is repeating the same story?

PENN: Well, there is some resonance in the mother's family. There are analogous triangles, which might cause her to both identify with Lisa and at the same time try not to show her too much favor.

## FAMILY INTERVIEW

BOSCOLO: *I see. Then you remarried and had two other daughters. And how did the marriage go from the beginning?*

MOTHER: *The marriage went fine in the beginning because I was always the one that would say "I am sorry!" "Let's try it again!" "Let's do this, let's do that, let's work this out, let's talk this over." I was the one who was always trying to undo any wrong things that were said and tried to understand all of his problems.*

BOSCOLO: *Did your husband understand you more at the time you were first married?*

MOTHER: *I don't think so. I think that he is a very unfeeling person. I mean, he may feel underneath, but as far as showing any feelings, he doesn't show any feelings, or any hurt, or any remorse. I mean, it's hard to live with someone who doesn't show any feeling.*

BOSCOLO: *I see. How old was Lisa when you got remarried?*

MOTHER: *Two and a half.*

BOSCOLO: *Was it at that time that Jack didn't like—didn't have a good relationship with Lisa? At the beginning did you feel he accepted her?*

MOTHER: *Well, I thought he did, but he was always very hard on her. And the more I objected to his hardness, the more he was hard, because the more he thought I was favoring her.*

BOSCOLO: *He thought you were favoring her. [to Father] But before the last two were born, how was your life with your wife and Lisa?*

FATHER: *We got along. There was numerous occasions I would come home from work and "Lisa did this wrong, take and discipline her," and this was almost from day one. Every time I would say something to Lisa, Betty would be on my back: "Leave her alone!" And she more or less, just every time I would speak to her, she would be jumping on me, and that just pushed everything further away.*

BOSCOLO: *Did you feel at that time like making contact with Lisa? Did you feel as if she was your daughter?*

FATHER: *Yes, I felt her as a daughter.*

BOSCOLO: *You wished you could have had a better relationship with Lisa at the time.*

FATHER: *Yes.*

BOSCOLO: *But Lisa was closer to the mother—too close to her mother.*

FATHER: *Yes.*

BOSCOLO: *And then, after you got married, when the second one was born, how old was Lisa?*

MOTHER: *Five and a half.*

BOSCOLO: *How did the situation change when Dori was born?*

MOTHER: *Well, it changed the situation where he was. He never really had much to do with the kids when they were babies because he was working two jobs, so I mean as far as the situation was concerned, it didn't change much because the only change was for me where I had far more responsibility and far more problems to deal with and less help.*

BOSCOLO: *You felt neglected?*

MOTHER: *I felt very neglected, like there was no support for me.*

BOSCOLO: *[to Father] For instance, when Dori was born, did you think that the birth of Dori would improve your rapport?*

FATHER: *I thought it would, yes.*

BOSCOLO: *Did the rapport with your wife improve when Dori and Diane were born, or did it get worse?*

FATHER: *Well, after Diane was born, it got a little worse.*

BOSCOLO: *A little worse?*

FATHER: *Because the day Diane was born, it was on a Sunday, and I took Betty to the hospital and I had to work that day. And she was quite peeved that I was not there and she was in the hospital.*

BOSCOLO: *Then if I understand correctly, when Diane was born, you had a good rapport with Diane and Diane with you, as your wife was saying before.*

FATHER: *Yes.*

BOSCOLO: *You were close to Diane.*

FATHER: *Yes.*

BOSCOLO: *While Mother was close to Dori and Lisa, and they were close to your wife. [To Mother] Why didn't things get better at that time?*

MOTHER: *Because, as I said before, I could not see a father favoring one child and*

*neglecting the other, and being mean to one and loving the other one up, and
saying that whatever she did was perfect and whatever the other one did was
never right.*

BOSCOLO: *The other one would be Lisa?*

MOTHER: *Yes. He picked on Lisa all the time.*

————————————

BOSCOLO: The mother is complaining because the father is not close to
Diane. She also complains because the father was never close to Lisa.
So she would like the father to be close to the daughters.

HOFFMAN: If your hypothesis is right, she is afraid of being a failure in
the eyes of her family, so she keeps trying to make her second marriage
work. But she is in a bind. From early on, she defers to this husband
and asks him to discipline Lisa. But when he does, she goes to Lisa's
side and he feels rejected. Then the mother gets scared because she feels
"This marriage may break up too."

CECCHIN: We can also see the bind the husband is in. The mother keeps
saying "You have no feelings, you never express anything, you are not
close to my daughters." And when he gets close, she says "You are still
wrong because you are playing favorites."

BOSCOLO: This makes a bind for Lisa too. On the one hand, the mother
seems to say "I want my husband to love Lisa, who is my first daughter."
At the same time the father says "My wife never permitted me to be
close to Lisa." And Lisa must feel confused and profoundly in the wrong
if she accepts the stepfather's advances, and she is in the wrong if she
does not.

### FAMILY INTERVIEW

BOSCOLO: *If Lisa were not born, let's say, if you didn't have Lisa when you got
married, and you didn't have any daughters, do you think the situation would
have been better?*

MOTHER: *It would have.*

BOSCOLO: *What upset you with your husband over and over again is that he favored
one of the daughters and did not favor Lisa. If Lisa were not there, if you would
have gotten married to Jack without having any children, and you would have
only Dori and Diane, do you think the situation would be better?*

MOTHER: *I think the situation would be a little better to the point that we wouldn't
have had to have the friction over me feeling that he disliked her so much and*

was always on her back and felt that she was always so wrong, and the situation would have been much better in that sense of the word; but the situation wouldn't have changed because the problems still would have been there of him favoring Diane and I would have had Dori and then I would have had to—I would have probably favored her. But I mean I have never liked, I've never favored any one child over the other. I've always tried to treat them equal, I've never . . .

BOSCOLO: But what upset you most is the fact that your husband didn't get along with Lisa.

MOTHER: Yeah.

BOSCOLO: Now I would like to ask a question to Lisa. We have talked about these fights between Father and Mother. The way you saw it—for instance, when they were fighting or had arguments—whose side did Diane and Dori usually take? [No answer.] You were not listening.

LISA: I was—didn't hear you—which side they were on?

BOSCOLO: Yes.

LISA: I don't know. On Dad's side.

BOSCOLO: Can you talk louder?

LISA: Diane was on my dad's side and Dori was on my mom's side.

BOSCOLO: How about you?

LISA: I was on my mom's side.

BOSCOLO: Were there times that, at least once in your life, you were on one side and your sisters were on the other side? This never happened?

LISA: No.

BOSCOLO: Not ever?

LISA: Not that I know of.

BOSCOLO: But Dori, on what side do you see her mostly, with you or with Diane? Is Dori closer to Diane or to you?

LISA: To me, I guess. I don't know, I never thought about it.

BOSCOLO: And you, Diane, what side is Dori mostly on, with you or with Lisa?

DIANE: I don't think she is with anybody more than the other.

BOSCOLO: You don't?

DIANE: No. I think she's sort of just—is there.

BOSCOLO: And Lisa, has she always been like this?

DIANE: I don't know.

BOSCOLO: She looks very sad—down, sad. Is that the way she usually looks?

DIANE: I don't know. [Diane and Dori laugh.]

BOSCOLO: [to Mother] Do you understand why Diane and Dori laugh? I don't understand. Do you understand why they laugh?

MOTHER: Because they are afraid to talk about each other, afraid to say how they feel. They don't want to commit themselves to any statement.

BOSCOLO: [to Lisa] Do you know why, when I talked to them, they laughed?

LISA: It's a way to hide the truth.

BOSCOLO: Beg your pardon?

LISA: They want to hide the truth.

BOSCOLO: *They laugh to hide the truth.*
LISA: *Yes.*
BOSCOLO: *What truth do they hide?*
LISA: *What they really want to say, so they just laugh.*
BOSCOLO: *Can you tell me what they don't want to say?*
LISA: *Yeah, but I don't want to say it either. I'm not going to say it. [Diane and Dori are laughing.]*
BOSCOLO: *Well, that's different. [to Mother] If I ask you, do you have an idea?*
MOTHER: *None of them want to say exactly what they feel and what they want to say. They want—*

---

CECCHIN: There is something mysterious here that you can only see on the tape. In the last two or three minutes, the mother's lips have been moving exactly in time with the sentences of Lisa. There was a technician doing the videotaping who got very excited because when he saw this behavior he didn't know whether the lip-moving came after the voice of Lisa or vice versa. They were so completely in sync.

HOFFMAN: In some way, the mother must be giving the daughter permission to speak by silently speaking her lines. That would be one way to signal it. At the same time that she says "You mustn't tell."

BOSCOLO: The mother said previously that they should all talk. Now she gives an injunction not to tell the secret. The girls are talking about something real, and she says "The girls are afraid to talk about their feelings," which is a message not to say anything.

PENN: But Lisa has just said it all. She says "They are laughing because they don't want to tell *the truth.*" And then she says "I am not going to say *it* either." How did you get her cooperation?

BOSCOLO: The sisters had been laughing all through the session, and I asked "Why are they laughing?" At that moment I joined with her against the sisters. So she gave me this piece of information, the "it." She led me to the secret.

HOFFMAN: But if you had said "It sounds to me as if they can't understand how sad you feel," I don't think she would have come forward.

BOSCOLO: I think there is also a question of timing here. You can feel the tension build, build, until at a certain point something cracks.

### FAMILY INTERVIEW

LISA: *I feel alone.*
BOSCOLO: *You feel alone. You have always felt alone as this, or lately?*
LISA: *All the time.*
BOSCOLO: *All the time. Also when you were a little girl?*
LISA: *Yes. I felt like I was in the middle of everything.*
BOSCOLO: *In the middle of everything.*
LISA: *And it would have been better if I wasn't here.*
BOSCOLO: *If you hadn't been born.*
LISA: *I don't want to sit here. [starting to cry]*
BOSCOLO: *No, I think it's important we talk. They laugh when you are crying. I want to talk to you so your sisters will listen.*
LISA: *[sobbing] I don't want to sit here, I don't want to. I want to get out of here.*

---

HOFFMAN: On the content level, was the information that Lisa had made a suicide attempt in your mind?

BOSCOLO: I think the question was more related to the fact that I felt Lisa was in a very bad situation. Her behavior in the session indicated that she was very down, very depressed, and I also thought she was in a position where she could easily get psychotic.

HOFFMAN: Why do you think Lisa was not actively psychotic?

BOSCOLO: We later learn that there was a grandmother—the mother's mother—who probably gave her the message that she cared for her. This would explain why Lisa went to live with her when she ran away. Also, if you look at the level of family pattern, you find that relationships are clear and distinct. The father and mother are very clear about whose side everyone is on, and so are the girls. In psychosis, people cannot so easily define their relationships.

PENN: But you were obviously worried; it shows in the seriousness of your tone and the sympathetic way you talk to Lisa.

BOSCOLO: Yes, and I think I was biased by the information I got from the therapist. I was concerned about Lisa and I don't think I was very neutral. It is hard to be neutral if you know that there has been incest and a serious suicide attempt and the family refuses to acknowledge it as a problem. For them, the problem was only that Diane was fighting with the father. The therapist is in a difficult spot.

PENN: One of the most effective pieces of information that has been introduced into the system so far is your confirmation of Lisa's dilemma. She says "It would have been better if I wasn't here," and you say "If you hadn't been born." It's as if she experiences all the time that she should not be there at all. It's a very powerful moment.

CECCHIN: By saying this, we touched on her feeling that she's useless there. You can see the effect: she suddenly sits up.

HOFFMAN: I wish you would say a little bit more about what you were doing there.

BOSCOLO: We can never know what would have happened in this family if Lisa had not been born. But it is important to see what kind of fantasies, what kind of ideas, the system has. By doing this, you tend to hit some of the myths, some of the premises of the system. It's possible that they could really be thinking that Lisa should not be alive. She may have tried to commit suicide because of a belief that her birth meant ruin for mother. But we are not looking for real answers to the question.

HOFFMAN: How do you explain the effect of this kind of probe?

CECCHIN: Hypothetical and future questions are very important because, if you are talking in cybernetic terms, they open up loops in the family. In the family, there are rules that govern what is allowed and not allowed. For instance, in this family it is forbidden to talk about many things. If you use hypothetical questions, you take the skeletons out of the closet. These questions—and also future questions—go against the rules that maintain these avoidances.

BOSCOLO: The family usually has the sensation of being stuck in an unending game. They have the idea that there is no way out. By using future questions, you introduce the idea that things could be totally different.

HOFFMAN: It's a way of introducing an idea about change without saying they should change.

BOSCOLO: It's a way of saying that there could be a difference. If Lisa had not been born, things would have gone differently. Lisa's birth becomes important information for the system. If you treat it like information, you can talk about it without being afraid of making her too upset. And then you bring out something real.

CECCHIN: A question we could have asked Lisa is "If you had not been born, what do you think would have been different in the family?"

BOSCOLO: Questions about the future have enormous impact on the nonverbal behaviors. You see much stronger responses to questions about the future than to questions about the past or the present. I think it's related to the fact that the family, over time, has developed a deterministic ideology. But when you ask about the future, you can't be deterministic.

Hypothetical questions put the whole family to work at making connections and finding solutions.

CECCHIN: For instance, if someone is suicidal, you ask "How long do you think you are going to remain suicidal?" That's a future question. Then you ask "If you die tomorrow, what will happen to your mother, father, sister?" et cetera. "If you die in one year, how do you think therapy will go? Suppose you continue to make suicide attempts all your life, what will happen to these other people?" You open up all the possibilities. Every family, when someone has a symptom, feels stuck in repetitive behaviors. If you say "You can die or you can stay the way you are; you can die later or decide to improve; you can also decide to stop dying," these possibilities can alter repetitive behavior.

BOSCOLO: Future questions have immense impact psychologically too. For instance, if a couple comes to treatment and each partner says they cannot stand to go on this way any longer, you ask: "How long will you be able to endure this situation—a year? two?" Then they get agitated because it's difficult for them to define their relationship around how long they will continue with this kind of behavior.

CECCHIN: If one of them says two years, you ask: "In two years, what will you do?" "I will leave him." Then you ask a survivor question: "Do you think your husband would survive?" Or you ask the husband: "Do you think your wife will survive? Who will survive best?"

CECCHIN: Then there is a punishment question that involves the future: "We understand you are angry with your parents and are punishing them. Your behavior is a punishment which everyone understands. How long do you think your parents will deserve this kind of punishment— fifteen, twenty years? life? Even in the Justice Department, they have a statute of limitations. Perhaps you have a limit. When will you be satisfied that they are finally punished?" Suppose a person feels humiliated or bad about himself. You can then say: "Well, punishment is necessary. You have worked for your punishment; punishment is necessary for your survival. But how long do you think you'll need to go on like that?"

HOFFMAN: These are interesting categories: survival questions, punishment questions. Do you have any others?

CECCHIN: Separation questions. They are the most frightening. "When will the children leave home? Which one will be the first to leave?"

HOFFMAN: How do you categorize the question that goes: "If you had not been born, would things be better or worse?"

CECCHIN: Existential questions: "If you didn't exist, if your children did not exist, how would you get along?"

BOSCOLO: I remember a question we used with a suicidal girl. We said

"Suppose you die, how long do you think it will take for your parents, your brothers and sisters, to forget about you? How long will it take—five years? three years? two weeks? You have a lot of choices." "A month," she said. And the parents said "Janey!" Then they all started to laugh. There's such a drama about suicide.

Another category of future questions are the ones that have to do with the relationship between the family and the therapists. Let me give you an example. I was the therapist on this case and I said to the family, "My colleagues behind the mirror are very pessimistic about your future because they don't see any big change in store. They agree more or less with Father's pessimism. Now, I don't agree with them. I agree more with the mother about the future. I think things will develop. But if in a year there is no change, then I will agree with my colleagues behind the mirror. I will become pessimistic like them." That was January, and we gave them a session a year later.

### FAMILY INTERVIEW

BOSCOLO: *Listen, Lisa, you said you always felt alone.*

LISA: *[still sobbing] I don't want to, I want to go.*

BOSCOLO: *Were you trying in the past to see if you could get close to your sisters, and your sisters didn't want to say it?*

MOTHER: *[trying to comfort Lisa] Lisa.*

BOSCOLO: *[to Mother] I will ask you: When Lisa was saying before "I was always alone," she started to cry—feeling she was nobody. Now, you know your daughter very well. Is she crying because she couldn't have rapport with her sisters? Why is she so alone?*

MOTHER: *Well, she felt that her father was against her and always picking on her; and because Jack and I fought all the time and she felt that she was the cause of the fights, and she felt that was to blame for the fighting, and I tried to stay what I would call neutral. I told her what was wrong and I said, "Listen to your dad, do as he says. If he says jump, jump; if he says lay down, lay down." You know, I tried to . . . try to make it even . . .*

BOSCOLO: *Did you try to see—for instance, over the years, did you try to tell Lisa to get, to try to get close to your husband? Have you tried to say "Try to be different. Let's see if you can try to satisfy Jack, or . . ."*

MOTHER: *Yes, I have. That's why I told her to listen to him. To do what he says and to try and understand. He works hard and he's tired. But problems came . . .*

BOSCOLO: *How would Lisa react when you told her that: "Try to understand that he works hard"?*

MOTHER: *During the last few years . . .*

BOSCOLO: *Did she try, Lisa?*

MOTHER: *She did at first, yes. She tried, she tried to do everything, she was actually a perfect child. She took care of her sister. She baby-sat. She had to take on a lot of responsibility. She cleaned the house. She did everything she was supposed to do.*

BOSCOLO: *Were they grateful to her, your other daughters, that she was doing all these things also for them? Were they grateful or not?*

MOTHER: *I think Dori was, but Diane was too spoiled to appreciate it.*

BOSCOLO: *She was too spoiled to appreciate it. [to Father] How about you? Do you agree with your wife? She said many times that Lisa tried to be good to her father, she worked so hard, et cetera, that Lisa tried . . .*

FATHER: *To an extent, I do.*

BOSCOLO: *To an extent. Do you feel she tried to make contact with you?*

FATHER: *She would try for a while, and then Betty and I would get into a fight or an argument, and because I said "Lisa, would you do this or that," Betty would be on my back: "Leave the kid alone. She doesn't have to do this" or "She doesn't have to do that."*

---

BOSCOLO: You can see how Lisa becomes a function of the parents' relationship. When she was getting along with her father, the parents would probably start to fight, perhaps to avoid closeness. And when Lisa would get close to Mother, then they would also start to fight. That's why Lisa says "I was nobody, but I was in the middle of everything."

HOFFMAN: It's such a clear description of the child participating in the triangle.

CECCHIN: This is a typical triangle where no twosome can persist. For example, Mother and daughter must have been so close to each other that Father felt left out. So the mother has to say to the daughter, "Go to your father." They can't tolerate having the father excluded, suffering. And when the daughter goes to the father, Mother gets on the father's back: "Leave her alone. You are doing it all wrong." And when the mother and father are getting along, the daughter gets the message: "I don't count. I don't exist." So no couple can form without damaging the third one. Everybody is interfering with everybody else. Everybody feels guilty when they are with somebody else. Everybody's accusing somebody else. They are all caught in the same situation.

HOFFMAN: The unconscious message of the mother is so explicit: "If he says jump, jump; if he says lay down, lay down."

CECCHIN: But it's not enough to think only in terms of Father, Mother, and Lisa. Mother also blames Father for spoiling Diane and Diane for being too close to Father. From the tone of her voice, you pick up that she suffered from this closeness, at least until six months ago. I wonder whether Mother's message isn't also a message to Lisa that she doesn't count as much as Diane.

PENN: Lisa's attempt to leave may have made things more difficult at home. Is your thought that Diane may then have become part of the triangle?

CECCHIN: One possibility is that after Lisa left, the father made advances to Diane. Since he cannot have his wife, he must have at least one daughter. And then Diane starts to act up, both in school and at home. Alternatively, Mother may have given a message to Diane that Father was incestuous, in order to break the relationship between Father and Diane. She may have given the message to Diane: "Look what your father did to Lisa."

We could say also that for a while there was an equilibrium. The mother had Lisa and the father had Diane.

PENN: And what about Dori? She didn't mind being left out?

CECCHIN: She was very happy being out. And so the family went along and the whole situation was quiet. But when Diane got close to Dori, the father was left alone.

HOFFMAN: And Mother was left alone too, in the sense that Lisa had run away to live with Grandmother.

CECCHIN: Yes. So the parents are left alone with each other and they fight more, and that's why they bring the daughters into therapy. But the girls are not cooperating, because the parents are saying "Come into therapy so we can triangulate you again." They want some good therapist who will put Diane back with Father, Lisa back with Mother, and split up Diane and Dori. The parents are the desperate couple.

HOFFMAN: The desperate couple is trying to break up the other couples.

CECCHIN: Yes. It's fascinating. The system was finding a self-healing solution. Lisa had found the grandmother; the two youngest girls found each other. And the parents are now looking for a therapist to reverse the process.

## FAMILY INTERVIEW

BOSCOLO: *Let me ask this thing. Lisa, when did you move out of the house?*

LISA: *I moved out a couple of times.*

BOSCOLO: *When was the first time?*

LISA: *About a year and a half ago.*

BOSCOLO: *A year and a half ago. Did you move out because of what you were communicating before by crying, when you were saying you felt alone and you felt nobody understood?*

LISA: *Part of the reason I just couldn't . . .*

BOSCOLO: *You couldn't do well in the family.*

LISA: *I just couldn't live there.*

BOSCOLO: *I can't hear you.*

LISA: *I just couldn't live there.*

BOSCOLO: *You couldn't live there.*

LISA: *My mom and dad would always say "Well, you just think the grass is greener on the other side." But they didn't listen, and I just couldn't stay there. And they just thought it was because it was just fun and I ran wild, but it wasn't. I just can't stay there.*

BOSCOLO: *You can't stay there. What was the main thing that disturbed you in the family, that made you decide to go out? Was there something specific?*

LISA: *Yes.*

BOSCOLO: *What was that?*

LISA: *It's better not to discuss it.*

BOSCOLO: *I see. It is something that you cannot discuss. But there was something, you say?*

LISA: *Yes.*

BOSCOLO: *I see. Do you think that your sisters know about this?*

LISA: *No.*

BOSCOLO: *When you say that there's something specific, do they have an idea what it is? I don't want you to say what it is. I am just asking if they have an idea.*

LISA: *They'd probably have an idea, but they don't know.*

BOSCOLO: *Who has more of an idea, Diane or Dori?*

LISA: *Dori; I don't know.*

BOSCOLO: *So you have doubt about whether your sisters know about this thing that made you decide to leave home. Do your parents know about this?*

LISA: *Yes.*

BOSCOLO: *They do know. But your sisters don't know.*

LISA: *No.*

BOSCOLO: *Have you ever had the idea or impulse of talking to them?*

LISA: *No.*

BOSCOLO: *Why?*

LISA: *'cause . . .*

BOSCOLO: *Why?*

LISA: *What they don't know won't hurt them.*

BOSCOLO: *I didn't understand. You were afraid of hurting them?*

LISA: *That's right.*

BOSCOLO: *But did you have any temptation at all to talk to them?*

LISA: *No, never.*

BOSCOLO: *If you would have told your sisters what you don't want to tell us—and it's important that you keep this private if you feel like it—if you would have been tempted to confide in your sisters about this, how would your mother and father have reacted if you would have talked to your sisters?*

LISA: *My father?*

BOSCOLO: *Yes. How would your mother and father have reacted if you had told your sisters the reason why you decided to leave home?*

LISA: *I don't know.*

BOSCOLO: *You don't know.*

LISA: *They would have been mad at me.*

BOSCOLO: *Who would have been more mad at you?*

LISA: *My mother.*

BOSCOLO: *Your mother. Did your mother tell you explicitly, Don't talk to Dori or Diane about this?*

LISA: *Not all the time, but she said it.*

BOSCOLO: *She said it. You, Dori, do you have an idea of what Lisa is talking about, that there was something making it intolerable for her to stay at home and she decided to leave? Do you have an idea what this is?*

DORI: *Just a tiny bit.*

BOSCOLO: *Huh?*

DORI: *Just a tiny bit.*

BOSCOLO: *A tiny bit? What is it, this tiny bit?*

DORI: *[silence]*

BOSCOLO: *[to Diane] You?*

DIANE: *A little bit.*

BOSCOLO: *When you know a little bit, a tiny bit, do you talk to each other about this?*

DIANE: *No.*

BOSCOLO: *Dori, Diane, you never talked about it? No. Why?*

------

BOSCOLO: There is one question I could have asked Diane at this point, a question important in terms of time. Since Diane says that she knows, I should have asked her *"When* did you know?" Because if it was six months ago, we could make a connection.

CECCHIN: When she broke off relations with the father.

BOSCOLO: That's right. That's an opening I missed.

HOFFMAN: Something you take so for granted is this technique of talking about the secret without talking about the secret.

CECCHIN: The fact that something is a secret is more important than the content of the secret. In a family, there are two or more people who have a secret. We are not interested in the content but in what effect the secret has on the other people. The secret has an effect, even if the others don't know what it is. We also know that when two people have a secret, this usually makes them more powerful than the others. We will often prescribe a secret that is totally meaningless from the content point of view, simply in order to create a couple. When we ask a couple to go out somewhere without telling anybody where they are going, we don't think it matters where they go. What's important is that they don't tell anybody. It's the fact of people going away together that has an effect on the system. If you are fascinated by the content, you miss the real issue. You ask: "When did you start to have a secret? Don't tell it to me. But who knows about it? How many people know? How long have you had this secret? How long do you think you will keep it? Or, do you think it will leak out by itself first?" And you keep saying "Don't tell me."

PENN: What about people who insist on telling you a secret?

CECCHIN: Years ago we fell into the trap of listening to somebody tell us something about somebody else. "I have to see you alone. There's something I don't want my parents to hear." You agree. You listen to them. Usually what they want to tell you is a very trivial thing. Their real purpose is to create an alliance with you and to break your relationship with others.

BOSCOLO: The family, as a family, is afraid that the content of a secret can be harmful. So by keeping the content from being known to others, they protect the family. But what we are interested in is the relationship structure around the secret. The family here tolerates my talking about the secret as long as I don't ask what it is. This family gave an injunction to the consultant not to talk about the sexual behavior. But here, during the session, I talk about the sexual behavior without talking about it.

PENN: You're making that same difference between information and data. The content of the secret is data and the way the secret organizes relationships is information.

BOSCOLO: This principle doesn't only apply to secrets. If you hear that somebody is delinquent or schizophrenic, this is data too. If you translate statements like this into process, into relationships, you get a very different picture. "What does it mean? Who knows about it? What effect does this delinquent behavior have on other people? What do you define as delinquent?" You change the meaning completely.

PENN: One interesting thing about a secret is that this can be the way a couple defines itself in a system where that's a particularly hard thing to do. As Haley says, a secret is often a coalition across generation lines.

CECCHIN: That's right. A secret also prevents communication from flowing freely within the family. People like Ivan Nagy (Boszormenyi-Nagy and Sparks, 1973) say that one of the most important sources of pathology is the presence of injustice in the family. Now, if there are secrets that allow some people to have information and others not to have it, this creates a kind of injustice. When a person feels pushed out of the communication system, you have a problem.

HOFFMAN: Another problem is when a therapist used to seeing individuals sees a couple and one of them talks to the therapist alone and says "I've been having an affair for ten years, don't tell my wife." It's a real problem for the therapist, figuring out how to get out from under the burden of that confidence.

CECCHIN: Suppose, for example, one member of a couple gives you a hint: "I want to talk to you alone." Immediately you say "I'm glad you brought that up." And then you say to the other: "Both of you, I'm sure, have something private that you'd like to tell me. But therapy can only go on if you keep your secrets. Having secrets is very important to the survival of the system."

BOSCOLO: If one person says "I have a secret" or "I don't want to talk about something," it is very important for the therapist to make a general rule for all family members. He should say that everybody should have some things that they keep private. You have to make general rules; otherwise you lose your neutrality.

PENN: In that way, the power of the secret is nullified, since your general rule puts it on the same level for all family members.


### FAMILY INTERVIEW

BOSCOLO: *But do you think—you, Dori and Diane—that this something that upsets Lisa so much and that brought her to leave home because it became intolerable for reasons she doesn't want to talk about, do you think that she did right to leave the home, or do you think she should have stayed home? [silence]*
*[to Diane] What do you think, for instance?*

DIANE: *I think what she did was okay.*

BOSCOLO: *She did what?*

DIANE: *She did okay leaving, because if someone can't stand living somewhere and they're not happy, I don't think they should stay there.*

BOSCOLO: *So, according to you, she did right to leave?*

DIANE: *Yeah.*

BOSCOLO: *But Lisa's leaving home, not being at home, is it better for you or for*

Dori, or worse? Would the situation in the family be better without Lisa, or worse?

DIANE: Well, there's not really any change.

BOSCOLO: There wasn't any change. But would you prefer—would you think, for instance, that Dori would have preferred Lisa to stay at home or to leave?

DIANE: I don't know.

BOSCOLO: [to Dori] What do you think?

DORI: I don't know.

BOSCOLO: You don't know. Lisa, where did you go? The first time was a year ago. Where did you go?

LISA: To a girl friend's.

BOSCOLO: To a girl friend's. How did your mother react when you decided to go, did she disagree with you, or not?

LISA: No.

BOSCOLO: She didn't want you to go?

LISA: No. She let me.

BOSCOLO: What?

LISA: She let me go.

BOSCOLO: She let you go.

LISA: But she didn't really want me to.

BOSCOLO: She tried to keep you at home?

LISA: No.

BOSCOLO: How long did you stay with your friend?

LISA: Just a couple of months, then I moved into another place with a girl friend.

BOSCOLO: With your girl friend? Do you have good girl friends?

LISA: No.

BOSCOLO: And then? Then you came back?

LISA: In the spring, 'cause I sprained my ankle somehow, I couldn't go back to work, so I had to go back home.

BOSCOLO: You couldn't go to work because of your ankle. You came back home, to this home? I mean to your family?

LISA: Yeah.

BOSCOLO: I see. But were you in doubt as to whether to come back or not?

LISA: I didn't want to, but there wasn't much else I could do.

BOSCOLO: I see. You felt sad outside? You were more isolated?

LISA: Um-hum.

BOSCOLO: You came back, and how long did you stay at home?

LISA: About three months.

BOSCOLO: Three months. And then what happened in those three months? Was it any better at home?

LISA: No.

BOSCOLO: You wanted again to leave.

LISA: Yes.

BOSCOLO: And then where did you go?

LISA: *I went to my grandmother's.*

BOSCOLO: *To see your grandmother. Whose decision was it to go to your grandmother?*

LISA: *Mine and my mom's.*

BOSCOLO: *Your mother's or . . . Mother suggested you go to your grandmother, and did you go willingly? I mean, did you want to go to your grandmother?*

LISA: *No.*

BOSCOLO: *And how long did you stay there?*

LISA: *I just moved out last week.*

BOSCOLO: *Then you came back home?*

LISA: *No. I got a place of my own now.*

BOSCOLO: *You have a place of your own. And how long did you stay with your grandmother?*

LISA: *Since the end of November till last week.*

BOSCOLO: *I see, so you stayed there three months. How was the life there?*

LISA: *Nice and quiet. My grandpa and grandma, they have their own ideas about things and they don't always—they're not the same as mine, but we got along okay.*

BOSCOLO: *But were they good with you, your grandmother and grandfather?*

LISA: *Yeah.*

BOSCOLO: *Did they ask you to stay longer there?*

LISA: *No.*

BOSCOLO: *Do you, Lisa, think that your grandmother and grandfather have some ideas about the reason why you were there? What we have talked about before that you didn't want to tell me. Do you have some ideas about that?*

LISA: *No.*

BOSCOLO: *You don't think they have any ideas?*

LISA: *I think they may have an idea. They know something's wrong.*

BOSCOLO: *Something is wrong. Did they talk to you?*

LISA: *Hm?*

BOSCOLO: *Did they talk to you about that? Did you talk to your grandmother?*

LISA: *No.*

BOSCOLO: *You didn't talk because you were afraid it would make your mother feel bad?*

LISA: *Well, they'd only tell.*

BOSCOLO: *I beg your pardon?*

LISA: *They don't need to know.*

BOSCOLO: *They don't need to know. Lisa, in these years you've been home, are there times that your parents talk about eventual separation? Was there a time they did that?*

LISA: *No.*

BOSCOLO: *They say they don't communicate well. Was there some moment that you were afraid they might separate, or if the problem came out that they might separate or divorce?*

LISA: *Well, they talked about it.*
BOSCOLO: *They talked about it.*
LISA: *Once or twice.*

---

HOFFMAN: Did you ask that because you guessed it, or did you know that they had talked about separating?

BOSCOLO: I think I asked because the mother, at the beginning, said there was such bad communication with the husband. This is what made me think about this idea of separation.

HOFFMAN: Could you talk a little bit about Lisa going to stay with the grandmother?

BOSCOLO: I thought she went to her grandmother because it was more acceptable for the mother—it was a more acceptable way to leave home. But although life was peaceful there, she said there was not a close relationship. Mother had already said that her own mother is not a very affectionate person.

PENN: But sometimes the relationship between a grandmother and a grandchild can be warmer than between the grandmother and the mother.

BOSCOLO: Yes. I think that may have been true. At least Lisa felt confident enough of her support to stay there.


## FAMILY INTERVIEW

BOSCOLO: *How did you feel about them talking about getting separated?*
LISA: *I was glad.*
BOSCOLO: *Hmm?*
LISA: *I was glad.*
BOSCOLO: *You were glad. How about Diane and Dori? Were they glad too?*
LISA: *I don't know.*
BOSCOLO: *How about Diane?*
DIANE: *Well, first I was sad; I didn't want them to. But now I wish they would just get it over with.*
BOSCOLO: *Get it over with? What do you mean?*
DIANE: *Well, just get their divorce and start a new life.*
BOSCOLO: *Start a new life.*
DIANE: *Especially my mom. I don't care about him.*
LISA: *At first I was upset, and now I don't really have any feelings about it.*
BOSCOLO: *If they would separate, who would go to Father, who would go to Mother?*
DORI: *[inaudible]*
BOSCOLO: *Beg your pardon?*

DORI: *We'd probably both go to Mom.*

BOSCOLO: *Who is both?*

DORI: *Diane and me.*

BOSCOLO: *And Lisa?*

DORI: *Lisa's on her own.*

BOSCOLO: *And who would go with Father?*

DORI: *No one. Nobody.*

BOSCOLO: *Nobody would go with Father. Up to six months ago, maybe Diane would go with father?*

DORI: *No.*

BOSCOLO: *A year ago? If they separated a year ago, two years ago?*

DORI: *If they were close, she would have went with him.*

DIANE: *If they got a divorce when I was close to him, I still wouldn't have gone with him.*

BOSCOLO: *You would go with . . .*

DIANE: *When we were close, I wouldn't have gone with him even if they had gotten a divorce.*

BOSCOLO: *You would have always gone with your mother?*

DIANE: *Yeah.*

BOSCOLO: *If they divorced while you were getting along with your father?*

DIANE: *Yeah.*

BOSCOLO: *[to Father] Are you surprised about this?*

FATHER: *Yes. 'Cause she would have went with me.*

DIANE: *I would not have.*

FATHER: *She had often said she would have went with me.*

BOSCOLO: *But if there was a separation, for instance, whom would you like to come with you?*

FATHER: *Both of them. Dori and Diane.*

BOSCOLO: *If they didn't want to come?*

FATHER: *Well, they'd have to go with their mother.*

BOSCOLO: *They'd go with their mother.*

FATHER: *Yeah.*

BOSCOLO: *What your daughters are saying now is that at some time the issue of your separation has come out. Do you agree with them, or have you really never thought about separation?*

MOTHER: *Yes.*

BOSCOLO: *They think about separation.*

MOTHER: *I had thought about it. Particularly in the last couple of months, I have definitely decided that there has to be a reconciliation, a complete understanding, or a complete withdrawal, because it can't go on like it is because it's just hell for everybody. [Cecchin knocks.]*

BOSCOLO: *Excuse me, I have to go.*

HOFFMAN: I take it that this break isn't the final break.

CECCHIN: Yes. We usually discuss together two or three questions that we don't want to miss before going out for the last break.

HOFFMAN: Why did you break then?

CECCHIN: I thought that we had enough ideas and that it would be useful to compare our opinions and see if there were some other questions. And we had gotten some very good information. The family is talking about the parents separating. The mother says "We have to reconcile or separate." It's a dramatic moment, a good time to leave.

HOFFMAN: Do you always take a minibreak before the final one?

BOSCOLO: Sometimes the supervisor, when he feels the session should end, phones in to the therapist with the message "You can leave the room when you want—for me the session is over."

HOFFMAN: Before we listen to your discussion, why do you ask the mother where the children will go in the case of a separation?

BOSCOLO: The sequence is that first you talk about the separation of the daughter from the family. Then you ask the mother "Do you think about separating too?" Then you talk about the separation of the children. We put them all on the same level; otherwise we're not neutral.

HOFFMAN: What would be the opposite of neutral?

BOSCOLO: Well, to have an idea about what the family should be like. This mother is saying "Something has to happen." She is talking about her marriage and she is saying "There has to be a reconciliation or a parting of the ways." In the beginning, she said that she was doing all the giving. It sounds as if a therapist told her to stop doing all the giving and was pushing her to leave this man. If we focus only on the marriage, we are doing something similar. We are implying that the marriage should change.

HOFFMAN: You're talking about ways to avoid therapist bias.

CECCHIN: Yes. It's easy for a therapist to like the mother. She is cooperative, she believes in therapy, she talks. The father sits and doesn't say anything; he acts as if he doesn't want to be there. So we have to work even harder to see the situation from the father's point of view.

HOFFMAN: How would you describe that point of view?

CECCHIN: The mother says they must have a complete reconciliation. However, there is a strong message that Father should be avoided because he is incestuous. So all the girls say that they don't want to go with him. The father is in a difficult position. He gets the message: "We don't like you. We have to avoid you." At the same time he hears: "But you must reconcile with us." How can he reconcile when he is getting these messages? If he leaves, everybody will say "Fine, we don't want you." At the same time, he will be accused of abandoning the family. And if he does try to reconcile, he will be accused of doing it the wrong way.

HOFFMAN: A lot of people would feel pretty judgmental here. It's hard to be neutral.

CECCHIN: We try to counteract this tendency by an exercise. A good experience for a team watching a family is to live through the sense of helplessness everyone in the family has. Sometimes we tell each person on the team to take the side of one member of the family. Or to blame everything on one member of the family. We say: "You blame everything on the father; you blame everything on the mother; you blame everything on the daughters. This will help us to understand how stuck everybody feels in this situation."

BOSCOLO: It's a way to get out of a moralistic position. From the system's point of view, you can see each family member either as a victim or an aggressor. This exercise contrasts all these different points of view. So the therapist ends up fighting against the game, not against the people.

PENN: You're saying that each position in the group is as understandable as any other, and all positions are absolutely integral to the game.

BOSCOLO: As we said earlier, if you think in terms of Logical Types, you're moving to a higher level, a metalevel. After understanding every position in the family in a linear way, you try to define the premise. There is a false premise on which all of this behavior is based, like Bateson's idea about the alcoholic who bases his behavior on the false premise that he has power over himself. We ask: What in this family is a shared premise that makes it impossible to find a solution? The father can do no right. The mother can do no right. The daughters can do no right. Obviously, there must be a premise on which they base their understanding of their relationships, their behavior, that makes it impossible to find solutions.

CECCHIN: Bateson says that a false premise tends to create vicious cycles, cycles that you can't get rid of. Take the anorectic situation where there is a premise that the mother cannot stop being a mother, and the daughter is fighting this premise. She says "I have to be a mother like you." So they each have this premise. The mother can never stop feeding the daughter because she has this fixed premise that she has to be a mother and the daughter can't stop challenging her. Nobody can find a way out.

PENN: So, in order for you to get to a metalevel, you first take linear positions. Then, out of that activity, you develop a number of premises that organize or connect those contradictory and linear positions so that they make sense. Finally you settle down on one reasonably general premise that seems to explain more of the behaviors than any of the others.

BOSCOLO: Yes, I think we go through a process like that.

PENN: Would you say then that these premises are partially learned from the families they come from and partly negotiated by their relationships in the present?

BOSCOLO: From their present relationships, from their history, and also from the general culture. You can have very powerful religious premises which are handed down by the culture in which a family lives. Or you can have premises regarding gender: what a woman is supposed to do, what a man is supposed to do.

CECCHIN: One universal premise we believe in is that a person can never leave the field under a negative connotation. Take the father in this family. He cannot leave with the connotation of being a bad man, an incestuous father. He's waiting to leave as a good father, a good man. The mother can never leave as a bad mother who married the wrong man, who gave her daughter to this incestuous father. And the daughters can never leave with the idea that they did something that destroyed the marriage.

HOFFMAN: At the time you saw this family, the current concern over issues of physical and sexual abuse of women and children was not so pronounced. But many people would have a problem with your emphasis on neutrality in a case like this. It is hard to see a therapist take such a hands-off stance with behavior that is not only morally repugnant but defined as criminal. Could you state in more detail what you mean by "neutrality"?

BOSCOLO: Neutrality is the result, over time, of the interaction between the therapist and the family. If you ask the family "What does the therapist think you should do?" or "Whose side is the therapist on?" and if the family cannot answer these questions, the therapist has achieved neutrality. They might say he's "tough" or "warm," but if they cannot state his position about what they should do, then he has achieved neutrality.

PENN: Why is it good to be neutral?

CECCHIN: It's a form of intervention—not accepting any definition or distinction along the lines the family is making. For example, if someone says "My son is schizophrenic" and you accept that, you're not neutral. At that moment you must say: "What does it mean to be schizophrenic? When did you decide your son was schizophrenic? Who agrees he's schizophrenic?"

HOFFMAN: Does circular questioning aid neutrality?

BOSCOLO: Circular questioning goes against the rules of the family system in terms of who is allowed to talk about what. In the reciprocal definition of a relationship, every system develops some rules. When you question a child and she doesn't answer but looks at her mother or father, she may be afraid she's going against the rule of the family if she talks. Since all family members hold positions in the family, asking circular questions frees them from holding onto those specific positions.

HOFFMAN: Neutrality is a very confusing term. People think of sitting way up on a mountain and being objective, dispassionate.

BOSCOLO: Every group has to deal with definitions of badness and goodness, of right and wrong, and sometimes they distribute these "qualities" among the members of the group. Maybe this happened when Adam and Eve lost paradise, because there was no badness there—only good. I believe neutrality is on a higher level than either positive or negative connotation. If you positively connote someone in the family, it could have a disturbing or a pleasing effect on the other members. That's one of the difficulties in using positive connotations. For instance, if you take the one in the family whom they feel is bad, wrong, or sick, and you say "No, he's good; he's helping the others," this cannot be accepted by the family. You have upset their sense of justice. So I think neutrality is an attitude on the part of the therapist that tends to rise above the family's tendency to distribute badness and goodness, right and wrong. I think this attitude has the effect of freeing people from fixed positions.

CECCHIN: But there are limits. Parents cannot be neutral. When you are a parent, you must say whether something is good, bad, permitted, or not permitted. You have to say "I don't agree with you; you make me angry" or "Everything is okay." You have to give clear instructions about what is right and wrong, according to your rules, so the child knows what to do. Unlike a parent, the therapist puts himself on a different level where everything becomes communication. That would be an impossible confusion for a child. But to a therapist, everything has to make sense as communication. So to be bad is an important message in the system; to be bad is as important and as valuable as to be good.

PENN: Sometimes parents decide that to be a good parent means telling the child that everything she does is good. Then the child can go crazy.

CECCHIN: Yes, you omit distinctions. It's the same as telling somebody "Everything you do is wrong." Even a teacher has to say "If you're a good student, I'll give you a prize. If you're bad, I won't; I'll wait till you improve."

HOFFMAN: You're pointing out a difference between education and therapy.

CECCHIN: Exactly. That's why we want to get away from educational therapy. If you're not neutral, you give instructions and advice, you tell people what to do and what not to do. Then you are an educator, not a therapist. The world needs teachers and preachers and policemen and parents to distinguish between what is good and bad, useful and not useful, but a therapist should not fall into that category.

HOFFMAN: Then how would you describe a therapeutic learning context?

CECCHIN: In systemic therapy, you try to undo all the work that, through the years, has gotten the family into trouble. I mean the usual, traditional way of education and teaching. Over time, a family develops some premises that are now giving them trouble. Through neutrality, through a systemic approach, you create a learning context where people can begin to find new rules, new premises for their organization.

HOFFMAN: You're saying that education is context bound—bound by culture, bound by family, bound by parents.

CECCHIN: Yes. When teachers come to us, we say "Don't ask us about this child. Treat him like any other child. If he's not doing well in school, flunk him. Don't think 'Poor boy, his family has a problem.' Judge him as a student."

BOSCOLO: You could say that the learning context of education provides labels while the learning context of therapy undoes labels.

CECCHIN: There are only a few moments in therapy, a few magic moments, in which you are able to grasp that therapeutic context. Most of the time you spend talking, looking, waiting for the right moment to be able to do that kind of work.

BOSCOLO: In a conference, when we talk about neutrality, immediately we see hands rising. This idea is not well liked. Inevitably you will have your own ideology, so it is impossible to be neutral.

HOFFMAN: Could you say that neutrality is also an ideology?

BOSCOLO: Yes, that's right. Neutrality is an ideology that I think we must underline, emphasize.

CECCHIN: Our ideology has been to see everything as messages, as communication. Neutrality allows us to get away from the tendency of the system to always make definitions and give labels to events. Neutrality takes away labels that define someone as good, bad, sick, healthy, grown up, not grown up, mature, intelligent, et cetera. Neutrality is the ability to see, in a systemic manner, the whole thing.

HOFFMAN: You mean that if someone shows stupidity and you say he is stupid, you are not neutral?

CECCHIN: Exactly. Neutrality means to get rid of the verb *to be*. The more pathological the system, the more wedded people are to that verb. In pathological systems, there are many definitions, like "You are crazy, you have a hereditary disease, your father was syphilitic." In these cases, you get very heavy causal explanations.

HOFFMAN: What other things characterize this stance you call neutrality?

BOSCOLO: We did some follow-ups on families we had treated and asked "What do you think about what happened in therapy and what do you think about us?" The answer was: "Well, we tried to understand what you thought about us, but we couldn't. We discussed it at home and realized that one day you would say one thing and another day another. We couldn't understand what you were doing." In that sense, the therapist was neutral because he allowed the family system to find its own solutions; he didn't introduce a specific solution or goal.

PENN: What strikes me is that the concept of neutrality is the central concept of your epistemology. Your methodology flows from it, other concepts flow from it, but it remains fixed.

CECCHIN: This is a learning experience for the therapist because, through time, you learn how to look at a system and appreciate it for what it is. Never expect the system to be different. It's important for the therapist and for the trainee to train themselves to see the system, to be interested in it, to appreciate this kind of a system without wanting to change it.

PENN: This concept challenges most views of "normalcy," since it directs one to accept, even admire, the most unusual solutions a family has found.

CECCHIN: Sometimes, in the beginning, you get a negative feeling about a family, but when you begin to see the connections in the system, your feelings change. Neutrality is to accept the whole system; it's not to be outside or to be cold. It's to feel a sense of compassion, interest, and curiosity about a family's dilemma: How did they get there? How did they organize themselves that way? We try to see the logic even in situations that are repugnant from a moral point of view.

HOFFMAN: For you, morality and neutrality are contraries?

CECCHIN: Yes, but both are necessary. We do not condone socially destructive behavior. We only introduce this different way to punctuate it.

PENN: How does the team teach or reinforce neutrality?

CECCHIN: An example: If you see that a therapist has become seduced by the mother in the family, you call the therapist out. You don't say "You are doing something wrong." If you do, then you are doing something wrong too; you're not neutral. You say: "We notice that the mother has succeeded in getting your attention more than the father and son have. Do you have any idea how she did it?" Use the word "how". Or: "What kind of technique did she use to seduce you?" So it becomes a very interesting suggestion. The therapist is not aware of it, so he begins to think about it. Then you tell all the other people behind the mirror, "Let's look at how the behavior of father and son is affected by this successful maneuver of Mother's." You say that in front of the therapist. You don't accuse him, you don't say anything; it's an experience. Perhaps the therapist himself will say: "Yes, I noticed the son is getting nervous— he doesn't look me in the face—and the father looks at his watch. Okay, now what do we do?" Then the therapist goes back in, but now with a different idea. You haven't connoted the therapist negatively—just helped him to look at the process and, in so doing, restored his neutrality.

HOFFMAN: There's no implication of fault. He's in the room with the family, and you're behind the mirror. Your context allows you to notice what his context doesn't so the mistake is not in him, but in the context.

BOSCOLO: It's important to remember that in our way of working it is the therapist who has more power than the supervisor. This is a rule we established a long time ago, that the therapist is the one who will finally decide what to do, what to say.

CECCHIN: Another point about neutrality is you always ask questions, you don't make statements. To make a statement means you're not neutral; you're defining something. You're saying "Oh, it's like that!" Instead, you question "How many years have you been like that? When did you decide to do things that way? How many years did it take you to forget about punishing your wife?" Punishment would be a word you picked up from them.

PENN: I call that a cue word, one that leads to an opening for questioning.

CECCHIN: Right. After you indicate it's their word, you can elaborate on it. Of course, you would never say a word like that unless they did. Then you challenge every statement that uses that word: "What does it mean to be highstrung? What does it mean to be crazy? What does it mean to be a mother?" People say: "I am a mother. A mother should behave like this." "Like how?" Sometimes people say we ask naive questions; they are too simple. Everyone knows what it is to be a mother. But I do not know what it means to *her*. Then, through these challenging questions, you get to the premises, to the basic ideas that are built up through time about what it means to be a mother or how to raise children.

BOSCOLO: That brings us to the process of joining. Some people who have seen us working have accused us of being cold. But the process of circular questioning produces a strong engagement. We had the notion that maybe our success with families in Milan depended on charisma, or depended on our name. Then I worked one or two days a month in a hospital in a small town where the families were not told who I was—they thought I was a member of the staff—and the families became engaged just as powerfully as they had in Milan.

PENN: How do you deal with less "neutral" professionals who may be involved in a case?

BOSCOLO: At first we used to ignore them, and I think this was a mistake. If the referring person is important—like a teacher or a psychiatrist who has been very active in the situation—we will tell the family to ask that person to call us. If another therapist is seeing a family member, we tell them to continue whatever they are doing.

PENN: So you don't necessarily ask them in; you just establish a communication loop.

BOSCOLO: That's right.

HOFFMAN: Do you ever bring the referring person behind the screen?

CECCHIN: Not usually, although in this case we did. The experience of being on the team helps us to develop a systemic position. But it's not always useful to get all these other people who are involved with the family to go through this experience. As we said before, if you are a parent, if you are a teacher, you cannot be neutral.

HOFFMAN: So it would not be helpful to include them?

CECCHIN: No. The team provides a special context in which everything is translated into some kind of information, a context in which we look at process, not content, in which we try to get rid of good and bad labeling. But, as we said, this doesn't apply to ordinary life at all. So we only include the parents or the referring professional temporarily, at the end of the session, when we share our ideas in a comment or message.

HOFFMAN: What do you advise trainees to do when the referral comes from the nonneutral institution they are working in?

BOSCOLO: The way we deal with the referring person or agency is related to the context. If there is a rule that you must send a written report to the referring person or if you have to have a meeting with him or her, you have to respond accordingly. The first thing a therapist who wants to learn the systemic approach must do is to analyze the context he or she is operating in. If the therapist is in an institution, he or she must determine the relations between the different subsystems in the institution and how the family, the institution, and the therapist all relate. These relationships will influence the kind of intervention that can be made.

CECCHIN: What I like to say to students is that it is very rare that you get the chance to be a therapist. Most of the time you are paid by the institution to be a teacher or a policeman or something like that. You're doing a job the institution asks you to do; and if you think that you're being paid to be a therapist, you're mistaken. But once you understand the context, you can wait for the right moment. If you are patient, there may be a chance to do something that will have an effect at the systemic level. But you have to accept the system you are working in as it is, the way you accept the family. You mustn't try to convince your colleagues of your way of working; you shouldn't get into fights with them, because, at that moment, you're not neutral.

BOSCOLO: When our first trainees went back to their workplaces, they tended to give the message to their colleagues: "We have a new theory that will make you more effective." The result was that they were wiped out.

PENN: What if they were faced with a decision to give medication or some other procedure that they couldn't believe in? What would you tell them to do then?

CECCHIN: Then, of course, you can't be neutral. All you can do is make it clear where you are coming from. For instance, if a person comes in who is breaking windows and acting crazy, you might give them medication and lock them up. Since at that moment you are being paid to be a policeman, you do that. Two or three days later, you go to see them and you say "Okay, now I want to understand how it was that you compelled me to act like a policeman. Let's find out what happened that you found yourself in the position of using me like a policeman." You don't say "What's wrong with you?" or "Let's try to cure you." That's an entirely different message.

BOSCOLO: Before we close our discussion on neutrality, I want to emphasize again what we said before about not using neutrality in one's personal life. It's a position to use only when you do therapy. I remember a trainee who said "I was driving on the highway and a car came up behind me and hit me. It was hard to find a positive connotation, but I did! I said 'This will help me to be more alert on the road.' " You have to protect yourself by protesting and getting angry; otherwise you won't collect any insurance.

### DISCUSSION BREAK

CECCHIN: *Why did the mother keep staying and not ship out?*

BOSCOLO: *I think there is another reason why the mother resents the father: because he picked on Lisa. That's because, when he got married, Mother and Lisa were always together. They were very close. Lisa resented the fact that Mother went* with another man, I am sure, at age two and a half. And she wanted the mother for herself. The father was a stranger. Then the two little girls were born.

CECCHIN: Lisa must have received very confusing messages. She is very close to the mother, who keeps sending her to the father. But the father is angry with her because he wants the mother. So she does not know what position to take.

BOSCOLO: I think that the confusion Lisa has always been in is this: As she grew up, she heard her mother complaining all the time about how bad Father is. When I asked her about the issue of separation, her answer was that she was glad, and that was the only time she smiled. She wished her mother would separate because if they separated, she could be consistent: Lisa could live with Mother and leave Father. Instead the mother confused her. She wants to have this rapport with Lisa and, at the same time, save her marriage.

CECCHIN: There were two marriages: Mother and Lisa and Mother and husband. Mother confused the whole issue because she wanted those two people to get along with each other. If they were separated, they probably would be okay. In fact, the daughter says that it would be better if they separated. It's the mother who gives the confusing messages. She wants the two rivals to love each other.

BOSCOLO: If we believe that Lisa left home because something happened that she does not want to disclose, we could ask "Do you think, Diane, that you might have to leave home for the same reason?"

CECCHIN: After asking Diane this question, I would ask the mother: "Why do you want so much for your husband to love your daughter? Weren't you enough for him?"

BOSCOLO: In reality, the mother wanted the daughter to love the husband because she is afraid he will leave her. It's interesting that when I asked if they would separate, who would go with whom, all three said they would go with Mother. The mother protested at the beginning because the father was favoring one girl. She had the other two, but that was not enough. She was jealous of the rapport between Diane and the father. The father should not have any girl. She should have all of them. It's a crazy game. I see Lisa in a very bad situation. The other two are in a less difficult situation because they made their own marriage, detached from the parents.

CECCHIN: We should ask ourselves: "Why does the father show incestous behavior toward the girls? What happened to him? What's the meaning of this incest? Why does he have to behave sexually with Lisa?"

BOSCOLO: We should ask Dori and Diane: "The same thing that happened to your sister, which you all know a little bit about but do not want to say, do you think the same thing could happen to you?"

CECCHIN: We should ask Lisa: "Do you think it could happen to your sisters?"

BOSCOLO: This is better.

DR. S.: Lisa feels like she needs to protect her two younger sisters. If she tells her secret, that is going to put them in jeopardy. So she is keeping quiet to protect them. I am wondering whether she feels they really need to be protected that much.

CECCHIN: *That's following the same idea, to ask: "Do you think it could happen to them? Do you think they need some protection?"*

BOSCOLO: *What is interesting is that the mother said that two months ago she decided to separate. There is something going on. Up to two months ago the mother had to keep everybody united, with the husband there. Now it seems that something has changed and the mother is interested in separation. [Dr. S., Boscolo, and Cecchin get up to leave.]*

---

HOFFMAN: These are heavy questions, asking Lisa if she thinks her sisters need protection, asking the mother why it's so important for the father to love Lisa, and asking if she wasn't enough for her husband.

CECCHIN: Since we began to use circular questions, we have become much more daring. When we break, as we do here, we are not just looking for a hypothesis about how the family organizes its ideas, we are also introducing some hypotheses of our own. We ask these strange questions. For instance, to Mother: "Don't you think you are enough for your husband?" That's a question that is very dramatic. It sounds like an interpretation, but it's put as a question: "Aren't you enough for your husband, that you have to give your daughters to him?" In another style of therapy, you would wait a long time before introducing such an idea.

PENN: One area you didn't cover previously concerns the background of the father. How does one account for his behavior? I was wondering why you never asked anything about him in the interview. Was he married before? What was his experience coming into this family? It's odd that you didn't address that.

BOSCOLO: I think it was an omission. Retrospectively, it would seem very good to ask some questions about the background of the father. This would balance the information we got about the mother.

CECCHIN: The danger is that we would connote him negatively: "Maybe there is some explanation why you are this kind of man."

BOSCOLO: It's interesting, I think, the way both the therapist and the supervisor become isomorphic to the family system. The family system isolates this man more and more. So the therapist and supervisor respond in a similar way. This is the power of the family—to make the therapist behave according to their rules.

## FAMILY INTERVIEW

BOSCOLO: *[coming into room] Your sister said she knows a little bit. But I would like to ask you, Lisa, do you think there is a possibility that the same thing that has happened to you, that has caused you to run away from home, might happen also to your sisters?*

LISA: *No.*

BOSCOLO: *You don't think it would happen?*

LISA: *[inaudible]*

BOSCOLO: *If it would happen, to whom would it happen?*

LISA: *It wouldn't—there's no—I don't see the point—*

BOSCOLO: *I make a hypothesis: if it would? Who is going to protect them?*

LISA: *It wouldn't happen.*

BOSCOLO: *If it would happen—here is a hypothesis—do you think your sister would leave home like you did?*

LISA: *I don't know. It wouldn't happen, so I don't need to think about it.*

BOSCOLO: *I see. [to Mother] One thing you say is that, for years, you tried to see the rapport in your family get better; you suffered very much from Lisa and your husband; your husband kept picking on Lisa, and you tried to make them get along better, but they couldn't. Why was it so important to you that Lisa have a good rapport with your husband? Was it more important for her to get along with him than for your other daughters?*

MOTHER: *Well, it was important that they have a good rapport too, but they weren't the ones that were suffering from the problem, they weren't the ones that were being hurt, and they weren't being, um, nobody was being mean to them. So, therefore, it was more important to try and see if I couldn't get Lisa and Dad to understand each other and to try and make a reconciliation to stop this constant dislike.*

BOSCOLO: *Were you also a little afraid that if this had gone on way back, that the marriage might have broken up? Because you had a marriage before that didn't go well. Was there some fear in you over the years that this marriage might also go on the rocks?*

MOTHER: *That's right.*

BOSCOLO: *So you tried to promote Lisa's getting into a better rapport with Daddy because you were afraid that Daddy might leave you, is that it?*

MOTHER: *No, I wasn't afraid that he would leave me, I was afraid of another failure; let's put it that way.*

BOSCOLO: *Another failure, on your part.*

MOTHER: *That's right.*

BOSCOLO: *You were afraid of another failure. Are you still afraid of this failure?*

MOTHER: *No, because I understand now that my attitude of feeling that I would be failing has to a great extent harmed my family. Possibly, if I had taken action*

*when they were younger, they may not have suffered the constant battling and
constant fighting.*

BOSCOLO: *How long have you had these ideas?*

MOTHER: *I have just come to this conclusion within the last year.*

BOSCOLO: *Did somebody help you have this idea?*

MOTHER: *We have talked with other people; we went with Lisa to see a psychiatrist,
with Diane to see a psychologist at Children's Hospital; and I've come to realize
that because your marriage don't work, don't mean that you are a failure as a
person.*

BOSCOLO: *I see.*

MOTHER: *But to sit by and not take action and not do something to—like I say, I've
tried over the years to solve the problem in other ways, like talking, trying to
communicate, trying to understand, make everybody happy—it just don't work.*

BOSCOLO: *So the psychologist is helping you with these ideas now.*

MOTHER: *To a certain point. Mainly, I've come to the decision myself that I'm not
a failure because it didn't work. It just didn't work, that's all.*

BOSCOLO: *So what do you think will happen in the future? How would you see it
going, with your family?*

MOTHER: *I think now it would have a bad effect on them because I can't see the
future being happy for them, being separated from their family and from constant
problems. I mean, this may be easier for them, but there's gonna be other problems. I can see where it could help and I can see where it might harm them.*

BOSCOLO: *[to Father] How do you see the future?*

FATHER: *Right now, it doesn't matter what I do. I'm in the doghouse. I'm always
catching hell, where it doesn't matter what I do.*

BOSCOLO: *Do you think that coming here to therapy is helping you?*

FATHER: *One minute I figure it's helping our relationship, next minute it looks sour.*

BOSCOLO: *How about you, do you think it's helping coming here?*

MOTHER: *Umm, yes, I do to a point. But then, if you can't communicate between
each other, then no matter how much [family's therapist] tries to help us, we
can't go any . . . you know, there has to be communication for [family's therapist]
to help us.*

---

HOFFMAN: One of the interesting things that has happened now is that
the other therapies are suddenly present in the room. The very first thing
Mother said to you was "We don't communicate." That obviously is a
phrase she has picked up from a therapist. It seems that Mother has a
very strong alliance with a therapist that she's seen along the way.

BOSCOLO: Well, from what they say, the mother had some contact with a
psychologist who saw Diane and with a psychiatrist who saw Lisa after

she tried to commit suicide. At that time we didn't see the importance of the contact between Mother and these experts. But, retrospectively, we can see how important this was. Before she saw these experts, she believed that she would be a failure if she gave up this marriage. So it's possible that the therapists had the effect of making her change her mind. This is an effect therapists can often have on families. It happens frequently that in individual therapy, the therapy can go "well" and the family, or couple, come apart.

CECCHIN: That's not in itself bad. What is bad is if they separate in a sticky, angry way, leaving confused children and guilt feelings that hang on for a long time. If the breakup coincides with the birth of a new way of thinking in the family, that's different.

BOSCOLO: You can see here the position of the father. He says that right now, anything he does is wrong. In the last few months, Mother and the three daughters probably became allied with the therapists. The result of this alliance is the isolation and expulsion of the father. And the father responds in a very logical way: "What can I do? Anything I do is wrong."

HOFFMAN: He seemed completely out of place in that therapy setting. I kept noticing the way he sat there, with a faraway look on his face and his mouth half open.

CECCHIN: He acts like a moron, an idiot. But we never know if someone is really a moron or an idiot. In a system, you often get an amplification of differences. If the wife defines herself as the one who is lively and expressive and the husband defines himself as the one who works hard and doesn't show his feelings, these characteristics become more and more pronounced over time. She becomes more talkative, more spontaneous, while he becomes more lifeless, more detached. The wife now is the one who appears to be intelligent and sophisticated. She has talked to many therapists, she knows all about growth, progress, change.

HOFFMAN: You're saying that their connection with therapy becomes part of the difference between them. But you become part of it too, because you tend not to ask him any questions.

BOSCOLO: I am obeying the rules of the system. It says "Please help us to amplify our differences," and I do. Ideally, if we see a father like that, we try not to be influenced by the system. We say only that he is a systemic idiot. We never think that someone is really stupid or really smart.

CECCHIN: We often see this gap between a couple where one member, especially the wife, has gone into therapy. After a while the wife introduces into the marriage a new language that creates even more problems of communication than they had before. The wife here keeps accusing the husband of not being able to communicate. But this doesn't make any sense to him.

BOSCOLO: That is why we are so careful not to introduce a specific set of terms into a family. We know that we are trying to introduce new maps, new connections. But we have to do it always with a question mark, without saying that our truth is better than their truth. We try to introduce our maps as doubts, as possibilities, in order to increase the loops in the system. That's what allows for the possibility of better communication, not talking like a therapist.

HOFFMAN: One of the great advantages of circular questioning is that it cuts down on therapeutic jargon.

BOSCOLO: It is important to do that because a member of a family who is in individual therapy can use therapeutic jargon as a weapon against other family members.

HOFFMAN: It's only fair to say that there are some family therapists who do this too.

BOSCOLO: True. And this increases the mental suffering of the whole family. We try to avoid this by communicating in such a way that the family does not know what we really think they should do.

CECCHIN: We always ask our questions with a naive face: "We don't know—it could be that way—why do you do that?" Always leaving the family with the sense that we have no solution.

HOFFMAN: One more question. What was your aim in asking Lisa if she thought that the same thing that happened to her would happen to her sisters?

BOSCOLO: We introduce the idea that since they are sisters they are subject to the same situation. If something like that could happen to them, perhaps she could protect them.

PENN: Introducing that thought also helps her to realize that the way she leaves home is important since her sisters may also have to leave home.

BOSCOLO: The main thing is to create the connection between the sisters. We want to give them the idea that they have the same problem and can protect each other. When parents introduce differences between the siblings, this can have a detrimental effect.

HOFFMAN: Are you saying that Lisa, because she was singled out, was especially vulnerable?

BOSCOLO: Yes. We had a hypothesis that Lisa might have been born out of wedlock. Mother said "My husband left before she was born." Then this man married her. She was probably ambivalent about sharing the daughter with her new husband and also wanted to protect the girl. But the doubt remained that her husband would have liked her more if she hadn't had the baby girl. At that point you could ask: "Suppose you had not had Lisa when you married. Do you think you and your husband would have gotten along better?" This would have been more direct.

## FAMILY INTERVIEW

BOSCOLO: *How about you, Dori and Diane, do you think you're doing well to come here?*

DORI: *I don't know.*

DIANE: *I don't know.*

BOSCOLO: *I would like to ask you one more question. Mother, you said you tried hard over the years to help Lisa to have a better relationship with Father, which would also help prevent the possibility of your marriage going on the rocks. But how about the relationship between Lisa and her sisters? There is not much cohesion between them, with Lisa on one side and Diane and Dori on the other.*

MOTHER: *I think there is. I think there is communication between them. They get along reasonably well when they're at home together. Up until Lisa moved out, they always tried to get along as well as any other sisters. I mean they talked to each other, they went to movies together; there wasn't a total lack of communication. Lisa communicates really quite well with Dori.*

BOSCOLO: *Lisa said she always felt isolated. Somehow she also felt isolated from her sisters. Isn't that so, Lisa?*

LISA: *Umm?*

BOSCOLO: *That you felt isolated from your sisters?*

LISA: *Yeah. They were always together. They were always together.*

BOSCOLO: *They stick together, both of them.*

LISA: *Yeah.*

BOSCOLO: *Did you feel over the years that you wished you could stick with them? To be with them?*

LISA: *Yeah.*

BOSCOLO: *In some ways you attempted, but you were not successful in this attempt.*

LISA: *No.*

BOSCOLO: *I will stop here now and I will have a discussion with my colleagues, and then I'll come back.*

---

HOFFMAN: During this break, you go into the process of hypothesizing that results in an intervention. As we are only transcribing the part of the discussion that leads directly into the final comment, could you say something in general about the process?

CECCHIN: Mainly, we try to be elastic enough to keep many possibilities in mind without fixing on one specifically. If we believe that there is any one right hypothesis, we can go crazy trying to find it. The main thing is to experience how stuck the family is. So, first, we brainstorm about how stuck they are, and only later do we look for solutions. Many students say "We should do this, we should do that." We say "No, wait, wait." It's too easy to move to solutions if you don't have the experience of being stuck.

PENN: What would you say are the elements that make up a good hypothesis?

BOSCOLO: I think the hypotheses draw from four sources. One is the data; two is the theory that you have; three is your experience seeing many families; and the fourth element is personality, what in analysis they call transference. For instance, what Gianfranco picks up in a family is very different from what I pick up. I'm more sensitive, more in tune with a certain kind of atmosphere. In terms of experience, for example, I've noticed that frequently the son or daughter from a previous marriage has more possibility of developing problems. Lisa seems to be in this situation. She looks like a second-class citizen in relation to the other sisters.

CECCHIN: And I'm always controlling what Luigi's doing. For instance, when he makes a statement like that, I try to say something totally opposite. I'm always aware of how easy it is to make a statement like "Every time you have an adopted child, you have these problems"; "Every time you have a sister who is beautiful, then the other one goes crazy." You have to be aware of this danger. This is an important issue in training. I feel it's bad teaching when you are too clever in giving your students your hypotheses about the family, because then the trainee goes into the session to prove that your hypothesis is correct. The implication is that there is some schema for assessing a family, and that once you know enough, you can find where on the schema a family falls.

BOSCOLO: We have to find the fit between the hypothesis and the organization of the system as it formed over time. There are infinite possibilities for hypotheses, but some fit better than others, some connect more of the data.

CECCHIN: The hypotheses are better when they are made by therapists who are circular and who respond continuously to the feedback of the family in the session. Then you have more of a chance to develop a hypothesis that fits because in that process there is a mirroring of the organization of the family.

PENN: But you do make assumptions based on the organization of the family, don't you? If the family has an adopted child, you ask yourself immediately: How does this family make secure connections over time? How can they be absolutely certain they belong together?

CECCHIN: Each family is going to be different, so every time you make such a hypothesis, it should be checked and questioned. Otherwise you create constructs similar to analytic therapy, where you look for oedipal complexes, paranoia, and so forth. For instance, when you say that Lisa has more of a problem than Diane because she comes from another family, you have to challenge that. It's better to have at least two competing hypotheses, then you can see if they confirm each other.

BOSCOLO: In this case, you could say that the fact that Lisa's position is worse than anyone else's may also be related to her isolation from the sisters.

CECCHIN: Yes. We notice that the other girls sit together while Lisa sits alone, outside that couple. We then look at the historical data and find she is the daughter of another father and we have a confirmation of that outside position.

BOSCOLO: The analogical data provides a link to the historical data.

CECCHIN: But we must be careful because the historical data can influence our perceptions. We should first look for the analogical pattern, the configuration in the present, and then look for the historical data to confirm it.

HOFFMAN: How do you know whether your hypothesizing has been successful?

BOSCOLO: We're not as concerned about the truth as about the fit. We use trial and error in making our hypotheses and our interventions. If the family changes, it means that there has been a fit between the family and our intervention. If they don't change, there is no fit. It's the family that tells you.

HOFFMAN: Sometimes one has the experience in a team of muddling and muddling, and then one person comes forward with an idea or a phrase, and everybody will sort of rise up together, saying, "Yes, yes, that's it." It's very peculiar, a kind of recognition. As though that formulation had always been there waiting to be discovered.

BOSCOLO: Yes, we get that experience. But it never happens when the discussion becomes competitive. For example, if we get into a struggle over which opinion is better or worse, or if we hear statements like "Why do you say that? Where did you get that idea?" this kind of recognition never occurs.

PENN: You're suggesting that one of the better ways for a team to manage its discussions is to express the ideas and hunches that they have without any need to agree.

CECCHIN: Yes. We instituted a set of rules last year that was very successful. We forbid our students to say "I agree with you" or "I disagree with you." Another rule was that when anybody said something, the next speaker should try to add something that was totally unconnected. One person might say "I see Lisa as very depressed, very upset." Another would say "I see Mother as a lost woman." These ideas are apparently disconnected. But of course it's impossible for them not to be connected, and the connection will finally appear when somebody comes out with a formulation with which everyone agrees. That's when you get an experience of recognition. Because everybody contributed to the final product.

HOFFMAN: It reminds me of that child's toy which is a whirling bowl and has colored lines on it. As it turns, it gets to be just a blur; and then, at a certain point, a geometric pattern suddenly springs out. I thought it was a good analogy for the way you arrive at an intervention.

CECCHIN: That's why, in this break, we asked two therapists from the clinic group to join us. We have found that you need at least four people for this process to be successful. You need to confront your own linear thinking with the linear thinking of someone else. Only then will a pattern emerge that will make sense at a different level of organization.

PENN: I would like to ask a question about consensus in the team. You have said that a team may have a rule that they must always agree; they then resemble a stuck family more than a team. A team is more task oriented and has a job to do. However, in observing your work together, you do seem to be in agreement most of the time. In the discussion breaks, one of you will say something, the other will then refine it or add something, so that this information structure seems to build itself and you end up looking very much in agreement. Now maybe you aren't, and it just doesn't show. But I wanted to ask you about that because there is a tendency in most groups that form teams to avoid open disagreement or to strive for consensus.

BOSCOLO: During the team process, we often do disagree, in the sense of having different points of view, but it may not look like disagreement because we avoid getting into power struggles. If you think in circular terms, power struggles do not arise. That is not at all the same as consensus because differences are allowed.

CECCHIN: There's another point here. You more often find a disagreement when you use linear, causal explanations. I believe that the father is more to blame, you say it's the mother, and someone else says it's the son. So we all disagree. But if we look for a systemic explanation, we look to see how all these linear explanations might connect. The process is not one of one idea knocking the others out but of one larger idea being added that contains all the others.

HOFFMAN: You said before that the therapist in the room has the final authority to decide what to do.

BOSCOLO: Yes. This rule allows the therapist to move freely at the interface between the family and the supervisor.

HOFFMAN: So that he or she is not a captive of the team.

BOSCOLO: Exactly. Otherwise there would be a problem in joining with the family.

PENN: The therapist is the one person in this whole therapy-family system who has to pass through the glass; she has to be at home on both sides of it.

HOFFMAN: I see. It's the position that determines what each party can or cannot do. There is no inherent hierarchy that says one component is better or more powerful than the others.

BOSCOLO: Yes. One more point about circular questioning: When we role-play families during training, we give trainees fifteen minutes to make up a script. Once the therapist starts the circular questioning, you see that after a while the script goes to pieces. Different information begins to come out quite spontaneously. With a real family, the same thing can happen. If the therapist is passive, no new information is introduced, and the family keeps on presenting its usual map. The circular questioning begins to break this map down and to introduce new connections. Seen from the point of view of resistance, you could say that the circular questioning doesn't go directly against the family's way of acting and believing, but it does make it hard for the family to stay the same.

PENN: Could you say another word or two about resistance? It's a concept that is being put into question.

BOSCOLO: You could just as well say that the therapist is resisting the family when the family doesn't want anything to change and the therapist is trying to make them change. Or if the therapist positively connotes the problem, here too you could say that the therapist is resisting. In that sense, I don't find it a very useful concept.

## DISCUSSION BREAK

*The team has been discussing the case for about
half an hour.*

CECCHIN: *There is something in the system that prevents Lisa from having a relationship with her sisters. This is supported analogically because they laugh when Lisa cries. For the moment, let's make this punctuation and give all the blame to Mother. From her point of view, it goes like this: For the first two years, Lisa and Mother were close, but when the new man appeared, Mother felt she would like to start a new life and not have Lisa interfering, so she probably became overprotective and rejecting at the same time. If Father didn't show love to Lisa, Mother would get furious. However, if Father and Lisa got too close, Mother would be jealous.*

BOSCOLO: *Lisa has many things to do. She must be supportive of Mother because Mother has made bad marriages; she has to be an auxiliary husband, an auxiliary wife, mother to her sisters, sister and mother to her mother, and once in a while she has to be available to the husband. By having all these roles, she's protecting everyone and keeping all the secrets. But no one is protecting her. In fact, she is blamed when the marriage doesn't work. Mother says "My husband only picks on you, not on the others. So you are no good. If you were not there, my marriage would be better."*

CECCHIN: *It's understandable that a psychotic break might be precipitated because of Lisa's perception: "I have no place, I should not have been born." Mother could be blaming the failure of both marriages on Lisa: "Without you, I could have had a contented husband." Perhaps even the first man left her because she was pregnant.*

BOSCOLO: *If Mother was not married the first time, she probably experiences a tremendous bond with Lisa and at the same time a rejection of her.*

CECCHIN: *The punctuation for the father is "Be the father but don't be the father," so he says "I'm always wrong, whatever I do is wrong." The situation worsened over the years, but finally Diane broke the relationship with the father, and the most powerful couple in the family became Dori and Diane. The establishment of this powerful relationship put everyone into crisis. The father, without Diane, becomes more alone, and Lisa is back with her mother because she cannot get close to her sisters.*

BOSCOLO: *There is one important piece of information. When you ask about the separation of the couple, Lisa answers by saying "I would be glad if you separated." She would finally get out of this paradoxical situation, out of these plural incongruent levels she is on.*

CECCHIN: *The two younger girls say, in response to that question about who they would go with if the parents separated: "In the past, we would have been torn, but now we would go with Mother." However, their tone is: "We don't care where we go because we are two, we are a strong couple."*

BOSCOLO: *We don't know if the mother is going to leave the marriage, we don't know what is going to happen, everything is very unstable. It's a dangerous situation for Lisa. So the intervention would have to put Mother and Lisa together. We should give them a ritual. We could say "We are impressed with the deep, affectionate bond between Mother and Lisa and Lisa and Mother, which has never been manifested openly. They have decided to go their separate ways, pretending that they don't get along together, and not showing their great affection. Now why did they do that? It seems that if they had manifested the bond between them, that would have made them a couple—mother and daughter—so happy, strong, and good that the other people would be completely left out, the husband and the two younger girls. They would not count as much as Lisa. So Lisa and Mother didn't display their bond out of their concern for the others. But we think they went too far. They went too far in fighting their tendency to be close, so now we think it's important that one day a week they do this ritual. One day each week is Lisa and Mother's day, and the others must stay completely out of that relationship on that day. Lisa and Mother don't have to tell anyone else what they are doing because everyone must realize that they went too far. They struggled to stay separate for the sake of the others, not to cut off the others. So Lisa and Mother, you did well not to manifest the affection each has for the other. But you went too far." I would see this intervention.*

CECCHIN: *I think it's good. Instead of commenting on the incest between Lisa and Father, the incest would be between Lisa and Mother. Instead of the secret being between Father and Lisa, it is between Mother and Lisa.*

BOSCOLO: *There are two families: mother and daughter, and then the second family. They always try to put Lisa in the second family, where she doesn't belong. Her family is her mother. So there must be a way that we can rebuild the first family. But where can we put the husband?*

CECCHIN: *You can say that both of them did an important thing for the husband. He would have married a woman and not have counted with her because of the strong bond between mother and daughter. But they didn't manifest their bond, for the sake of the father as well as for the two younger girls who, otherwise, would have counted for nothing in the family. I would stress this very much in the intervention so that the girls understand that if Lisa and Mother had not denied their deep bond, they would be completely left out. They two have to thank Lisa because she helped them feel strong and happy. But Lisa and Mother went too far, so now they must stay together one day a week, and the two girls and Father must leave them alone."*

BOSCOLO: *What about putting mother and daughter on the same level? They were both very lonely; they had to hate each other, fight being together. Mother tried to keep herself from her daughter—even kick her out—because she was afraid her husband would be upset and the two younger girls would be jealous. Both Lisa and Mother tried so hard to separate, but in reality they are deeply united.*

CECCHIN: *Also, if they had manifested their affection, it would have been a threat to this family since Lisa comes from another family. If Mother had manifested* her bond with Lisa, the second family would not be as important as the first family.

BOSCOLO: Now we get to the positive connotation. Before we saw the negative side of mother, but now we see the positive side. She has to get rid of Lisa in order to create a new family. To marry again, she has to deny her marriage to Lisa. So Lisa must behave in a way that helps the mother to appear separated from her, indifferent to her.

BOSCOLO: Also, in the cases we have seen where a family is constructed from two previous marriages, the child who goes from one family to the next is bound to have more problems.

CECCHIN: And if the previous family is made of only three people, it's very difficult to handle.

TEAM MEMBER: What about Diane's hostility to her father? She says "I don't want to talk to you, I don't want to see you, I want you out."

BOSCOLO: Diane is the pathological leader in the family because she is the one who is loved by Father, and Mother is very concerned about it. She's the one Mother and Father fight over, and that's why she has most of the power now, while Dori stays back. You can make a symmetrical situation: for example, if Mother and Lisa get close to each other, the second family will disappear; or, if Father and Diane got too close, then the first marriage is finished. So Diane has to fight the relationship with Father.

TEAM MEMBER: Will they obey the ritual?

BOSCOLO: Yes, because it comes from outside the system, from a meta-level. Lisa and Mother's relationship has always been related to one person, the husband, who was not at a higher level but on the same level and was jealous of their relationship.

CECCHIN: We must not in any way ask Mother and Lisa to get along with each other. They can spend their day not talking, even hating each other; the important thing is that other people don't know what they are doing, that they create a secret between them. They don't have to enjoy each other, only give a message to the children that they are together. So, here, Mother and Lisa give a message to the others that they are a couple. They can on that day do whatever they want; the important thing is that no one interferes. We can even say that on that day, the two daughters should not even talk to the mother or Lisa. Total silence. Only Mother and Lisa should talk, if they want to. And if they are asked what they are doing, they can respond: "It's our business."

BOSCOLO: That's one intervention. Let's see if we can make another intervention putting all three girls together: three girls on one side and the parents on the other.

CECCHIN: I think Lisa would like to be with her peers, no?

BOSCOLO: But before getting there, she should have a little piece of her mother. Suppose, now, you create an incest between Mother and daughter. It's not a real solution for the family; the real solution is for the siblings to be together and the parents to be on the other side. But before that, I think Lisa is longing for her *mother, who keeps rejecting her. So I think she should be with the mother for a while to get a little more of a feeling of her mother, and then in the future we can design a ritual that puts all the children together. But next time, not now.*

CECCHIN: *If this one works.*

BOSCOLO: *Of course. Next time we could change the punctuation with a new intervention. We could ask the three girls, Lisa, Diane, and Dori, to meet once a week for half an hour, and each talk for ten minutes, while the others listen. Putting the mother and daughter together cannot be a final intervention. Do you have any doubts?*

CECCHIN: *No. If mother and daughter can find time to be together it doesn't matter if they aren't friendly. I think as soon as they begin to define their relationship, Lisa will probably be angry at her mother's lack of support for her. But at least she will have a clear understanding.*

BOSCOLO: *If she does, we can give her the explanation that Mother couldn't support her because she wanted to create this new marriage, and as that becomes clear, perhaps the daughter can forgive her.*

CECCHIN: *And then there is more possibility of a relationship. So the next time they should all come together so we can give the girls this ritual.*

---

HOFFMAN: During the beginning of this discussion you take very simple positions. Most of your opinions seem to side with Lisa and make the mother the villain.

CECCHIN: Yes. Usually we begin with linear-causal statements related to one or two members of the family. Here, as you see, we decided to attack the mother. Then, in time, the hypothesis becomes more and more general and a pattern appears. We leave the linear explanations and go on to a more circular description.

HOFFMAN: One can follow the way you develop your hypothesis, but it's not clear how you arrive at the intervention. It seems to appear from nowhere.

BOSCOLO: This is the way we engineer an intervention. We had agreed that this was a dangerous, unstable situation. There was a pause and I introduced an intervention based on one punctuation of the situation. Gianfranco could have refused it, and so could the other two therapists who had joined us, but instead they accepted it and refined it.

PENN: I like this intervention because the couple is placed back in the family rather than any one person being singled out. It doesn't, for the moment, challenge the younger girls; it allows Father to feel he's not the problem; and it repairs the mother and daughter relationship. But most importantly, it challenges the idea that the first family must be obliterated for the sake of the second. It validates that first family which, in a sense, had been denied.

BOSCOLO: The first marriage—mother and daughter—was a bad marriage because after Lisa was born the father left and ruined the life of the mother.

PENN: Okay, that's the premise; very clear. Now what's the logic that follows?

BOSCOLO: According to this premise, Mother felt that when she remarried, this first marriage was dangerous to the new marriage and the new daughters. The logic is in using this idea to explain what happens. If this marriage should not have occurred, then this explains why the girl is suicidal, why the mother is ambivalent toward the girl, why Lisa accepts the position of being excluded, why the mother offers Lisa to her husband. When we turn the argument around and say that this marriage was good, all the little pieces that we talk about change their signs.

PENN: You're talking about a reversal of the premise, from bad first marriage to good first marriage.

BOSCOLO: Yes.

HOFFMAN: Why did you stop Luigi from making the other intervention?

CECCHIN: Because we had to deal with the situation in the present. The idea of putting the children together seemed like an intellectual exercise, out of place.

BOSCOLO: I think I proposed this because we were in a training context and I wanted to suggest an idea that the staff could use in another session. We decided on the first intervention because Lisa was in the most danger and we felt she needed a clear message from her mother. Second, we had to consider the fact that we had two families that were not yet integrated. Because of this, the second intervention would have been premature.

## INTERVENTION

BOSCOLO: *My colleagues and I have discussed this situation and we're very impressed. What impresses us most is the strong bond that there is and always has been between Lisa and Mother and Mother and Lisa. But we have a question: How is it that the strong bond, the deep rapport that has always been between Lisa and Mother, Mother and Lisa, has not been manifested openly over the years? Our experiences tell us that in situations like this, where Mother and Lisa, Lisa and Mother, have fought all their life not to show openly the strong bond between them, this strong bond they have toward each other, this deep affection, they have not shown it openly to each other for the sake of the other members of the family. They did it for Father, for Diane, and for Dori. Now, why? Because we feel if they would have openly manifested their strong bond, their strong relationship, the other members of the family would have been excluded. Father* married Mother to be with her, and he would have been left out. Diane and Dori would have been second-class citizens if this bond would have been manifested openly. So we think you did well, Mother and Lisa, Lisa and Mother, not to openly show the strong bond between you. In the past, Mother was often disappointed if Lisa and Father did not get along, and Lisa was upset because she sensed Mother's disappointment. So Lisa and Mother, Mother and Lisa, always found ways not to be deeply satisfied with each other over the years, for if they had been satisfied, they would have made a very strong couple and their positive relationship would have manifested itself, leaving out the other members of the family, Father and the two girls. The two girls should thank Lisa and Mother for having fought against the love they feel so deeply for each other.

Lisa was the firstborn, and Mother lived alone with her the first few years, and this was the ground, the preparation, for a very strong relationship. Both of you, Mother and Lisa, have always tried not to show your strong positive feelings you deeply hold for one another. This has been for your sake, Jack, and for Diane and Dori. But we think that Lisa and Mother went too far. They went too far in trying to avoid showing these strong bonds between them. We have discussed all this and we would like to recommend that Mother and Lisa, Lisa and Mother, would have one day a week that would be their day. For instance, you could take Wednesday. Each Wednesday would be the day that Mother and Lisa, and Lisa and Mother, would be together. And Father, Dori, and Diane should understand this and cooperate by staying away from the two of them that day. This would allow one day a week for Mother and Lisa, and Lisa and Mother, to stay together. They can do anything they want—talk, not talk, go out, not go out—they will decide what to do, what to say—fight, not fight— anything.

What is most important is that this is their day, because they went too far in not manifesting their bond, their love for each other. So you two girls and you, Jack, should let them have one day. In that day, for instance, if Dori and Diane have something to say to Mother, they shouldn't say it on that day but save it until the next day or until another day, because that day is Mother and Lisa's day.

Whatever Mother and Lisa do that day, that one day a week, must be kept between them. If Father, Dori, or Diane are curious and want to ask Mother and Lisa "What did you say to each other? What did you do that day?" they must restrain themselves and not ask. If they ask, then Mother and Lisa should say "We are not supposed to tell you what we did or said today." Is it clear, Lisa? All right. One day a week. It is important to have only one day a week, no more. It might happen that you feel, because of the increased rapport between you, that you may want more time together, but it is important that you do not take it. The risk would be that Father would be isolated and Diane and Dori would be second-class citizens. So, in sum, we think that Lisa and Mother went too far in helping Father, Diane, and Dori to feel that they are the important part of the family. So they should have one day a week, Mother and Lisa, to spend together,

*and the others should let them have this day. If Mother and Lisa begin to feel*
*they want more than one day, then you must talk to [family's therapist] because*
*we think it is too much. At the moment, it is important to have one day.*

---

HOFFMAN: Diane looked very angry.

PENN: The most touching feedback was from Lisa, who smiled very quietly. Just lifted her head and smiled.

HOFFMAN: I think Father looked relieved. He nodded and came alive.

BOSCOLO: You could see the competition emerge between Diane and Lisa when we gave Mother to Lisa. It made Diane furious. Even when the girls run after Father, it's Mother they always think about. They go with Father because Mother sends them. They do it to please Mother. But, in reality, they both want Mother.

PENN: What impact did you expect this intervention to have on the family?

CECCHIN: We know from experience that a mother and daughter who are caught in this kind of situation will experience tremendous relief from an outside permission that says they can be together. But the important thing is what happens to the other people. The father is also relieved and, if he is relieved, his behavior with Lisa will be different. If his behavior with her is different, his behavior with his wife is bound to be different. And it is likely that the two younger girls will become jealous and make more demands on Mother. If Diane shows jealousy, Lisa will feel relieved because she'll feel "I count too." The two younger girls have been giving the message: "Lisa doesn't count, she doesn't exist." So the angry reaction of Diane can give Lisa enormous reassurance. That's the only way Lisa will be able to leave home: if she's sure her mother loves her.

You can only leave home if you know that people are going to miss you. And if Lisa can leave the field, the others will be able to leave too.

BOSCOLO: I want to say something about the ritual. We made Lisa the priority in this family. Since Lisa can't make sense out of her relationship with her mother, we supply a ritual for the whole family to follow. The ritual introduces two experiences: first, the experience of a relationship between mother and daughter one day a week, where Lisa can finally find out if her mother will accept her or not; and, second, an experience in which Lisa can permit her sisters to have her mother on other days.

HOFFMAN: The interesting thing is that in your prior discussions everybody was negatively connoted, and with this intervention it all snaps into place and becomes nonblaming and nonpejorative.

BOSCOLO: It's due to a jump of levels, it's more systemic.

HOFFMAN: But how do you get there?

CECCHIN: The most compelling fact was the first marriage between mother and daughter, which was denied. When we change that by putting the two women together, everything begins to make sense. Lisa and Mother can love each other, the father can be generous, the younger daughters can permit their sister a piece of the mother, so everybody feels good. This system had created a context where all the meanings were bad, everybody was bad to each other. Now we create a context where everybody can be good to each other.

PENN: When you go through this process of creating a positive connotation, doesn't it influence how you feel about the family?

CECCHIN: In general, you do identify with that "positive" feeling toward the family. And you have to really believe what you're saying, so it's not a maneuver, not a trick.

HOFFMAN: So what would you say most characterizes a systemic intervention?

CECCHIN: Suppose you have a system where everybody feels bad about everybody else: "My husband is a brute," "My wife is a shrew," "My daughter is a demanding idiot," et cetera. Everybody has bad feelings about each other and about themselves. The perceptions are "This is real, my wife is like that, really!" And people get trapped in these perceptions. There is the feeling that there is no solution and there is no way out. But there is always a solution. The solution is to change the family's epistemological view of their relationships.

HOFFMAN: In other words, you go from the behaviors to the context of the behaviors—the premise about the first family in this case—and you move to a level of logical type that allows you to see all the behaviors as having a certain rightness, no matter how destructive their effects have been.

CECCHIN: That's right.

PENN: What happened next with this family?

BOSCOLO: The family's therapist saw the family three more times. Mother and Lisa did the ritual, but Diane was very angry and tried to stop them. Gradually her hostility lessened and she and Lisa got closer. Lisa, who had moved out on her own, found a boyfriend. The mother told the therapist that Lisa and her husband did not want to come in for therapy, so the therapist recommended taking a recess. The next time we went there, which was nearly six months later, we asked if we could see them for a follow-up session. This time only the parents came.

PENN: How did you handle this second meeting?

BOSCOLO: The problem for us was how to continue to give a message to the family that this was not therapy. The "consultation" as such was over, and we did not want to pull them back to us. So we decided to utilize circular questioning in a very monotonous way, as if we were following an interview schedule. We told them we do follow-ups half a year after ending with a family, for research purposes, and that we would ask them standard research questions.

HOFFMAN: Were there any surprises?

BOSCOLO: We were pleased to hear that Lisa was much happier, had a job, and was living with a boyfriend who wanted to marry her. The girls were all much closer, according to the mother, and she and Lisa now had a very good relationship. However, the relationship between the parents had deteriorated, and it seemed as though the father felt even more outside than ever.

PENN: Tell us about the next session with the family.

BOSCOLO: We went back a year and a half later and asked to see the whole family. They all came, plus a new member, Lisa's baby son. She was married. But we could not tape the session because the father wouldn't allow it.

PENN: Will you summarize?

BOSCOLO: I greeted them the same way as before, thanking them for coming. The father said: "Is your friend behind the mirror?" I saw that he was very angry. He said he didn't want Gianfranco watching us, so I asked him to come and sit in the room with me and the family. Then the father got up and closed the curtains so we could not take a picture. He unplugged the audio, and I really began to get nervous. So I said to him "Excuse me, but if you do not want to be interviewed, it's all right." He said "Sit down!" I sat down and started to ask questions. I asked how things were, and they said that Diane had become more and more rebellious, demanding to leave the home and either live alone or stay with Lisa. The more the parents opposed her, the more rebellious she became. I asked Lisa if she wanted her sister to come and live with her, and she said yes, but felt it would be bad for her parents, so she was ambivalent. The situation had escalated to the point where Diane refused to go to school and finally took refuge in a psychiatric hospital. She had said "I'm not leaving here until you give me permission either to live by myself or go to my sister's." During the session she was angry but coherent. She didn't look crazy. She had gone to the hospital voluntarily and now wanted to leave. Lisa was uncomfortable, and I was curious about why Lisa was so upset. My emotional response was disappointment. I felt she should be grateful to me, so I was thinking like a therapist. I asked her some questions, and she said she was married, doing well with her husband, et cetera. So I asked why she was so angry. I had to resolve this doubt. She looked at me and said "Because you left your work unfinished!" She pointed to Diane. "You helped me, but then you left us with this." All the family nodded, agreeing with Lisa. They were angry at us because they felt we had helped them but had gone away without finishing the job. We went out and discussed what we should do. We felt we were in a classic paradox. Our dilemma was this: if we were to do therapy we would be wrong because we were consultants; however, if we did not do therapy we would be wrong because the family was unhappy. This is the way we got out of our bind.

After our discussion, I went back to the family and, in a tone that sounded very much like a prayer or a litany, I said: "I have had a discussion with my colleagues, and we understand why you are angry. We also understand why Diane decided to go to the hospital, why she doesn't want to stay home, and why she wants to either live by herself or with Lisa. Further, we understand why, on the one hand, Lisa would like her to move in with her and, on the other hand, can't allow this to happen. And we understand why the parents do not want Diane to live on her own or with Lisa. We understand all these things, but we cannot tell you our understanding of all these 'whys' because we are not your therapists."

The effect of this was dramatic. They all sat as if hypnotized. I paused and said, "We agree with you that the work is unfinished, but we cannot finish it because we are not your therapists. All we can say is that we think you should get in contact with a family therapist here. If you decide to do that, then we will tell the therapist all the things we understand about your family, because the therapist will be able to do therapy. But we cannot tell you, because then we would be behaving as though we were therapists, which we are not."

The family responded positively, got up, said thank you, and shook our hands. I had the feeling that the family understood everything. It was a very powerful intervention, more powerful than if we had told them what we understood about them.

HOFFMAN: What was it that you "understood"?

BOSCOLO: It was clear that the relationship between the father and Diane was very bad. She preferred to go to a hospital rather than be near him. Lisa could not take her in because she didn't want the mother to be left alone with the father. That's why the father wanted total control over the session. He said, in effect, "If we have another session like the last one, where you stole one daughter from me, it's possible that you'll steal the next one too." The mother's position was that she wanted to be close to her daughters, but she also wanted to keep this man. By saying "We understand," we were able to point to each individual's private concern without making anything explicit.

HOFFMAN: Did you intend to instruct the therapist the family might then see as to the content of these "whys"?

BOSCOLO: No. Any future therapist should be free to embark on a new search with the family, which would be a totally different family if and when they next came in. This intervention merely addressed the dilemma we were in, by explaining to the family why we couldn't work with them. If the family did decide to come back, they could call the therapist and the therapist could start a new relationship with them, freeing us from the job of being consultants. The intention is never to use the prescription again; it is said at the moment to obtain an effect.

CECCHIN: We have used this intervention in public institutions with students. Public institutions have a bad reputation in Italy. For this reason, a therapist from this kind of agency doesn't count. The family looks at the therapist as useless, thinking "If we went to an expensive center we could be cured; but you can't cure us here." The therapist in that spot can use this same technique. He can say "I have some idea of what's going on, and I understand why you did that and that and that, but I cannot tell you because I have no position in your eyes—you don't trust me. For this reason, what I say can make no sense to you. It is not your fault. If I were the director of this institution, perhaps I could help you. But I'm not. So I think you should wait, and if you are willing, we'll have a few sessions together until there is some spontaneous sign that you trust me. But it has to be spontaneous. When you have a feeling of trust in me as a therapist, which is very difficult considering the circumstances, then I'll tell you what I understand. Only then would it make sense to you."

HOFFMAN: In this interview, did you feel that you had lost control of the session?

BOSCOLO: No. There is an old idea that the therapist should always have control, but we don't believe that. The control is always shifting, because to control an interview means that you create a system that is fixed. You have to offer yourself as a cybernetic loop, so that they can utilize you. Usually, in the beginning of therapy, we appear to take a lot of control, we are very active, we make interventions. Later on, we might start to comment on how confused, uncertain we are. Finally we might say "We really, honestly have nothing to tell you, we have no ideas." And then we would let them decide whether to stop right there or to go on.

PENN: Did you think this family was in a worse or better place than when you first saw them?

BOSCOLO: You can't say if they were in a worse or better place. All you can say is "At the time I observed the system, there was no better solution." Also, when there is a crisis, it can go either way. The escalation they were describing could have had a very negative result. But we also have to remember that the system is evolving. We tend to believe that if we can help a family to get unstuck, they will themselves go on to find a balanced solution.

HOFFMAN: What things made you feel hopeful?

BOSCOLO: Well, Lisa being married and out of the house, of course. And the family seemed much clearer about their relationships. There was a lot of definition, a lot of agreement. In the first two sessions, the wife was antagonistic to the husband, but now she agreed with him. The whole family agreed with him except for Diane.

CECCHIN: What was impressive was the way the father suddenly became the leader in the situation. He was setting the rules: "Now we do it this way." This man sat dumbfounded in the previous session, and here he is saying "This is my family, these are my daughters."

HOFFMAN: Which could be seen as bad or good, depending on your point of view. Using hindsight, is there anything here you would have done differently?

BOSCOLO: I think the intervention we made in the first session was a mistake, because we displaced the therapist. This is always a difficulty. The therapist, when he invites the consultant to come in, gives the message to the family: "I'm stuck, so I need a person who is better than I am." He puts himself down. We could have directed the first intervention to the therapist, saying "This is our way of seeing the situation, and now we want to give you two pieces of advice." The first piece of advice would have been to give the therapist the idea of putting the mother and daughter together. The second piece of advice would be to tell the therapist that she should discuss this with the family during their next meeting, and that she and they must come to an agreement about whether they want to follow this advice or not. I think that would have reinstated the therapist.

HOFFMAN: They would be following your advice even if they decided not to take it.

BOSCOLO: Yes. And this might have reestablished the positive relationship between the therapist and the family. If they had had a therapist, the family might not have reached the impasse they were in, which I perceived as very dangerous. Diane probably wanted to stay in the hospital to avoid the situation that Lisa was in before. She was indicating "If I go home, I'll get into the same relationship with my father." And the parents were fighting to get her back. The situation could have gotten worse, in that the girl might have had to escalate her symptoms to stay in the hospital.

HOFFMAN: As far as you know, this didn't happen?

BOSCOLO: No.

HOFFMAN: Another question. In this country, professionals who work with families and children are now required to file a complaint with the authorities if there is any suspicion of physical or sexual abuse in a family. I realize that it is not within your usual repertory to become what you call a "social control agent." But you state that there are times when a therapist does put on this hat. Why, given the high probability of Diane being harassed, if not abused, by her father, would you not have recommended to the clinic that an investigation be made of the situation, or, at the least, refused to go on with the consultation? Alternatively, why would the clinic or the other professionals who were involved with this case not have taken action?

BOSCOLO: Regarding violence in the family, I think the issue poses a very serious challenge to people who want to maintain a systemic perspective. In the cases where violence is an open fact and legal action has been taken, or will be, violence is then part of family communication. It should be addressed as such. A fall-out of this situation is that the therapist often has to change hats, from a therapist hat to a social control hat. The conversation with the family will center around the consequences for therapy of the change in the therapist's position.

CECCHIN: In the cases where violence is only suspected, the problems are more difficult to resolve. The therapist has to become a detective. The systemic therapist is not usually interested in "the truth," but rather tries to construe a new reality with the family. His concern is to find meanings for all behaviors that will hopefully help family members to change in ways that obviate the need for the violence to continue. He takes his time doing this and is not constrained by a sense of urgency. But if he is suspicious and for ethical and legal reasons is constrained to change into a detective, he then has to act accordingly.

BOSCOLO: We tend to feel confused when we see that family members are perpetrating a crime and trying to conceal the truth. We go back to our former idea of therapy as a battle between the patient and the therapist, with each trying to outsmart the other. For years we have been trying to get out of that position.

CECCHIN: In regard to our behavior in Canada, let me share a historical perspective. At the time we interviewed this family, in 1980, the attitude of the professional community towards the issue of physical and sexual abuse was quite different than it is today. In Italy, therapists would not report abuse to the authorities in order not to break the bond of confidentiality with the client. The same bond is present in the relationship between the priest and the person confessing. It was only in 1984, in Italy, that anyone knowing about sexual or physical abuse to minors was required to report to the police. In the last few years, it has also begun to happen that professionals can be reported to the police for not reporting abuse.

BOSCOLO: At the time we interviewed this family and discussed the case with the other professionals involved, the issue of reporting the case to the police did not come up. We assumed that the therapist and the consultants were bound by the client's right to confidentiality, and that our task was to change the undesirable behavior in the context of therapy. When we showed this tape at workshops and conferences in the early '80s, questions about the issue of reporting did not arise. It has only been recently that audiences have begun to ask such questions. In the last two or three years, the attitude of the professional community has changed massively. The pendulum has shifted, with the professionals becoming more and more like detectives, looking for evidence of abuse.

PENN: One last question. In Milan, do you ever have the problem of the family getting too attached to a therapist?

CECCHIN: In Milan we always work with many therapists. We can substitute one therapist for another and the family doesn't seem to notice. Sometimes a therapist the family doesn't know will come into the room. "Who are you?" "I've been behind the mirror, watching you." "Fine." It doesn't seem to matter. And the family develops an affection for "you" in the plural. They keep referring to what "you" said. You are in the room alone, but they know that the comments are made by you and the team. Systemic therapy doesn't seem to need the same kind of personal involvement with the therapist as other therapies.

PENN: What you're saying is that consultation is not consultation versus therapy, but that those two things together are different ways of changing human systems.

CECCHIN: Which brings us to the elimination of the concept of therapy. Lyman Wynne says "There is no therapy, there is only consultation." When you see a family, you consult with the family system. "Therapy" belongs to the medical model, when you take a piece of the body and you cure it. Family therapy in the systemic sense is always consultation.

BOSCOLO: There is something here that goes even deeper. If you use the word therapy, you define the family as having a problem. Implicitly, you accept pathology. If you introduce the word consultation, you become free of all that.

# PART 3

# *The Anorectic Store*

## INTRODUCTION

T HIS CONSULTATION takes place in four sessions over a period of two years. As in the other consultations in the book, the primary objective of the Milan Associates is to teach their treatment model to colleagues, using consultation as a vehicle. Since Boscolo and Cecchin are functioning fundamentally as teachers, they are free to be critical as well as innovative in their work. In each session we see them respond with a change of direction, based either on the presentation of new information or a recognition of an earlier omission. They always feel free to reformulate their hypotheses when a different aspect of the family's dilemma is revealed.

This consultation with the S family illuminates issues of the referring context, delineates triangles and their changing shapes in a family over the period of treatment, and highlights Boscolo and Cecchin's concept of the premise, a deeply structured family belief that accounts for the family's definition of the problem and indicates how it can change.

## Presenting Problem and Referring Context

Sue, the twenty-three-year-old daughter in the S family, has suffered from anorexia nervosa for the last six years. The family has three other children: Jane, twenty-five; Kate, twenty; and Joe, fifteen. The father is retired and stays at home. Sue and her parents have crisscrossed the United States and Canada looking for therapists, or a therapy, that would cure her. During this time Sue has undergone a lengthy behavior-oriented hospitalization and the family has sought consultations with therapists noted for their work in anorexia, but nothing has produced the elusive cure. All these therapists have failed to help Sue and her family. Consequently, the family dislikes and mistrusts therapists. Mr. S loudly expresses this attitude in the first session when he attacks Cecchin and "the others" for not knowing what they are doing. Mr. S seems to be determined to protect his family from disappointment—that is, from further therapy.

Cecchin responds to the chaos in the family and to the father's attacks with circular questions, making comparisons among the therapies and tracking the family's ideas about therapy. At one point Sue volunteers: "If I had made up my mind to get better a long time ago, I wouldn't be sick." This is a positive statement which is contrary to the family's negative premise regarding therapy.

It is important to note that in the Milan treatment model in general, issues of the referring context are always taken into account, often before the team approaches family dynamics. The teaching consultations of the Milan Associates are distinguished by the fact that the therapeutic context is included. Their focus on this important feedback loop in their treatment model has advanced their understanding of the "significant system": the network of meanings and relationships organized by the problem. The idea of the therapeutic context encompasses not only the referring professional(s) but all of the therapy the family has been exposed to. The experience of many therapies results in the creation of an idea about therapy in the system that can represent, isomorphically, all the splits, agreements, or disagreements found in the family itself. To ignore the meaning of earlier therapies for the current therapy would be to assume that a family is isolated from its own history. The questioning procedure in the Milan model always focuses on these other therapies. When the system's understanding of its therapeutic history becomes clear, the questioning turns to the particulars of the current therapy and how the ideas for it began in the family—who thought of it first, who was most reserved about the idea, who was most enthusiastic, and so on. The idea of "therapy" as it exists in the family is never assumed; rather it is treated as a theme that can both give and respond to information.

There is an interesting background for this idea. From early on, the Milan Associates perceived family therapy as sitting at the interface between the family and society. Boscolo tells a story about the first family therapy conference in Milan, in 1968, which was attended by Nathan Ackerman and Ronald Laing. At this time, most Italian psychiatrists were Marxists, and they clamorously attacked Ackerman because he represented himself as exclusively interested in family dynamics. They much preferred Laing's social context punctuation, for it fit their ideology; they felt psychoanalysis and its derivatives to be "bourgeois." However, a group of these Marxist psychiatrists came to the Milan Center to learn the Milan Associates' "technical instruments" for dealing with family problems. The center's reputation had spread, and the Marxist psychiatrists were using conventional means to treat people who were not getting better. The Marxists' dilemma proved to be a very interesting one; as they learned the Milan techniques, they also came into contact with a different epistemology—one that was not only neutral but was tolerant of many non-Marxist worldviews. The Marxists felt that it was important for therapists to be politically conscious, for they had the power to introduce social norms to a patient, ally with a patient against society, or ally with society against a patient. But these interface problems between the patient and society were not resolved when the Marxists learned the Milan techniques. Instead, the methodology served to challenge Marxist solutions. Nevertheless, the Marxists taught the Milan team an important lesson: that it was not possible to have a therapy that did not include the relational context of the family, both social and professional. The act of therapy must represent *all* of those contexts.

Returning to the S family, the family had constructed a position to deal with all these failed therapies. During the interview it becomes clear that their discounting stance is in the service of asking that the therapists—but not they themselves—change. So the collection of therapies itself becomes an integral part of the way the family stays together. The hypothesis is that therapy poses a risk of separation for this family. The parents handle this danger by one of them competing for an illustrious therapist whom the other will find reason to disapprove of. This "game" protects their premise that the family must stay together. The parents' major area of agreement is when they agree that the therapist or therapy has failed. In that sense, they agree on when to agree and when to disagree.

In order to address the S couple's relationship rule about therapy, the Milan team asks them to come back the next day after agreeing on which group will attend the session, the parents or the children. The rationale given to the family is that the daughters are in conflict and will not grow up because they have the idea that the parents will not be able to get along without them. If the children choose to return, the consultants will try to disabuse them of this idea; and if the parents choose to come back, the team will investigate how the children are getting the messages that support this idea.

The mother and father return the next day and are given the "secret couple" task: they are to have a secret date each week over a period of time. No one is to know where they go, and they are not to discuss their activities or whereabouts on their return. This ritual accomplishes two important things. First, it puts all the children on the same level. Each one, in his or her own way, is struggling with the problem of how to leave home without worrying about the parents. Second, all the triangles in the system are subordinated to the couple's secret time together. In addition, the S family is asked not to have therapy for six months to relieve them of their distrust of therapists and to give them the time to explore new possibilities on their own.

## Triangles and the Premise

A triadic assessment is one base from which to construct a hypothesis, but a premise is the theme or idea the problem triangles struggle with. The triangles in a family may change—certainly in response to therapy—but the premise is difficult to change, retaining its position as a key issue the family has yet to resolve.

Before we explore the changing triadic structure in the S family around their particular premise, remember the Milan team's views on labeling. Anorexia is a challenge to any therapeutic model, so it is important to remember that the Milan team will accept it as a label like any other and convert it into interactional process, or descriptions of behavior. They are particularly alert for indications that the family understands that a person's illness is a way of behaving with others. At that time, both the therapist and the family can begin to view the "illness" as a decision to behave in a certain way and members of the family begin to react as if the anorectic is a human being and not exclusively "a sick person." The Milan team feels this is the moment when change begins.

Over the course of the four consultations, the assessment of the triangles in the S family takes some interesting turns. The consultants move from the triangle of Mother, Sue, and Jane in the first session to Mother, Father, and Sue in the third session. At the conclusion of the work with this family, still another triangle emerges, which will be discussed later.

From the analogical and verbal material in the first interview, the Milan Associates conclude that Sue and Jane seem to be in a struggle for their mother that promotes competition between them. This form of competition results in neither daughter being able to separate from the family. Their competition is expressed around a theme of staying/leaving. The consultants, tracking the two girls' movements—their attempts to leave home and their subsequent returns—develop the notion of the pseudostable child and the pseudofugitive child. Both positions increase the bond with the parents, whether they threaten to leave or to return. The logic of this behavior is that one child must appear to leave and the two positions must alternate, since neither by itself is a solution. The result of this behavior for the family is that it makes staying together acceptable, since one of the children is always preparing to leave. This rationale promotes a more inclusive definition of the stay/leave oscillation in that it allows the family to remain together and not separate.

Boscolo and Cecchin then introduce future questions that address the stay/leave oscillation. For instance they ask: "Which of the four children would decide to stay home to be close to the parents?" This and other future questions concern the family's expectations for their children, thereby creating connections the family has not foreseen or talked about.

The Milan Associates see a premise as part of a family's belief system. When people try to create a world too similar to the one they know, they create a self-fulfilling prophecy. But if you ask future questions, as in this case around separation: who will be the first to leave the family, marry, and so on, you are asking questions that the premise does not allow. These questions introduce the idea that the premise can change or at least be modified.

Changing a premise is a rare and demanding event, as Gregory Bateson has indicated in his essay, "The Cybernetics of Self" (Bateson, 1972). In this essay Bateson describes the alcoholic's premise, "I am in control of my drinking," which must be proved over and over again in each ensuing alcoholic bout. In order for the premise "I am in control" to change, the alcoholic must "hit bottom," finally recognizing that he or she has *no* control. Then the premise shifts from constant attempts to prove control to accepting the fact of having no control.

The Milan team feels that if you say, for example, "Don't change! Remain the same! Be more depressed, anxious, anorectic, even though you may die," that statement is the verbal equivalent of hitting bottom. By prescribing this "bottom," you create the possibility of a new solution.

Boscolo and Cecchin say in this case discussion that families have general premises, particularly about separation and death. How the idea of death is perceived in family relationships and the way it will be experienced in the future is in accordance with how these ideas have evolved during the family's history.

To go back to this case, the third session takes place six months after the "secret couple" ritual. Sue's behavior has changed but is still upsetting her family. During this time she has begun to see a therapist, in what appears to be a steady involvement. However, her parents are still quarreling over her: Father attacks her for having "garbage" friends; and Mother defends her, saying that she probably has such low self-esteem she doesn't think she deserves better! The Milan team feels it is important not to further separate the family, as they did in the "secret couple" intervention, and recommends that the family stay together. Time, they say, will take care of things, and the *normal time* to separate will come by itself. They describe Sue's therapy as an important way of slowing down the separation process. Essentially they want to give the family the time to reorganize its behavior in response to the consultation and to counteract the injunction from the many therapists the family has been involved with that staying at home is abnormal. In line with this idea, they also tell the family that Sue no longer is anorectic, even though she still shows anorectic behavior. Boscolo and Cecchin then go on to talk about the longer intervals between sessions that characterize their work. In the beginning of therapy, they see a family more often, perhaps taking three sessions to make an intervention. Then, after an appraisal is made of what, in each case, would be an appropriate time lapse, they let the family go for a prescribed interval which may be for a period of several months or a year.

## Follow-up, One and One-Half Years Later

There is a follow-up one and one-half years later. During this interval, Sue has continued to see her individual therapist and the family has been seeing a psychiatrist. A large change has taken place. Mrs. S has opened a chain of stores that sell sports clothes. This proves to be a successful venture for the family, for not only are they making money but each daughter either has a store of her own or works in the main store. Father, too, works in the main store. The explanation given by Boscolo and Cecchin for this change is the following. For years, Mrs. S had tried to make her husband become a good provider, with the result that the family had been on the verge of bankruptcy several times. In fact, on one occasion Mr. S was compelled to sell their family home. At these times Mr. and Mrs. S went to Mrs. S's wealthy mother to borrow money. This was a humiliation for Mrs. S because she was the only one of three sisters whose husband was not rich. During these years Mrs. S had a dependent relationship with her mother, and Mr. S had a cozy relationship with her, often visiting for tête-à-têtes. Consequently, not only did Mother not do what her sisters had done—marry a rich husband—but her husband and her mother were in an alliance. The opening of the stores untied the S family from the grandmother and established a clear boundary between Mrs. S and her mother. Mrs. S had finally separated herself from the financial and emotional bonds that tied her to her family of origin.

In the S family, the central issue seemed to be the mother's separation from her family of origin and her sense of her own independence and autonomy. According to Paul Dell (Dell, 1982), change does not come out at the level of the system but at the level of its individual members. The family does not change all at once; instead, there is continuous feedback between the individual who changes and the system. In this family, it was the mother who made the first dramatic change, breaking the domination of her mother and organizing the family's business life.

This outcome raises two questions. The first question is around the continuation of the family's closeness or "enmeshment." For instance, would a structural family therapist react to this solution as inadequate since the family is still basically living together? Or could this family be seen as a healthier, though still enmeshed, family? This case also shows unambiguously that women, as well as men, are organizers of systemic solutions, and that these solutions are characterized by interpersonal success and ingenuity.

The second question has to do with the scope of the Milan Associates' working hypothesis. Although they do get some of the family of origin information, at least in regard to the mother's family, they do not work it into a multi-generational hypothesis on which to base their questions and interventions. They stay focused on the separation of the children from the parents rather than move to, or include, the separation of the nuclear family from the families of origin. Yet in the discussion that follows the outcome in regard to the stores, they use the information about the extended family to account for what took place. This brings up a further idea that one does not always have to work with more than a partial hypothesis to create changes across the entire family.

# THE CASE: CONSULTATION AND CONVERSATION

## Session 1

HOFFMAN: Why were you called in to see this family?

CECCHIN: They had a twenty-three-year-old daughter, Sue, who had been defined as anorectic for the previous six years. During that time the family had gone to many different professionals, including Hilde Bruch in Houston. They were finally referred to a clinic where they worked with a therapist, Dr. H, for a few sessions but decided not to come back. Then, when we were going to this workshop, this same therapist wrote a letter to the family. In it she said: "We have two Italian doctors visiting us who are famous for their work in anorexia, and if you want to come back to the Institute they will see you for a consultation."

PENN: How long had the family been out of treatment?

CECCHIN: About six weeks.

HOFFMAN: How long had the family seen the therapist?

CECCHIN: Over a period of three or four months for five or six sessions. Some Milan-style interventions were tried, but the family's response was to leave treatment. So I see it as a challenge on two counts. The family says "Let's see what these doctors can do," and the former therapist is saying "Let's see how the Italians do it."

HOFFMAN: What was their experience with Hilde Bruch?

CECCHIN: Hilde Bruch only referred them to a hospital. When the girl, Sue, was there, she was fed and gained weight. Then the hospital recommended she go home and enter family therapy.

HOFFMAN: When you saw her was she underweight?

BOSCOLO: No. At this point she looked fine, but her behavior was anorectic behavior; she was always worrying about food. She became anorectic just as the oldest sister, Jane, left home. There were three sisters in the family. Jane, twenty-five, had been back and forth to college. There was also an overactive younger sister, Kate, twenty, and a brother, Joe, who was fifteen, and who was quiet and a bit heavy. The father, who was "retired" and living at home, said he was slow in school.

PENN: What about the therapist?

CECCHIN: She was behind the screen. The therapist who is seeing the family usually comes into the room with us. However, since she was the "fired" therapist, we decided that perhaps she should stay out.

### FAMILY INTERVIEW

*FATHER: Is Dr. H (family's former therapist) coming in?*

*CECCHIN: No, we asked her to stay out. Do you prefer her being here?*

*FATHER: No, I just thought she was going to be here. It really doesn't matter.*

*CECCHIN: Dr. H gave us a briefing of the sessions she had with you and told us what's been happening. I understand that you have been having problems for a long time and have seen many different therapists.*

*MOTHER: For a long time.*

*CECCHIN: What's the problem in the family now? Can we start from scratch? What's the problem in the family now?*

*MOTHER: Sue has anorexia, and that is what the problem is. She's sick and it creates a problem within the family because maybe the other members of the family don't want to accept her illness. Instead of helping her, there's a lot of fighting, and that makes everything worse.*

*CECCHIN: Sue, do you agree with what your mother says—that you have a sickness?*

*SUE: I think yeah.*

*CECCHIN: Since when?*

*SUE: Since I was seventeen.*

*CECCHIN: Now you're twenty-three.*

---

BOSCOLO: The mother said that Sue has anorexia and that some people in the family won't accept it. I think it would be good to ask "Who does not accept it?" because the struggle in the family may be that the mother believes Sue is anorectic and the others in the family don't believe it. The issue could have been addressed by asking this question: "Who believes you're anorectic? Who does not? And among those who believe, who believes it the most?" If you believe someone is anorectic, a lot of behaviors are allowed. For example, if the anorectic throws a plate in your face, and you believe she is anorectic, she's not responsible. If you don't believe it, you become angry.

CECCHIN: Here we are talking about process again, not content. We don't care if it's true that she has anorexia or not. Otherwise we would fall into the epistemological error of the family. We want to know who believes or doesn't believe in her anorexia. We are attentive to the process of how this belief works in this particular family.

BOSCOLO: Here is a good example of the attempted solution becoming the problem. Anorexia has been increasing in the last thirty years. One explanation is that when fashion models became so slim, many adolescents started to go on diets. The problem begins when the one who becomes too thin, or anorectic, provokes feedback in the family. They begin to worry, Is she sick or not sick? This feedback creates the problem.

PENN: I was wondering about the sibling structure of this family, particularly the relationship between the three girls, since two will often form an alliance leaving out the third. Does that tend to be the anorectic one? What is her relationship to her mother?

BOSCOLO: Though we have seen this in some cases, we have to be careful not to generalize. The girl who becomes anorectic tries to make some sense out of the relationship with her mother. She experiences a sense of betrayal—of her mother not being there. Usually it's when another sister does something different—leaves home for a job, marries—and the mother calls her every day. The child remaining is now hoping for total love from the mother. When this doesn't happen, the girl decides not to eat, and that involves the mother exclusively with her, but *without* resolving the problem. This usually happens in a family where food becomes a way of giving messages. If you are in a family that uses a psychosomatic language and you want to give a message, you develop a stomachache or a headache. In Italian or Jewish families, food is a big thing. If your wife doesn't cook well, you say "She doesn't love me any more." In this family, food is a way they communicate, and therefore someone might logically develop anorexia.

CECCHIN: I think there are many different typologies that describe anorexia. Sometimes the most important triangle is the anorectic, the mother, and a sibling. Sometimes it's the anorectic, the mother, and the father. We've seen a few cases when the anorexia started when the father retired and stayed home all day. Another possible triangle could be the anorectic, mother, and mother's sister or the daughter of the sister of mother. Another typology, and I think this is the worst, is when the mother clearly prefers another sibling, another sister, and the anorectic girl is supposed to make a couple with father. When she enters adolescence, she starts to become anorectic. I believe these cases are the most difficult because the anorectic never gets her mother.

BOSCOLO: We tend to put the mother in the center of the triangle, but sometimes, when there are many siblings, the sibling relationship is more important. In some instances, one sibling leaves the house because he or she cannot be tolerated by another sibling. In adolescence, siblings sometimes create such a strong subsystem that parents become peripheral. Of course, when one sibling leaves, the question of who Mother is going to choose becomes very important.

CECCHIN: Another typical situation is a woman who becomes anorectic after her marriage. Because she is so connected to her mother, she tries to get away from her: "I'll find a man who's better than you. I don't need you." The man goes crazy because he tries to be a mother to her, a father, a husband, but the more he tries, the worse it becomes. Eventually the girl returns to her mother for a while; then it gets worse, she leaves; et cetera. No one can understand what's going on.

HOFFMAN: How would you describe the triangles in this family?

CECCHIN: It's not clear yet, but we might start with a hypothesis that the most significant group is the three girls. If two get close, another is excluded. Often, when there are three siblings—male or female—more or less the same age, the most important group is the siblings.

PENN: But you had no hypothesis for this family at this point?

CECCHIN: No.

## FAMILY INTERVIEW

CECCHIN: *You've had this disease for a long time. Who decided it was anorexia?*

SUE: *I did.*

FATHER: *Who said it was a disease?*

CECCHIN: *Mother.*

FATHER: *It's not a disease.*

MOTHER: *Whatever it is.*

CECCHIN: *You don't agree with what your wife said?*

FATHER: *No. Anorexia is not a disease.*

CECCHIN: *How do you see it?*

SUE: *A sickness, illness.*

FATHER: *It's a mental disorder, a psychiatric problem, an emotional . . . call it whatever you want. A disease can be classified as something, like, if you have typhoid.*

CECCHIN: *So it's not a physical disease?*

FATHER: *No.*

CECCHIN: *It's a mental sickness.*

FATHER: *You can call it what you want. Call it emotional or . . . what is the definition between emotional and mental? Is there a difference between the two?*

CECCHIN: *Not very much.*

---

PENN: Are you doing something in the session we can't see? The father seems to be attacking you.

BOSCOLO: There is a disagreement between the wife and husband about therapy and about the definition of the problem. The father doesn't agree with the mother that they need therapy, so he starts to attack the therapist.

CECCHIN: It's clear that he doesn't want anyone to interfere with the family. The mother goes around looking for therapists, but the father wants to be the boss in his family. So he says "What are you doing here? I don't want anybody coming and competing with me for all these women."

## FAMILY INTERVIEW

CECCHIN: *What about your daughter? [To Sue] Do you agree with what your parents are saying? It is a sickness, an emotional sickness?*

SUE: *To some extent, yes.*

CECCHIN: *Your mother was saying that this brings problems into the family. What kind of problems?*

JANE: *Well, that's a hard question to answer.*

CECCHIN: *What kind of problems do you see your younger sister giving to your mother?*

JANE: *To my mother? She makes my mother feel guilty about everything. My mom doesn't have her own life because she's always so worried about Sue, and that's not fair 'cause she's always worried about Sue and Sue is getting all the attention. Everyone isn't getting an equal portion from the parents 'cause it's always directed specifically to Sue. That's where the greatest concern is. Because she's sick.*

CECCHIN: *You say the parents, or your mother in particular?*

JANE: *Mother in particular. More my mother than my dad, although I think both of them when it comes right down to it. And it causes problems for the other children, like Kate and Joe, because they're younger. I'm sure they feel a little neglected. I'm older and I don't have that same feeling. I've been on my own for a long time; it doesn't make any difference to me, really.*

CECCHIN: *Do you live outside the house now?*

JANE: *No, I live at home now, but I used to live on my own. I just recently moved back home, but that doesn't create a problem for me as much as maybe for Kate and Joe.*

CECCHIN: *You say Sue makes your mother feel guilty. What does she do to make her feel guilty?*

JANE: *She picks her face.*

SUE: *But I think I'm a good excuse for everyone, because whenever anything goes wrong, it's my fault. Like last week, Kate and my mother had a fight. So I happened to be at home, and the first thing that happened was that Kate threw it right into my mother's face: "It's all her fault," meaning me.*

CECCHIN: *How does she manage to do that?*

SUE: *Oh, because, you see, Kate had a temper tantrum, and 'cause she couldn't handle her anger, she just brought me right into it. "It's Sue's fault. If Sue wasn't sick—"*

KATE: *No, that's not true.*

SUE: *Yes, I think it is; and she got mad at me because of you.*

MOTHER: *No. You know what happened? We had a letter to come here, an invitation to come here. And I thought we were very fortunate to have this opportunity, so I told Jane and Kate about it. And their attitude was "I'm not coming," and this upset me because I thought we're lucky, we got a chance, and maybe it'll trigger Sue into . . . I could never give up the chance. So I think because I wanted so badly for them to come, it was their way of maybe punishing me. Not you. [to Sue]*

KATE: *That's not right. I told you exactly why I couldn't go, and you started to tell me all the things you wouldn't have said to me if Sue wasn't present.*

MOTHER: *No, Kate said she didn't want to go because she said she had to work. The two hours of coming here and returning were going to interfere with her work, so she said she's not going to lose the two hours of work. But that was just an excuse.*

---

HOFFMAN: This family is being very noisy, very chaotic. One of the questions a student will ask about circular questioning is what to do when a family won't shut up or somebody gets very hostile, or when a child is screaming or running around.

BOSCOLO: You can respond to that specific behavior by asking questions of another family member: "How do you explain this behavior?" But I think that when we talk about circular questioning there is the danger of becoming too rigid. First, if all you do is circular questioning, you become like a robot. Second, you can create a problem in joining. The therapist can become too mechanical in asking these questions, so there is a danger of hypercircularity. It becomes like a symptom. Sometimes the therapist uses circular questioning, sometimes he takes a break. Taking a break allows him a chance to be quiet and think—it isn't always necessary to listen to what the family says. I try to see if all the information that came up in the last couple of minutes contributes to some pattern that connects. It gets me out of the family at that moment. So I will let one person talk just to protect my own thinking, or I will ask dyadic questions.

Also, at the beginning of the session, the therapist may decide not to control the family's interactions. Sometimes it's good to let them respond in the way they would if the therapist were not there. At the same time I notice how they sit down, how they look at each other. I tend to pay more attention to the analogic behaviors than the words. I will often make a hypothesis based on the analogic behaviors during these first minutes, then I will test the hypothesis by using circular questions.

PENN: In this session the mother sits forward and all the girls begin to compete for a position near her. I would suspect a triangle between the mother and at least two of the daughters.

CECCHIN: Yes, and immediately you see one premise: that you cannot share the mother. You get the idea that all the children have this fantasy about possessing her exclusively. The premise of this anorexia is that mother should be all mine.

BOSCOLO: The father has the same idea; that's why he is so interfering. Even the mother is not able to handle this situation; she is offering herself, but she doesn't know how to give herself to anyone.

PENN: Luigi said just now that anorexia can develop when the father retires. He depends on the mother to join him in his new activities, but if the children are still home, he becomes a rival.

CECCHIN: Yes, he becomes a child. He is also saying "I've been working all my life, waiting for this moment when you can take care of me." But the wife indicates that she liked it better when he worked.

BOSCOLO: Some retired fathers think that all these years the children had their mother, and now they feel it's their turn. That's when trouble can start. It can be an escalation between the anorectic and the father. In this dynamic, you'd see hostility between the father and the daughter.

## FAMILY INTERVIEW

SUE: *Then my mother said to Kate, "Well, then move out." So then Kate threw back: "Oh, I'll move out if you bring me food, because I'm on a student loan and don't have any money." I live in an apartment by myself.*

MOTHER: *She just moved out in January.*
CECCHIN: *How far are you from home?*
SUE: *Not far, because I like that area.*
CECCHIN: *How often do you go home to visit your parents?*
SUE: *I'm not going home, ever.*
CECCHIN: *But you went home last week.*
SUE: *It makes me a mess.*
CECCHIN: *Before last week, how often did you go home?*
SUE: *About once a week, every ten days.*
CECCHIN: *Did you keep in touch by phone?*
*[Boscolo phones in.]*

---

HOFFMAN: What did Luigi want to say to you?
CECCHIN: He called me out because he felt we were involved in tea-party talk.
BOSCOLO: No, I think I wanted you to test the hypothesis that the daughters were competing for the mother.

## FAMILY INTERVIEW

CECCHIN: *So, before, Kate was saying that if Sue didn't have this problem, you could get more of the parents. Jane, you said "We're not getting our share," didn't you? Then I asked "Which of your parents would you like to have more of?" and Kate said "Mother." Now, I would like to ask Sue "Which of your brothers and sisters would like to have more of your parents?"*
SUE: *Kate.*
CECCHIN: *Which of the children is missing the parents more?*
SUE: *Kate.*
CECCHIN: *You say that. [to Jane] Kate said that Sue's problem makes the others not have enough of their parents. Do you say Kate suffers more?*
JANE: *I don't think any of them suffer. I think my parents are there when they are needed to be there.*
CECCHIN: *So you don't agree with what was said?*
JANE: *No, not really.*
CECCHIN: *It's not true what they say?*
JANE: *Well, for a time it was.*
FATHER: *The truth is only in the mind of the one that speaks it. Her interpretation*

*of what she thinks won't necessarily be the same as her sisters'.*

MOTHER: *But I agree with Jane and I agree with Sue. There was a time, definitely, where I was so concerned with her that it's true.*

CECCHIN: *When did this time end?*

MOTHER: *I think when Sue moved out. When she was away [in the city], I was always worried.*

CECCHIN: *So, since January this problem is over?*

MOTHER: *Well, it's not over.*

FATHER: *What problem is over?*

JANE: *It's still there, but we don't see it because when she phones she talks to my mother; she doesn't talk to any of us.*

CECCHIN: *Is your brother also having the same problem of missing the parents?*

SUE: *I don't know.*

FATHER: *Ask him. [to Joe] What problem do you have?*

CECCHIN: *Do you have the same problem your sisters are having? Jane and Kate said that before Sue moved out, there was this problem. Mother is always looking after Sue—Father too—and they felt somehow they weren't getting enough of their parents, their rightful share . . .*

JOE: *No.*

CECCHIN: *Do you have enough of a share of the parents?*

JOE: *Yeah.*

FATHER: *Look at the doctor, don't look at me.*

CECCHIN: *[to Joe] How do you explain the fact that they have a problem and you don't? They notice this kind of thing and you don't notice it?*

JOE: *I don't know. I have them enough.*

SUE: *He spends most of his time with Dad.*

CECCHIN: *He spends most of his time with Dad? Is Dad also involved with Sue, or not?*

MOTHER: *I'll tell you how Joe was involved. Joe didn't like the fact that Sue was binge eating and vomiting, and where Joe got involved was not that he was lacking his mother and father, but his problem was that he didn't want to use the toilets because Sue was vomiting in them. This is how he got involved. So he always liked Sue—they were good together—but her illness made him stay away because he didn't want to use the toilets.*

CECCHIN: *You explained that he has his father. [unclear sentence] He's not making his father guilty?*

SUE: *If he does, he doesn't show it.*

CECCHIN: *[to Jane] Is Kate or are you more upset about not having enough of the mother?*

JANE: *It was that way too for a while, but I don't think now—*

SUE: *They forget that when they need help, we're all there. They forget that if one of them had my problem, then everyone would be there for them the same way they're there for me.*

CECCHIN: *Suppose you didn't have anorexia and you were as healthy as your sisters.*

*Who would want to be closer to Mother then? Which of you three sisters would like to be close to Mother?*

FATHER: *[snorts]*

SUE: *Probably me.*

CECCHIN: *Why?*

SUE: *Because I always felt—*

FATHER: *No, that's not the question. The question is: If you weren't sick, if you were in the same category as your other two sisters, if all three of you were healthy, which one of you would want your mother's attention more?*

SUE: *Probably nobody.*

CECCHIN: *Probably nobody would care about Mother?*

SUE: *It would probably all be equal. I would probably care the most because I'm not like them. They seem to care about themselves more than anyone, and ever since I can remember I've always cared about everyone.*

---

BOSCOLO: If we had a hypothesis at that time, it was probably that the girls were fighting over Mother. Reviewing the tape now, it seems that the other sisters are not as attached to the mother as Sue; they don't care that much. The sisters are not competing with her for Mother. So this is the time we should switch our hypothesis. We should ask: "Who else might threaten her relationship with her mother? Is it the brother? the father? Should we move to the extended family?"

CECCHIN: The boy is very comfortable.

BOSCOLO: We were experiencing a continual stuckness in the session because this hypothesis of fighting between the sisters was not correct.

PENN: But then you asked the question "Suppose you didn't have anorexia, who would want to be closer to Mother?"

CECCHIN: Yes. "Probably me," she said. That is very honest, very strange. If she were really competing with her sisters, she wouldn't say that, she would say "My sister."

BOSCOLO: But it's very interesting that she says "It would be me," because that indicates that it is not anorexia that keeps her close to her mother. She also says that, in the past, the sisters wanted to share the mother, but lately they don't care. However, she and Jane do seem to compete, since when one comes home, the other leaves, and vice versa.

CECCHIN: There are many elements that confirm the idea that they are competing with each other, so we are seduced by it.

## FAMILY INTERVIEW

CECCHIN: *Before the anorexia, which of the three daughters was closest to Mother?*

JANE: *Don't look at me.*

SUE: *Me, because I was still in high school.*

FATHER: *[laughing] Jane was never close to my wife, never. That's why I laugh—because it's true.*

CECCHIN: *Is that because she was the first daughter and was very independent?*

FATHER: *No, she was jealous.*

CECCHIN: *Who was jealous?*

FATHER: *There was a complication between the two of them [Jane and Mother].*

CECCHIN: *For what?*

SUE: *For him.*

FATHER: *I don't know. As far as one demanding more attention than the other or who would care more, I don't think either one of them would make much difference.*

CECCHIN: *Before this problem happened, Jane was . . .*

FATHER: *She was independent.*

CECCHIN: *She was independent. Was she ever close to you?*

FATHER: *Well, up to a certain age.*

JANE: *Yeah, till I was four. You see, I have never been close to either my mother or my father and I've always gone my own way; and I remember thinking all the time that I wish I had more guidance from my parents than friendship, because I needed someone to talk to as a parent rather than a friend, and I still, to this day, don't really talk openly to either.*

CECCHIN: *Why? Because they behave like—*

JANE: *Like friends. Always.*

CECCHIN: *Who more, Father or Mother? Who behaves more like a friend?*

JANE: *Both. I feel very distant from both of them.*

CECCHIN: *You said Jane was very attached to her father.*

FATHER: *At a certain age.*

CECCHIN: *Sue, you say Jane was very attached to Father at a certain age. She said when she was four years old she stopped. Do you agree?*

SUE: *I don't think so, because when I was born I remember her hating me as much as she hated my mother.*

MOTHER: *Well, we were both in the way because then she had to share her father. See, she didn't like me because she had to share her dad with me; then, when Sue came, she didn't like Sue because now she had to share with two of us; when Kate came, it didn't matter because she was already in school and had her own world starting. Also, Jane wouldn't let me touch her: I couldn't breathe too loud, I couldn't breathe on her.*

JANE: *I'm still not affectionate to my mother or father, I'm just not an affectionate person. I don't like to be touched, I like to do my own thing. I remember when*

*Kate came along Kate was my center of attention. When Kate was born, she was my best friend because I was like her mother. Except one time when I answered the phone, she went crazy on me; and ever since then I didn't like her because she tried to hit me. I picked up the phone and she got really mad at me because it was for her and I never said "Just a minute." I just put the phone down. And I remember screaming for you to come because she was beating me up.*

CECCHIN: *When was that?*

JANE: *About four years ago, when she was going out with this real idiot.*

FATHER: *All her boyfriends are idiots.*

CECCHIN: *And then you broke with her?*

JANE: *She wouldn't pay attention to me any more because she was going with this boyfriend.*

*[Family talks about recurrent fights between Jane and Mother.]*

CECCHIN: *[to Mother] If you stand up and she [Jane] resists, who do you ask for help?*

MOTHER: *Nobody helps me. I'll discuss it with him, but he's no help because I don't think he wants to be involved. He doesn't want to get involved.*

CECCHIN: *What about with Kate? Does he help you?*

MOTHER: *No, Kate doesn't say anything. She will see what's happening and she will have her own feelings about it, but she will not express herself openly on who's right, who's wrong, why is this happening.*

KATE: *That's because I don't talk to you like you're my parents.*

MOTHER: *Oh well, maybe she talks to you, but as far as I'm concerned . . .*

CECCHIN: *If there is this conflict between Jane and Mother, who wins?*

FATHER: *Why does there have to be a winner?*

JANE: *There's not a winner.*

CECCHIN: *Your wife said if she has to impose something important, if she has to impose her will, that means there's a winner.*

FATHER: *In the sense that the girl—you know, she's twenty-five, she's not a girl any more, she's twenty-five years old. So how can there be a winner? How can you impose . . . It's impossible.*

JANE: *The way I see it, Mom doesn't give in, but she always stops when she doesn't want to argue any more.*

FATHER: *That's what I said: there is no winner.*

JANE: *Then, in a couple of days, it works itself out.*

CECCHIN: *The problem goes away?*

MOTHER: *It's never really solved, there is never a conclusion. And I believe that the problem is basically between my husband and I. These children have learned how to manipulate because that's what has happened to my husband and I. I can communicate and I can talk and talk and talk. He doesn't want to face the problem. He . . . that's exactly how he handles it. It's never really solved.*

CECCHIN: *Who's the best manipulator of your husband of all four children? Have they learned how to manipulate your husband?*

MOTHER: *They are all manipulators in this house.*

*CECCHIN:  But make a classification—who is the most brilliant in this activity? Who manipulates your husband the most?*

*MOTHER:  Who manipulates the most?*

*SUE:  Joe.*

*MOTHER:  Who manipulates my husband? I think the best manipulator . . . well, Sue, of course, has become very good at it because of her illness; but I can't call it the same kind of manipulation. Her manipulation probably affects me more. I think Jane . . . not that she's manipulating, but there are ways that she has learned—punishment. I know because I feel punished an awful lot, a great deal in the house, and I don't know that Sue is. I feel that from a very young age, when we were first married, Harold used to punish me, in a way. If we were dressed up, going to a party, if he got angry with me for something, he wasn't going to the party. If I wanted to go to a show, his way of punishing me was saying "I am not going." And this used to affect me, and I do believe that the children have learned this form of punishment. I believe Jane punishes Sue and me in the same way that he does. [Boscolo calls in and Cecchin takes a break to talk with group behind the screen.]*

------

HOFFMAN:  What did you talk about during the break?

BOSCOLO:  We shared impressions of the family. We see that the son, Joe, is sitting close to his father, touching him from time to time, while the women are sitting separately. The father seems to want everyone for himself but never supports his wife, and in the fight between Mother and Jane, the daughter wins all the time. Jane and Father are together. But what was missing was the answer to why, at seventeen, Sue decided to be anorectic.

CECCHIN:  I think that at this point we had become dissatisfied with our hypothesis, which was based on our observation that the symptom of anorexia starts when one of the parents—most often Mother—starts to prefer one child over the other, and denies this preference. The danger of this hypothesis is that we like it too much. After a while all anorectic families look the same. Here we decided to ask a future question that we have been using a lot lately that deals with the family's expectation of their children. We ask "How are your children doing? How well are they growing up?" And we ask hypothetical questions along the line of: "What do you expect will happen if X or Y changes?" "If Sue did not have anorexia, would the other girls fight to be close to Mother?" "If your brother became a problem, would Father worry more about him than he does about Sue?"

These questions create connections; they reveal myths, self-fulfilling prophecies, and expectations which, in the family, are usually not talked about. Here they led us to an understanding of a premise in the family around leaving and staying, which seemed very important. We also decided to ask questions about the family's experience with therapy.

PENN: The questions you are asking now reflect the change of hypothesis you made. They introduce the notion of separation—whether or not the children will be able to leave the family. Can you state your new hypothesis?

CECCHIN: The whole idea is that these people are all enmeshed with each other; they compete for each other. For example, the father comes in and wants to control the session, the girls are competing for the parents, the parents are competing for the children, everybody wants to possess each other—that's their way of living. The idea that people might leave is unthinkable for them.

HOFFMAN: If you ask "Who might stay?" then you imply others might leave.

CECCHIN: Introducing the possibility that some people might stay and others might leave allows us to see how they react to the concept of separation. We pay a lot of attention to the one who appears to be trying to escape—the "fugitive," as we call him or her.

PENN: This is the first time you've spoken of the fugitive. So often we only notice the one who stays behind. I wonder if you would talk more about that.

CECCHIN: We call one the pseudofugitive, because usually in a family like this there is a pseudofugitive and a pseudostable. The pseudostable child stays home, thinking "This is the way I get love from my parents." The pseudofugitive one discovers that by moving out, threatening to leave, threatening to get married, she has a tremendous effect on the parents, especially the mother. The mother begins to be very interested in that child, so the one who plays the fugitive usually gets a lot of attention.

HOFFMAN: Who in this family is the fugitive?

CECCHIN: Jane is the fugitive; she's been that way since age four. She found out that there's only one way to become interesting to the parents: to leave. The other, Sue, is stable, always there.

HOFFMAN: That's why she says "Since birth I have been taking care of my parents; I'm the only one who worries about them." Jane was four when Sue was born. That's when Jane became fugitive. And Sue became anorectic when Jane first left home.

PENN: Even the fugitive only appears to leave. In point of fact, Jane recently returned home and Sue moved away.

CECCHIN: It's interesting that there is an escalation of the differences between the two positions. Sue has become more and more stable, to the point of staying in the home, even dying there. Instead of finding a boyfriend, she finds therapists; and Jane becomes more and more fugitive, saying "I don't care about my parents, I'm independent."

BOSCOLO: For example, if someone leaves the family, the leaving can provoke different reactions in those who stay behind. A person who is left may start to have different feelings toward the person who went away, may start to feel "Maybe I love him" or "I care for her."

CECCHIN: But this is based on a premise. You must identify the premises in a system to have an idea of what is going on.

HOFFMAN: Well, here there seems to be a rule that if you leave, you are more loved then if you stay. Father came home to stay: he's less loved. Jane leaves: she's more loved. What about the boy? I don't see his part in this.

BOSCOLO: The boy is totally self-possessed. He feels very comfortable, for he's the only boy in the family. So he has a closeness with Mother and with Father. Father probably sees him as the next male in the family. And for Mother, he's a boy, so he's more important than the girls. He doesn't have to talk or run away.

HOFFMAN: Who cares more for Jane, Mother or Father?

CECCHIN: Both care for her. However, it would not be correct to say that the one who is the fugitive is more important. She is only important in the eyes of the one who stays. And the one who is the fugitive is jealous of the one who stays.

HOFFMAN: So we get to the premise: they are struggling to find a solution about staying and leaving. If you leave, it's not a solution—you're always coming back.

BOSCOLO: But if you stay, it's not a solution because everybody thinks more about you if you leave. Like the movie *L'Avventura*, where a man leaves and everybody searches for him; but the moment the woman finds him, she loses interest.

PENN: The premise in this family must be that leaving and staying must always alternate. Neither alone is a solution; both must exist, with one always replacing the other.

HOFFMAN: That could be an explanation of the pursuer-distancer cycle, where one partner is always trying to get hold of the other, who is always running away.

BOSCOLO: The problem is hard to define with a pursuer-distancer concept. It's a systemwide premise, not a couple premise. The whole system works to solve this problem, but any solution only increases the problem.

HOFFMAN: What you're saying is that the way this family stays close is through an alternation of doubt: "If I leave, will the one who stays be preferred? If I stay, will the one who leaves be preferred?" This oscillation continues, keeping everybody involved.

PENN: If you state this premise in terms of an internal recursion, it might sound like "In order to be preferred, I must leave; but if I am away too long, I must return to be sure I am preferred." If this is the premise you are trying to modify, one assumes that your questions will focus on these issues around staying and leaving.

CECCHIN: Yes. But we have to introduce a totally different idea, which is: Is there any possibility to get out of this circuit? They don't like to stay together, but they feel somehow they have to.

CECCHIN: I'm fascinated by the idea that each family with a problem has a basic premise, unique to them, that they have to resolve.

BOSCOLO: There is one basic premise that people must resolve around separation. If you accept the idea that relationships are not permanent— that mother and child is not a permanent relationship, that husband and wife is not permanent, that people die—that's a basic premise. People in enmeshed families try to deny this issue, or test it. They try to separate as an experiment, then come back to resolve the same issue; but in doing that, you often produce symptoms. The way death is lived within the system, the way it is perceived and experienced, is in relationship to a premise that has been established before the death. And the way it will be experienced in the future is in accordance with this premise. There are some premises about death that say that the person should not have died, and he or she is kept alive in some fashion. Or we see in some families that the dead one has a powerful pragmatic effect: "What would he think if he were alive?" or "What advice would my mother give to me if she were alive?"

HOFFMAN: Is this another example of the pseudofugitive, when people die and the family won't accept their death?

CECCHIN: Yes. When someone dies, he or she can become more important than when they were alive.

BOSCOLO: Let me give you an example. Five or six years ago, a woman came to us who was psychotic, paranoid. She became psychotic after her mother's death. This woman had some sisters, but it was never clear which of them the mother was closest to. So this woman was always unsure. Then her mother developed a tumor. Our patient left her husband and stayed in the hospital for a month, becoming a full-time nurse for her mother. She did much more than her sisters, and she always waited for her mother to show her approval. Before her mother died, she asked her, "What do you think of me?" I can't remember exactly what the mother said, but after saying it she died. After that, the woman became more and more delusional, ignored her husband, and finally became fully psychotic. We saw her alone and, in the first few sessions, she said she was in daily contact with her mother. Her mother sent her messages— how this should be, how that should be, what she should think—that kind of thing. The first question we asked her was: "What does your mother think about what we are doing here? Is she glad that we are taking care of you, or not?" She said, "Well, I'll have to talk to her, and maybe next session I'll tell you what my mother thinks." Throughout the therapy we included the mother because the mother had a tremendous pragmatic effect on the woman. She was dead, but this woman did everything in relationship to her. If we made an intervention, we would say that it was very important for her to tell us what her mother thought about the intervention.

In psychoanalytic literature, the premises explaining psychosis or schizophrenia are all around separation and death. For instance, a schizophrenic system has crazy premises about how to deal with separation. In our previous example, the mother is dead, but the daughter behaves as if she's alive.

HOFFMAN: No wonder so many family therapists have based their whole therapy on unresolved mourning. In many families the problem seems to be attached to somebody that is not allowed to die.

CECCHIN: You find out immediately that, in certain families, they are not able to resolve the impact of the death and it becomes a nodal point.

PENN: Even in instances like unforeseen chronic illness or accidental death, the premise in the system about how to deal with separation has to be addressed. The system has developed or continues a premise about separation that will adapt to any form of leaving or death.

BOSCOLO: Yes. If you talk in terms of Bateson's ideas about premises, you talk about structures laid down in childhood. They are "hard-programmed"; they explain how a person tends to repeat the same kind of relationship his parents had. If a person has had parents who separated or divorced, there's more of a probability that this marriage will divorce or separate. If a person had two parents who were overclose, he or she will tend to repeat this.

PENN: It's as if the system has to keep looking for an epistemological solution for some particular issue that was not achieved by the previous generations.

CECCHIN: I agree. For example, a woman might feel the need to divorce at age twenty-five because her mother divorced at twenty-five, but she didn't do a good job. Perhaps, if it had been a real divorce, the daughter wouldn't have to do it again. It was not the solution to the problem of being together or being separated, so it keeps going until the problem of how to be together or separated is resolved.

HOFFMAN: That's like the notion of karma.

BOSCOLO: If you say it's only imitation, divorcing because your parents divorced, you espouse the analytic concept of repetition compulsion. We say something different. We say you have to repeat what is already hard-programmed into the system, but with the aim of trying to resolve the issue, not continue it.

CECCHIN: From your experience in your family the first few years of life, you acquire a way of seeing the world, and this becomes a premise. This premise then becomes a self-fulfilling prophecy; you tend to re-create a world similar to the one you are in. But in terms of this family, if we ask them, "Who is going to be the first to leave the family? get married?" et cetera, then we are introducing an idea that their hard-programming does not allow. They are attempting to resolve the issue of how they can be together or not together, who can be fugitive, who can be distant, et cetera. When you ask future questions about this issue, you can see the family respond quickly because you have introduced the idea that the premise might change.

BOSCOLO: That is rare. Most times the interaction doesn't touch the premise. It's very hard to change a premise. As we said before, you have to hit bottom. That's why the prescription of a symptom can be effective—it gives a hint that things could be different. A statement like "Don't change, remain the same; be more anorectic, even though you might die" is the verbal equivalent of hitting bottom. By prescribing this absurdity, you suggest the possibility of a new opening.

HOFFMAN: At this point you decide to ask about how the children are growing up.

CECCHIN: Yes, and I start by asking if anyone else has a problem. To try to take the identified patient label off of Sue.

### FAMILY INTERVIEW

CECCHIN: [coming back in] Does anyone in the family, besides you, have problems?

SUE: I think Jane does.

CECCHIN: How do you see this problem?

SUE: If she's in a bad mood, she puts everyone in a bad mood. She doesn't care.

CECCHIN: You mean she has this influence on others?

SUE: *If she's upset about something, she'll yell at you. She'll yell at everyone and make everyone upset. Even in a department store, because Jane is in a hurry and everyone should know that—no patience.*

CECCHIN: *What about Kate?*

SUE: *Kate takes things seriously, she hides everything. And she has bad temper tantrums too: she goes crazy.*

CECCHIN: *And your brother?*

SUE: *He's picking up everyone's habits. Like, see, Kate. When I was at home, I couldn't touch the food if I was making the salad, and so the other night my dad was eating off of a spoon, and so Joe started, "I'm not eating. I don't want it. . . ."*

CECCHIN: *[to Father] How do you see your children growing up? Are you satisfied with the way they are growing up? Do you see any problems for the future? Let's talk about your son—how do you see him doing? As a father, what do you think of your son?*

FATHER: *I think he'll be okay. The girls—I have no idea.*

CECCHIN: *So you think he's growing up all right?*

FATHER: *Well, so far. He has his problems in school, but he's got a good business head.*

CECCHIN: *How does he get along with his friends? Does he have a good social life?*

FATHER: *Well, not yet. He plays hockey, he goes to the Y, the community center. He assimilates with other kids.*

MOTHER: *Not enough.*

CECCHIN: *Do you see him getting along with the other kids?*

FATHER: *He gets along, but he could expound on it a lot more than he does.*

CECCHIN: *Does he talk to girls? to boys?*

FATHER: *If he talks to girls, he does it very discreetly; but he doesn't want anybody to know that he talks to girls—he's shy. But you have to understand that my children are segregated, they went to parochial schools for so long.*

*[Father makes a digression on the subject of parochial schools.]*

CECCHIN: *How do you see Kate growing up?*

FATHER: *Kate? I don't see her too often. She leaves early and comes home late.*

CECCHIN: *Do you have an opinion? Do you see her growing pretty well?*

FATHER: *I would think no. I'm not satisfied, but there's not much I can do about it.*

CECCHIN: *What disappoints you? What dissatisfies you—her behavior?*

FATHER: *Well, she's strong-willed. They take after their mother: if you don't do things their way, they'll scream, rant, and rave, and probably end in an argument. I think she's pretty strong-willed, yeah.*

CECCHIN: *So you're not very satisfied with the way she is growing up?*

FATHER: *Is any father completely satisfied?*

CECCHIN: *Sometimes they feel very glad—*

FATHER: *Well, so far, no, I don't. I think she's good in school, but she has to learn to realize there are more important things than what she's been doing. If you put a pair of skis on her head, she'd be happy.*

CECCHIN: *How is she getting along with her friends?*

FATHER: *Well, I think she gets along fine with friends, provided they do what she wants them to do.*

CECCHIN: *She's bossy?*

FATHER: *Quite.*

CECCHIN: *A boyfriend?*

FATHER: *A whole bunch of them. They call at one, two, three in the morning— you name it. Last few weeks, last few months, it hasn't been so bad.*

CECCHIN: *You don't like that? You'd like her to settle down with one?*

FATHER: *No, I don't think so. I don't think she knows what she wants to do at this point; she's very oblivious as to how to do it.*

CECCHIN: *So she's kind of scatterbrained?*

FATHER: *Well, in a sense, yes.*

CECCHIN: *What about your other daughter? How do you see her growing up?*

FATHER: *I don't know what to tell you about her. It's like going to a gypsy and you look in a crystal ball: it's either cloudy or it's clear because of what day it is. That's Jane.*

CECCHIN: *She's twenty-five. [to Mother] Do you have an idea?*

MOTHER: *Kate, I think, has got problems. Okay, I'm not happy with what I've seen happening with Kate because she's got a lot going for her, but she's not using it to the right advantage for her. She knows what she wants, but she's not going about it in the right way to get it. She wants to go into the world of fashion. She's not working toward that goal: she's having a good time, and the day is going to come when she is going to want us to give her all this money to get her fashion career. Socially, Kate was stuck for a while. She seems to have moved on, but people use her. She is aware of it, but she isn't doing anything to be selective and have a relationship with people where nobody is using her and she's not using them. No, I'm not happy; I worry. But I think Kate maybe just has to grow up a little more and decide what she wants out of life and go about getting it in the right way. She doesn't work, and yet she's having a marvelous time. She's skiing all the time. I would like to see Kate settle down and say "I have to work." I would like her to show me that she can get a job, work, save some money, and show me that she's gonna deserve this education that she wants.*

CECCHIN: *What about your son?*

MOTHER: *Joe? Joe had problems. He had problems in school. He was not learning, he was doing what he wanted to do. He would not accept discipline in the school. Anyway, I created quite a scene. I demanded from the school, finally, that he be tested and see if his ability was average. It was, but he did not learn any of the basics. After fighting for three months, I got him into a learning assistance program, and now he is learning to accept responsibility. He still is not doing homework the way he should because he wants to get the marks. He's learning.*

CECCHIN: *What about Sue before she decided not to eat? How was she growing up till that point, at age seventeen or so?*

MOTHER: *All right, I'll tell you what it was with Sue. Sue was very good, always good, and the reason was because she saw Jane giving me problems; and I think at some point Sue decided, when she was very young, she was not going to give me problems, she was going to be good. And I don't know when that happened, but I bet that's what happened. And after that, I think Sue decided she wanted Jane to love her so much that when they had an argument Sue didn't argue back. Sue would go to her room and punish herself because it was her fault this argument happened. She was feeling a lot of guilt.*

CECCHIN: *When did you leave home the first time to go out and work?*

SUE: *My first job?*

CECCHIN: *When you left home. Weren't you out of your home for a while?*

SUE: *When I went to the university.*

MOTHER: *She left home when we had a terrible argument . . .*

CECCHIN: *Moving out—*

SUE: *First, at the university when I was eighteen; but when I first moved out of the house for a long period of time was when I was nineteen.*

CECCHIN: *You know, in families like yours, sometimes one of the children decides "I will stay close to my parents. When everybody moves out, I'll stay close to my parents." That child wants to be close to the mother, especially if there are problems. Which of your children, do you think, would stay home closer to you? Which of the four would make the decision not to leave but to stay close to the parents?*

FATHER: *None of them.*

MOTHER: *I don't think any of them would right now.*

CECCHIN: *If one had to stay, which one is most likely to stay?*

MOTHER: *Sue would be the one, because Sue wanted to assume the responsibility. When her anorexia began, it began because of a problem between her father and I. I understand it started long before that, but I think that when that happened, Sue's world was shattering. Her image of family was being shattered; the family has to be together, and I believe Sue decided she had to do something drastic to keep the family together, and she did. She stopped eating. She was always close to the one she felt needed her, without thinking about herself. And that's why Sue's sick.*

CECCHIN: *[to Jane] How do you see the relationship between your father and mother? Is it a friendly relationship? Are they friendly with their children? How do you see it through the years? What is your opinion?*

JANE: *They like each other and they know how to get along with each other. But from my point of view, I don't know why they're together, really, because their relationship is ridiculous. But they know how to live with each other, so they can live that way . . . they enjoy it, I think they really enjoy it.*

CECCHIN: *You said "I would never accept such a situation, but they enjoy it." When did you make that discovery? Is it a recent thought?*

JANE: *It's recent—when they were having problems. I wasn't even home. I was away living at the university, and I never really knew what was going on; and now, see, I never considered myself like that.*

CECCHIN: *Kate, what would you say?*

KATE: *Well, I would say I just thought about it recently because she told me about a couple of weeks ago. I asked her why she never goes out anywhere, because I know she likes to dance and go and have fun; and she said because if she does, then he'll get mad at her. And he's very jealous of her because whenever I go to exercise classes and I come home, even my girl friend asked me why he says "Where's your mother? Where is she? What's she doing?" when he knows where she is. He laughs, he knows he's foolish, he knows that she is coming home; but he does it all the time. The other day a man phoned and asked "Is Mrs. S there?" Yes, you were jealous. That's why you don't want her to go anywhere.*

CECCHIN: *Is your father jealous of men or women?*

MOTHER: *And women.*

KATE: *Men and women. He doesn't allow her to have any friends or anything like he does. [Inaudible, overtalking.]*

CECCHIN: *[to Kate] You talk so much about it that you don't want to think about it?*

MOTHER: *That's right. She has gotten so involved . . .*

KATE: *Gives me a headache to think about it.*

CECCHIN: *[to Joe] What about you?*

JOE: *[after a long pause] If he doesn't want to go out, he doesn't have to go out.*

CECCHIN: *How do you see your dad and mother as a couple? They are married, they stay together.*

JOE: *[silence]*

MOTHER: *Speak.*

JOE: *It's— [hesitates]*

FATHER: *Don't look at me.*

CECCHIN: *You agree with Jane, Kate, or Sue?*

JOE: *Kate.*

FATHER: *Are you saying that to give the doctor an answer or is that your own opinion?*

MOTHER: *Can I interject here for a minute? I believe he does feel like Kate, because a few months ago when I wanted to go to a movie and Harold didn't want to go, I remember Joe saying to him "Why don't you take Mom to a show?"*

JOE: *I did?*

MOTHER: *This happened, and it really affected me because—*

CECCHIN: *Before you said "My husband is jealous of women." Which women?*

MOTHER: *Oh, my girl friends, any of my girl friends that I talk to. If we start having an argument, he'll say, "Go phone Louise, go phone Mary," whichever one of them happens to be closer.*

SUE: *That's 'cause he doesn't have any friends to talk to.*

CECCHIN: We've heard Kate saying that her father is jealous of her mother, that he wants her present all the time. When she's out, he keeps saying, "Where's my wife?" This information could make you think more and more in terms of the hypothesis that Sue and Father are in competition for Mother and that they are in a symptomatic escalation now that Father has stopped working and is in the house all day.

HOFFMAN: Did you know at the time that the father had retired?

CECCHIN: No, this is in hindsight. This father had sold his business, or lost it, several times, and he had also sold the family home a couple of times, much to the mother's distress. One gets the impression that her family is quite wealthy; also, he had at times apparently made a lot of money, so that he doesn't really have to work. But this behavior is apparently very aggravating to the mother.

HOFFMAN: You have another piece of evidence for your theory, which is that Father is not only competing with Sue for Mother's attention, but with the women who are Mother's friends.

CECCHIN: Yes. A good question to have asked would be: "How about Sue? Is she jealous of Mother's friends, too?" This would further validate the hypothesis that Father and Sue are both trying to get a bigger share of Mother.

HOFFMAN: It's interesting that in your hypothesis making, you leave out the information around the marriage, when the mother says that Sue's anorexia began when she and the father were quarreling a lot, and offers her own hypothesis—or maybe she is just quoting one of the therapists they had seen—that Sue got sick to keep the family together.

CECCHIN: That hypothesis could be true, but it is only one punctuation. It seems to be a more popular one with American family therapists.

HOFFMAN: Yes, it's as though we have a built-in idea that the symptom helps to keep the family together, through being a kind of glue for the parents' marriage. You tend to assume that having a share of the mother is the motivation for the same events. And I think you place much more of an emphasis on the sibling group competition, which now also includes the father.

CECCHIN: I agree that this is a difference between the way we tend to think and the way you think over here. But we are more and more leaving these triadic hypotheses behind to look for a system-wide premise like the one about staying or leaving.

HOFFMAN: Here you go on to ask about the context of therapy.

CECCHIN: Yes, we had decided during the last break to include that question after the one about the children growing up.

FAMILY INTERVIEW

CECCHIN: *This brings up a problem regarding therapy. Your family has been participating in many different therapies, so some of you must be disappointed. Who in the family is more disappointed with therapy?*

SUE: *I think Jane is.*

JANE: *I think I am.*

FATHER: *What kind of therapy?*

CECCHIN: *Any kind of therapy; you must have seen eight or ten people by now.*

FATHER: *They've been trying to treat us. Not us—I shouldn't say that. They've been trying to treat her for something they know nothing about. First of all, the doctors she originally went to—the original doctor here—they knew as much about anorexia as I know about electrical mechanics: zero. The doctors didn't know what they were talking about.*

CECCHIN: *What about in the other city?*

FATHER: *There the doctors knew what to do, they didn't fool around. They treated Sue. They said: "This is the way it is and this is what you're going to have to do; and if you don't do it. . . ." You work on a merit system, you have privileges.*

CECCHIN: *[to Sue] What is your opinion?*

SUE: *Oh, they knew how to handle it.*

FATHER: *But where did they know how to handle it? They had experienced the anorectic patients, they had experience with it.*

CECCHIN: *Yes, but that experience didn't work.*

FATHER: *Oh, the experience worked. But don't you understand, Doctor? When I phoned her doctor, I phoned her therapist, they were well aware of what her problem was. They had said to me that she wants to go home; they have gone as far as they can go with her. She has gained weight, she is in a good frame of mind, and she can go home provided that therapy is available, that she can continue with the anorectic therapy. We brought her back here, which was the worst thing in the world, because the doctors here have no idea of what the problem is; and if they do know what the problem is, they don't know how to treat it because they've never seen it; if they've seen it, they can't recognize what it is.*

CECCHIN: *Did you think about going back to the city?*

FATHER: *I told Sue to go back to the city. She doesn't want to go back because she knows they can help her, so she is fighting the anorectic condition. [to Sue] This is my opinion, not yours. The first time I told you to go back, you said you're not going back: "I'm not staying here." And when I got to the city to bring her back, I told her "Sue, things have not changed at home. You have to learn to live and accept things the way they are because people are not going to change for you; they just won't do it." She said "I understand." Did you not say that? "I understand. I'm better. I think with the therapy available, I'll get better." Did you not say that, Sue?*

SUE: *Well, you talk for me, you know exactly what I'm thinking.*

FATHER: *Did you not say that?*

SUE: *Hm-mm.*

FATHER: *And then when she came home, the proper help was not available here. The therapists here do not know how to handle it.*

CECCHIN: *What kind of expectations do you have? What would you like therapy to do?*

FATHER: *Well, it's not what I expect, it's what I've been told. These people are supposedly the top authorities in this country on anorectic recovery, who have been trained by a supposedly . . . again, I never met the lady. Do you know of a Dr. Bruch, Dr. Hilde Bruch in Houston, Texas? She is supposedly an authority on anorexia. My wife and my daughter went to Houston, they saw her. She then recommended a clinic in Canada, which we did send her to, and, by all means, she did progress. And when I went to bring her home, she looked good. But they also told us that she had to have proper therapy.*

CECCHIN: *Would you like her to get back to that therapy?*

FATHER: *If the therapy were available here, I would say fine; but she cannot find anybody here to relate to the problems that she has.*

CECCHIN: *What opinion do you have of the therapy?*

MOTHER: *[to Sue] Would you express your opinion on the therapist you're seeing now?*

CECCHIN: *Perhaps we don't need all the details. It's important, but perhaps it's better to know the general view. Who at the moment is the most disappointed with the therapeutic situation?*

SUE: *I am. They don't know beans, the different doctors.*

CECCHIN: *You are the most disappointed of all?*

SUE: *Well, I don't think they should be practicing medicine.*

CECCHIN: *What kind of expectations do you have? Do you still hope that somebody can help you or are you giving up?*

FATHER: *Did the doctors in the city help you?*

SUE: *No. Mrs. R did. The doctors fed me.*

CECCHIN: *No. Your position is that no one could help you, right?*

SUE: *Yes, a therapist could help me in another city, and I'm calling her today. Here, they don't understand anorectics because they don't work with them on a daily basis. So when you try to explain something to someone, they take it for what you said; they don't take it that maybe it's the anorexia . . .*

CECCHIN: *So you still have a little hope?*

SUE: *Well, of course I have. I'd be dead now, I would imagine.*

CECCHIN: *You're very disappointed, but you still have hope?*

SUE: *I'm angry, probably at myself more than anybody else, because if I had made up my mind to get better a long time ago, I wouldn't be sick.*

FATHER: *Do you also think that if you had stayed in the city, you'd be—*

SUE: *No. I think if I had come home and not moved back into the house, and moved into my own apartment immediately, I never would have gotten caught up in the web again.*

FATHER: *But you were aware of what was going to happen when you came home.*

CECCHIN: *[to Mother] What about you? What is your feeling about therapy?*

MOTHER: *I'm terribly disappointed about the therapy here. She is seeing a therapist now, and he is trying to help her, but he does not understand anorexia at all. He is trying to help her as a person with an illness: but she is two people. The anorexia always comes out, and he doesn't understand it. In the city, the therapist she had at the clinic went out and interviewed many therapists before they decided on a therapist they felt could help her.*

---

BOSCOLO: We usually give names to our families in order to remember them. This one we called the Tea Party Family because in the sessions we noticed they were always smiling, looking at each other, and feeling very comfortable. You can observe a splitting between the verbal messages and the analogical messages in the family. Verbally, they talk about problems, symptoms, disappointments, et cetera; but, analogically, they seem very happy, very close.

CECCHIN: They imply "Even though we are in serious trouble, we can laugh about it." The therapist cannot respond to either message without disqualifying one of them.

BOSCOLO: If our hypothesis fits this family, then the therapist may join the tea party with the aim of engaging the family. However, at a certain point he must change the tone between himself and the family. He must introduce some drama in order to break the game. Otherwise, this tea-party talk could go on forever.

CECCHIN: They're united against any kind of therapeutic intervention. Father protects this family from any outside interference, so that every therapist is regarded as bad and not helpful. But instead of getting derailed by the content, we ask: "Do you feel disappointed? When did you decide it was bad? When did you decide you had no hope?" At this point, in response to the questioning, Sue said, "If I had made up my mind to get better, I wouldn't be sick." This is contrary to the family's negative perceptions of therapy.

BOSCOLO: Sue said at one point she had seen thirty doctors. You can see two systems evolving here: the "family system" and the "system of therapists." The therapists, by definition, have the goal of changing the family. But in this case the family says the therapist should change since they are not being helpful or competent. So we must ask: Why does the family continue to look for therapists if they are all incompetent?

Usually what a family wants from a therapist is for him or her to change the patient, but not the family game. When the family game changes, then, automatically, there is no longer a patient and no need for a therapist. What can happen over time with a family and therapist is that the family becomes attached to the therapist and the therapist becomes like a family member. Once the therapist becomes part of the family, the family can't change; because if it changes, it loses the therapist. So, in time, the therapist becomes essential. That's why some therapies become interminable.

CECCHIN: In this case, it's different. You describe a family where they want the therapist to become a Dr. Homeostat who will keep the family the same. But this family finds one therapist after another, all over the country, and eats them up, digests them, and throws them out. And if you are prestigious, the meal becomes more exciting. It's striking, the way the parents compete for therapists around Sue's problem. If Mother likes them, Father doesn't; if Father approves, Mother disapproves. In order to really go into therapy, both would have to agree; but they only agree on the fact that the therapist is never right. If they agree, they go against the rule of the system, which is: they are never to agree.

BOSCOLO: This point of Cecchin's, about the parents' inability to agree, is an interesting one. When we see parents continuing to disagree on how to raise their children, sometimes our first intervention is this: "We see that both of you disagree on how to deal with John or Mary, and each thinks his or her way is best. Now, we think that both of your ways are very good, excellent ways to deal with John . . . but only if you were separated. For instance, if John were with you, your way would be best; or, if John were with Mother, her way would be best. The problem here is that you disagree. So the only thing we can offer is this, and you will have to carry it out. If you agree to do it, we will give you a prescription, we will tell you what to do. And this is the only condition for therapy; otherwise it is useless. Go home now and don't discuss this with each other. In a week or two, you must come back, having decided whether or not to accept our prescription. If you agree, we will start therapy."

CECCHIN: If they agree, this is the prescription: On Monday, Father takes care of the child; on Tuesday, Mother, et cetera, alternating the days of the week. You remind them that they are perfect as long as the other one is not there. Of course, they agree with that. Now they are doing something you told them and they are obeying your rule.

BOSCOLO: But once they have agreed to come in and follow your prescription, they have already changed the rule of their relationship.

## FAMILY INTERVIEW

CECCHIN: *[to Sue] Were you disappointed in therapy too?*

SUE: *I don't know.*

CECCHIN: *I see that everybody came here today. How was that possible? Who insisted most on coming?*

FATHER: *These two were very reluctant.*

CECCHIN: *Who insisted most that they come?*

FATHER: *Their mother. This was a big argument for two days. It just about led to blows. It did lead to blows in one instance. She [unclear which one] threw a plate at her [unclear].*

CECCHIN: *So it is your wife who is more—*

FATHER: *My wife is looking for a rainbow.*

MOTHER: *I am not, Harold! I know it's going to take a long time, but I've got to have help.*

CECCHIN: *What about your son?*

FATHER: *He didn't give a damn. But I told him we're going to go, and he said "Fine." Don't forget that when you're dealing with the three girls, you're dealing with three young adults with minds of their own; and if they want to come, they'll come; and if they don't want to come, stand on your head, and they won't come.*

CECCHIN: *How did your wife succeed this time?*

FATHER: *I don't know if she succeeded or not. They came under duress.*

CECCHIN: *What about you?*

FATHER: *Me? It makes no difference. I think it's a waste of time, for the simple reason that I don't think—and I still have to be proven wrong—that if they would show me a little bit of hope that they know how to treat an anorectic, then I'm all for it. But so far they've struck out one hundred percent. They have not even tried to come close to what the problem is.*

CECCHIN: *I would like to have a discussion now with my colleague. [Exits.]*

---

HOFFMAN: What did you talk about during the break?

CECCHIN: We mostly discussed the relationship between the family and the therapists, including the consultants. In the beginning of our work, the hypothesis was related to the dynamics of the family only, but now we include in our hypothesis the relationship between the family and the therapist. This is a very important part of the hypothesis. In the past, when we neglected it, we had failures.

PENN: It's true that yours is the only method in the family field that explicitly addresses the therapists' own context and the context of the other professionals.

BOSCOLO: Yes. We try to take into account three levels. One level is the family system. The second is the relationship between the family and the therapist, and the third is the family/therapist/consultant loop. It's very complicated to design an intervention that takes into account all three. In the case of a family like this, we might give the message that we were confused. We might say "One of us thinks one thing and the other thinks the opposite, and we don't know which way is best." Or I could say "There is something I am in disagreement about with my partner. I don't think that you parents will ever agree on therapy. Of course, any therapy you both agree on would be effective, but I doubt you'll ever agree. You'll just keep going to therapy without agreeing."

PENN: In that way you put the parents in a small bind. If they disagree with you, then they agree, and if they don't agree, they are saying they can agree on therapy.

CECCHIN: We could say "You have a problem, and we could help you if you trusted therapy; but because of your experience, that is very difficult for you. Therefore, what I say you won't trust, because you don't trust therapy. So we are in a bad situation. We would like to share our conclusions, but you don't trust us. We understand. However, I'm going to tell you anyway." We essentially say they are immune to therapy.

BOSCOLO: I remember another intervention we made in a family with an anorectic. The whole family believed she was anorectic because she was not happy with her job. We decided that what we had to respond to was the family's explanation for her anorexia. So we said: "We have had a discussion and we see that all of you feel she started not eating because of her work. We agree that this is very possible. Of course, if it is not due to her work we would say something very different—but we agree that this explanation is the most probable. Now, the problem at this point is that we can't do therapy." The family looks at us—after all, it is the first session. We continue: "It would be useless for us to do therapy. What we recommend is that she get fired or quit her work. If she quits her work and the problem is due to that, then the problem will be gone. Only if she quits work and nothing improves will we offer you another session." We stop there and ask the family to call us if this happens.

About six months later we receive a phone call from Mother requesting a session. I ask Mother how things are, and she says her daughter is going to get married soon and the mother is afraid she will start not eating again. I ask how her weight is. The mother says it is perfect. I ask if she has quit her job. The mother says no, but she is doing fine; there are no problems and she is very happy. The mother then asks to see us for "preventive" reasons—in case she ever has the same problem again. I say that we can't do preventive therapy because we cannot know what will happen in the future. That was the end. In this case it was important to target the relationship between the family and therapy.

HOFFMAN: I remember you once spoke about the political situation in Italy in the seventies. The mental hospitals had been closed and psychiatrists were thought of as agents of social control. You told us that this contributed to your becoming acutely aware of the therapeutic context.

BOSCOLO: Yes. I was trained as a doctor in the U.S., and when I went back to Italy and met with Italian psychiatrists, I felt as if I had come from another world. In the States, I had learned to understand patients, to diagnose, and to do therapy, while in Italy there was an antipsychiatric revolution. It was important to look at patients with symptoms at another level, the level of society. It took some time to integrate these two levels, and I think this has had an effect on our work. As a result, we are extremely sensitive to different levels of systems: individual, family, society, and the interactions between all these levels.

CECCHIN: In the U.S. during the seventies, there was no awareness that the action of every person contributes to the whole. In Italy it was very clear that everything you do is a political action. Therefore, when a patient has a problem and you have to lock him up, it's a political action.

PENN: What's interesting is that you didn't end by taking a position like Laing, saying that the schizophrenic is good and the psychiatrist is bad; you emerged with an appreciation of the relationship between the two.

BOSCOLO: I agree. At the time I was reading Bateson and was familiar with the positions of Szasz and Laing. But if you work with Bateson's ideas, you think in terms of punctuation. Traditional psychiatry punctuates problems in a particular way. The organic psychiatrist sees problems deriving from biochemistry or from genetics. The psychoanalyst sees problems coming from the first few years of childhood. These are linear-causal punctuations. Laing put this punctuation upside down. He said (as the antipsychiatric movement did in Italy) that the individual has a problem because society is sick and that the healthy people are the ones in the psychiatric hospitals. This pushed us toward the concept of a metalevel.

PENN: At that time, were you with Selvini?

BOSCOLO: No, not until 1967. In 1968 the first conference in Italy on family therapy was organized by the group that Mara and I were part of in Milan. The conference took place in southern Italy and the foreign guests were Nathan Ackerman and Ronald Laing. The Italian psychiatrists that attended were mostly Marxists, and they attacked Ackerman because he was only concerned with the level of family dynamics. Ackerman felt that psychiatrists should help those who were sick with their sickness. But the other people were very sympathetic to Laing and his punctuation. I was very confused, but it was then that I began to understand the importance of different levels.

Our first trainees in 1977 were very knowledgeable in psychiatry and psychoanalysis, and they also belonged to this antipsychiatric movement. In fact, they were in the forefront—very sophisticated. When they first came to us, they said "We have come here because we have been part of a social revolution, and now we need to have some technical instruments so that we can treat the patients who don't get better. Psychoanalysis is no good because it's bourgeois."

CECCHIN: For them, it was always a dichotomy: you are either a Marxist or a bourgeois; you cannot not be political. It's similar to the idea that you cannot not communicate. They felt you have to be on one side or the other, even if you don't say anything. So they came to us and said: "We don't know which side you're on, but we don't want to know. We only care about your techniques." The point is that, slowly, they found we offered a third solution: through technique, you reach epistemology; through technique, you learn to think. But the fact that we were not Marxists and that they had to come to a private center and pay to learn was very hard on them.

HOFFMAN: Why were they so interested in your techniques?

BOSCOLO: They didn't believe in individual psychotherapy. They too thought in terms of "systems," and family therapy seemed to be congruent with their philosophy.

CECCHIN: In that 1968 conference, Ackerman was seen as a reactionary because he said: "I saw this couple for two or three years. Before I saw them, they really didn't enjoy sleeping together, and now they do. I consider this a big success." The people at the conference said: "This is a sad story. It's ridiculous for a human being to spend two or three years helping other people to sleep together. That's like saying that a normal family is one that fits the American system. And what's the American system? The system that supports the multinational corporation that needs to sell something to this family." Because they felt that Ackerman was in the service of this system, they couldn't accept his ideas.

BOSCOLO: I think Ackerman was just unlucky. The husband in the session he presented worked for IBM, so when Ackerman showed the tape, suddenly there were two hundred people screaming "That's a success? Because he makes a quickie with his wife while he makes missiles to kill the Vietnamese?" And Ackerman, who was a master of big groups, said, "I agree with you," and they quieted down. He said: "I agree about Vietnam, missiles, IBM. But the only weapon I have is a vote. You might have revolutions, but in America the only thing I can do against the Vietnam policy is vote." So everyone started to laugh a little. He said, "Every time I go to vote, I assure you I'm against IBM, et cetera." He was a master. He said: "I take issue with you that the couple sleeping together is not a result. To me, it is a result. The wife had not been able to make love for three years. After they could make love, the wife had a child. To me, to make love is better than not to make love. That is my bias. To me, it is a result."

But his bias was my bias too. I had trained for seven years in the United States to become a psychiatrist, a psychoanalyst, and I realized when I went back to Italy that I was thinking in terms of dyads: the therapist and the patient. In Italy it became a triad: family, therapist, and society; and the therapist was at the interface between the family and society. Then I began to understand the dilemma for the therapist. The therapist, often not conscious of what he is doing, may introduce societal norms to the patient, or ally with society against the patient, or ally with the patient against society. The Marxists were aware of these possibilities too.

HOFFMAN: What you picked up was that the therapist could restabilize the system in such a way that the problem never went away. In other words, he or she could make it just tolerable for the problem to continue—with medication, sessions, et cetera. It would be a leap of thinking to consider the psychiatrist as homeostatic, one who preserves the game.

BOSCOLO: The way we got to the problem of the referring person—from our paper of the same name (Selvini Palazzoli, Boscolo, Cecchin, and Prata, 1980)—was in coming up against cases where there was no motivation for treatment or where we couldn't collect the information. We tried to find a hypothesis to justify this behavior in the nuclear and the extended family system, but we couldn't. Then we had a flash. We recognized that the behavior of the family could be explained by the relationship to the family of the referring doctor. For instance, the family might be very attached to the referring doctor and the referring doctor might feel very important in treating their case. Even though she sent the family to us, she remained very important. And the family couldn't tell us why they were reluctant to come because they didn't want to give us the message "We don't want you" or to offend the referring doctor. So the family would stay with us, but without getting engaged. That's when we made the hypothesis about the referring person.

CECCHIN: The referring persons, whether we're talking about an individual or an agency, are not bad. They are in this business for the purpose of helping people. But sometimes such a group evolves into an institution whose main purpose is its own survival. People spend their time in meetings, talking to each other, gossiping. They forget about the patient; the patient becomes secondary. It's a natural process. One shouldn't see it negatively, that the institution is bad or that they're trying to kill people. It's obvious that the institution helps the patient and the patient helps the institution.

PENN: The first "problem" to treat would be the homeostatic effect of the other professionals.

BOSCOLO: Yes. For example, if the therapist needs to survive as a therapist, he or she has to help people. If the therapist is to remain in his or her position, the patient must remain in his. That's the usual basis for a stuck therapy. In this case, instead of beginning the session by saying "What's the problem now?" we say "What happened to your system that you got yourself into the position of needing therapists? What happened to your self-healing capacity that you need someone else to take care of you?" You get the history of everyone else who entered the system as a therapist and further complicated the problem. Then the whole thing begins to make sense.

HOFFMAN: Let's get back to the intervention. Since we will not be including the team discussion, we will have to ask you how you arrived at it later.


### INTERVENTION

CECCHIN: [coming back in] Let us share our observations with you. In this family, we see much division among the four children. Sue has always been in a conflict with Kate, Kate with Jane, et cetera, so that the three girls have never been unified. And your son is isolated from his sisters; he stays with his father, perhaps because Mother is not close to Father. We know from our experience that if the girls get together, it's easier for them to grow up and leave the family, be independent, and lead their own lives. But when the children are divided, as in your family, there is a reason behind it. The reason is that they believe if they remain divided, they will not have to grow up and leave. So they remain little children because they feel their parents still need them. In order to be sure their parents are not lonely, the children don't get along with each other. This keeps the parents focused on them and their problems in growing up, and not on their own loneliness.

However, in this family there is some confusion. In this family, the parents have their own disagreements, but the way they live together could go on forever without changing. Father is jealous of Mother, Mother doesn't agree with Father, but somehow they still have a life together that will never change: it will always be the same. But the children have it in their mind that, without them, the parents would not know what to do. This is a tremendous misunderstanding between the parents and the children. It's not a question of anorexia, because if Sue didn't have anorexia, one of the other children would have some other problem. She developed anorexia because she was the most sensitive one at the moment. If she didn't have anorexia, maybe Joe would have problems—perhaps a problem at school or behavior problems—who can say? The important thing is that the four children cannot get together to leave home as long as they have this idea that they must do something for their parents, who in our opinion don't need their help. You have a good relationship—you fight and enjoy fighting, you enjoy your disagreements—you don't want to separate. Jane understands this because she said "They enjoy their fighting. That's how they get along."

Now we have a problem. If we were in Milan with a family like yours, we would ask the four children to come back for a session in order to understand how they have this idea that their parents can't be without them. And it isn't only Sue who has this idea that she must stay with her parents, it's all four of them.

FATHER: You're giving them ideas. Next week we could be in Milan.

MOTHER: No, it's true.

CECCHIN: If we were to ask Father and Mother to come without the children, we would see that all the messages you give to the children support this belief, perhaps without knowing it. But the messages are clear: Stay around, don't leave us, we need you, we don't get along with each other, et cetera. You probably give this message without wanting to. After all, you have your own life without the children, your own style. Since we are going to be here for three days, our proposal is that we would like you to go home and think over what we have said. If you decide you want to continue, we will give you the opportunity to make the following choice: either all four children come back here for half an hour to talk to us about their problem with their father and mother, or you, Father and Mother, come back and discuss the problem. We are indifferent as to who comes, the parents or the children.

MOTHER: Not all of us together? Just one or the other? Well, I think it's more important for the children.

CECCHIN: Don't discuss it now. Go home and think about it. We will give you this *opportunity; that's what we would do in Milan. We are going to be here until Saturday, so you have time.*

FATHER: *What about Sue?*

CECCHIN: *Sue has to decide at the moment if she will give up this problem.*

FATHER: *Well, for how long?*

CECCHIN: *There is no doctor, nobody who can make that decision for her.*

MOTHER: *So, in other words, if the family problem gets better . . .*

CECCHIN: *If this conviction of the four children that they must do something for their parents goes away . . .*

FATHER: *We planned on going to California next week, just my wife and I and my son were going. [to Mother] You know that, two weeks ago, two of them decided they were coming with us.*

SUE: *Not two weeks ago, so sorry. I've been going since December. [Family gets up to leave.]*

CECCHIN: *[to Mother] How come your son didn't decide to stay home with them? How come the two of you have to go with one of your children?*

*[Family exits session in a good mood. Mother says to Cecchin: "You should stay here."]*

---

HOFFMAN: What was the reasoning that went into this intervention?

CECCHIN: Since they dislike therapists, this is like a test of trust. If we were in Milan, we would ask them to come back, to see if they would or not. We would say "We have some ideas that explain what's going on, especially how the children have divided the parents."

PENN: It's the same idea: they must agree on a decision to come back or not.

CECCHIN: Yes. In this case, if the children come back, we would try to help them get rid of their crazy idea. But they have to make the decision.

HOFFMAN: You also put the family in a position where they can't avoid differentiating along the generation line. Whether the parents come or the children come, the point is made. Or even if nobody comes. Would you call this a structural move?

CECCHIN: No, because we aren't at this point thinking primarily in terms of the family dynamics. We are focusing on therapist/family dynamics. Somebody else has always made the decisions for them about therapy. That's why you have the tea-party effect. The therapist pushes and pushes and they just sit and joke. We are saying "We aren't sure what to do because we aren't in Milan. And we will only be here till Saturday. But if you like we will see either the two parents or the four children. You decide. It's up to you."

HOFFMAN: By leaving everything up to the therapist, the couple's disagreement over therapy doesn't have to surface either.

CECCHIN: That's right. The mother takes the initiative, the father goes along, but there's never any resolution of their basic split. If they come in, they will have had to deal with that split, because they have to agree to come in. And if they don't come in, they will have dealt with the split in another way.

PENN: This intervention asks them to agree on which subsystem will come to see you. In making that decision, it would be hard for their old normal divisions to take place. I see them as positioned by the intervention to do something different.

BOSCOLO: Yes, the therapist is asking them to choose. But the therapist must remain neutral. This is essential because sometimes a family therapist, without being aware of it, may be on the side of the parents against the children or the children against the parents. Or the therapist may prefer one outcome more than another. It's important for him to be genuinely indifferent.

## Session 2

HOFFMAN: Since we are not going to include the transcript of this session except for the end, could you tell us what happened?

CECCHIN: The parents came in alone. It was two days later. There was some good feedback about the last session in that they all went out to eat afterward and, unlike their usual pattern, didn't have an argument.

BOSCOLO: We had decided to get more information about the extended family. It became even clearer that Mother was extremely tied in with her mother and sisters, even though the father got along better with the grandmother than she did. The mother said that her mother was jealous of her sisters, who had married successful men. It looked as though the grandmother felt more comfortable with this daughter because she had so many troubles. This was when we found out that the father had a history of starting businesses and selling them when they weren't successful. Sometimes he would also sell the family house. Even though he had apparently made money doing this, the mother wasn't too happy with him. He was not working at the time we saw the family, and she felt he should work. The grandmother had told the mother she was afraid the husband was getting "mental" from sitting in the house all day without enough to do.

CECCHIN: We asked about the way the children fit in, and it seems that they are always around so that the couple is hardly ever alone. I ask the question "Which of you gives more messages to the children, 'Come in and exploit the situation' ?" And they both agreed that the children constantly take advantage of both of them. During our break, we took the idea that the children believe that the parents would separate if they didn't interfere and made it the framework within which to prescribe a "secret couple" ritual, where the parents go out secretly and alone.* Here is the transcript of the last part of the interview.

## INTERVENTION

CECCHIN: *What we saw the last time is that the situation is rather serious—more serious than perhaps you perceive it. For the children, it is a dangerous situation. Sue has a problem around eating. The other girls present a kind of irresponsible behavior—living without any sense of reality is a very dangerous situation for the children. Why? Because they have the idea that, without them, without their behavior, without their presence, the two of you could not stay together. That's their idea. What we see is that the two of you have found a way of life, a marriage; the two of you have no complaints about each other. We also see that you do not present yourselves as a fantastic couple; you do not show everybody what a successful couple you are. We see that's very good for your mother-in-law because she tends to be kind of jealous. You are the preferred daughter, and the fact that you have problems can be helpful to her. But we see that this kind of situation is not very good for the children. It's a serious situation. So now we have a suggestion to give, a kind of ritual. For the next several months—let's say six months—we don't think it's important for you to come to family therapy; we think it's important for you to stop. However, you should do one thing: once a week the two of you should choose a couple of days, without saying anything to the children, and take a trip somewhere. Just disappear from circulation. You can leave a note on the table saying "We are going to be out until Tuesday at five."*

FATHER: *She would never do that.*

CECCHIN: *We know it's extremely difficult; it's difficult for her, and difficult for you too.*

FATHER: *Because I'll give you an example. Let me explain for a second. We're going*

* This is a version of the "invariant prescription" used by Selvini Palazzoli and Prata in a research study they have been conducting (Simon, 1987).

*away next Thursday. Jane has said already to stock the fridge, make sure every-thing is there.*

CECCHIN: *But you say nothing. You can stock the fridge before you go if you want to make sure they don't die of hunger. But they should know nothing about it. And then the two of you disappear. You don't have to go around and enjoy yourself; you can even go to different places for those two days if you don't like to stay together. The important thing is that they receive the message that the two of you are doing something they don't know about. This is very important. It is based on our experience with situations like yours.*

FATHER: *Good idea. I like that idea.*

CECCHIN: *And when you come back, you arrive five o'clock Tuesday. They will ask you "Where have you been? What did you do?" If they ask you, you say "What we did is our business."*

FATHER: *I left home the other day for an hour or for two hours, and my son came to me and said "Where were you?" I said "None of your business." My wife then said "Why can't you tell him where you were?"*

CECCHIN: *If you are together, you say "It's my husband's and my business." I know it's a sacrifice, but it's necessary for you to do this. Perhaps you don't perceive how dramatic the situation is.*

FATHER: *I perceived it a long time ago.*

CECCHIN: *So you "choose" to take a trip every three or four weeks; you prepare beforehand and then disappear without saying anything. The important thing is that they don't know what you do. And when you are out you don't have to enjoy each other. Suppose you don't feel like staying together: you can go in one town and you can go in another, visit friends, even stay together . . . anything. The important thing is they shouldn't know where you are. Don't go to visit your sister because then your sister will tell them where you are. You must only see people who won't say anything. When you go home now there are two possibilities. If they ask you about this meeting, you can say "Dr. Cecchin told us we cannot say anything about what has been said during the session. He told us that we shouldn't say anything about it."*

MOTHER: *But what about Sue? Sue doesn't live at home. Will she get better?*

CECCHIN: *Yes. We have the experience that if people are successful, many problems go away. In 80 percent of the situations where we saw families like yours, if the parents were able to do this, they were successful. There is a chance that a problem like Sue's would get better even if she were not at home because she knows everything that happens at home. She left home because her sister came back; everything she does is in relation to what happens at home. She will know about it; you don't have to tell her.*

MOTHER: *I don't even have to phone and say "We're going out of town for a few days"? Just don't say anything to Sue?*

CECCHIN: *To anybody. Perhaps you can say to them "Let Sue know."*

MOTHER: *Oh, let the children tell Sue that we've gone away?*

CECCHIN: *Yes. But you mustn't instruct them because then it becomes: "Where are*

*you going? Why do you call them and not me? I should be treated like them."*
*If Sue's not present, one of the children will take charge of advising her. My*
*colleague was saying it's important not to go anyplace where others may tell the*
*children, so it's better to find other solutions. The important thing is to go home*
*and say "Dr. Cecchin told us this is something that should be kept between him*
*and us."*

FATHER: *They won't ask us what happened.*

MOTHER: *Oh yes, they will, and Sue will be phoning to find out what happened.*

CECCHIN: *So then, in four or five months from now, you call up Dr. H [therapist].*
*You come back with some notes on the reaction of the children to this kind of*
*behavior. Each of you notices something—perhaps somebody broke the lamp.*
*So you take notes without saying anything to each other, and then you bring all*
*this material to Dr. H in five or six months, and she'll be in contact with us.*

MOTHER: *Do you mean that just by doing this, these children are going to grow*
*independent and go their own way and Sue will start eating?*

CECCHIN: *Eighty percent do. But this is extremely difficult.*

MOTHER: *How will that make Sue get better? How will she start eating?*

CECCHIN: *Sue is like the others who come between you. Sue said, "Mommy, let's*
*stay together, you and me." She wanted to separate you and your husband.*

FATHER: *In utopia.*

MOTHER: *They're jealous because he and I are together.*

CECCHIN: *She's stuck in this fantasy that the two of you cannot live together alone.*

MOTHER: *And when they see that we are . . .*

CECCHIN: *That you are together—you don't have to show you are together . . .*

MOTHER: *And then . . . ?*

FATHER: *They're on their own. We're gone. They don't even know where we are.*

CECCHIN: *However, if you really get together, it might be dangerous for your mother.*
*She might not have such a comfortable relationship with your husband or feel*
*so needed by you. That's why I'm saying it's good that you don't show it. Don't*
*worry if you don't enjoy your husband and if you don't enjoy your wife during*
*these two days. Perhaps you'll get bored with each other, will go to different*
*places.*

MOTHER: *And you're going to keep in touch with Dr. H?*

CECCHIN: *Dr. H wants you to call in four or five months to see if you succeeded or*
*not. You can tell her if you've succeeded or not.*

MOTHER: *Tell me, with Sue and her therapist, how should we be reacting? Should*
*we not be involved with Sue?*

CECCHIN: *You say "You're going to a therapist. It's your problem; don't tell me*
*anything about it."*

FATHER: *My wife gets involved.*

CECCHIN: *Let Sue take care of her therapy.*

MOTHER: *By herself, and me not to be involved.*

CECCHIN: *If she says "I don't like my therapist," you have to say "That's your*
*problem."*

MOTHER: *Make her own decisions. And what about Joe? Joe and him are like this [makes a sign for closeness].*

CECCHIN: *The four children are all in the same boat: one is anorectic, the other is Daddy's boy, the other is manipulative, the other is confused. And so they're all in the same boat.*

MOTHER: *And Kate shouldn't come to the resort with us, should she?*

FATHER: *Nope, nope.*

CECCHIN: *No, that is not part of this project. Everyone knows where you're going. You do what you feel like. I can't tell you anything about that.*

FATHER: *What you're saying, in essence, is that when you decide to leave, you don't tell anybody; you leave a note on the table: "We've gone."*

MOTHER: *This'll work. I bet you it will too. I'll write you a letter.*

*[Couple gets up to leave.]*

---

HOFFMAN: How did the process of reaching this intervention go?

CECCHIN: We agreed on the ritual, but then we had a discussion about how to respond to this family's distrust of therapists. We decided to tell them not to see any family therapist for six months. This was important because they had dropped so many other therapists. We gave a lot of double messages: Forget about family therapy for six months—however, here is a prescription, implying that you are in therapy. Don't come into therapy—however, it's all right for the daughter to go to an individual therapist. By giving all these messages, we tried to break the pattern they were in with therapists. From our point of view, it was highly significant when they took the initiative in deciding to come back to us.

BOSCOLO: There is another piece to this intervention, which is the use of statistics. Since this is a family that fires its therapists, we introduce a higher-level framework. We say that in 80 percent of cases the intervention works, in 20 percent it doesn't. They are very competitive, and we hope to use their competitiveness by setting up the 80 percent statistic.

PENN: It seemed to me that this prescription was a continuation of the original task that divided the family into two groups. The prescription would carry them over that period of time when you prescribe no family therapy, but it still keeps a division between parents and children, with all the members of each group being on the same level.

BOSCOLO: Yes. Notice how theatrical we are when we put all the children in the same boat. Since the family wasn't being very serious, we thought it was very important to dramatize the situation. If it's a tea-party family, you want to avoid becoming a tea-party therapist.

HOFFMAN: The father responds to the intervention very positively in contrast to the mother, who seems a bit down.

BOSCOLO: Yes. Here you see how the intervention confirms the hypothesis that we made when we observed that the father can never get close to the mother because she has all these connections—with her daughters, with her mother, with her sisters. So the intervention put Mother and Father alone together, and Father said "I like that." And the mother confirmed the hypothesis by looking sad.

CECCHIN: You can see the problem with this intervention, which is in some respects purely structural. Even though we say that the parents don't have to stay together, that they only have to appear to be together, the reality is that we are putting them together. This makes Father happy and Mother unhappy. So this is the limitation of this idea.

PENN: The prescription severs all those triangles the father and mother are part of, both within the nuclear family and in the extended family as well. Of course, it is harder on Mother than Father. In retrospect, would you have looked for a more balanced intervention?

BOSCOLO: Possibly. The feedback of Mother's sadness suggests that another intervention, based on a slightly different hypothesis, might be more effective. The hypothesis would be related to the fact that Sue started to have symptoms after the father sold his businesses and started to stay home. During the session, the mother said that her mother thinks her husband is getting mental in the sense that he stays in the house all day bickering, complaining, and being bored. One can guess that at that time he started to compete with Sue for the possession of Mother. Father is jealous of Mother's relationship with Sue. He has said several times that Sue wants her parents to separate and that she wants to live in utopia with Mother. He cannot accept that Mother can be a mother for the children and a wife for himself. He wants her all for himself, and Sue apparently wants Mother all for herself.

PENN: How would you change the prescription?

BOSCOLO: We could have given the following prescription. Since both Sue and Father want Mother, one day a week Mother is to relate only to Father; one day a week she is to relate only to Sue; and on the other days everyone is to behave spontaneously.

CECCHIN: This ritual would have given Sue an important position in the system and also would have permitted the mother to remain close to her. You can see from the mother's face that the idea of going out with her husband alone is not attractive to her.

BOSCOLO: That's because Mother, according to this hypothesis, is in an untenable position. Any time she's with Sue, she's wrong because she's not with her husband; any time she's with her husband, she's wrong because she's not with Sue. But the ritual offers a way out. It fixes a set time for Mother to be alone with Sue and a set time for her to be alone with Father. If you introduce a sequence in the Father/Sue/Mother triangle, you take Mother out of the paradoxical position she is in.

PENN: Being ordered to behave spontaneously is a paradox too, but a benign one. This is a good example of a ritual that makes use of time.

BOSCOLO: I'd like to get back to what Gianfranco said about the limits of the structural intervention. Here there was the danger of imposing the idea that parents and children should separate. In many cultures with three- or four-generation families, the children can grow up and stay with the parents and not have it get in the way. I like the second intervention because it responds more accurately to the configuration in this family rather than to an idea of what is normal.

CECCHIN: If we were to think of one characteristic that seems to organize the families we see, it would be that the structure is governed by a rule of threes. If a dyad tries to go off alone, there's always another person that will interfere. So we don't think in terms of parents and children or generation lines or marital or parental subsystems but more in terms of triangles.

HOFFMAN: You're going against this rule of threes when you take a couple and isolate them.

CECCHIN: Yes. That's why, when we wish to strengthen a couple, we will warn them that they must not become too strong or the other people will suffer; or we ask permission of the others for them to be alone. We will use an educational fantasy: one day Mother takes care of the child and the father does not interfere; the next day, they switch. You tell them that each is a good educator alone, and therefore they must take turns. But your secret purpose is to break the rule of threes.

HOFFMAN: Do you care, by the way, if the parents actually do this secret couple ritual or not? In other words, suppose they came back and told you they couldn't do it. That Mother had to tell Sue where they were going, or she found out?

BOSCOLO: If they fail, they still bring you a lot of information. You find out if Mother refused to do it because she had something else to do or because the children interfered or the father didn't feel like it. And then you might give a counterprescription: "We believe that you should stop this ritual; it was premature, and we think you should wait."

CECCHIN: In some cases this intervention works very well. But in very serious cases there is the danger of getting into a power struggle. Sometimes you have a crisis because the children do not permit the therapist

to have this kind of power. The patient increases the symptomatic behavior, escalates, gets hospitalized. This is also to protect the parents. If
this happens, we abandon the prescription and ask the whole family in.
And then we decide what to do next. Here, as you will see, we did
provoke an escalation. The next time we see this family, Sue has begun
to behave very badly and is interfering with the parents' lives even more
strongly than before.

## Session 3

HOFFMAN: How long had it been between sessions?
BOSCOLO: It was six months. Some time after the last session, Sue asked
  one of the therapists who had been behind the screen to be her therapist.
  In the time between the meetings, she started to do some shoplifting,
  and she began to go out with all kinds of boys, bringing them home
  drunk and giving a message of being sexually promiscuous. The therapist
  said the mother called him a lot, trying to interfere with the treatment.
  In our presession discussion, most of what we talked about related to
  the handling of the individual therapist. We finally decided to have him
  sit in the session.
HOFFMAN: Why would you do that?
BOSCOLO: Because he has become part of the system. He is activating
  Mother, activating the girl and probably the rest of the family as well,
  without being able to see his impact on the case because he only sees
  the girl. So we treat him like the therapist in an impasse consultation—
  we put him with the family.
HOFFMAN: Who was in this session?
CECCHIN: The parents; Sue, who was now back living at home; and Joe.
  The two other girls were living in a city away from home. The focus was
  on Sue. Father began to describe the "garbage" she was bringing home,
  meaning boyfriends. Mother then defended Sue on the grounds that her
  self-esteem was so low that she didn't feel she deserved any better.
PENN: Had the parents obeyed the prescription?
CECCHIN: Yes, they had. They kept to it pretty well, although a couple of
  times the mother hinted to Sue where they were going or where they
  had been.
PENN: What reason did Sue give for moving home again?

CECCHIN: She didn't say, but we felt it was related to the prescription to the parents to go out alone. She went home and began to behave in such a way that she interfered totally with their relationship.

PENN: Was the father still not working?

CECCHIN: Yes. He's giving a lot of double messages to his daughters: "Try to leave but don't really leave." So does the mother. It doesn't seem to matter if these girls go to some other city or if they have boyfriends or not. The only outside relationships that seem to be allowed are the ones they make with therapists. You have the feeling that the couple would be very depressed if the children all left, especially Father.

HOFFMAN: Overall, how did you assess the position of the family? Had they regressed? Was there some movement? Or were they just standing still?

BOSCOLO: We felt there had been a shift. The daughter's behavior had changed, and although she was still a problem, it was a different problem.

HOFFMAN: You mean she wasn't acting different than many other irritating young women?

BOSCOLO: Yes. When we see this in therapy, it's a sign of change, and we have a positive reaction to it. In Milan, when there has been a shift in the family, we recommend termination. We tell the family that we see no more psychiatric problems, only life problems or human problems. Let's play the intervention. It will give you some idea of how we initiate termination.

### INTERVENTION

CECCHIN: *In your family, which has been very close and intimate, people have stayed together for a long time. And then there was an injunction—I don't know where it came from—that you should separate. Somebody told you, or you got the idea, that you should separate, that you should work hard to separate. But we think you're doing too much in that direction, trying to be free from each other. You just have to wait, psychologically, and the time will come when everybody will be on their own. It's like a plant that is growing; you can't push it, it has to grow by itself. It is a physiological phenomenon. So I can see that all of you, especially Father and Mother and Sue and Jane, want to go against this tendency to separate. We think it's a very good thing you're doing. For example, Sue is doing everything not to fall in love with boys—that's one good way not to grow up. We see Jane—as soon as she falls in love with a boy, she immediately pushes him out—that's another good way not to separate. We see the father,* who says "I will kick you out of the house" and never does it. One day it will happen, but he's slowing down the process. Mother is slowing down the process by going to therapy sessions with her daughter, and especially by looking for therapists. A good way to slow down the process is to look for therapists. As long as you are seeing a therapist, you won't grow up. Then, as you said, Sue is going out with "garbage" people, so she cannot get involved with anybody important. So somehow we feel that you are very sure of what you are doing. We feel it's not a psychiatric problem any more. You have been pushing very hard to separate and individuate, instead of waiting for the normal time to come by itself; and you're doing very well. If you were our patients, we would say we are not going to see you any more because it's not a psychiatric problem; time will take care of the problem by itself. You are a very close family, and of course you have difficulty in growing up, which means separating and having everyone find his own way. Father finds it difficult to separate from the daughters; Mother finds it difficult to separate from the daughters; the daughters find it difficult to separate from the parents. It all takes time. It could be ten years, five years—we don't know. But you can never push this kind of a process. It cannot be pushed.

MOTHER: So then you don't consider that Sue has anorexia any more?

CECCHIN: No.

MOTHER: She does not have anorexia?

CECCHIN: That's what we decided. Now the problem is different.

FATHER: [to Sue] Then you're cured.

CECCHIN: However, she's working hard to slow down this kind of push that you have inside of you making you feel you have to separate. I don't know where this idea is coming from. It seems to me it'll happen by itself. No one needs to make any effort. However, you're doing very well in cutting down this pressure that you have to do something.

MOTHER: Do you suggest Sue continue with her therapy?

CECCHIN: She has to make up her own mind.

MOTHER: That's for her to decide.

CECCHIN: When she says "I'm going to therapy," it means "I'm not yet ready to separate." It's a slowing-down process which is very useful. So it will slow down this separation that has to come naturally. When the time comes, it will come by itself. But you have been pushing too much. Father says "Get out of the house"; you say "You should become autonomous"; she says "I don't want to talk to my parents because I worry them too much." Everybody's trying to do something. Jane goes to the city and says "I must be here by myself." Everybody makes a big effort, and we don't know why. Time will take care of this problem by itself.

MOTHER: As far as Sue goes, she still does not eat properly.

CECCHIN: It's not anorexia.

MOTHER: She still vomits.

CECCHIN: Most people eat in a bad manner.

FATHER: *Well, that's for her to decide whether she's going to continue with her therapist.*

CECCHIN: *[to therapist in the room] It's a good idea if she comes to you; it's like saying "Let's not push this separation." If she stops seeing the therapist, then she'll find another man; perhaps she would get married—that would be separating. Obviously she's not ready if she goes to a therapist. She's not going to marry him—he's her therapist. You approve of her seeing a therapist, so everything remains the same. It's a good thing. It would be pushing too much to separate. It's not a psychiatric problem; it's a kind of idea that came to you: "We have to separate." That's what we feel.*

FATHER: *I don't know if I'm going to wait that long.*

CECCHIN: *Sometimes it takes all of your life. Some people go all their lives without separating; they do well, anyway.*

MOTHER: *It's not a terrible problem.*

CECCHIN: *You made a problem out of it. This family decided you had to separate to be independent. I don't know how you got this idea. Anyway, we see it as not a psychiatric problem; it's not a problem of growing independently. For every family has a different time—you have to realize that. You want to do it faster than your time.*

FATHER: *That's quite possible. The message is: "Be yourself. Let it happen."*

CECCHIN: *Let it happen, without pushing, without worrying about independence.*

FATHER: *Okay, Doctor.*

MOTHER: *Thank you. It's really a pleasure to meet you.*

---

HOFFMAN: Why do you tell this family at this point that they no longer have psychiatric problems? Is this a way you terminate?

CECCHIN: Originally the family comes because they need a psychiatric label. The family itself has already started the labeling, and they need someone to confirm their diagnosis. You go along with that idea to a certain extent when you accept them as patients. You accept their definition of having psychiatric problems, but you immediately begin to challenge this definition. Slowly, through the process of therapy, you try to change the label into behavior. For instance, you ask: "What does it mean to be anorectic? What do you do to your brother? to your mother?" When you feel pretty comfortable that the family is able to translate their own label into action, when they understand that a person's illness is a behavior, then you can view anorexia as a decision, and people begin to react as if the anorectic is a human being, not a sick person. That's the moment when change begins. Finally you step out altogether and say "This is no longer a psychiatric problem," and you take the label away completely. You tell the family that because they no longer have a psychiatric problem, it is useless for them to keep coming to you. But you say they have a lot of life problems—this girl will still fight with her mother, will probably not eat, et cetera. The important thing is that you have described them as behaviors attached to life problems rather than to psychiatric labels. You don't say "You're cured." You change the language from sickness into behavior, and people will react differently. The behavior becomes a message about what's going on in the family. Then you can withdraw completely.

PENN: How do you recognize a change that will allow you to pull out?

CECCHIN: When the family makes changes that do not follow your suggestions. For instance, when a structural therapist tells the family to make changes, that is a change we would not consider valid. In that situation, the change stays attached to therapy, and if the therapist withdraws, the family may fall back into the same situation.

HOFFMAN: One of the surprises of this approach is that the family sometimes comes back and reports that everything is different. You find out that they thought of their own solution. Then they fire you because they thought of their own solution.

CECCHIN: That's the best solution, right?

HOFFMAN: Yes. The family defines you as no longer necessary. They drop out, but that is a way of leaving that is very different from the traditional termination process of "mourning" for the therapist.

CECCHIN: What is important is not to end the therapy by saying "Now you're cured," "Now you're better," or "Now you've improved, so we can finish the therapy." That really keeps the patient hooked, because he may come back later saying he's not through. You must not put yourself in the position of the therapist who decides someone is cured or not. You have to say "The only thing I can say, as an expert, is that it's not a psychiatric problem."

PENN: I don't believe other innovators in family therapy have thought out the issues in termination in exactly this way. They rehearse relapses, reoccurrences, et cetera, but they do not give up their authority.

CECCHIN: Well, we sometimes build in a little bridge. The family says "If something happens, can we come back to you?" And we say "Of course, I'm here. But we would prefer that if something happens, you don't call us for at least six months." That way you take away from the temptation to create another psychiatric problem. You ask for six months of leave, trusting they will manage.

HOFFMAN: In this intervention, what are you trying to do?

BOSCOLO: In the first session, we said that the parents must be giving the children messages to interfere with their relationship, and we imply that this is why the children don't grow up. But we didn't tell them that the children have to grow up. What has happened is that the entire therapeutic community keeps telling them they should separate and that the children should leave home. So in the intervention, we reverse that. We turn around the concept of separation by saying: "You have this crazy idea that you have to grow up, to be independent. We don't understand where it's coming from" (of course, we know very well) "but we appreciate your effort to go against this crazy idea. You're doing beautifully."

CECCHIN: When the therapist talks about time, saying that the process of growing up may take five, ten years, he introduces a flexible time. The "growth therapist," the one who says to people that they should leave home, find an apartment, et cetera, this therapist communicates "The time set by your family is no good; you should follow my time." When the family doesn't change, the therapist will say that the family is rigid. But the therapist is more rigid than the family.

PENN: Can you comment on the time intervals between these sessions, and if this has changed since you first started to work this way? I'm thinking of Selvini's "Why a Long Interval Between Sessions" (Selvini Palazzoli, 1980).

CECCHIN: In Milan, we started to see people at intervals of a month if they had to come from far away. Then we saw that they were doing better than the people who came more frequently. We realized that if you give an intervention, a ritual, say, the family needs time to elaborate on it and weave in their own fantasies and ideas. If you make an intervention and see the family two or three days later, or a week later, it's too early. It's still your hypothesis, your intervention, and you impose your own ideas on the family.

HOFFMAN: That could stop the process too.

CECCHIN: Yes. Giving time allows the family to reinvent their own map and to do something original. If you're always there telling them what to do, you interfere with their self-healing process. If you do structural therapy, for instance, you have to see the family every week because you want them to do what you tell them to do; you have to monitor them. So it makes sense, in structural therapy, to schedule meetings every week, and it makes sense to us not to see families every week. However, even the monthly interval has begun to seem rigid. Since we have biweekly training groups, it gets too comfortable for us. We have to fight that. In several cases we have felt that perhaps we should shorten the interval, especially in the beginning.

BOSCOLO: Or lengthen it.

CECCHIN: But not in the beginning. In the beginning, we tend to see families every two weeks, not every week. The two-week interval can be very good, especially when you're not yet coupled to the family. So we have two or three sessions without an intervention. Then, for example, in the third session, we make an intervention, after which we tell them "We will see you in two months."

BOSCOLO: The first few sessions should be at shorter intervals because engagement is very important. If the family gets too engaged, however, what we see is that the ties with the extended family diminish. In a given family, we might notice that the grandmother is very important; but if the family gets too involved with the therapist, she becomes less important. You could say that the therapist becomes bigger than the grandmother.

PENN: So the therapists can sometimes replace the extended family.

BOSCOLO: Exactly. So if the family is very engaged with us, we tell them that they can see the therapist once a month. In the last few years, the intervals have at times become even longer—six months, a year.

HOFFMAN: What determines how often you would see a family?

BOSCOLO: It depends on each case. If we decide to set an interval of a year, we might have the hypothesis that in this instance time is very important.

CECCHIN: The idea is to be able to perceive what the time of the system is. If the family's time is fast, you have to move with them—you can't slow down their time. Sometimes it happens that you are pushing them too fast. Then you have to slow down.

HOFFMAN: Sometimes people communicate that by not showing up for an appointment. At least, it often feels that way.

CECCHIN: Yes. They might call you up and say "Can we postpone the session? Our daughter has to go to school." Usually you accept their request immediately; you don't ask questions because it's clear that the system needs a little rest.

PENN: If they cancel the session, you define that as their need to have more time or take a rest. What if they want to come sooner?

CECCHIN: We usually say that we can't see them; we have to meet on the date that was appointed. Sometimes the family goes into crisis after an intervention and they call for an earlier appointment. The danger is that if we agree, we may block the possibility of change.

HOFFMAN: What if you perceive that the family doesn't want to come in because they don't like what you are doing?

BOSCOLO: One intervention would be to invite those who are willing to come in to help us understand why the family is giving this message. If you see part of the family, you can get information on why they think the family, as a whole, is reluctant to come in. If they are all together, it may not be possible for them to reveal this.

HOFFMAN: But what if the parents call and say that the children are busy or the father can't take off from work? In other words, when it seems clear that they are using stalling tactics?

BOSCOLO: One way we handle this is to accept this request by saying "All right, today we will see only you and your oldest son; next time we will see your husband and your youngest son." You take charge of the process, and then you can allow it.

HOFFMAN: When you give an intervention that seems to touch a lot of the spokes on the wheel, the family will often not show up for the next session, or only some of them will. I get a little bit nervous about this and don't always know what to do.

BOSCOLO: If they don't come to a session, we try to have a session on the phone. Since we don't set up appointments ahead of time, we have to call anyway; but in these cases, we ask a few questions and make a quick hypothesis with the team. In this way, we have a two- or three-minute phone session. Depending on the reason they give for not coming, the therapist might say that they are doing very well in deciding not to come and connote positively the family's wish to slow down treatment.

HOFFMAN: With more traditional methods, you feel like a failure if your family doesn't keep coming back. With this method, every response is new information (even when you don't appreciate it) and gives you a better understanding of how the system works.

CECCHIN: Right. One of the myths of therapy is that a good patient comes back to you all the time or that a good therapist gets a family to come back all the time. If they come back, it shows they have good motivation; but the motivation may be only to see you—it may not be a motivation to improve. It may be a dependency or a situation where the therapist and the patient are putting each other in double binds. If a patient keeps coming back to you, it may be because he or she may not have the freedom to send you away.

HOFFMAN: That's a problem in some training settings, because if you are supervising students in an agency and some of the families come only once, it looks bad in the statistics, even though you think that there has been a change and everything has gone well.

BOSCOLO: Some years ago, if the family didn't come after two or three sessions, we felt we were failures. Then when we started to do follow-ups, we noticed that some of these cases that dropped out were among those that had the best results. We called these therapeutic dropouts. In trying to understand this phenomenon, we noted that a system had two characteristics: one, the tendency to remain stable; and the other, the tendency to evolve. The idea we had in the case of the therapeutic dropout was that the information that was introduced in those few sessions made the family change so much that they had to drop out of therapy to preserve the system.

PENN: You said before that you like to initiate termination somewhat before the family expects you to. But the rule seems to go the other way too: they can terminate before you expect it.

CECCHIN: Yes. At the two extremes, there are the families that drop out and the families that become chronic patients. In the first situation, you can never have much impact. In the second, you lose your capacity to be a therapist and become a family member. The heart of therapy is to remain between these two solutions.

## Session 4

PENN: This is a year and a half later. What had you heard about the family before you saw them?

BOSCOLO: Formally, this is a follow-up session. The others were therapy sessions. The clinic called the family and said that we were here and that we would like to see them.

PENN: Had the therapist at the clinic continued to see Sue?

BOSCOLO: Yes, and also the family had seen a psychiatrist here. Apparently things were going very well. There had been some interesting changes. The mother had taken the initiative and used her resources to open a chain of stores selling exercise clothes. The husband was in charge of one of the stores and went there every day. The two younger daughters were employed there as salespersons. Jane, the oldest, was just opening up a branch in another city. Only Joe was left out of the new enterprise. He had put on weight and was now two hundred pounds.

CECCHIN: The mother was the one who made the biggest change. She was blossoming. In the other sessions she seemed worried, tense, upset.

HOFFMAN: Since we won't be including the transcript of this session, except for the closing bit, could you give us your impressions of the interview and some speculations about why this change took place?

CECCHIN: This change is most likely related to the change in the relationship between the nuclear family and the extended family. For years the wife tried to make her husband provide for the family, and the husband kept putting the family in danger of bankruptcy, which meant that they always needed to go to the grandmother, who is very rich. The solution they found—the solution of the store—is a good one because it unites the nuclear family. Now that they have this idea of a network of stores, the mother can show the extended family that she is independent.

PENN: In the second session, in a part we deleted, the mother said that she was afraid of success in relation to her mother and sisters. What do you think changed that?

BOSCOLO: My speculation is that the work that was done in the first three sessions had the effect of introducing many connections between family members. If you look at the way the daughters now talk about the father and the way the parents now talk about the daughters, it's as though the system became more intelligent. At some point a certain clarification of relationships came about within the nuclear family and, after that, they were able to find agreement as a system. So when they fight, they have fun now. Everybody's smiling while they're fighting, and that's the way they enjoy life. It changes their relations with the outside systems too. The store was a fantastic solution.

HOFFMAN: You're implying that a shared premise in this family was that Mother always had to stay in a certain relationship with her mother. She couldn't be too successful, so it was in a way useful for her to have an unemployed husband and a sick child. In return, she was the grandmother's favorite.

CECCHIN: In a previous intervention, we suggested that Mother, in not being successful, was doing a lot for her own mother. This may have jogged her a little bit.

BOSCOLO: I would feel better if we had made an intervention in this session telling them to go slow because if they are too happy, too successful, something might happen in the other families. It comes out later that the grandmother thinks the stores are a terrible idea and keeps telling the mother to sell them.

CECCHIN: You could also ask Mother the question: "Some time ago you told me your mother was jealous. Is she jealous now of your success? What about your sisters? Do they enjoy your success? And your nieces and nephews—would they want to enter your business?"

PENN: A good future question would have been "If Mother continues to be this successful, what will the girls do to help her with her relationship with her mother and her sisters?" And then something analogous for the father. I always had the secret sense that she married this man for her mother.

CECCHIN: Or the man married her for her mother.

PENN: I wondered why you didn't get information about the father's family. The only thing we know about the father is that he went into business with his brother at one point and that the partnership broke up. It tends to be true in every marriage—sometimes for geographical reasons, sometimes emotional reasons—that one family of origin is more dominant in the marriage than the other. I was curious why you had decided not to ask the father about his brother or the rest of his family.

BOSCOLO: That was an omission. I think we thought that the mother's family was the more important, so we left out the father's.

PENN: The reason I brought this up was because the mother said, in the second session, that the trouble started when the husband went into partnership with his brother. It was never clear what was what or why it ended.

BOSCOLO: It's possible that the "fear of success" that the mother said the husband had was in relation to his brother. If he became too successful, this could have put down his brother. And if this fear were validated, it could have been used as part of an intervention.

HOFFMAN: Just for the record, one must include the possible contribution of the other therapists the family members were seeing during this time period.

CECCHIN: Yes, therapists can become convinced that all changes must be due to the work they alone did and forget about the many other influences the family is responding to at the same time.

HOFFMAN: Let me ask a more general question here. When you see a systemwide change, as here, do you feel that the family changes suddenly, as if it were a single unit, or do you believe that the changes come about piecemeal? Often it seems as though one person will start doing something different that attacks an underlying premise, a premise that is attached to the problem; and then everybody else changes in relation to the premise which has changed.

BOSCOLO: Let me put it like this. I believe that the change doesn't come out at the level of the system but at the level of its members. It's extremely improbable, in any case, that the change in two or more people will come about at exactly the same moment.

HOFFMAN: But there's a tendency to treat a family as though it were a unit that could undergo a conversion all at once. I think it's important to keep coming back to the idea that the family is made up of individuals and that if one changes, this may trigger off the others.

BOSCOLO: Inside the individual there is the same process. A person doesn't change totally, suddenly, but there's a change of an idea or in a job, and these then have a repercussion effect on the rest of the personality.

HOFFMAN: It may be something in between, like the interplay between nature and nurture, with change moving back and forth from the level of the individual to the level of the system. But could you describe the process of change in this family, as you saw it? the stepwise shifts? For instance, the first shift was when the parents came back the second time. The mother would have come anyway, but somehow you convinced the father. You got them to agree about therapy, which was a major step.

CECCHIN: Yes. Then, in the second session, the prescription to the father and mother to go out together had the effect of triggering Sue to come back home and remain stuck there, bringing in undesirable men and interfering with her parents' relationship.

BOSCOLO: The family clearly made the most progress after the third session. The intervention addressed the family's preoccupation with time; they were always talking about time when they said people had to leave, become independent, grow up. So the intervention hit this point. We said "It's good that you stay together—daughters can stay at home, Father can stay at home," because the mother was always giving negative messages about this, especially to Father. Of course, no intervention can have an effect unless the family is engaged with the therapist. But within this frame, the therapist said two things. One: Why should you hurry to become independent? It will come about in time. Two: You don't have to grow up. This may have freed family members from continuously fighting each other on this issue.

HOFFMAN: You've also freed this family from their negative preoccupation with therapists. They don't talk at all in this session about illness or about therapists, and that was one of the major topics in the first session.

PENN: Do you agree with the Palo Alto group that there is a particular customer—that one member of the family is apt to be more anxious or more uncomfortable? Here it seemed that the father was quite at ease with the situation and the girls were comfortable; it was only Mother who wanted to change.

BOSCOLO: I think that's a punctuation. There are other punctuations.

PENN: Well, I was thinking about the conversation that we had about the mother in the beginning and how she was in this paradoxical situation, so that if she was with her husband, she couldn't be with her daughter;

and if she was with her daughter, she couldn't be with her husband. The first and second interventions put the parents on one level and the children on another. The next thing that happened was that the symptom changed from anorexia to a developmentally higher symptom, if you will, which was acting out sexually. Anorectics don't usually act out sexually. Somehow the parents didn't get terribly upset about that; what they got upset about was that the children were not independent. So you counteracted that issue with your take-your-time intervention. The whole group then relaxed and the mother did this amazing thing with the stores.

BOSCOLO: She had been in the position of being a mother who had to take care of a sick daughter. During the third session the labeling of sickness was taken out—there was no more psychiatric illness. That may have allowed her to manifest her energy outside the family.

HOFFMAN: I want to stress again what you said about the punctuation. Here we are talking as though everything was done through the mother, but if you look back at the process, it was always multilateral, prismatic. It took every point of view into account. When we use a particular punctuation, we have to remember that the more clear it is, the less it is true. Anyway, I think that was a very nice example of therapeutic process moving through time.

PENN: For closure, I think we should include the last part of the session.


### FAMILY INTERVIEW

CECCHIN: [to Mother] What does your mother think about this business?

MOTHER: My mother thought I was absolutely insane. She said to me: "It's not going to work with your children. Why are you trying to protect your children? They need husbands, not a business. You're going to make them into business-women and they need husbands; and you're going to tie them to you more." And she's right. See, what I thought—and I'm wrong—I thought it would make them independent, mature, to have a business; and at the same time, I would be buying my freedom because they would be . . .

CECCHIN: So did you buy your freedom?

FATHER: No, we got in deeper.

MOTHER: We're more enmeshed than ever. It's not my mother—she's smart. I was not so smart.

CECCHIN: [to Father] Did you also discuss this with your mother-in-law?

FATHER: No, I just fight with her. I like to argue with her.

CECCHIN: Do you fight about this issue also?

FATHER: Never.

MOTHER: *My mother is telling me to sell the business.*

CECCHIN: *How do you take the disapproval of your mother? Before you were so concerned about it. How come now the disapproval of your mother doesn't bother you and before it bothered you so much?*

MOTHER: *Do you know what my mother tells me? To sell the business, because she thinks I'm going to end up sick. She's worried about me, with the emotional problems that are happening, because, in the end, from all the fighting that he creates, that they create, I have to end up . . . see, it all comes back to me.*

CECCHIN: *I have the impression, however—and also my colleague—that you are doing pretty well.*

FATHER: *Oh, we're doing real well.*

MOTHER: *Great. And this is what is so disturbing. . . .*

CECCHIN: *I mean, is there an issue that they're going to delay their marriages?*

FATHER: *Well, if I'm the cause of that, I'm going to change.*

MOTHER: *You say you're going to change? Great!*

SUE: *All these things we're fighting about, they can be solved like this. How? Well, if my father would quit saying that we're stupid, we're this and that; if he treated us like adults, we could be adults and we'd treat him like an adult. When he treats us like little babies, we get upset and we can't help it because: one, if you talk like adults; two, instead of fighting, discuss things and then come to an answer. . . .*

CECCHIN: *But then there would be a danger that, perhaps, you would separate.*

SUE: *There definitely would be a danger; of course there would be.*

CECCHIN: *You are a very close family. Perhaps you wouldn't like that idea.*

SUE: *Exactly.*

CECCHIN: *For example, by fighting with him, he keeps you infantile, as you said. You keep attached; and they keep you little nasty girls that push the boys away from you. [All talk.]*

SUE: *No. I watched this three weeks ago one Sunday. I woke up and there was no fighting, and it was nice. Everyone was out washing cars and everyone was talking. And I thought to myself, It's not going to last. And two hours later, there was a fight because the family couldn't go that way for too long. And all I'm saying is that if people all started changing a little at a time, instead of drastically . . .*

KATE: *I don't want to change. I don't want to move out.*

CECCHIN: *[to Father] The point is, if you change and everybody's quiet, then perhaps everybody will feel like leaving home, doing something different, which is premature. You're very close to each other, you love each other. [Father tries to interrupt.] It's a very close family, very difficult to separate.*

SUE: *But that's why I say "a little at a time."*

CECCHIN: *If you spend the day talking and fighting with your father, in the evening you don't feel the desire to talk to a boy.*

SUE: *No, definitely not.*

CECCHIN: *[to Father] And you have this business that takes away your daughters— public relations—worrying about them, this kind of life. If it gets too quiet, they'd get bored, they could go on their own. [All talk, laugh.] The way we see it, from our point of view, is that you are doing very well.*

MOTHER: *The family's doing well?*

CECCHIN: *Delaying solutions.*

SUE: *But why? Okay, why?*

CECCHIN: *Because you're very close to each other. The pain of leaving each other is too much.*

FATHER: *Who says that?*

SUE: *For how long is this going to go on?*

FATHER: *Who gave you the impression that we're a very close family?*

KATE: *Well, Jane isn't around anymore.*

SUE: *Sure she is, she's on our payroll. Sure, she's around—she calls all the time.*

FATHER: *The only one who's close is my son and I, we're very close.*

CECCHIN: *You're very close to your daughters.*

FATHER: *No way. I'm trying to get away from them. Why should they move out when everything is so good?*

SUE: *How long is this going to go on?*

CECCHIN: *It's very hard to predict. There will be a point when everybody gets bored of being so close and everybody will do something else. But it has to happen spontaneously; you can't make it happen.*

FATHER: *I'm trying.*

MOTHER: *But why is he . . . every day, he's trying to push them out of the house. . . .*

CECCHIN: *But when they go out, he pulls them back.*

FATHER: *Oh, I don't pull them back. No way.*

GIRLS: *Yes, you do; yes, you do.*

FATHER: *Well, move out and see if I pull you back now. [laughing]*

CECCHIN: *Everybody will be ready. Because you are not stupid people—you're intelligent, you know how to live. So, one day, when everybody gets bored being together . . .*

FATHER: *But why would they move out when everything is so good?*

CECCHIN: *That's right.*

KATE: *I don't have any money.*

CECCHIN: *You can very well cut down on their salary; you can cut down to twenty-five dollars.*

FATHER: *That would cause a war. I said I was going to deduct their expenses from the wages: you should have heard them riot—wow.*

MOTHER: *If these girls are adults and you want to treat them like adults, now they've got a salary, why shouldn't they understand that they should contribute to the household because they're getting paid a salary? Why should he have to take it out of their salary when . . .*

KATE: *We do have a salary and we do contribute to the household. If we weren't there, who would he fight with?*

CECCHIN: *Anyway, I don't think the two of you can do anything now to make them become adults.*

FATHER: *I'm not trying to make them become adults.*

CECCHIN: *If they want to be adults, they could be adults tomorrow.*

FATHER: *That's right. I said that a hundred times.*

CECCHIN: *So you have to wait. When it's the right moment—*

FATHER: *I won't live that long.*

MOTHER: *Why do I have to put up with this nonsense every day because he's fighting with them to move out?*

CECCHIN: *All this about "move out" means nothing now. They will move out when they are ready, when they feel mature. You can't mature them by telling them.*

FATHER: *I can try.*

CECCHIN: *That's how your daughters describe you. You say something, perhaps to start a conversation because you get bored; probably you talk about moving out, like you do with your mother-in-law, you can sell the house . . .*

MOTHER: *What about me? I'm not ready to leave my house. I am not ready, and you cannot make me move out of my beautiful house into a two-bedroom apartment.*

FATHER: *The doctors come from Italy. Why don't they stay at my house? We'll rent them rooms.*

CECCHIN: *The point is that, of the four of you, no one is ready to live separately from the others.*

MOTHER: *[laughing] Okay, Doctor, why does he change the subject all the time? When you're talking . . . like she just said, we were talking, and then he makes silly remarks. This upsets the girls. It upsets me too, only I understand it already. He says silly things; you can't have a conversation with him.*

CECCHIN: *If the family is very quiet—everybody doing their own thing—there is a sense, after a while, that there is no family anymore. So he comes in, he does the job of keeping everyone together with silly remarks.*

---

HOFFMAN: Let me stop this for a moment. I take it that you weren't planning to make a formal intervention?

CECCHIN: No, because this is a follow-up. But I am pushing them just a little bit, telling them to go slow. And they react very sensibly; they don't think I'm off the track at all.

PENN: It's very subtle, this business of doing a follow-up.

BOSCOLO: Yes, it's very difficult for the therapist to step from the position of therapist to the position of the one who does the follow-up. When I called in to Gianfranco the first time, I told him to remember that this was a follow-up and to try not to talk about problems.

PENN: It's impossible. Why didn't you decide that Luigi should do the follow-up?

CECCHIN: We should have thought about it. A follow-up should be done by someone who is not connected with the family. But it's hard for the therapist not to get seduced back. You have a lot of difficulty around separation, especially when the family has done well. If they say everything's okay, it's like saying "We don't need you anymore." Their job is to get you back, and the best way to do that is to talk about their problems.

BOSCOLO: Also, it's difficult for the therapist to leave the family. If he has fallen in love with the family, then he has to go through a mourning process, perhaps even more than the family.

HOFFMAN: In this method, you don't have to work through termination issues with the family, but you perhaps ought to do this for the sake of the therapist.

### FAMILY INTERVIEW

CECCHIN: [to Sue] Why are you taking him so seriously?

SUE: He bothers me. I can't believe how stupid he is. One minute he flashes it, he tells everyone he buys this and he buys this. And you sit there and you tell us and you hound us about money, money, money. And then when you're around people, like these Italian doctors, you tell them "Why don't you stay at my house? I've got a big house." You want everyone to know you've got a big house and you're so rich.

FATHER: But that was a way of telling that I want to get rid of the house.

[Boscolo phones in.]

———————

HOFFMAN: Why did you phone Cecchin?

BOSCOLO: I told him to say to them "I've tried to leave for ten, fifteen minutes, but I cannot leave—it's such a close family."

HOFFMAN: Did you think he needed help?

BOSCOLO: He needed someone who could get him out. He was like Sue, saying "I can leave at any moment" and staying there.

CECCHIN: It's like Italian opera. You sing, "Partiame, partiame"—"I'm going, I'm going"—for two or three acts while you just stand there.

BOSCOLO: I wonder if it would have been more effective, since it was at the end, to enter the session rather than talk to Gianfranco on the phone. I could have remained standing while I asked him to come out. It would have been more powerful, I think.

## FAMILY INTERVIEW

*[Everybody talking, Cecchin breaking in.]*

CECCHIN: *I have the experience with you— I want to say something, and here I cannot leave you. [to Mother] Probably you have the same experience all the time?*

MOTHER: *Well, sometimes, now and then, we need to get away.*

CECCHIN: *You can do it if you want—you go to Los Angeles—it's not difficult.*

SUE: *I'm going.*

MOTHER: *I say if everyone would stop fighting and we could get on and open all these stores . . .*

CECCHIN: *You cannot do anything to change it—you should not make the effort— because at the moment when people are ready to do something different, they will.*

MOTHER: *This will all stop?*

CECCHIN: *One day it will stop without you saying anything.*

MOTHER: *So you don't think we're so sick? Sue isn't sick, Kate isn't sick, and we're not sick?*

FATHER: *Nope, we're saddled with kids and that's the way it is!*

*[The family leaves amid much laughter, everyone talking at once.]*

---

PENN: What finally happened with this family?

CECCHIN: They didn't go back into family therapy, although the last we heard, the girl was still in individual therapy. They said she was doing well. The girls were still circling around the home.

BOSCOLO: Not everyone would have been satisfied with these results. They were still an "enmeshed" family, as shown by the fact that the girls were not yet out. This is one position. But to frame your goal this way is to risk imposing your idea of what is normal. It's possible that you can have an "enmeshed" family that is healthy, where nobody has symptoms.

PENN: David Reiss has done some interesting studies of the way families relate to each other and to the larger world outside the family. In this case the family's style is characterized by a trait he calls "consensus-sensitive." That means that they are always thinking: "Do they agree with me? Do they not agree with me?" And that's how this family was: they were a consensus-sensitive family. That has now shifted, so that they don't have as rigid a paradigm controlling the way family members behave—it's not as constricting. They have a family that goes out into the environment—the stores are going across the country, and the girls are going to manage the stores. That is bound to make them less consensus-sensitive, less enmeshed.

BOSCOLO: It's possible that they started to be less addicted to consensus after they became successful, but I think they still remain within that style. The difference is that it's in a workable rather than an unworkable form.

HOFFMAN: In general, what do you think you did in this case that was especially helpful?

BOSCOLO: When I think about it, the most important aspect was the concept of time. I like to use time interventions because I think that one of the sources of "pathology" in families is the rigid ideas about time people impose on their relationships. Suppose two parents decide that the children, after the age of twelve, have to show adult behavior. From that moment, if the child does not act grown up, all the behavior is labeled negatively. A time intervention would be to say in one session "Children should become detached from their parents, and therefore we think that you should separate." In the next session, as in this case, we say: "It is not yet time to separate. You are moving too fast." By alternating these two elements, you introduce flexibility. There is a time for separating, there is a time for not separating. If you introduce this leeway into the system, people can begin to make their own choices about when to leave or stay.

CECCHIN: One thing I particularly like about this case is the many techniques we used for pushing for change and then backing off.

HOFFMAN: I call that "rocking the system."

CECCHIN: Rocking the system. Pushing the parents to go out and then telling them all to stay together.

HOFFMAN: But the *timing* of your move (this is another aspect of time) was in response to the family's time. After that first change, the daughter came home and was bringing in these drunken boys. That's when you slowed them down.

CECCHIN: Yes. But in general, I think this illustrates two broad categories of intervention that we use. One is when we try to change the belief system by challenging the premise on which the problem behaviors are based. The other category is pushing for change and then stepping back.

With these two methods, when you succeed in triggering a change (I don't think you can ever say you "caused" a change), the family finds its own answers. This is the originality of systems. For instance, this family began to relate to a store instead of a symptom. This is not the kind of solution a therapist thinks of. A good example of a therapist idea is the idea that a son or daughter should take an apartment and become autonomous. Being "autonomous" is a repetitive map that the therapist imposes without taking into account the self-healing properties of the system. Here the system found the idea of a store where people could be both dependent and independent. It's a metaphoric solution, because if you can handle money and run a store you can be independent. But you don't have to be literally independent yet. The question we should now ask is why we think this solution is better than the symptom.

BOSCOLO: Because this solution introduces a new element. Before, the parents kept giving money to the children, all the time complaining that they were acting childish and dependent. Through the store, the children learn to work for their money. That sets up a very different arrangement.

CECCHIN: Another thing. When Sue was anorectic, she was representing the problem all by herself. The solution of the store put the girls together. They found a configuration that would represent the same dilemma but spread it more evenly.

HOFFMAN: As opposed to one girl being caught in an endless oscillation—stay/leave, stay/leave.

PENN: That's the dilemma—should they stay or should they go? The store is a way of moving them to a higher level of organization, one that resolves an either/or dilemma in favor of a complementary configuration that places the opposites in the service of the whole.

CECCHIN: That's a very beautiful idea. If the therapist believes that the problem should be resolved, that's a mistake, because that's one of those human issues that should never be resolved. One way to try to resolve it—a way that is not so much pathological as primitive—is for one person to have a symptom like anorexia. But if you move to a higher level of organization, the same problem can be played out a different way.

# PART 4

# *The Girl Who Got Stuck to Her Mother*

## INTRODUCTION

THE FOLLOWING CONSULTATION departs from the format used throughout the rest of the book. Boscolo and Cecchin were their own interviewers because the session was taped during a workshop in a clinic in Germany some time after the interviews about the other three cases had been finished. Because it is an excellent example of the circular questioning process, we wanted to include it. However, the four of us were unable to sit down together at that time to review the session and so the interviewing protocol is different.

The case represents a vivid illustration of the use of "openings," which are a key component of circular questioning. An opening is an expression of the meaning system in a family. It can occur in many forms: as an idea, a word cue, a theme, or a piece of analogic behavior. Whatever its form, it acts like an indentation, or an "opening," into the way a particular family organizes its pattern of thinking, its behaviors, and the combination of meanings they collectively represent. For example, a father may say "My daughter is too independent." The idea of independence is an opening; it is a word that is heavily invested with meaning for this family; and though a complaint is usually directed to a problem person, the opening has hidden distributions throughout the entire system.

As we see in this consultation, Boscolo and Cecchin follow all openings with questions—circular questions, future questions, existential questions, and so on—until they feel the questions have perturbed the system enough to invite the family's rethinking or reorganization around the idea presented. Often the openings are not completed, meaning they do not require a conclusion; rather they act to disrupt the thinking pattern of the family by suggesting new connections and different possibilities. Alexander Blount has written that the family therapy of the Milan Associates is "meaning driven." That idea—that this is a therapy that constructs meanings—is nowhere more apparent than in the careful delineation of their use of openings.

Furthermore, openings in sessions accrue; they add up and become more complex and richly integrated as the session develops. Each opening intensifies and thickens the one before it until a pattern emerges—the family's pattern, which displays increased variation and color as the openings are processed.

## The First Opening: The Rule of No-Talking

This consultation was done at a clinic in Germany and was conducted in English with the help of a translator. Gerte, the identified patient, is a twenty-one-year-old woman who is working and living at home; her younger brother, Karl, is a student; her father works and her mother is a housewife. Gerte has always had trouble connecting with anybody but her mother and was recently hospitalized for four months following a psychotic episode.

Boscolo begins the consultation by asking what the problem in the family is now, and the family responds that Gerte is the problem. He continues in his usual manner, asking who noticed the problem in Gerte first. The family replies that she has had the same problem since childhood: not being able to sleep or make contact with other people.

When a family designates a problem as being so longstanding, since childhood, the therapeutic team is immediately aware that it will not be easy to produce change in the family, for time amplifies and deepens the problem as the behavioral sequences are repeated over and over. However, at this early point in the interview, the Milan Associates are most concerned with what kind of information value the problem has for other people, what kind of relationship definitions have accompanied the problem. By asking who noticed it first, the therapist describes the problem as existing as a psychological reality only when someone notices it, only when it is interactional or co-created among members of the family. Karl, the son, answers that his mother was the first to notice Gerte's problem, and states that his sister talks only with his mother and not with "us," the men in the family.

Karl thus offers the therapist the first important opening in the session: there may have been an early split in the family, with Gerte remaining close to her mother and the two women remaining distant from Karl and his father. This opening, which yields the basic configuration of the family, occurs during the first three minutes of the session and then occupies (through many permutations) the first half of the consultation. Karl immediately offers another interesting description, one he cannot possibly remember, since he is two years younger than Gerte. When Boscolo asks how long it was before the parents noticed that their daughter had a problem, he answers: "Perhaps some months." This has several meanings: he is not allied with his sister, which confirms their split; and since his birth, their relationship has always been polarized in the mind of the family—he is the nonsick member and she is the sick member of the family. Since an opening always is some form of offering from the family, these further questions provide more information concerning the early split in the family.

Now the father volunteers information that is different from Karl's. Karl has said Gerte had less difficulty at home than at school, but Father describes her as getting "stuck" to her mother, implying that she did have difficulty at home. Boscolo asks a circular comparison question: "Who got stuck the most, Gerte or the mother?" This is an important elaboration of the split in the family, for it allows the therapist to feed back the family's descriptions of "stuckness" within the structure of a comparison question. This feedback provides a double description, and it becomes clear that it is not possible to get stuck alone: one must get stuck to someone *who may also be stuck!*

"Stuckness" implies a relationship; it is the expression of a mutual recursion. This recursion adds an element of surprise, as it is something the family has not thought of; and it flips the explanatory coin, looking at the other side. If the family members look at the other side—why Mother got stuck to Gerte—they must reconstruct their explanation of the family problem. Clearly they are not ready to do that at this point. This kind of com-

parison usefully addresses the other side of the family's presented problem.
If the family is ashamed, one inquires: "What is the last event around
which someone in this family felt pride?"; or, if the family is too serious:
"When is the last time you felt playful?"; or, if a family is disconnected
and comes together for the therapy, one asks them to comment on this
unusual coming together and its meaning to them now, and so on.

It is during the exploration of the first opening that Gerte communicates
to her mother that she does not want to talk about her problem. This
behavior highlights what turns out to be a theme or a premise in the family:
*There should be no talking, everyone must keep secrets.* What follows is a
communication between Gerte, the therapist, and Mother, a communication
whose larger meaning suggests that the family system houses contradictory
ideas and treats them as though they were not contradictory but the same.
The communication is worth describing since it contains the family's logic
and illustrates the performance of the linguistic sequencing that keeps Gerte
fixed in her problem role.

In response to Mother's saying that Gerte doesn't like to talk about her
own problems, the therapist asks Gerte if she agrees with her father, mother,
and brother that she has the problem. She agrees, adding, however, "But
I have already . . ." She doesn't finish this sentence, but Mother does: ". . .
overcome it." Her mother continues: "She *thinks* she has overcome her
problems. . . . But in reality I don't think so." This communication could
be viewed as a mutually shared symbiotic thought between Mother and
Gerte, the attempt to express a difference on Gerte's part that has been co-
opted by her mother, the judge of "reality." Again, the therapist asks: "Do
you agree with what your mother said?" And again Gerte agrees, only this
time, in fact, she has agreed to the idea that she has *not* overcome her
problem. Nevertheless she goes on to state that she *has* overcome her problem. Boscolo asks: "*When* did you overcome the problem?" and she says:
"After my disease." Father adds that she *feels* she has (and Mother adds
that she *thinks* she has) overcome her problem, both disqualifying her
attempt to make a distinction that allows contradiction. This confusion
between overcoming or not overcoming the problem dominates this exchange, but is treated by Father and Mother as though it were conclusive—
she thinks and feels she has overcome the problem (but she has not!).

This is an example of a co-created family reality that sustains a rule: You
may not talk about secrets. Gerte cannot clarify the contradiction in the
family about whether she has or has not overcome her problem without
breaking the no-talking rule. If one talks, contradictions may become clearer
and secrets may be shared that could prove dangerous. Gerte begins by
reminding her mother that she does not want to talk about her problem,

but she does not refuse to answer the therapist's question of whether she agrees with other family members that she has problems. Once she has succumbed and is talking about overcoming her problem, her mother reminds the family and the therapist that Gerte's "reality" is confused, inferior to the larger "reality." So disqualified in her reality, Gerte can only agree with both realities—that is, the contradiction—that she has overcome her problem and that she has not overcome her problem.

## The Second Opening: Who Else Has a Problem?

Having disturbed this sequence and what it protects, Boscolo leaves it to reorganize itself and pursues another variation. Now, under the frame of the first opening—the description of an early coalition between Mother and Gerte that has split the women from the men and may not be talked about—Boscolo pursues two subopenings: who got stuck to whom, and Gerte's message to her mother that it was important not to talk. This work takes place in a short time and expands the relationship information around the first opening. Recognizing that there is to be no agreement on whether or not Gerte has overcome her problem, Boscolo asks her if anyone else in the family has a problem. This is a challenge to the distributions the family has made. They say, in effect: Gerte has all the problems; we have none.

It is also a challenge to the polarization the family has made around that distribution: there is one bad member and three good members. This polarization is similar to the earlier one that described the children as sick and not sick. As expected, Gerte answers that she sees *no* other problems. Boscolo then switches to a hypothetical mode and begins to use "if" questions. The future questions allow the discussion of a forbidden topic and provide a safe and indirect way of answering a question that could not be posed directly. "If someone else were to have a problem, who would that be?" is conditional enough to provide control; whereas "Who else has a problem?" is a direct assault that would be turned away. Gerte answers this hypothetical question about other problems by listing Mother, then Father. Boscolo continues by asking about her brother. According to Gerte, Karl would not develop a problem in the future.

Boscolo persists. If he asked Father if Karl would develop a problem in the future, would he provide an answer?

"Perhaps," replies Gerte.

Mother interrupts, saying she doesn't quite understand. This interruption can be viewed as either a misunderstanding of the wording or of the content of the exchange.

The German translator-therapist immediately "explains" Boscolo's question in German to Mother.

Subsequently, Father offers another digression, asking "Do you mean who could first develop or first overcome a problem?"

Mother elaborates Father's digression, saying that according to Gerte, the parents can help her overcome her problems in the future.

Again, a "translation" is required before Gerte's statement is accepted: Mother, then Father.

This idea of others in the family having problems is quite obviously a totally new idea, and the family uses the language difficulty as a way of responding to the difficult question. As Cecchin says in the discussion, you can clearly see how, through using this language difficulty, the family reinstates its own belief system, its own explanations, which finally allow them to conclude that *if* a problem should come up within the family in the future, the ones who could solve it would be Mother, Father, and then brother.

Boscolo is content to rest here; he has accepted the family statement of opposites: the daughter's view that Mother and Father could develop problems and the parents' view that they could never have problems because they could always resolve them. He does not discuss this contradiction but rather accepts it. Then he moves to a variation on the theme of "other problems"—Karl's growing up. He asks Gerte if her brother is growing up well, "without problems." She replies that he is. Again, Boscolo uses the hypothetical mode, asking her what her parents might reply to this question. Again, there is a linguistic difficulty, so Boscolo asks the question of Father. Father's first response is to remark on how *tall* Karl is growing. However, in the next sentence he agrees that, of course, he has problems, but they are not serious. He has friends and gets along well in school. The parents speak only positively of their son, and Mother immediately compares him with the negative characteristics of their daughter. This is the amplification of opposite attributes that has been going on for years. This polarization around the good, well son and the bad, sick daughter represents one of the rigid patterns often seen in psychotic families that are covered by the pseudomutual agreement that all is well in the family except for this problem person.

In an effort to break this idea that Gerte is bad and Karl is good, Boscolo switches the question to a closeness/distance one, asking: "Who is Karl closer to, Mother or Father?" He learns that Karl is closer to Father, sometimes close to Mother, and never close to Gerte, since they quarreled some years ago. This line of questioning challenges the family's thinking pattern which tends to form itself around opposites: the bad child and the good child, the sick child and the nonsick child. Closeness and distance are negotiable ideas, and they change over time, while opposites remain opposites.

## The Third Opening: Sibling Jealousy

The closeness/distance questioning has unearthed another secret—that Gerte is not at all close to her brother and does not talk to him. The switch in questioning that occurs at this point is important to comment on here. Boscolo begins asking Karl if he knows his sister's *reasons* for not talking to him. The boy replies that he doesn't know her so well. Then Boscolo switches his mode of questioning. Instead of asking dyadic, circular questions, he asks one person to comment on another person's reasons for keeping a secret or to offer their explanation of why someone wishes to keep a secret. The content of the secret is immaterial; the important thing is to perturb the family's rule about not talking. Though not a direct challenge, it promotes talking about the explanations and boundaries of the secret. Boscolo then asks Karl whether his parents know Gerte's reasons. Everyone agrees they all know them. Boscolo inquires what their explanation is for Gerte's choice to stop talking to her brother: "What are her reasons?" not "What is her secret?". Father says he cannot answer because it might hurt her "in her heart." Mother interrupts at this point, saying Gerte doesn't want to reveal herself to anyone but her mother. The problem is Gerte's isolation, and now a colleague at the new job wants to get her to talk to him, so she wants to give up her work. Mother establishes control again by redefining the original problem and the family's relationship to it. In the discussion, Boscolo comments that the mother and daughter have been stuck all their lives, and the parents feel that Gerte controls them now. A premise emerges around control. Boscolo feels that their idea has been the following: If they rebel against Gerte, she will break down. They fear her violent reaction. This fear of violence creates a covert relationship system that defines and imprisons everybody. Neither the mother nor Gerte can go out and talk to another person. The situation where the family does not want to talk for fear of revealing secrets presents, as we have seen, a dilemma for therapy. The idea of talking and not talking must be dealt with if the therapy is to continue. Otherwise the family will come to therapy and *not* talk in just the same manner that they manage not to talk to each other at home.

It becomes clear to the Milan Associates that the mother is behaving exclusively toward Gerte; it is as though she had only one child. What systemic meaning does this show? This relationship definition, no matter where it exists in the system, describes the theme of intense jealousy. Extreme dyadic exclusion is always a statement about jealousy. However, jealousy is a premise, an interactional premise: who is jealous of whom? who was jealous of whom first? then who? if a new dyad were to be jealous in the future, who would they be? and so on. Jealousy is thus a systemic expression of these triangular structures, for there is always someone else each is jealous of. In this system, jealousy may be in the sibling dyad, but not exclusively. It is likely also to be in the mother/daughter dyad because of their exclusive closeness. It is an idea that permeates the entire system, an idea with a history and a future.*

Sibling jealousy is thus the beginning of the third large opening in the family. The family has just been reassuring the therapist that the problem definition is the mother and daughter stuckness! When Boscolo gets too close to the reasons Gerte has for not talking to her brother, he receives the news of the unacknowledged and untalked-about sibling jealousy. He uncovers it by asking about the history of the family: *When* did the father see that Gerte got stuck to his wife? Father, in one sentence, confirms the hidden opening: "At about [the] time . . . he was born." His explanation: "A kind of jealousy. A kind of jealousy, I think."

When Boscolo asks whether Mrs. T would agree, Mrs. T replies that jealousy is part of the reason. But she can't talk about the rest "because she [Gerte] doesn't want it."

Again the rule is invoked, and the family attempts a retreat from Father's jealousy distinction. Gerte says: "I don't say I agree or not." Mother says: "We didn't talk about that in the family." Finally, Father gives in: "I can't . . . remember. It's long, long ago." Now they all obey the rule not to talk.

---

* This is an important point to enlarge on since the women in this case, as well as in parts 2 and 3, seem to be the subsystem whose extended families became the focus of the hypothesis construction. The capacity to form a relationship must not in any way be regarded as exclusively female; old assumptions that women are the gatekeepers of the family in charge of the socialization of children must be avoided. We also note that in these three consultations it was the women who initiated therapy and who showed more inclination to change.

## The Fourth Opening: Talking, Not Talking

For the fourth opening Boscolo uses "the other side of the coin," finding an opening around talking that the family will respond to since "talking/not talking" is still the presented dilemma. He asks questions about how Mother and Gerte spend their "stuck" time together. Karl says Gerte and Mother always talk to each other, since Mother has no job and now Gerte is giving up her "profession."

Then Boscolo asks whether Gerte talks more when the men are home or away. When either of the men talk to Mother, is she temporarily unstuck? What does Gerte do then?

Sometimes she gets angry and leaves the room, they reply.

The focus here is what Gerte will do if she gets "out of control." All the feelings Gerte holds—anger, disappointments, jealousy—are feelings the family is forbidden to have; they seem to be dangerous feelings for this family. It is as though Gerte's position in the family requires her to collect these feelings, and in that manner free her family from them.

Boscolo continues talking about the opening of talking/not talking. He asks Karl if Gerte asks Mother to keep secrets from Father, from him. This variation on the talking opening provides important information that the family has not openly discussed among themselves. As the line of questioning proceeds, it is clear that, though Gerte keeps all secrets, Mother does not keep *all* secrets. Mother says it is very difficult for her because "I have too many sorrows and sometimes I must confess." Then once more Boscolo switches to a hypothetical mode to ask Gerte what she would do if her mother could not keep a secret from her father. Karl then says that *sometimes* Mother and Gerte argue about Gerte taking up her profession again. Mother wants it, whereas Gerte wants to stay at home. When Boscolo asks when was the last time Mother was angry at Gerte, Father volunteers that it was when Gerte gave up her job. Mother replies that she wasn't angry because Gerte was ill. Father says "You were shocked," and Mother agrees: "I was shocked."

The pattern in the family is that Mother and Father always agree; no anger is expressed; and the illness becomes the explanation that allows Mother to not express feelings that are forbidden for the family. The second important piece of information resulting from the pursuit of this opening is Mother's statement that the only time she gets angry at Gerte is when she is aggressive or hostile toward her father. "Then I'm angry, and I tell her it's not good for the family when she shows herself so hostile toward her father, because her father likes her too, but he cannot show his feelings."

It is interesting to speculate on this particular piece of information about their relationship. If this is the *one* event where Mother will admit feeling anger toward Gerte, is it possible that Mother, in fact, wants Gerte to move closer to her father? Gerte, sensing this, possibly remains "stuck" to Mother so she will not be pushed toward Father. Is this an underlying secret? What reason might Mother have for emptying the place beside her that Gerte occupies? Who might be its next occupant? The questioning around the talking opening continues on the variation of who keeps secrets best in the family, but by now the cat is out of the bag. Mother does not keep all the secrets Gerte tells her because of the weight of all her sorrows, which she sometimes must confess. Further exploration reveals that Mother does tell secrets to her son and husband, with the caveat that they must not tell Gerte. Her explanation is "There are more sorrows than secrets." Mother's sorrows, she feels, are a form of secrets that must be told, but not to Gerte. The danger in this revelation is that it changes the relationship between Gerte and Mother. Gerte now knows that her mother does not keep her secrets!

In the discussion, Boscolo makes an interesting comment about his pursuit of this opening. He says that the therapist's active obsessive questioning puts into crisis the family's repetitive patterns and roles. The therapist asks questions and accepts each answer without making interpretations. These questions, which continually introduce opposite, other-side-of-the-coin punctuations, go against the rigid family rules. The family is now, in fact, engaged in talking about not talking, and a secret has been revealed: Mother talks about some of the secrets Gerte tells her because she has many sorrows.

## The Fifth Opening: The Hospital Stay

Every opening or theme put forward by the family contains many sub-openings or variations. We have tracked some of the most conspicuous openings in the interview this far. Several important ones are left for the reader to discover. But the next opening, concerning Gerte's stay in the hospital, produces interesting information when combined with the opening concerning Mother talking about her angry feelings toward Gerte because the girl is not close to her father.

Speaking of the four months during which Gerte left work and spent time in the hospital, Boscolo asks how the atmosphere at home was without her. Father speaks first. "Terrible." He continues: "I think those were the worst days of my life." Mother relates that Gerte didn't want to live any more before her hospitalization. Karl confirms that Father was the most depressed. He says Father was depressed and pessimistic. The parents say they constantly thought of Gerte when she was hospitalized, even to the point of neglecting Karl. Father adds: "When she is outside, I constantly think of her. What happens to her, what might she do, and so on. I'm constantly thinking of that." The entire family admits to being uneasy when Gerte is out, whether in the hospital or at work. Boscolo turns to Gerte, asking her if she were to feel well, leave the family, and get married, how would they do without her. And then he asks her an existential question: Suppose you were never born, how would the life of Father, Mother, and Karl go without you? Gerte turns down the first question but answers the second one promptly, saying that things would have been much easier for them. Karl immediately tries to rescue his sister, saying No, he wouldn't have been happier if she had not been born because there are other sorrows. Boscolo inquires about the attribute of sorrow in the family—how sorrowful they are—and, finally, he asks: "Who's more sorrowful, your father or your mother?" Karl says: "Father." Father has always been more sorrowful. Boscolo ends this inquiry by asking the children whether their parents would be even more unhappy if they had no children.

During this questioning, we find out that Father was most depressed at Gerte's being "out" of the home and that he is the most sorrowful member of the family. Up until this point such descriptions seemed to belong more to Mother. This new information, combined with Mother's *only* expression of anger at Gerte—her refusal to spend time with her father—confirms the interview's latest hypothesis: that Mother wishes Gerte to not be so stuck to her! However, it is not clear whether Father would fill the space beside Mother that Gerte occupies. The next opening clarifies who the occupant of that space might be. It is here that another person is introduced who will make all these questions make sense: The mother's important sister.

The existential questions toward the end of this opening confirm the identified patient's inner view that everyone would be better off without her. But the next question, asking whether the parents would be even more unhappy if they did not have children, seeds a new idea about the parents: However unhappy they seem, they would be more unhappy without their children. This question plants the idea that the parents have some unhappiness or sorrow that is *exclusive* to them and does not involve their children.

Both questions act as an antidote to the existential condition of the identified patient. If an existential question is asked, it must be followed through in this manner because the unspoken has been spoken: They would have been better off without me. It must include the antidote thought, which is: Your parents have exclusive problems that do not involve you, and they would be *more* unhappy without you.


## Postsession Team Discussion


The first part of this discussion is a free expression of all the therapists' linear and causal hypotheses; nothing is omitted or censored. Slowly, as the discussion proceeds, the patterns become more complex and more connected until a general hypothesis emerges. The thrust of the discussion is to understand Gerte's psychotic behavior, linking it to the most obvious family pattern—the tendency of this family to keep secrets.

The team tries to reach consensus on a general hypothesis that includes different possibilities so that many ways of intervening may be considered. In consulting with families in schizophrenic transaction, it can take two to three sessions before the therapists are able to reach a consistent, systemic hypothesis. When the team does not easily reach a consensus but begins to experience discomfort, repetition, confusion, or when new ideas stop occurring, then the team process must be stopped until the next session.

The Milan Associates utilize three different classes of hypotheses in their discussions. One class refers to who is with whom in the family; this is an appraisal of the alliances, coalitions, or "marriages," as they are sometimes called. The second class of hypotheses refers to individual and family premises and myths. In the case discussed in part 1, the identified patient struggled with the myth of the perfect marriage. The third class of hypotheses is based on the analysis of the communications in the family and other systems. This class describes the double-bind language in this case, which allowed the family to talk without talking.

The discussion combines all the meanings the different openings have suggested. The therapists remind themselves of the family's reaction to therapy: no one wanted to come except Mother. The team struggles with two ideas: how to positively connote Gerte's behavior and how to reframe the relationship between the family and the therapy. Since only Mother is motivated to come to therapy, team members strive to find the link between their hypothesis about the family and their hypothesis about the family and the therapeutic relationship. One member of the team feels it would make sense to invite only two family members to attend the next session. This is isomorphic to the family's struggle with their exclusive dyadic relationships and their avoidance of open triangular structures. The team suggests the family decide on which couple should come to the first session, which to the second session, and so on. The team remembers that the family talks about secrets but wants to keep them private. Another idea emerges: that after the family decides which couple should attend the session, they are to decide as a group which secrets they do not want talked about. This is consistent with the system's presentation; it discloses the system's rule about talking while forbidding talking. While Gerte says she does not understand the intervention, the rest of the family behaves as if each clearly understands it.

This consultation illuminates the clear relationship between the Milan Associates' thinking and the line of questioning in the interview. The follow-up to the case is disappointing, for although the family returned in "couples" several times, Gerte did not improve significantly. In the fall of the next year, she began to attend a day hospital on a daily basis, and the family dropped out of therapy.

The issue of how the consultation connects the family to ongoing therapy is a delicate one. If the consultation is too good, the family has a hard time giving up the consultants; if the consultation fails to provide new information, the therapy remains uninformed by the consultation.

The work of Boscolo and Cecchin has been largely represented in English through the use of teaching consultations, although the form of these consultations has undergone consistent change. The importance of the consultation issue lies in the fact that we teach each other well through consulting to one another! Consultations offer colleagues around the world the opportunity to learn from each other through the investigation and presentation of consultation maps, for in a consultation, the model must be clearly theorized, enacted in the session, and fully discussed. It must represent all the participants in and values of the meaning systems of the family, the referring context, and the clinic requesting the consultation. In the last ten years, no other group has been as available to this idea of mutual work through teaching consultations as the Milan Associates.

# THE CASE: CONSULTATION AND CONVERSATION

The following interview is an intake consultation that took place in September 1980 during a series of workshops conducted by Dr. Boscolo and Dr. Cecchin in a clinic in Germany. The case was presented to the consultants by a member of the clinic staff who had been in contact with the family. He reported that the family had been referred to the clinic for an evaluation with the idea that they would then go into family therapy with a local psychotherapist.

Gerte, the identified patient, is a twenty-one-year-old woman living at home. Her brother, Karl, is a nineteen-year-old student. The father is a civil servant and the mother used to work, but for most of her married life she has stayed at home as a housewife.

Very little information was given to the consultants. Gerte has had problems since early childhood. She has always been quite isolated, both at home and outside the home. She avoids contact with people and her mother is the only person she is close to. One year before, she started working as a receptionist but became increasingly distressed and anxious. A few months later she was hospitalized in a psychiatric hospital, following a psychotic episode characterized by restlessness, sleeplessness, and paranoid delusions. She stayed there several months. After the case presentation, it was decided that Boscolo would interview the family with the help of a therapist-translator, and Cecchin and the clinic staff would watch the session behind a one-way screen.

BOSCOLO: Let me begin by explaining how we start our consultations. I tell the family that Dr. Cecchin and other colleagues are behind the mirror. The reason I give is that one therapist alone does not have as great a capacity as a team to understand the complex interactions presented by the families who come to us.

CECCHIN: We also explain that we understand them better because we, "as a group," correspond to them "as a group." The thinking is the product of a relationship system that comprises both groups. We introduce the concept that out of such a system can come ideas, connections, that one person alone can never achieve.

### FAMILY INTERVIEW

GERMAN THERAPIST: *Since all of you speak English, we could conduct the session in English.*

BOSCOLO: *Do you speak English?*

GERTE: *A little.*

BOSCOLO: *A little.*

MOTHER: *She's learning at school.*

GERMAN THERAPIST: *That way we won't have to translate everything. Maybe only when something is not clear?*

BOSCOLO: *All right. Names? The ages? Your name?*

GERTE: *I'm twenty-one.*

BOSCOLO: *Twenty-one. Your name?*

GERTE: *Gerte.*

BOSCOLO: *Gerte?*

GERMAN THERAPIST: *Gerte.*

BOSCOLO: *Gerte. And you?*

KARL: *Karl.*

BOSCOLO: *Karl.*

KARL: *Nineteen.*

BOSCOLO: *Nineteen. You are the only two children. Yes. I see. Can you tell us what's the problem now? The problem—why you are here?*

GERMAN THERAPIST: *Do they know about the setting?*

BOSCOLO: *Yes. I want to describe the setting. You see, there is a microphone here. There is a mirror. Dr. Cecchin, from Milan, and other colleagues can observe from there what is going on here and eventually Dr. Cecchin might call me during the session to have an exchange. The reason that we do this is that in our experience the inclusion of a team of colleagues gives us the possibility of understanding better the situation of people who come to us for help. This is the main reason. So it might happen that Dr. Cecchin might call me during the session.*

GERMAN THERAPIST: *Also, there is a videotape—*

BOSCOLO: *Oh, yes. We have a videotape and this is a camera. We make a videotape and we watch the videotape, as I said before, in order to understand and help the persons who come to us. I would like to start by asking generally what is the problem that brought you here today?*

FATHER: *I think it's mainly a psychological problem, that my daughter is—well, depressed—*

MOTHER: *She was scared.*

FATHER: *When she started work she was there for some time, for about twelve months or so, but then she had to give up work.*

BOSCOLO: *What work?*

MOTHER: *She couldn't sleep any longer.*

FATHER: *She was a receptionist at a firm, and she couldn't sleep any longer and in the end we had to send her to a hospital.*

BOSCOLO: *When was that?*

FATHER: *The beginning of March. It was a kind of psychosis and, well, she stayed there for about five months while she made a little progress. The main sickness seemed to abate in degrees, but still there is a psychological problem.*

BOSCOLO: *So, you said that the problem is Gerte, hmm?*

FATHER: *Yes.*

BOSCOLO: *And when did you notice the problem in Gerte? When was the first time you noticed Gerte having problems? Was it twelve months ago? Or was it earlier?*

MOTHER: *Since her childhood.*

FATHER: *Since her childhood.*

BOSCOLO: *Since childhood.*

MOTHER: *She could hardly sleep in her childhood—she couldn't sleep—and since she started school she had to take tablets for sleeping and she always had difficulties in making contact with other people.*

BOSCOLO: *Other people.*

FATHER: *That's part of the problem.*

MOTHER: *And she has isolated herself also in the family.*

BOSCOLO: *Who was the one who noticed first that Gerte had a problem in childhood? Who noticed it first?*

---

BOSCOLO: I ask who was the first to notice the problem with Gerte. This is a standard question. It is based on the concept that a problem is not something inside the person, inside Gerte. The problem may have an organic or physiological aspect, but for our purposes, it is more important to find out what kind of information value the problem has for other people. So you ask other people "Who noticed it first?" The problem exists as a psychological reality only when somebody notices it.

## FAMILY INTERVIEW

KARL: *Of course, Mother.*

BOSCOLO: *Mother noticed first?*

KARL: *Certainly. Yes.*

BOSCOLO: *You said certainly—*

MOTHER: *I am the only person—*

BOSCOLO: *Excuse me. Is it because you remember that day that Mother started to notice a problem in Gerte?*

KARL: *Yes, I think that because she always is with my—talks with my mother. She doesn't talk very much with us.*

BOSCOLO: *Do you remember that it was Mother who noticed first?*

KARL: *Yes.*

BOSCOLO: *How old was your sister when Mother noticed this problem? How old was she? Do you remember?*

KARL: *She was—umm—*

BOSCOLO: *Hmm?*

MOTHER: *It was some years ago.*

KARL: *Some years ago. Yes. I don't know exactly.*

MOTHER: *She even told me—didn't talk about it in her childhood, but later when she was perhaps fifteen or sixteen she began to tell about her problems to me.*

BOSCOLO: *[to Karl] You said Mother was the one that noticed first that Gerte had a problem. How long after did your father see that Gerte had a problem? How long after?*

KARL: *Perhaps some months—*

BOSCOLO: *Some months after. Would you agree with your son?*

FATHER: *You cannot date it exactly. It's—*

BOSCOLO: *I see. [to Karl] How about you? When you—how long after did you realize?*

KARL: *Perhaps the same time.*

BOSCOLO: *Perhaps the same time. And the problem that has been noticed when Gerte was a child, you said it was in her childhood, over the years there was a change. Were there some times, some months or years, in which you didn't notice any problem?*

KARL: *No. I don't think so, but by the time it developed and became more grave.*

FATHER: *Graver and graver.*

BOSCOLO: *Yes. What would you say in the past—what was the problem as it appeared to you? Gerte's problem in the past?*

KARL: *In the past, perhaps she had some difficulties in school.*

FATHER: *At school.*

KARL: *At school.*

BOSCOLO: *Difficulty. What sort of difficulty? Learning or in relationships?*

KARL: *Yes, learning and getting contact with the others.*

FATHER: *With the other pupils.*

BOSCOLO: *Did she have more difficulty at school or at home?*

KARL: *I think in school. At school.*

FATHER: *At school, yeah.*

BOSCOLO: *At school. At home she did not have difficulty.*

KARL: *Not so much.*

BOSCOLO: I ask the son how long it was before the father and mother noticed that the daughter had a problem. The son answers: "Perhaps some months." It is interesting that even though the son was born two years after the daughter, he answers by giving full details about the early life of his sister. He never once says "I don't know, I was too young, ask my parents."

CECCHIN: Immediately you get the idea that the boy has some kind of interest in defining the sister as being the sick member of the family. He gives a careful description of what is wrong with her. This tells you that he is not allied with her. If he were, he would be eager to defend her: "What problem are you talking about?" Instead he confirms that the sister represents the sickness in the family. A split between the brother and sister is revealed by this behavior.

BOSCOLO: The problem of splitting may have started when the son was very young, two years old, because he found himself not with a sister but with a sick person. He had a sick person to take care of.

### FAMILY INTERVIEW

BOSCOLO: *Where did she start to have difficulties? At home or at school?*

FATHER: *Well, she stuck to her mother. She stuck to her mother, especially.*

BOSCOLO: *She got stuck to her mother. Would you say you would agree with your husband?*

MOTHER: *She refuses to get in contact with her brother and her father. Her father is only there to help her to get along at school and so on.*

BOSCOLO: *But when you said that she got stuck to her mother, who got stuck the most, Gerte or the mother?*

FATHER: *Gerte.*

BOSCOLO: *Gerte, yes. Did your wife also get stuck with Gerte?*

FATHER: *Oh, yes, she got stuck too, but I think that there was a good relation between us, between the adults and my son, there was a good relation—*

---

CECCHIN: The question "Who got more stuck to each other, mother or daughter?" represents an attempt to introduce the concept of circularity, of mutual recursiveness. The family describes Gerte as the one who has the problem of being stuck and the therapist introduces the idea that stuckness does not exist without somebody else to be stuck to. This statement introduces another way of looking at things, and if you look at the faces of the people at this moment they seem quite surprised at the question.

BOSCOLO: Another example of introducing an opposite punctuation, especially in a depressed family like this one, is for the therapist suddenly to ask: "When was the last time you had some good moments?" This introduces an opposite feeling.

CECCHIN: When the father was compelled to say "The mother got stuck with Gerte," this suggests that he sees the difference between mother and daughter and the relationship between mother and himself and the son. He says mysteriously: "Yes, my wife was stuck, but there was a good relationship between the rest of us." So it seems that the question is already having an effect.

What the father is saying is that the stuckness between mother and daughter somehow is related to the relationship between himself, his wife, and his son.

BOSCOLO: Another possibility is that when the father answers in this way, he is saying "Yes, she was stuck, but between us, between the adults and my son, there was a good relationship."

### FAMILY INTERVIEW

BOSCOLO: *Is there something that Gerte wants to say to her mother?*
GERTE: *No. I don't want to say.*
MOTHER: *She doesn't. She doesn't want to tell anything about herself. She doesn't like to tell anything about her. [to Gerte] I think you refuse.*
GERTE: *Yes.*
BOSCOLO: *I just wanted to see, you know.*
MOTHER: *She doesn't like to tell about her problems—what is her problem.*

---

BOSCOLO: Here you will notice the first clue to a theme that comes up over and over again in this family: people are not allowed to talk, and everyone keeps secrets. But it is Gerte who has the job of maintaining and reinforcing this family rule.

CECCHIN: Yes, and what is interesting is that the mother comes in so quickly to remind her that she does not want to talk about her problems. It is almost like a hypnotic induction.

## FAMILY INTERVIEW

BOSCOLO: *Well, perhaps—I understand. Perhaps I'll ask Gerte. Now, I asked before of your family "What's the problem in your family? Why are you here?" So they told me that they noticed that you had a problem since you were a child and also lately. Do you agree with them, with your father, with your mother, with your brother that you have problems? Or don't you agree?*

GERTE: *Yes. I agree.*

BOSCOLO: *You think you have a problem?*

GERTE: *But I have already—*

MOTHER: *Overcome it. She thinks she has overcome her problems. Yes? But in reality I don't think so. You always—umm—*

BOSCOLO: *Do you agree with what your mother said?*

GERTE: *Yes. I do.*

BOSCOLO: *Do you think you've overcome the problem?*

GERTE: *Yes. I have overcome it.*

BOSCOLO: *You've overcome the problem.*

MOTHER: *But you are not able to get in contact with other people, other than with your mother. That is a big problem.*

BOSCOLO: *So you think you have overcome the problem.*

GERTE: *Yes, I think so.*

BOSCOLO: *When did you overcome the problem? When was that?*

GERTE: *After my disease.*

BOSCOLO: *After your disease.*

MOTHER: *She has to take—*

BOSCOLO: *Excuse me. I would like to know when, what year did you—in what year did you overcome the problem?*

GERTE: *Twenty-one.*

BOSCOLO: *Twenty-one? You mean when you were twenty-one?*

FATHER: *After her recent illness she feels she overcame her problem, if I understand correctly.*

MOTHER: *Yes, she thinks so.*

---

BOSCOLO: Here I ask the daughter if she agrees with my analysis of the problem. She says "Yes, but I have already . . ." and she looks at her mother and her mother looks at her, and the mother answers for her, saying "She thinks she has overcome it." The mother then adds that she does not agree that the daughter has overcome her problem. So I ask the daughter "Do you agree with your mother?" and the daughter in effect says "I agree with two contradictory statements," that she has overcome and that she has not overcome her problem.

CECCHIN: There is a confusion between overcoming the problem and not overcoming the problem. Mother and daughter become mixed up in talking about it. This is a characteristic example of a double value—a value that keeps flipping between two poles.

### FAMILY INTERVIEW

BOSCOLO: I see. Do you—Gerte, do you see other problems? You agree that you had a problem, but do you see other problems in the family?

GERTE: At the moment I have not got one.

BOSCOLO: How about the others? Your brother, your mother, your father?

GERTE: I don't know.

BOSCOLO: You don't know. Is it more "yes" that you see problems or "no"?

GERTE: I don't see any problems.

BOSCOLO: You don't see any problems. For instance, if you see a problem in your father, mother, your brother, who would be the most likely to develop the problem in your family?

GERTE: Mother.

BOSCOLO: Mother? Most likely she would develop a problem, Mother. And then who else? After Mother, who?

GERTE: Father.

BOSCOLO: Father? How about Karl? You don't think that Karl might develop a problem in the future?

GERTE: No.

BOSCOLO: Why not? [pause]

GERTE: I've never discussed problems with him.

BOSCOLO: If I ask Father, for instance, do you think he could give me an answer about this? You said, if it will come out that there are some problems—maybe Mother will show problems, then Father, but you don't see Karl developing problems. You say "I don't know." If I ask Father, do you think he can give me an answer?

GERTE: Perhaps.

BOSCOLO: Perhaps. What answer, do you think?

MOTHER: I didn't understand quite—

BOSCOLO: Gerte doesn't expect—eventually, if there are problems in the future, maybe Mother, Father will have problems, but she doesn't expect Karl to have a problem in the future.

GERMAN THERAPIST: [translates]

FATHER: Do you mean who could first develop a problem or first overcome a problem?

BOSCOLO: Develop.

GERMAN THERAPIST: *Develop it. He thinks she might have misunderstood this. She might have heard you say who could first overcome the problem instead of develop the problem.*

MOTHER: *She thinks I could perhaps overcome her problems—her parents could overcome her problems.*

BOSCOLO: *Ah. They could overcome the problem.*

MOTHER: *Yes. Yes, to help her.*

BOSCOLO: *And then Father will—*

MOTHER: *Her father will—*

BOSCOLO: *[to German therapist] Can you ask her if I misunderstood which is which?*

GERMAN THERAPIST: *[translates to Boscolo] She understood you to say "solve the problems." If there should be problems who could best solve them?*

FATHER: *Mother, Father, then brother.*

---

CECCHIN: When you ask the daughter "Do you see any other problem in the family?" she does not even understand the question. She is so used to being the carrier of the problem that the therapist has to repeat "What about other people?" This is a totally new idea for the family.

BOSCOLO: I try to get an answer: If someone did have problems, who would be more likely to have one? They say definitely: We do not see any problems; she is the one who has the problems.

When the daughter is pressed by a hypothetical question—Who would be most likely to develop a problem?—then she answers. She says first the mother, then the father, not the son. This answer may give rise to the hypothesis that over the years the parents have presented the son as the healthy one, the good one, and the daughter as the one who has the problems. Since the son is always acting as the comparison for the daughter, this makes it impossible for the son to become a problem.

CECCHIN: The idea that the mother could develop problems—i.e., that somebody else other than Gerte could be a problem—creates real confusion. The German translator has to enter and translate because Mother begins to say: "I do not understand what you are talking about." In this session you can see how the language difficulty is utilized regularly when difficult questions come up.

Here you can see how the family finally reinstates their own belief system, their own explanations. They cannot accept the idea that somebody other than Gerte could develop a problem. After a lot of confusion with the language they come to a final conclusion that if another problem should come up within the family, the people who would be able to solve it would be the mother, father, and then the brother.

BOSCOLO: Which means that the only one who could have another problem is the daughter.

## FAMILY INTERVIEW

BOSCOLO: *Gerte, how do you see Karl? How do you see him growing? You said you haven't noticed a problem in Karl. Is that so?*

GERTE: *I didn't understand.*

BOSCOLO: *You never noticed any problem?*

GERTE: *If Karl has problems?*

BOSCOLO: *Yes.*

GERTE: *I don't know.*

BOSCOLO: *You don't know. How do you see Karl growing up? Do you think he's growing well or not well?*

GERTE: *He's growing well.*

---

CECCHIN: At this point the therapist has decided to give up his previous line of questioning. In some way he has already created confusion to the point that the family has to clarify their view of the problem.

There's a concept of perturbation embedded in a process like that. You don't need the family to agree with your ideas. You've already frightened their organization. If you insist that they agree, you put yourself in a symmetrical, adversarial position. Usually the therapist is the loser when that happens.

BOSCOLO: This is a good example of taking a neutral position. The therapist accepts the daughter's view that the mother and father could develop problems. He also accepts the parents' view that they could never have them because they could always resolve them. The therapist accepts both views and doesn't discuss them. He keeps matters in a kind of uncertainty rather than entering a discussion about which of the two positions is right. This uncertainty can be very therapeutic.

CECCHIN: There is also the connecting of these opposites by the therapist. This can have a positive effect. First because he accepts these opposites, and second because by accepting them he suggests the possibility of a synthesis or a new position that reconciles them.

### FAMILY INTERVIEW

BOSCOLO: *Hmm? He's growing well. If I ask this question to your mother, to your father, if they have noticed in the past sometimes that Karl has some problems, what do you think your father and mother will answer?*

GERTE: *I have not understood you quite.*

GERMAN THERAPIST: *[translates] She cannot say it. She says that she cannot understand.*

BOSCOLO: *[to Father] How about Karl? How you see Karl?*

FATHER: *He's a young man growing up to be very—to become very tall.*

BOSCOLO: *To become very tall.*

FATHER: *Of course he has problems, but I think they are not so serious, not in the least so serious as Gerte's problems are. They are problems of a young man, I think.*

BOSCOLO: *What—problems that you are a man?*

MOTHER: *Of a young man.*

FATHER: *Of a young man. Of a young man.*

BOSCOLO: *For instance?*

FATHER: *Well, how to enjoy his years best and—umm—*

MOTHER: *To get along in school.*

FATHER: *—to try to get along at school and to get good marks at school.*

MOTHER: *To get the best marks.*

FATHER: *Well, perhaps he tries to get into contact with some young ladies. Just normal things and the other problems, I can't say—there aren't any, in my eyes.*

BOSCOLO: *[to Mother] How about in your eyes?*

MOTHER: *I agree with my husband. He has—he had never big problems at school and with other children. He has a lot of friends.*

BOSCOLO: *A lot of friends.*

MOTHER: *Yes. Enough friends, I think.*

BOSCOLO: *Or too many?*

MOTHER: *No, not—and he is independent enough to go abroad. He went abroad some years ago on his holidays with some of his friends and this is a lack of hers. She doesn't want any friends.*

BOSCOLO: *I see.*

MOTHER: *She only sticks to me.*

---

BOSCOLO: The mother says "Gerte always sticks to me." She says this in the context of talking about her son, who she says is independent. You notice the pattern here: any time they talk about their son and they find positive characteristics, they spontaneously compare them to the negative characteristics of their daughter. You can see that this process has been going on for years. It can really become a form of brainwashing for the daughter, a kind of hypnotic induction, suggesting that she only has negative qualities, that she's the black sheep of the family. And there is a continuing amplification process making the son seem more and more normal and the daughter seem more and more abnormal.

CECCHIN: People in this kind of family only exist in relation to their opposite. You're good only if your sister's bad; you're bad if your brother's good. You exist only in relation to another person. This keeps the system extremely bound up. There is no space for individuality where people can be something that is not necessarily related to somebody else.

BOSCOLO: This is a typical example of the rigid patterns that can be seen in psychotic families. The therapist is talking to the parents about the way they see both the daughter and the son and they keep on repeating that the daughter is bad and the son is good in a very rigid fashion.

## FAMILY INTERVIEW

BOSCOLO: *I see. May I ask Gerte a question? Who is Karl closer to, Mother or to Father?*

GERTE: *Closer?*

BOSCOLO: *Karl is closer to your mother or to your father?*

*[Family speaks in German.]*

GERTE: *I think he had a closer contact to Mother.*

GERMAN THERAPIST: *Connection to Mother.*

BOSCOLO: *To Mother? It's always been like this? Also when he was a little boy he was closer to Mother or was he closer to Father?*

GERTE: *In one side he's closer to Father because they have the same interests.*

BOSCOLO: *Ah, yes. On one side. On the other side?*

GERTE: *Perhaps if he has problems he will ask Mother.*

BOSCOLO: *They said before that you have been always closer to your mother. That you have been stuck with your mother, that's what they said. Do you agree with that?*

GERTE: *Yes, I do.*

BOSCOLO: *Have you been close to Father sometimes?*

GERTE: *If I have problems at school I turn to Father.*

BOSCOLO: *You turn to Father when you have problems at school.*

MOTHER: *He could help her.*

BOSCOLO: *Umm—do you think that Karl has been—*

FATHER: *Independent, independent.*

BOSCOLO: *Yes, but in the past, did you see Karl closer to your wife or to you?*

FATHER: *Well, if he wants to have anything, he went to my wife. [Family laughs.]*

MOTHER: *He had wishes. Special wishes.*

FATHER: *Well, I did not verify all his wishes.*

KARL: *But I think—umm—neither closer to my father nor to my mother. It's the same thing.*

BOSCOLO: *The same thing. Also when you were a small boy?*

KARL: *Yes. Perhaps, as they said, if I wanted to have something I turned to my mother.*

BOSCOLO: *I see. And how about with your sister?*

KARL: *I never had a good contact with her. A good relationship.*

BOSCOLO: *You haven't had it, you don't have it.*

KARL: *No.*

BOSCOLO: *When was the last time you had a good relationship with your sister?*

KARL: *Some years ago. We quarreled always and now we don't talk anymore.*

BOSCOLO: *You don't talk anymore.*

MOTHER: *It's hard for him. Yes? Because she doesn't want.*

BOSCOLO: *She doesn't want what?*

MOTHER: *Want to talk.*

BOSCOLO: *To him?*

MOTHER: *Yes, and to us either sometimes too.*

---

BOSCOLO: Here, in order to get away from the idea that Gerte is bad and Karl is good, I ask about closeness. Is Karl closer to Mother or Father? Asking about closeness and distance fits in perfectly in a family where everything exists only in relation to its opposite, but instead of being pejorative, it is merely descriptive. So we find out that Karl is close to Father, although sometimes he goes for problems to Mother; that Gerte goes to Father for problems at school but is closest to Mother; and that brother and sister have never been close.

CECCHIN: This is a good example of staying with the family style but introducing a difference—in this case, we are making comparisons between relationships, but they are not comparisons of "good" versus "bad," so we are cutting into this dichotomy.

BOSCOLO: This also cuts into the singleminded focus on Gerte, since everyone must be included in a description of closeness and distance.

## *FAMILY INTERVIEW*

BOSCOLO: *[to Karl] What explanation do you give for the fact that your sister doesn't want to talk to you?*

KARL: *Perhaps we are so different in interests and—I don't know an exact explanation.*

BOSCOLO: [to Mother] *What explanation do you give? In the past there was some kind of relationship between them. They quarreled but there was one.*

MOTHER: *I think she doesn't want to talk about the reason. She could herself give the reason, but she doesn't want to talk about it.*

BOSCOLO: *Do you agree with your mother?*

GERTE: *Yes, I do.*

BOSCOLO: *I see.*

MOTHER: *I know her.*

BOSCOLO: *You said that there are reasons that Gerte doesn't want talked about. If she doesn't want to have them told, I don't want to hear them, but what I would like to ask is: What do you think these reasons are that Gerte knows but doesn't want to talk about? Do you know what these reasons are, Karl? You tell me the reason because Gerte doesn't want to talk about the reasons. At certain points she didn't get along with you, she didn't talk to you. You understand.*

KARL: *Yes. I suppose I do.*

BOSCOLO: *Do you have an idea about the reasons?*

KARL: *I don't know why.*

BOSCOLO: *You don't know why?*

KARL: *I don't know her so exactly.*

BOSCOLO: *Do you think that your mother knows these reasons?*

KARL: *Perhaps.*

BOSCOLO: *And your father, do you think he knows these reasons?*

KARL: *Umm—it's more possible that she knows it.*

BOSCOLO: [to Gerte] *Do you think your father knows these reasons that you don't want to talk about?*

GERTE: *I think so.*

BOSCOLO: *How about your mother, does she know these reasons?*

GERTE: *Yes, she does.*

BOSCOLO: *She does.* [to Father] *Do you know these reasons?*

FATHER: *Yes. As far as I can explain to myself.*

BOSCOLO: *Why did she decide at a certain point to stop talking to the brother? Do you have an idea why? I don't want to hear the reasons because I want to respect Gerte's—*

FATHER: *I have my—I can't explain.*

BOSCOLO: *Do you have an idea why Gerte doesn't want to bring these reasons here? Do you have an idea why?*

FATHER: *I know that.*

BOSCOLO: *Could you say why without telling the reasons that Gerte doesn't want talked about?*

FATHER: *She doesn't want them to be told. She doesn't—she doesn't want to tell us about her reasons.*

BOSCOLO: *But you have an idea why.*

FATHER: *Oh, yes.*

BOSCOLO: *Can you say? Tell me your idea? You don't have to talk about the reasons.*

FATHER: *Well, it might hurt her. Now—*

BOSCOLO: *It might hurt—*

FATHER: *Hurt her.*

MOTHER: *Hurt her.*

FATHER: *In her heart.*

BOSCOLO: *In her heart, if you tell me why.*

FATHER: *Yeah.*

BOSCOLO: *[to Mother] Do you agree with that?*

MOTHER: *I agree, yes, that she cannot tell the reasons to us.*

BOSCOLO: *Yes. I don't want to hear the reasons. I respect Gerte's wish that she doesn't want us or me or her brother or—but the question I ask is why do you think Gerte doesn't want these reasons to be known?*

MOTHER: *Because she doesn't want to reveal herself. She doesn't want to show her feelings to anybody except to me. As I told you, she isolates herself and it's our big problem that she has now a job, but she doesn't want to stay there because there is a colleague who wants to get her to talk with him and she doesn't like it—*

FATHER: *Talking with other people.*

BOSCOLO: *Talking with other people.*

MOTHER: *—and so she wants to—get up—*

FATHER: *No, no, no. To give up—*

MOTHER: *To give up the work.*

FATHER: *To give up work.*

---

BOSCOLO: At this point, the previous refusal by Gerte, seconded by Mother, to talk about her problems becomes generalized into a clear family pattern. In this family having secrets is connected with the presence of many types of prohibitions. For one thing, talking is dangerous. It is also probably not permitted to have a feeling of possessiveness or to be jealous. You can see how reluctant everyone is to discuss why the relationship between Karl and Gerte is not close.

CECCHIN: This is where we move from direct questioning of the person to asking another person what they think the first person's reasons for keeping something secret might be. Or we will ask them to give us their explanation of why the person wishes to keep the secret. The content of the secret becomes immaterial, but we don't allow the family to block this exploration. In this way we disrupt the family's fixed rule about not talking without challenging it directly.

BOSCOLO: Another family premise that surfaces here relates to the issue of control. Father says his daughter has been stuck to Mother all her life. The mother cannot get unstuck. They cannot control Gerte, she controls them. Their theory is that if they rebel against Gerte, she will break down. Their fear of a violent reaction by Gerte creates a violent relationship whereby a person can be a prisoner, can be nailed down by another all her life. The mother cannot go out, cannot talk to other people.

CECCHIN: You could have another hypothesis, that the mother must not have more than one child. If she has two, they compete with each other as though only one of them can survive, and the mother behaves as if she is available for only one person. The parent-child relationship must be exclusive, dyadic, the third party has to be eliminated.

BOSCOLO: In this case it is as if the mother has to take care of the sick daughter. The father has to stay out, and the son takes his father's place. These roles tend to become fixed forever, like a straitjacket.

CECCHIN: Yes. The mother stays with the daughter because she is stuck to her. Karl, because he feels sorry for his mother, cannot leave her. The father cannot go to anyone because there is no room for him. They can go on forever in this kind of situation. The four of them never learn to live together as a group.

BOSCOLO: To paraphrase Pirandello, I think one can say these are four characters in search of a therapist who can free them from their fixed roles. The daughter is supposed to have all the negative qualities, the son all the positive, the mother has to be the victim of the daughter, and the father has to sacrifice himself by staying alone.

## FAMILY INTERVIEW

BOSCOLO: *I meant to ask this; you got married, at a certain point Gerte was born, then three years later—*

MOTHER: *Two years later.*

BOSCOLO: *Two years later Karl was born. When did you notice first that Gerte got stuck to your wife? At what age?*

FATHER: *At about—at about that time, when he was born.*

BOSCOLO: *At the time when he was born you noticed this. Before she wasn't.*

FATHER: *No.*

BOSCOLO: *I see. Just after he was born. In your mind what explanation did you give? Did you give some explanation?*

FATHER: *A kind of jealousy. A kind of jealousy, I think.*

BOSCOLO: *A kind of jealousy. If I would ask a question to your wife about that, what explanation would she give? Would she agree with you?*

FATHER: *I think she would.*

BOSCOLO: *Yes? What about it, would you? You agree. It was jealousy that made Gerte—*

MOTHER: *Part. Part of the reasons.*

BOSCOLO: *Part.*

MOTHER: *Yes. But I don't—*

BOSCOLO: *Is there some other part, Karl?*

KARL: *[unintelligible]*

MOTHER: *That's part of the reason. The other part I can't tell you.*

BOSCOLO: *You can't tell me, because—*

MOTHER: *Because she doesn't want it.*

BOSCOLO: *Ah, because she doesn't want it.*

MOTHER: *She doesn't want it.*

---

BOSCOLO: You notice that I ask a mind-reading question here: "If I asked this question to your wife, what answer would she give? Would she agree with you?" The father said "I think she would" and the mother agrees. This is a pattern throughout the session: any time I ask a question the parents always agree. They have no differences of opinion, for instance, on the subject of why brother and sister are totally different.

## FAMILY INTERVIEW

BOSCOLO: *[to Father] Well, do you—so it's very important that you don't tell the other part of the reason, because Gerte doesn't want you to tell, but I'd like to ask, do you have an idea what is the other part of the reason?*

FATHER: *Of course. I have my reason.*

BOSCOLO: *Related to the fact that Gerte got stuck to Mother. You have—but it's better that you don't tell it, but do you think that also Karl knows the other—*

FATHER: *I think so.*

BOSCOLO: *You think so. Do you, Karl?*

KARL: *Yes, perhaps.*

BOSCOLO: *Perhaps.*

KARL: *I'm not quite sure it is this.*

BOSCOLO: *You're not quite sure. But what do you think of the explanation that Father—the one that they could say, because Father and Mother couldn't give one explanation? Your father gave one explanation that Gerte got stuck to Mother when you were born. Right? So Father said—the explanation he gave was that*

Gerte was jealous of you, that you were born, and Mother agreed. Then there are some other things that they did not want to say. Do you agree with this explanation that your sister got stuck because she was jealous of you?

KARL: I don't know what I should say right now. It's possible, yes.

BOSCOLO: It's possible.

MOTHER: We didn't talk about that in the family.

BOSCOLO: Do you agree with the explanation that your father, your mother gave that you got stuck with Mother when he was born because you were jealous of him? That's what Father and Mother say.

GERTE: I won't say that.

BOSCOLO: You won't say it. You don't agree.

GERTE: I don't say I agree or not.

BOSCOLO: Ah, you don't say if you agree. [to Father] Well, when this started—when you noticed, for instance, that Gerte got very close to Mother, got stuck with the mother after Karl was born, how would you describe her being stuck? She stayed all the time, close to her mother?

FATHER: I'm sorry. I can't—I can't remember. It's long, long ago.

BOSCOLO: Well, let me ask this question to you both. Can you describe this thing that they say that Gerte was stuck to the mother—would she stay all day long—all day long would they stay together? They never left each other?

KARL: Yes. She always talks to her mother if she has problems or if there is—if something has delighted her or if she's distressed, always to her mother.

BOSCOLO: Always to her mother, so her mother has always to listen to her.

KARL: Yes. And now she has no profession and so she talks the whole day to her mother.

BOSCOLO: I see. Does she talk more to the mother when she's alone with your mother or when you or your father are there?

KARL: When she's alone.

BOSCOLO: When she's alone she talks more?

KARL: Yes.

BOSCOLO: Okay, now when, for instance, your father comes home or you come home do you talk to—does your father talk to your mother or you talk to your mother, for instance?

KARL: Yes, of course.

BOSCOLO: And what happens when you talk? Gerte—what does she do, Gerte? She unsticks herself, at that moment?

KARL: Yes. She doesn't take part in the conversation.

BOSCOLO: What does she do?

KARL: She—she's silent.

FATHER: She becomes silent.

BOSCOLO: Does she listen?

MOTHER: She leaves the room.

FATHER: She listens.

BOSCOLO: Listens.

MOTHER: *No, she doesn't listen, but sometimes she leaves the room.*

BOSCOLO: *Sometimes she leaves the room.*

MOTHER: *Yes.*

BOSCOLO: *She leaves the room because she's upset?*

MOTHER: *Because she doesn't—*

FATHER: *She doesn't want anybody to interfere with—between her and Mother.*

BOSCOLO: *Does she get really openly upset sometimes when you try to talk to your wife for instance or when your son tries to talk to your wife?*

MOTHER: *Sometimes.*

BOSCOLO: *What does she do the most when she's upset?*

MOTHER: *She gets very angry sometimes, but I don't know if she wants that talked about.*

FATHER: *I'm afraid she doesn't want to talk about that, but we talk about that.*

BOSCOLO: *She doesn't want to talk about that. But what would happen if instead of saying that she doesn't want to talk about it—Suppose that you or your wife talked about it, what would happen? Suppose you were to tell us things that Gerte doesn't want told. What would happen?*

FATHER: *Well, she would get very, very angry.*

BOSCOLO: *What would she do?*

FATHER: *I think she would be very disappointed or she might be disappointed.*

BOSCOLO: *What would she do if she were there? What could she do? Ask Mother. What could she do?*

*[conversation in German]*

FATHER: *Well, she doesn't want to listen to—*

MOTHER: *She loses her—*

BOSCOLO: *Do you think she would lose her self-control?*

KARL: *No, no.*

MOTHER: *Sometimes.*

KARL: *I don't think so.*

BOSCOLO: *You don't think.*

KARL: *She might do anything—nothing perhaps, but she's angry. That's all.*

BOSCOLO: *You think that your parents are too concerned about this? Too concerned, too worried about what Gerte could do?*

KARL: *Yes, of course.*

BOSCOLO: *They are too worried?*

KARL: *They are the parents. They are of course worried about everything she does.*

---

BOSCOLO: Here I ask what Gerte can do when she is upset. I am trying to see what Gerte does to intimidate her mother and father to the point that the mother agrees to stay close to her and the father remains distant. What they say is that she hasn't done anything really threatening. It is possible that the parents' fear of Gerte's reaction is an alibi for keeping separate.

CECCHIN: Again, you have these prohibitions. It's forbidden in this family to be jealous; it's forbidden to be angry; it's forbidden to be disappointed. There is something dangerous in having feelings. It looks as if the only one who is allowed to have these feelings is Gerte. She is the one who can be disappointed; she can be angry, and she can be jealous of her brother. She is delegated to have all the feelings that the other family members cannot admit to. So she's the depository of the bad feelings, the dangerous feelings. It's a fascinating position.

## FAMILY INTERVIEW

BOSCOLO: *Does it also happen, for instance, that Gerte doesn't want Mother to say something to Father?*

KARL: *Yes, that's possible.*

BOSCOLO: *Does it happen sometimes that Gerte tells you "You mustn't tell this, either to my brother or to my father," does it happen?*

[conversation in German]

MOTHER: *Always, she says.*

BOSCOLO: *Always. What does she say?*

MOTHER: *She—she never wants that I check anything to find out what she tells to me.*

BOSCOLO: *And when she tells you, you—*

MOTHER: *In secret.*

BOSCOLO: *You keep the secret.*

MOTHER: *Yes.*

BOSCOLO: *You always keep the secret?*

MOTHER: *Very difficult to say because it's very difficult for me. Sometimes I have too many sorrows. I have too many sorrows and sometimes I must confess.*

BOSCOLO: *Let me ask Gerte, does it happen sometimes that Mother is unable to keep this secret? Does it happen sometimes that Mother did not keep a secret and talked to Father about something that you didn't want her to talk about?*

GERTE: *No. I don't think so.*

BOSCOLO: *You don't think so. You think that Mother has always kept the secret.*

GERTE: *Yes, I think so.*

BOSCOLO: *Suppose that Mother would not be able to keep some secrets? What would you have done if Mother had to tell Father something that you didn't want her to tell, what would you do?*

MOTHER: *What would you do if I was not able to keep a secret?*

GERTE: *I would be cross with you.*

MOTHER: *You would be angry with me.*

GERTE: *Yes.*

BOSCOLO: *You would be angry with her. Does it happen, Karl, sometimes that you see Gerte angry at Mother? Does it happen sometimes? Does she get angry at Mother?*

KARL: *No. Perhaps sometimes, but not often.*

BOSCOLO: *Sometimes.*

KARL: *Often it's—sometimes it's about seeing if she can take up her profession again, because Mother wants that and she insists—*

MOTHER: *I want her to have patience because she isn't allowed to get under stress— to get stressed, and I was very angry with her yesterday because she wanted to give up the job I had found for her. It is a good thing for her, I think. She cannot always stay at home, but she wants to always stay at home.*

BOSCOLO: *And you got angry at her.*

MOTHER: *I got angry with her because—*

BOSCOLO: *What did you do when you got angry?*

MOTHER: *I told her that I'm very, very sorry, I'm sorry that she gives up this job and so she made a compromise, she said she would go to her job twice a week, but it is not enough for me. I think it's very bad for her if she stays at home always and always looks in her grammar books. That doesn't give her anything.*

BOSCOLO: *So you got angry? This time it's about work—the job you found. You got angry.*

MOTHER: *Yes.*

BOSCOLO: *When did you get angry the last time before that? When did you get angry before?*

FATHER: *When she gave up the other job.*

MOTHER: *No. I wasn't angry with her.*

FATHER: *You were shocked.*

MOTHER: *I was shocked, but I wasn't angry because it was not her fault, it was her illness.*

---

BOSCOLO: When the mother says she isn't angry, the father says: "You were shocked." He suggests a way out and then she says: "I was shocked." Again we see the same pattern: Father and Mother always agree. The mother borrows the words from the father. She then says: "I wasn't angry because it wasn't her fault, it was her illness." The illness becomes the explanation which allows the mother to avoid expressing the feelings which are forbidden in the family. Moreover, she takes away all responsibility from Gerte.

CECCHIN: Yes, but this not only takes the responsibility away from Gerte, it takes it away from the parents. If you take away the responsibility of giving orders to a child, or of asking a child for something, you give up the responsibility of being parents. The parents give the responsibility for the child to somebody else, like a therapist. This is a pattern we often see in chronic cases.

BOSCOLO: Yes, but how do you explain that in this case the parents don't help the therapist? They offer more secrets than information.

CECCHIN: This is their contradiction. If they could express their feelings, or tell their secrets, they wouldn't need a therapist.


## FAMILY INTERVIEW

BOSCOLO: *I understand, so when was the other time in the past that you were angry? You said "I was angry this time."*

MOTHER: *Sometimes I'm angry when she's too aggressive, hostile toward her father and sometimes toward her brother, but mostly toward her father. Then I'm angry, and I tell her it's not good for the family when she shows herself so hostile toward her father, because her father likes her too, but he cannot show his feelings.*

BOSCOLO: *Do you get angry when she gets hostile?*

MOTHER: *To her father because I tell her that her father cannot show his feelings.*

BOSCOLO: *But do you get angry also about the fact that she is so close to you? She is so stuck to you? Does that make you angry or does that not make you angry?*

MOTHER: *No, I can understand that because she hasn't anybody besides me, but I should like that she has—*

BOSCOLO: *So that doesn't make you angry. Never made you angry?*

MOTHER: *No, but I should like her to have a friend.*

BOSCOLO: *All right, but it doesn't make you angry if she doesn't find a friend and she is stuck to you. That doesn't make you angry, you said.*

MOTHER: *No. That can't make me angry because it's not her fault.*

BOSCOLO: *Does this make your husband angry? Does sometimes your husband get angry that you are so stuck to Gerte—Mother is so close to Gerte and Father feels left out?*

FATHER: *Never.*

MOTHER: *No, I don't think so, but I—he is depressed because—*

FATHER: *Sometimes I feel—I'm disappointed and I'm depressed when I find out that I can't get into close contact with her—*

BOSCOLO: *With whom?*

FATHER: *—then I feel depressed.*

BOSCOLO: *With whom?*

FATHER: *With Gerte.*

BOSCOLO: *How about with your wife?*

MOTHER: *No. No.*

FATHER: *No, with Gerte.*

BOSCOLO: *Yeah, I understand—with her. I understand. How about with your wife—*

MOTHER: *No.*

BOSCOLO: *—because if your wife is so close to your daughter—*

FATHER: *Well, I can't understand that. I can't understand.*

BOSCOLO: *—don't you feel sometimes a little left out by your wife?*

FATHER: *Never. Never. Well, I can't understand it, but I must respect it because she does so much for her.*

BOSCOLO: *Yeah. Do you feel sometimes that Father should feel a bit left out by your mother?*

KARL: *No, I don't.*

BOSCOLO: *You have never left him out.*

KARL: *No. No.*

MOTHER: *He's only depressed because Gerte doesn't find any way to him. She's not able to find a way to her father.*

BOSCOLO: *That's what depresses him.*

MOTHER: *Yes. And also that depresses me.*

BOSCOLO: *It depresses you.*

MOTHER: *Yes.*

BOSCOLO: *When did you start to see your husband depressed about Gerte not having a good rapport with him? Is it a long time?*

MOTHER: *Some years ago.*

BOSCOLO: *Some years ago.*

MOTHER: *Yes. I can't tell exactly the day 'cause it's a long time.*

BOSCOLO: *Because way, way back he could not have a rapport with Gerte.*

MOTHER: *When she was a little child—*

BOSCOLO: *Little child.*

MOTHER: *—she talked to her father, but when Karl came, then—later on, she got stuck to me.*

BOSCOLO: *She got stuck to you.*

MOTHER: *Only to me.*

BOSCOLO: *Before Karl was born there were two years in which Gerte was not stuck to you, how was your husband with her? Was he with her?*

MOTHER: *Perhaps, yes.*

BOSCOLO: *Did he like to be with her?*

FATHER: *I liked her very much and I still like her very much. She's my child—* [knock on door]

BOSCOLO: *Excuse me for a minute.*

----

CECCHIN: The therapist is trying very hard to introduce to the family the idea that father and son could also feel left out. This means that they could also feel sentiments of jealousy and competition. But you see a massive denial. The only thing they feel is depression, they feel disappointed because the daughter doesn't get close to them. Again, the only one who can have angry, jealous feelings is Gerte. The mother accuses the daughter of being angry, saying "anger is not good for her." But when the therapist asks her: "Do you feel angry about your daughter?" she says "No, I only feel disappointed." So the daughter is angry and possessive and jealous and the other people are only depressed and disappointed.

BOSCOLO: Carl Whitaker has described "psychotic" families in terms of the white knight and the black knight. One person has to be all black, the other all white. He says that in therapy the task is to make them all gray. In this family Gerte is the black knight and all the negativity has to belong to her. The others are all white.

CECCHIN: When this process starts, when one of the family members begins to collect the negative feelings of all the other members, the process tends to amplify itself. The more Gerte becomes the jealous one, the sick one, the sticky one, the more the other people become free from these feelings. The only feelings they can have are the feelings of being hurt by the behavior of the other person. This gives us some idea about how the white knight and the black knight originate in a system like this. These differences tend to be amplified over time.

However, what we are saying seems in contradiction with the common finding that psychotic families usually give "no difference" answers and tend to make statements which equalize everyone. Here we see, instead, a major difference which tends to get amplified—the difference between the good and the bad. How can we reconcile these two ideas?

BOSCOLO: One explanation is that there is one member who has all the negatives and the others all the positives. This major difference escalates in time, making two homogeneous groups—one in which everything is negative and the other where everything is positive. In the positive group, as in this family, the members are strong, good, loving. There are no differences between them. The only difference is between they who are good and perfect and their daughter who is jealous and possessive.

CECCHIN: I think this explains why, when the designated patients start to get better and more independent, thus getting out of the negative position they occupy in the family system, then you see that the other members of the family start to become depressed. Either they develop symptoms or they resist this change.

BOSCOLO: Another point to be made here is that Cecchin called me out and asked me to ask Gerte if the mother ever asked her to keep a secret from the other family members. He wanted me to find out who else in the family keeps secrets.

## FAMILY INTERVIEW

BOSCOLO: *Let me ask you this question. As we said before, there are many secrets that you want Mother to keep.*

GERTE: *Yes.*

BOSCOLO: *Also here today, Mother, a few times, has said, I cannot say this because Gerte told me I must not say this.*

GERTE: *Yes.*

BOSCOLO: *All right. Also it seems that sometimes Mother has difficulty in keeping all the secrets that you tell her to keep. There are some difficulties there. Do you understand?*

GERTE: *Perhaps.*

BOSCOLO: *Perhaps. I understand that perhaps Mother has some difficulties in keeping all the secrets that you tell her to keep. Does it happen sometimes—this is Dr. Cecchin's question—does it happen sometimes that your mother asks you to keep a secret?*

GERTE: *No.*

BOSCOLO: *Never happens that your mother tells you something and she tells you, Don't say this to Daddy or to Karl. Never happens?*

GERTE: *No. Never happens.*

BOSCOLO: *Never happens. How about—about Karl, does it happen sometimes, for instance, that Mother spoke to you and she asked you not to say anything?*

KARL: *Oh, no.*

BOSCOLO: *All that was said to Gerte, was this said to you?*

KARL: *No.*

BOSCOLO: *This never happened? That Mother tells you something and she tells you don't tell this to Gerte?*

KARL: *Perhaps if she can't keep a secret or—but that's very seldom.*

BOSCOLO: *Very seldom. When was the last time, do you remember, when your mother asked you—told you something and told you not to tell it to Gerte or to Daddy?*

KARL: *Perhaps a month?*

BOSCOLO: *A month ago. And what did she tell you, your mother?*

KARL: *I don't remember.*

BOSCOLO: *You don't remember, or you want to keep a secret too?*

KARL: *Yes.*

BOSCOLO: *You want to keep a secret too. All right. Now you keep a secret because you feel otherwise your mother will get upset if you tell me now what your mother one month ago told you not to say? To whom, I just want to know to whom. She didn't want you to tell that to whom, to your father or to Gerte?*

KARL: *To Gerte.*

BOSCOLO: *Ah, to Gerte. All right. So, it is important that you keep a secret too.*

KARL: *But it's not really a secret. It wasn't very important. It was only the thing that she had too much—too many sorrows—*

BOSCOLO: *No. It's important that you don't say.*

KARL: *No. She had too many sorrows and she wanted to tell me something, but—*

BOSCOLO: *This was one month ago or was it also before? Does it happen sometimes in the past over the years that she comes to you and she has these sorrows and she tells you how sorrowful she is? She tells you. And she tells you not to— don't tell this to—*

KARL: *Yes. Very seldom.*

BOSCOLO: *Oh, seldom—to Gerte. [to Father] How about you? Does it happen sometimes that your wife talks to you and she tells you, Don't say this to Gerte or to Karl?*

FATHER: *I can't remember.*

BOSCOLO: *Never happened.*

FATHER: *It may have happened, but I can't remember. It was not so important.*

BOSCOLO: *Do you remember that it sometimes happened that you told your husband, Don't say this to Gerte or to Karl?*

MOTHER: *I don't like to discuss that because it's not good, I think.*

BOSCOLO: *You don't like to discuss—No, I just want—It's important that you don't say the secret, but I just want the answer yes or no if it sometimes happened that you told your husband something, you told him keep the secret. Don't tell Gerte or Karl. Did it happen, yes or no?*

MOTHER: *It may have happened, but very—*

BOSCOLO: *It may have happened. Stop. Stop. Stop because it's important that each one has a right to secrets.*

MOTHER: *There are more sorrows than secrets. More sorrows.*

KARL: *Yes. She has sorrows.*

MOTHER: *Because sometimes I can't keep the sorrows to myself.*

FATHER: *You have to talk about it and have to discuss it.*

---

CECCHIN: This question about who tells secrets is aimed at distributing throughout the family the negative attributes. It looks as if Gerte is the only one who keeps secrets, which is bad. So the therapist asks whether Mother also asks Gerte to keep secrets. Does she behave like her daughter? In this way the therapist tries, without being pejorative, to overcome the white/black, right/wrong dichotomy.

BOSCOLO: Yes, the active, obsessive questioning of the therapist puts in crisis the repetitive patterns and roles of the family. The therapist asks questions and accepts each answer without making interpretations. Through these questions, which continuously introduce opposite punctuations, he goes against the rigid family rules.

CECCHIN: You can see that the son is now beginning to open up a little bit under this persistent questioning. The therapist never gives up, he keeps insisting. And this insistence represents a very active neutrality—the therapist does not accept the negative attributes of the daughter and the positive attributes of the son. His behavior is almost intrusive. This contradicts the idea that some people have that the Milan approach is somehow passive.

Here the son first admits that he keeps secrets, then he says "but it's not a real secret, it wasn't very important." Again, when there is an admission from family members who are supposed to be "good" that there might be something not very good about them, then they apologize, they try to minimize the fact.

BOSCOLO: Words are changed. A "secret," which is negative, becomes a "sorrow," which is not.

The questioning also provokes an attitude of "giving up" on the mother's part: "I don't like to discuss that because it is not good." She begins to reveal herself more openly. The things which are not good should not be discussed. We go back to the idea that bad things belong only to Gerte, and so things which are not good should not be discussed. But by talking like that she is describing her behavior at a more inclusive level. She is defining herself as one who doesn't want to talk about bad things.

*FAMILY INTERVIEW*

*BOSCOLO: Are there some times also when, as a husband and a wife, you and your wife have something that you feel like keeping for yourself? Is there something that you keep for yourself or somehow there is nothing that you—no secret between you?*

*FATHER: Well, I think there is no real secret between us, the main problem is—the main problem is the sorrow we have with this child. That's the problem we are going to discuss from morning till night.*

*BOSCOLO: Yes, we are discussing that, but my question is that very often parents have something—they have something between themselves that they think is important children don't know. Is there something between Mother and Father, between both of you, is there something that sometimes you don't want to tell to your children? Is there some secret between you? It very often happens.*

FATHER: *I think we have no time to have any secrets.*

BOSCOLO: *Do you think, Karl—*

MOTHER: *Not too much—*

BOSCOLO: *Do you think, Karl, that they have something that they have not told you?*

KARL: *No, I don't think so.*

BOSCOLO: *How about if they would have something? Do you think it would be right or wrong, what do you think?*

KARL: *Perhaps it would be right if it doesn't concern me, if it isn't very important for me.*

BOSCOLO: *But does it happen sometimes, for instance, that Gerte asks Mother about—when you [Mother] talk to your husband— when you are talking—what you talk about? Is she curious about what you talk about, both of you when she is not there or Karl is not there?*

MOTHER: *I think she doesn't like me to talk to my husband, I think, and she wants to interrupt me if I talk to my husband.*

BOSCOLO: *Does she ask sometimes what you talk about with your husband when she is not there?*

MOTHER: *No. But I only remember she doesn't like that, if I talk to my husband.*

BOSCOLO: *I see. For instance, does it happen sometimes that you talk to your husband or your husband to you—without the children around?*

MOTHER: *Yes. Sometimes. But we have too much to do. I think—it's too much— he's too much engaged in his profession, in his work. He has to work from—*

KARL: *I think they have the right to talk if we are not there. It's only natural—*

MOTHER: *Yes.*

BOSCOLO: *Do they talk?*

KARL: *Yes. Perhaps.*

FATHER: *You know, we have one main problem. One main problem.*

MOTHER: *Yes.*

FATHER: *That's the problem we are talking about.*

MOTHER: *And sometimes we have the problems that we don't get along with our work. We are overworked. He's overworked in his profession.*

---

BOSCOLO: Here I ask whether husband and wife have secrets between them and connote this idea positively. A mother and father having secrets could be a positive thing.

It's interesting that when I ask the parents whether they have secrets, Father says they have no time to have secrets because they have no time to talk. He is very quickly followed by Mother who blames Gerte for not permitting them to talk. Again, if there is some difficulty between the mother and father the fault is Gerte's. So there is a battle here between myself and the family. The family wants to maintain the myth of the black knight. I am trying to counteract this myth. But I don't do it in a confronting manner, I do it by changing questions rapidly. The family has to defend itself but it doesn't feel challenged in an open manner. With this kind of technique, it's much more difficult for family members to hold on to their construction of reality.

CECCHIN: Since the therapist does not give interpretations, but just asks questions which are based on a hypothesis, the family does not know what the therapist is thinking about. He just keeps asking questions about different things. As a result, they don't know how to orient themselves, how to fight the therapist.

### FAMILY INTERVIEW

BOSCOLO: [to Father] What do you do? What is your profession?
FATHER: I'm a civil servant.
BOSCOLO: You're a civil servant. And you?
MOTHER: I'm a housewife only, but I'm too much engaged in my sorrows with the family and with the house and I—sometimes I don't get along.
BOSCOLO: Have you always been a housewife or was there some time that you worked outside?
MOTHER: Some time I was a legal assistant too, but it was very long ago.

---

BOSCOLO: Mother says "sometimes I don't get along." I interrupt her and start to talk about something else. My feeling is that I was caught by the powerful rule that it is forbidden to criticize or find something negative in the couple.

### FAMILY INTERVIEW

BOSCOLO: [to Mother] When was the last time you worked?
MOTHER: Oh, it was very long ago.
BOSCOLO: When?
MOTHER: Umm—twenty-four years, or twenty years.

FATHER: *Twenty-four years.*

BOSCOLO: *Twenty-four years, but you were married when you stopped working.*

MOTHER: *Yes. When I married, I stopped working.*

BOSCOLO: *Just after you were married or after Gerte was born?*

MOTHER: *No. Just after I married because I didn't like my profession.*

BOSCOLO: *Yes. But have you thought about going back to do something outside? For instance, in all these years, over the last twenty years, was there some time that you thought about going out and finding work or something like this?*

MOTHER: *Yes. I sometimes regretted having given up my profession, but I have not much time to reflect about that.*

BOSCOLO: *But do you think, for instance, if there would not have been children you would have worked?*

MOTHER: *Perhaps, yes. If I had no children.*

BOSCOLO: *I would like to ask about how many rooms you have in your—what is it, a house or apartment?*

MOTHER: *We built a house when she was two years old.*

BOSCOLO: *Two years old.*

MOTHER: *Then he was born in our new house.*

BOSCOLO: *Ah, he was born in your new house. How many rooms do you have in that house?*

FATHER: *Quite a lot.*

BOSCOLO: *Oh, you have many rooms.*

FATHER: *I think about twelve or thirteen.*

MOTHER: *Ten.*

FATHER: *Altogether.*

BOSCOLO: *Where does Karl sleep?*

MOTHER: *In the same—*

FATHER: *On the same floor as we do.*

BOSCOLO: *On the same floor.*

FATHER: *On the same floor, yes.*

BOSCOLO: *Yes. But he has his own room?*

FATHER: *Yes.*

BOSCOLO: *His own room? And how about Gerte?*

MOTHER: *She has her own room, I have my own room, and he has his own room.*

BOSCOLO: *Ah, you have four different rooms? You don't sleep in the same room?*

MOTHER: *No, since several years we don't sleep in the same room.*

BOSCOLO: *Since when?*

MOTHER: *Several years, I think perhaps ten years.*

BOSCOLO: *Ten years.*

MOTHER: *Perhaps ten years or so—*

FATHER: *That's because I'm a heavy smoker and she can't stand the smell.*

MOTHER: *Yes, he goes to bed very late, and I don't like that.*

BOSCOLO: *Were there other reasons that you decided on sleeping in different rooms?*

FATHER: *No.*

MOTHER: No.

BOSCOLO: No?

FATHER: That was—that was the main reason.

BOSCOLO: That was the main reason. And does it happen during the night sometimes, in the last ten years, does it happen that one went in the other room, the
  other person's room or—[Family laughs.]

BOSCOLO: Gerte, do you understand?

MOTHER: No, she doesn't understand.

BOSCOLO: Daddy and Mother said that for the past ten years they have not been
  sleeping in the same room, so I asked them if some nights, for instance, Mother
  went to Father or Father went to Mother's room. Do you think they did?

GERTE: No, I don't think so.

BOSCOLO: You don't think so. How do you know? Has Mother told you she never
  went in Daddy's room or—

MOTHER: That wasn't a subject that we talked about. We didn't talk about that.

BOSCOLO: Excuse me. You [Gerte] said, I don't think so, when I asked whether in
  the past ten years Mother ever went to Father's room or Father went to Mother's
  room during the night. How do you know that they never did? You stayed awake
  all night for ten years?

GERTE: No. I think so, only.

BOSCOLO: You think so. That sometimes because they said that you had some problems sleeping at night, does it sometimes happen that you stay awake and listen?

GERTE: No.

BOSCOLO: That if Mother or Father moves around?

GERTE: No. I never listen.

BOSCOLO: Never listen, but what makes you feel so sure that neither one went to
  each—to the other room for the past ten years, at night? What makes you so
  sure?

GERTE: Because each one has his own room and I don't think that they are walking
  around at night.

BOSCOLO: Suppose it comes out instead that some nights, during these ten years,
  they met in either room, what would be your reaction? Suppose they tell you,
  look, some nights we slept together, either in Daddy's room or in Mother's room?
  Would you like that or wouldn't you like that—to hear that?

GERTE: That's indifferent.

BOSCOLO: It's indifferent. Do you think, Karl, that in those ten years that sometimes
  either Mother or Father went to the other room or—

KARL: I don't think so, but I think it's as well that it's indifferent. It's normal that
  couples sleep together and—

BOSCOLO: It's normal?

KARL: Yes.

BOSCOLO: Yes, it's normal, but do you think it happened—

KARL: No.

BOSCOLO: —over the past ten years. You don't think it did happen. Do you think there was intimacy? That there was some intimate rapport between Father and Mother over the past ten years?

KARL: I'm not so well informed about that.

BOSCOLO: You are not well informed. Now, you said sometimes that Gerte has difficulty in sleeping? You said—you mentioned when she was a little girl. It was also over the years she had sometimes some difficulty in sleeping over the night?

MOTHER: She always had to take some medicine and this sleeplessness has perhaps caused her nervousness.

BOSCOLO: Yes, but since when has she been sleeping less? For many years?

GERTE: Yes.

BOSCOLO: Now who—you [Gerte] say yes. Who usually gets up at night when you hear that Gerte is not sleeping?

MOTHER: No.

BOSCOLO: When you want to see or talk to her does she come to your room?

MOTHER: No. I—I try to wait until morning. I didn't want to begin such a bad custom to come to her room and I didn't like her to come to my room because—

FATHER: A bad habit.

MOTHER: A bad habit.

BOSCOLO: When was the last time she came to your room?

MOTHER: Perhaps ten years ago. She slept in my room for perhaps one or two years because she had so much anguish and fears and so many—

BOSCOLO: So for two years you slept together.

MOTHER: Yes, well, perhaps one or two years.

BOSCOLO: And then after that, you slept with her father?

MOTHER: No, no, he had his own room.

BOSCOLO: His own room.

MOTHER: A room of his own, yes.

BOSCOLO: Did it ever happen that Karl slept with you?

MOTHER: No, never, because he had no problems in sleeping. He always slept very well, I think, or mostly, and she always was full of fear and anguish of the future. She always thought that—

BOSCOLO: In the past few years, which is also lately, did she ask you to sleep together? She comes to your room at night?

MOTHER: No, in the last time she has slept alone by herself, but before her illness she always had fears of the future, of what may happen in the future, and she didn't see any sense in her life. That was her great problem and she always told me she had perhaps gone into the wrong profession.

---

CECCHIN: This is an interesting interchange. First, the mother says Gerte does not understand about the parents' sleeping arrangement. The therapist falls into the trap of believing the mother and tries to explain to Gerte what he meant to say. Gerte, we know, is obedient to the system. Under this questioning, where the therapist is trying to get her to comment on the situation, she makes a very concrete, simple statement, saying that each parent has his or her own room and they don't walk around at night. Without laughing, without smiling, because smiling means to understand. Smiling also means to understand that the parents are lying when they say that the reason they have not slept together for the last ten years is because of Father's smoking.

It is quite clear that there is something else going on. The family is implying there is something else by smiling and laughing but Gerte is under an injunction not to see this kind of thing, because the parents have to be perfect. Parents don't lie. Parents don't contradict each other, even if it is obvious to everyone that they do. So the girl has to go out of her way to defend this idea of the parents' perfection, to the point of appearing totally stupid, or perhaps totally psychotic.

BOSCOLO: I fell into a trap here. When the mother said that Gerte didn't understand, I think I should have asked the mother, father, and son how they knew she didn't understand. Then I could have asked a hypothetical question such as "Suppose she did understand?"

*FAMILY INTERVIEW*

BOSCOLO: *You said she had been working—you found a job for her, when was that?*

MOTHER: *That was after her illness because she is not able now to work in her former profession. It was too much stress for her and now she has a job, it is not paid, it's—*

FATHER: *A part-time job.*

BOSCOLO: *But did she work regularly more or less in the last few years or she has not worked?*

MOTHER: *She went to school first until she was eighteen—*

FATHER: *Nineteen eighty-one.*

MOTHER: *She went to school. To a language school and then she got a job as—*

FATHER: *Receptionist or—*

BOSCOLO: *Did she have difficulty in keeping the job?*

FATHER: *Well, the main problem was contact with other people.*

MOTHER: *She got no contact and she was—I heard she was too—she was not quick enough in working because she had too many problems with herself. She had to—and since she got ill she couldn't concentrate any longer. She couldn't sleep any longer and she had to stop.*

---

CECCHIN: Notice how the therapist changes the subject, suddenly, without bringing the previous subject to a close. This pattern happens frequently. The explanation of this pattern is that the therapist begins to explore certain areas of behavior, like sleeping at night. When either the resistance of the family becomes too high or he feels that he has already shaken the belief system of the family, then he chooses to stop and to change the subject. But the moment that he stops is not related to the fact that the subject he has been discussing is exhausted or that he has reached some conclusions. In point of fact, every change of subject seems to happen before the subject has been completed. This is an important feature of the systemic interview. The therapist tries to open up possibilities in a certain area, to disturb the thinking pattern of the system, to suggest different connections, different punctuations, and then leaves the system in that area and changes the subject completely. This allows the system to elaborate these changes by itself, perhaps not on a conscious level.

BOSCOLO: This fits in with what family members usually say during follow-up calls. When asked about what they think the therapist did, they say: "We don't know. We tried hard to understand what the therapist meant, what he wanted to know, what he thought about us, but he kept changing topics so we never understood what the point was."

CECCHIN: Your choice of topics can be of a general exploration that takes place in a first interview. You talk about night life, then you talk about work life, then suddenly you move on to social life. There are a series of topics that any therapist has in his own "bag." It's easy to choose a topic to change to. The important question is when to do it. We believe that the "when" is very important for the therapeutic effect.

### FAMILY INTERVIEW

BOSCOLO: *When she was in the hospital, how long—did she stay a long time in the hospital?*

MOTHER: *Five months. From March to July.*

FATHER: *June.*

BOSCOLO: *For five months, I see. Five months in the hospital. How was the atmosphere at home without—*

FATHER: *Terrible.*

BOSCOLO: *Terrible?*

FATHER: *Terrible. [pause] I think those were the worst days of my life.*

MOTHER: *She didn't want—*

BOSCOLO: *Those five months.*

FATHER: *When she—when she—*

BOSCOLO: *It was the worst five months of your life.*

MOTHER: *When she came to the hospital—she didn't want to live any longer before she came to the hospital.*

BOSCOLO: *Yes, but you said in those five months when Gerte was in the hospital were the worst months in your life.*

FATHER: *Oh, yes, of course.*

BOSCOLO: *For whom was it more terrible in the family?*

FATHER: *For the parents. The parents, I think.*

BOSCOLO: *How was the atmosphere in those five months?*

KARL: *Such as he described. He was very distressed—depressed.*

BOSCOLO: *Who was more depressed, your father or your mother?*

KARL: *Perhaps Father, but—*

BOSCOLO: *Perhaps Father.*

KARL: *—but you can't say exactly. He was more excited openly. He always—*

MOTHER: *Yes, perhaps because he is—*

KARL: *He is pessimistic.*

MOTHER: *—a pessimist by nature—and perhaps I have some hope for the future. I will always keep some—I try to keep some hope.*

BOSCOLO: *You say he's more pessimistic.*

MOTHER: *He's more pessimistic, yes. I try to—keep some hope.*

BOSCOLO: *When Gerte was in the hospital, your wife was for five months without Gerte. Didn't Karl lift her spirits up?*

FATHER: *Well, I think we neglected him a little.*

BOSCOLO: *You neglected whom?*

FATHER: *Him.*

BOSCOLO: *How did you neglect him?*

FATHER: *Because we always thought of her.*

MOTHER: *We visited her five times a week. Five times a week.*

FATHER: *Four or five times a week.*

BOSCOLO: *But, for instance, did you notice that it happens sometimes, for instance, that Gerte is at work and Karl is at home? The way you see it, for instance, whose company does your wife seem to enjoy more, Karl only or when she's with Gerte?*

FATHER: *It's difficult to answer that question.*

BOSCOLO: *Well, does she enjoy more the company of Gerte or Karl?*

MOTHER: *I can't say because it's impossible to say that.*

FATHER: *We like both of them.*

BOSCOLO: *It's not a matter of—when one is outside for work—*

FATHER: *Well, when she is outside, I constantly think of her. What happens to her, what might she do, and so on. I'm constantly thinking of that.*

BOSCOLO: *I understand you, but how about your wife?*

MOTHER: *I too.*

KARL: *Yeah, she does the same.*

MOTHER: *I'm full of sorrows because I don't see much chance for her. I'm full of sorrow what she might do in the future because she—she's not willing to get into contact with other people. I think that's very important for her. I should like her to—*

BOSCOLO: *But doesn't it happen sometimes, Karl, when you are at home and your sister is not at home because she's at work or the time she was in the hospital, that you see, for instance, that your mother talks to you and she feels relieved?*

KARL: *No. I don't think so. Every time she is outside my mother is worried, Father is worried, and we can't talk in a very carefree way.*

BOSCOLO: *Do they sometimes talk to you about this worry? Do they talk to you sometimes? When they talk to you they always talk about Gerte? They never talk about anything else?*

KARL: *They want to talk about something else, but—*

BOSCOLO: *Not so often.*

KARL: *Not so often.*

BOSCOLO: *Do you feel sometimes you're tired of Mother coming to you or Father talking about Gerte? You feel tired?*

KARL: *No. I can understand that.*

BOSCOLO: *You understand. Now I would like to ask a question to Gerte. Suppose one day you feel well, you get out, you get married—this is a supposition, a hypothesis we make—and you leave the family, how do you think their life would be without you?—how do you think the life of your mother, your father, and your brother would go without you?*

GERTE: *How they would live without me?*

BOSCOLO: *Yes. Without you. Do you understand the question?*

GERTE: *If I'm independent?*

BOSCOLO: *Yes, suppose that all of a sudden you become independent, you leave, you go out and you become independent. What do you think would happen to your mother or father?*

GERTE: *Nothing.*

BOSCOLO: *Nothing? Do you think it would be a better or worse atmosphere without you? Hmm?*

---

CECCHIN: The therapist inquires about how things were at home when Gerte was in the hospital. The father said: "It was terrible." This was surprising because he kept saying that when she was at home he could not have contact with her, she never talked to him, they were always separated, she talked only to Mother. Now he says that the time when the daughter was in the hospital were the worst days of his life. It's a very strange statement. When the husband describes how terrible it was he could either mean how much he missed his daughter or how terrible it was to be alone with his wife, without a daughter in between. There are many implications in this word terrible. It must be extremely threatening to the family to be without Gerte.

BOSCOLO: It is possible that Father needed Gerte at home either as a buffer in his relationship with his wife or because he was incestually attached to her. This could be one of the family secrets. He seems to be competing with son and wife about who suffers the most from Gerte's illness.

When I ask the father if Karl lifted his mother's mood when Gerte was in the hospital, the father gave a tangential answer. He said that they neglected the boy. He seems to deny any possibility of emotion between his son and his wife.

CECCHIN: Father has already said he was depressed when Gerte was away and now he says that Karl also needed to be cheered up. So both men became depressed. This is very odd. The daughter is always with the mother, but when the daughter is away, the ones who become lonely and depressed and abandoned are the father and Karl, not the mother.

BOSCOLO: From the beginning Gerte has been told she is bad when she is at home because she immobilizes Mother, splits the parents, and does not work. Now she is told she is bad when she is away from home because her family suffers even more. There seems to be no way out for her.

CECCHIN: The question "Who suffers the most when Gerte is not there?" brought out the feelings of Father and son, but not the feelings of the mother. So the therapist changes his tack and instead of saying "Who suffers?" he says: "Which of the children do you enjoy the most?" hoping that this will bring some statement about feelings from the mother. And we get the same answer, which is nothing.

Here we have another fascinating implication. In this family, everyone is full of sorrow when Gerte is not there, and nobody can talk to anybody else because they are constantly thinking about Gerte. So it looks as if she is the connecting element in the family. There is no possibility of communication between Mother, Father, and son. When these people haven't got Gerte, they can't even talk to each other. So she's absolutely necessary.

### FAMILY INTERVIEW

BOSCOLO: *I'll give you another question. Suppose you were not born, that your father and mother had only one child, Karl, and you were not born. According to you, if you were not born, how do you think the life of Father and Mother and Karl would go without you?*

GERTE: *It would have been much easier.*

BOSCOLO: *Much easier? You mean happier?*

GERTE: *Yeah.*

BOSCOLO: *Who would be the happiest if you were not born and it was Father, Mother, and Karl? Of the three, who would have been the happiest if you were not born?*

GERTE: *All three.*

BOSCOLO: *Hmm?*

GERTE: *All three.*

BOSCOLO: *No. Give me a classification. Who would be the happiest if you were not born and it was Father, Mother, and Karl. You said their life would be easier and happier. That's what you said. Who would be the happiest? You understand the question?*

GERTE: *Yes, I understand.*

BOSCOLO: *Who would be the happiest?*

GERTE: *I don't know.*

BOSCOLO: *Just put a guess, Mother, Father, Karl?*

GERTE: *Difficult to say.*

BOSCOLO: *Difficult to say. How about you, Karl?*

KARL: *I think if she—*

BOSCOLO: *Who would be the happiest?*

KARL: *—would get married then we'd be happy because the problem would be—*

MOTHER: *Resolved.*

KARL: *—resolved.*

BOSCOLO: *I would like to ask everyone the question. If Gerte were not born— supposedly not born—and your parents had only you as a child, would you agree with Gerte that life would have been easier for the three of you? That you would have been happier?*

KARL: *No.*

BOSCOLO: *You don't think so.*

KARL: *Perhaps the sorrows would not have been because of Gerte. The sorrows would have been because of me or because of something else.*

BOSCOLO: *You mean because your parents are very sorrowful patients?*

CECCHIN: Here we see an interesting and significant slip of the therapist. Speaking to the son, he said: "You mean because your parents are very sorrowful *patients.*" I think that here the therapist loses neutrality because he is aligning himself with the children against the parents. He is getting tired of hearing all these defensive statements by the parents. He wants to put them in the position of patients like the daughter, but since he's supposed to be neutral and to avoid negative connotations, his unconscious rebels and comes up with a clear Freudian slip.

## FAMILY INTERVIEW

MOTHER: *It would be other sorrows, probably.*
KARL: *It would be other sorrows.*
BOSCOLO: *Because they are very sorrowful.*
KARL: *There are always sorrows.*
BOSCOLO: *There are always sorrows. Who's more sorrowful, your father or your mother?*
KARL: *Father.*
BOSCOLO: *Always been your father?*
KARL: *Yes.*

---

BOSCOLO: This interaction between the therapist and the family brings to my mind the part in *Paradox and Counterparadox* where we said that interviewing a family in schizophrenic transaction is like entering a labyrinth. You think there is a door, but when you open it, you find yourself in front of a wall. What you think is a window is a door. You don't know what is what. These interactions give us a good example of this confusion. At a certain point I ask the son: "Your sister says that if she hadn't been born the rest of the family would have been all right. Do you agree?" I expected the son to agree, but he doesn't. He says that there would be sorrow anyway, and he thinks that he also would be sorrowful. And then he says that his parents are sorrowful and that Father is more sorrowful than Mother and then somehow the family inevitably has to live in sorrow. Only the daughter says that the family would not be so sorrowful if she were not there. So it seems that the daughter is in this respect more optimistic than the rest of the family. It is not clear whether life would be sorrowful for the parents in any case or whether it is Gerte that makes life sorrowful. Following these thoughts the therapist gets lost in the labyrinth.

CECCHIN: Here we see a familiar pattern within the family, which is to disqualify any statement implying that Gerte might have a positive value. Even the possibility that Gerte's absence could create more happiness is disqualified. There is no chance for her to count. She cannot even leave the family and believe that this could have a positive effect.

BOSCOLO: I would like to underline the rigidity of the roles. The daughter says: "If I were not alive, my parents would be all right." But the son, who occupies the role of the healthy and rational one, is forbidden to agree. He must say the opposite to his sister, in order to avoid being like her.

Another possibility is that there is in this family a myth of perfection and goodness. If Gerte is not there they cannot talk, as the brother said, "in a carefree way," they cannot have fun together, because that would be bad. They must all the time think and suffer about Gerte being ill. To paraphrase Descartes, their motto could be: *Suffero ergo sum.*

### FAMILY INTERVIEW

BOSCOLO: *He gets easily upset, he gets easily emotional? Is that it?*

KARL: *He's a little bit pessimistic.*

BOSCOLO: *Pessimistic. All of them pessimistic?*

KARL: *Not very, but—*

FATHER: *[unintelligible]*

KARL: *No, I'm just giving my opinion. Not very pessimistic but—*

BOSCOLO: *Now I would like to ask another question. Suppose your parents could not have children? You were not here and she was not here—like some people do not have children—how would you have seen the life of your parents without children?*

KARL: *I think a couple isn't happy if it can't get children. I think it's the aim of every—*

FATHER: *Marriage.*

KARL: *—every marriage to get children.*

BOSCOLO: *You think they would be less happy than they are now?*

KARL: *I'm not quite sure, but I think so.*

BOSCOLO: *[to Gerte] How about you, do you think that if your parents did not have children they would be more sad than what they are?*

GERTE: *It's difficult to say.*

BOSCOLO: *It's difficult to say.*

CECCHIN: It's striking to see the effect of the question: "Do you think your parents would be less happy than they are now?" The son says: "I'm not sure, but it could be, I think so." This is a very tricky question because they have been talking for the last ten minutes about how unhappy they are. The therapist introduces the idea: "Could you be even more unhappy if you didn't have the children?" which is again reversing the statement which was made before. The question that was made before said: "Do you think your parents would be happier not to have children?" Now it is: "Do you think they would be even more unhappy if they did not have children?"

BOSCOLO: This implies that parents having crazy children are much better off than having no children. So the children don't even have the choice of suicide because they will make the parents more unhappy than they already are.

## FAMILY INTERVIEW

BOSCOLO: [to Mother] I would like to ask another question. You said before that sometimes you felt over the years the need or the desire to go to work, for instance. You worked before getting married but then you had a family which you had to take care of. Sometimes you would get tired over the years. You have Gerte, who talks to you a lot, and you have your husband, who's very pessimistic, or is sometimes pessimistic, and who gets worried. So sometimes—you know— you might have said, over the years, "I felt like I wanted to go to work, but I didn't go to work because of the situation." Is that so?

MOTHER: Yes.

BOSCOLO: Do you have some person outside the family that could make you feel a little better sometimes, someone you could talk to, like your parents or relatives?

MOTHER: Yes. I have my parents and my sister.

BOSCOLO: Your sister.

MOTHER: And I owe much to them because I can speak to them and talk to them about my sorrows. To my sister above all.

BOSCOLO: To your sister. Your parents are alive?

MOTHER: They're still alive, they're over eighty now.

BOSCOLO: They're eighty.

MOTHER: But I can talk very much to my sister. She is two years younger.

BOSCOLO: I see. Yes. Where are your parents?

MOTHER: In [town].

BOSCOLO: *Far away from here?*

FATHER: *Thirty miles.*

BOSCOLO: *I see. And how many brothers and sisters do you have?*

MOTHER: *I have only a sister. One sister.*

BOSCOLO: *I see, how old is she?*

MOTHER: *She is two years younger than I. She is twenty-one, yes? I think.*

BOSCOLO: *How old is she?*

MOTHER: *Twenty-one. No.*

FATHER: *Fifty-one. Fifty-one.*

BOSCOLO: *Ah, fifty-one. [Family laughs.] She's married, your sister?*

MOTHER: *No, she's not married. She's a teacher.*

BOSCOLO: *Are you close to her? You have always been very close?*

FATHER: *Well, she's her best friend.*

BOSCOLO: *Ah, she is her best friend. Does she live close by?*

FATHER: *No, the same place.*

BOSCOLO: *I see. She lives with her parents.*

FATHER: *Yes, with her parents.*

BOSCOLO: *You have obviously been very close.*

FATHER: *Oh, yes.*

BOSCOLO: *So you feel she's important for you, this sister—*

MOTHER: *She's like a friend to us.*

FATHER: *She is like a friend. Yes.*

BOSCOLO: *Would you say, for instance, that your sister-in-law is the one who has the best chance of lifting the mood of your wife, for instance?*

FATHER: *Beg your pardon?*

MOTHER: *Lifting the mood?*

BOSCOLO: *Does she have more of a chance of lifting Mother's mood?*

GERMAN THERAPIST: *[translates]*

FATHER: *Oh, yes, I think she is a bit more optimistic than I am.*

BOSCOLO: *Does Gerte like when your sister comes to talk to you? Does she like that?*

MOTHER: *Not always.*

BOSCOLO: *Not always. Does she talk to—*

MOTHER: *In spite of the fact that her aunt is very fond of her, she is not so fond of her aunt, I think. She always clings to me.*

BOSCOLO: *Does she seem to—do you like your aunt?*

GERTE: *Yes I do.*

BOSCOLO: *Do you like when your aunt talks to your mother or do you sometimes feel a little upset about—*

GERTE: *But I don't like—I do like when they talk, but I don't like when they talk about me.*

BOSCOLO: *You like when they talk, but you don't like it when they—so, do you find that Mother doesn't keep secrets with her?*

GERTE: *Yes. Sometimes.*

BOSCOLO: *Do you think she is more successful, your mother, in keeping secrets with your aunt or with your father?*

GERTE: *I did not understand.*

GERMAN THERAPIST: *[translates] She can't say.*

BOSCOLO: *I see. How about your family? Your parents, are they alive?*

FATHER: *They died some years ago.*

BOSCOLO: *They died some years ago. And how many years ago about? How many years ago did they die?*

FATHER: *About three or four years. My father died three years ago and my mother four years ago.*

BOSCOLO: *Do you have brothers and sisters?*

FATHER: *I have one sister, she is married.*

BOSCOLO: *How old is she, your sister? How old is she?*

FATHER: *She is fifty-one.*

BOSCOLO: *Fifty-one, like—*

FATHER: *Like her sister.*

BOSCOLO: *Her sister. Is she married, your sister?*

FATHER: *Yes, she is.*

BOSCOLO: *She has children?*

FATHER: *Two girls. Yes. Young women.*

BOSCOLO: *Young women. Is your husband close to his sister or—*

KARL: *They live in a little village about fifty miles away and therefore the contact is not as close as it is with her sister.*

MOTHER: *Yes and because they have another way of life. Her husband is —*

FATHER: *But I like her.*

MOTHER: *Yes.*

BOSCOLO: *Yes, what way of life do they have?*

MOTHER: *They have sort of—*

GERMAN THERAPIST: *[translates] Ah, they are farmers. They are farmers.*

MOTHER: *Farmers.*

BOSCOLO: *It is more often that your sister comes to see you or you go to see your sister?*

FATHER: *Well, I think she often comes to us.*

MOTHER: *She comes to us more often. Yes.*

BOSCOLO: *How is she? Is she lively?*

FATHER: *Oh, yes.*

KARL: *Yes.*

BOSCOLO: *She is optimistic?*

FATHER: *Oh, yes.*

KARL: *Yes.*

MOTHER: *She blames me sometimes because I didn't—I didn't—*

BOSCOLO: *She blames you.*

MOTHER: *Yes. Sometimes she blames me, she says I must entertain myself, amuse*

*myself, I have too many sorrows and she doesn't like that. I said "I don't but—
I cannot forget my sorrows."*

BOSCOLO: *Does she blame your husband too, sometimes? Does she ask—does she
blame your husband too?*

MOTHER: Sometimes, yes. Sometimes.

BOSCOLO: *What does she say about your husband?*

MOTHER: She says he is too—[in German]

GERMAN THERAPIST: Pedantic.

FATHER: Fastidious.

MOTHER: *Yes. And he works too much and so on. He never gets rested.*

BOSCOLO: *Does she try to help you sometimes if she sees that Gerte is stuck with
you, you are stuck with Gerte, does she try to stick herself with Gerte—*

MOTHER: Yes, she tries.

BOSCOLO: *—so she can unstick you from being stuck with Gerte?*

MOTHER: *She tries to help me in my problems. She tries to stick to her too, but
Gerte does not always want that. Sometimes she doesn't want that.*

*[Family speaks in German.]*

---

CECCHIN: It's fascinating to see how the mother describes the sister as the
only one she can talk to. It seems to be a rule that people in this family
think all the time of the people who are not present. An example, when
Gerte was in the hospital, everybody was thinking about her. When
Mother is with Gerte, Mother thinks about her sister who is not there.
They are always thinking that the one who is not there is the one with
whom they can communicate best. This is another characteristic of many
psychotic systems.

BOSCOLO: An interesting slip here is when the mother said: "My sister is
twenty-one." This is exactly the age of her daughter. She says: "I can
talk to my sister who is twenty-one." In reality, she spends most of her
time with her daughter, who is twenty-one, thinking about the sister,
who is fifty-one.

What comes out very clearly is that Mother is very close to this younger
sister. This is confirmed by Mother's mistake when she said her sister
was twenty-one. Her closeness helps us to understand why the father
felt so sad and so sick when the daughter was in the hospital for five
months. The hypothesis is that as long as the daughter is at home sick,
she succeeds in making a family. If the daughter is not there, sticking to
the mother, then the mother will stick to the sister so that the sister
displaces the husband, and the family unity will be threatened. The
husband needs the daughter to be there to interfere with the "marriage"

between wife and sister-in-law. Gerte is also needed at home to keep the parents distant from one another, especially at night.

CECCHIN: If the daughter were a healthy daughter, probably she could not fulfill this function. This fits into the idea of the problem-determined system, which exists as long as Gerte is the problem. The moment you destroy the problem of Gerte, you destroy the system.

BOSCOLO: It looks as if everybody is working very hard to keep this kind of system alive. This could be an explanation of what we usually call resistance. Resistance is an expression of the conservation of the organization of the problem-determined system. As long as Gerte is the problem, the system remains what it is.

CECCHIN: Yes, this system is organized around the sickness of Gerte. The system exists as long as Gerte maintains her symptoms. If Gerte changes, or somebody else changes, you don't have the same system any more. If Gerte changes they would be very happy, or perhaps they would be very upset. They could feel dead. They would not be the same people any more. They would have to organize a different system.

### FAMILY INTERVIEW

BOSCOLO: *Now, I would like to ask another question. You said she has been in the hospital for five months; did she have treatment before? There was treatment?*

MOTHER: *Yes, there was a treatment for four weeks and some years ago for [unintelligible]. She went to a—*

FATHER: *Specialist.*

GERMAN THERAPIST: *Did she see a psychiatrist?*

MOTHER: *[in German]*

GERMAN THERAPIST: *A neurologist.*

BOSCOLO: *He gave her some drugs, medicine?*

FATHER: *She was given some drugs, pills.*

MOTHER: *Yes, she has—I brought it with me. This is for the night.*

BOSCOLO: *The night, yes.*

MOTHER: *This is for the day.*

BOSCOLO: *Yes. And did she have psychotherapy? Did she have talks with—*

MOTHER: *I want her to have psychotherapy, but she doesn't want it. She refuses.*

BOSCOLO: *She refuses it, I see.*

MOTHER: *But I think it would be necessary for her.*

BOSCOLO: The therapist at the end of the session starts to ask questions about the relationships with the hospitals and the experts. Usually in the beginning of the session we inquire about the relationship of the nuclear family, then we extend the context to the extended families. Finally we explore the relationships with the experts, including ourselves. As one can see we proceed centrifugally: from the nuclear to the extended family, to larger systems. We proceed centrifugally also in terms of time. We start exploring present events, then we go into past events and future solutions.

CECCHIN: This interview pattern can be used by the mother or the father to reestablish their beliefs, and we see, in fact, the mother immediately taking out the pills, throwing them on the table, and reestablishing the definition of Gerte as the crazy one, the only one in the family who is sick.

BOSCOLO: But in cases with a history of chronic psychosis the therapist has somehow to accept that one member of the family is different, otherwise the family does not get engaged. So at the end, after the therapist has unsettled the family system through all these questions we were talking about before, he hooks the family by accepting their map, their diagnosis, often made by other experts. Then the family can trust the therapist again and develop a positive rapport.

CECCHIN: The family can trust you, but the daughter can't. I think the daughter feels betrayed again, because during the session you tried to give her some chance to exist and at the end you accepted the definition of the family again.

BOSCOLO: It could be. But the rapport with the daughter could have been established during the session with the help of the circular questions and the neutrality of the therapist. It is also possible to use the final intervention to correct the loss of neutrality.

CECCHIN: This is a question of a very fine equilibrium.


## FAMILY INTERVIEW

BOSCOLO: *Who advised you to come here?*
MOTHER: *[in German]*
GERMAN THERAPIST: *[unintelligible] counseling.*
BOSCOLO: *Counseling.*
MOTHER: *I went to this office.*

BOSCOLO: *Yes. They advised you—and when you have been told to come here with the family, then you are here with the family. How was the reaction when you told your husband and your son and Gerte about coming here?*

MOTHER: *Nobody wanted to come here.*

BOSCOLO: *Nobody wanted to come here.*

MOTHER: *Nobody wanted to come here because—*

FATHER: *It was a sacrifice.*

MOTHER: *—they have no time and she doesn't want to tell about herself.*

BOSCOLO: *She doesn't want to—*

MOTHER: *—to—to talk about herself, and he has no time and he too has no time because—*

BOSCOLO: *—but this depends upon time, also —*

FATHER: *Especially on time.*

BOSCOLO: *Suppose you had the time, for instance, suppose—*

FATHER: *Well, I'd come at once. I'd do everything I could to help her if I had enough time, but I think I spent a lot of time on her.*

BOSCOLO: *How about you, Karl?*

KARL: *Yes. I would have come too, but tomorrow I have to write a test and it was a little bit difficult for me to come.*

BOSCOLO: *Now suppose, for instance, suppose—this is a consultation to see if there is a problem—suppose we think that maybe it is indicated for you to come, for instance, for some encounters with—*

GERMAN THERAPIST: *Some meetings.*

BOSCOLO: *Yeah. Some meetings, then what? Do you think it would be possible or not?*

MOTHER: *It would depend how often this would be, because it's very difficult for us to come by car because we are bad drivers. Very bad drivers.*

BOSCOLO: *Is there a way—I understand this problem you have about work and all the other things. You have the car and—but when you were told to come here today as a family—you told them that you got an appointment, and what reaction was there about coming here—what expectations do you have in coming here? Do you understand what I mean?*

MOTHER: *Yes. I hoped that we'd get some advice to better the situation in our family.*

BOSCOLO: *Who do you think in the family has more hope about that?*

MOTHER: *Yes.*

BOSCOLO: *This work here with—who has more hope?*

MOTHER: *I have more hope.*

BOSCOLO: *Second, who has more hope?*

FATHER: *Who has the most hope? You.*

MOTHER: *Yes.*

GERMAN THERAPIST: *And who has the second most hope, then?*

MOTHER: *Nobody, I think. Perhaps Karl.*

BOSCOLO: *How about you, Karl?*

FATHER: *We must have some hope, otherwise we wouldn't have come.*

BOSCOLO: *[to Gerte] How about you—suppose we think it would be helpful for you to come here for a few meetings?*

MOTHER: *Would you like to come? Would you have some hope, Gerte?*

GERTE: *No.*

BOSCOLO: *Do you think—you don't think there is hope?*

GERTE: *I don't think.*

*[Family waits while Boscolo and the German therapist break for a discussion with the other consultant.]*

———————————

CECCHIN: The frequent hypothetical questions and the vagueness of the answers as to the family's motivation for coming to therapy create an atmosphere which is not real. "Probably you're not even here, probably you don't have a problem, probably this is not a consultation, probably we'll ask you to come here for some meetings. You didn't want to come here, you don't know what you are here for anyway. Is it a consultation? Are we discussing a problem? Or are we not discussing any problem?" So the session ends with the same vagueness, the same confusion that the family brought to it, without the therapist attempting to confront directly the system and their incongruence, their confused thinking, their organization.

BOSCOLO: The family relates to the consultant in a paradoxical way. They put him in a double bind. They are there, but they are not too hopeful about being there. They have a problem, but they have to keep it a secret. Suppose the therapist says "You don't want to be here so let's stop." The family would say "But we have a problem." If the therapist tried to relate to the problem, the family would say "But we cannot talk." So the therapist tends, too, to relate to the family paradoxically.

Mother says she is the only one who has hope coming here. Probably the mother would like therapy to get unstuck from the daughter, allowing her to be closer to the sister. But the father doesn't want therapy because he is stuck to his work. The son is stuck to his outside life. Father and son probably came there because the mother had pushed them to do so. The only one who wants to change the situation is the mother because she wants to be with her sister and her daughter won't let her go. That's probably the motivation of this family to be there.

CECCHIN: During this session we saw the mother as the one who defended this kind of pathological situation. Now suddenly we see her as the only element who can change it. This hypothesis can be very useful because it pushes us to find some way to utilize her motivation.


## DISCUSSION BREAK

CECCHIN: *It was a very interesting family, much better than what we expected. They accepted most of the questions. There is an especially interesting story about secrets. Secrets are present all the time in this family. Gerte goes to an extreme limit in making the secrets ridiculous. A psychotic person usually does bring to an extreme the problem which is in the family. And here the problem is that there are a lot of secrets going on. The only one who would talk about secrets and who would accept that they were there was Karl.*

GERMAN THERAPIST: *And which he said were not secrets.*

CECCHIN: *A secret is a way to show that you have a relationship, a special relationship. Secrets create power. If people have secrets, they have power over the other people. Here you see the couple, the married couple, they don't have any secrets. Only Mother and daughter have secrets, but the mother betrays the daughter all the time. Probably the real secrets are between Mother and sister. It's interesting that in the end it came out that the most important person in the family is Mother's sister. The mother lit up when she talked about her sister. There was a complete change of mood. The mother and the sister live close by. They see each other all the time.*

GERMAN THERAPIST: *She's unmarried. The sister is a teacher.*

CECCHIN: *Unmarried teacher.*

GERMAN THERAPIST: *Unmarried teacher.*

CECCHIN: *So she is a much better husband than her husband. I also noticed that Gerte answers very cautiously so as to be sure that she doesn't offend anyone. She seems to be very much aware of what is going on. Probably she is less psychotic than she appears, than the family describes. Behavior problems like that might be due to her medications.*

---

BOSCOLO: At the beginning of the team discussion, the team members start making simple observations, simple linear-causal hypotheses; and then, step by step, they get into more complex patterns until finally a more general systemic hypothesis emerges. Simple hypotheses, at the beginning, are usually about who is with whom in the family, that is, alliances and coalitions.

CECCHIN: We also try to give a meaning to the psychotic behavior in relation to other behaviors. We start to link the psychotic behavior of Gerte with the most obvious family pattern: the tendency and the ability to keep secrets.

## DISCUSSION BREAK

BOSCOLO: *I was very impressed when I asked the question about the four months that Gerte was in the hospital. One would expect that the family would give some messages that they felt relieved since she has been in treatment. Instead they were very unhappy when the daughter went to the hospital. The father said those were the worst four months of their life. This was because everybody kept thinking about the girl. There was no relief, and I felt at that moment how important this daughter is for the family system. The brother added also that the parents are very worried people, that they need to worry, and that the father worries the most. We have to try to understand why she is so essential for the system.*

---

BOSCOLO: My first contribution to this discussion relates to my surprise and to my strong emotional response to the unexpected reaction of the family following Gerte's hospitalization. I expected they would feel relief since she was taken care of by doctors and they could have a break at home. Instead they felt terrible for the entire period she was in the hospital. I emphasize here the issue of emotions, both the family's and the therapist's emotions; since people who watch us working often state that we are very cold and intellectual, hung up on thinking and ignoring feelings. Emotions are often brought up in the team discussion and are linked to patterns and premises in the family of the therapist and, sometimes, to patterns and premises of the team itself.

## DISCUSSION BREAK

CECCHIN: *The father is very fond of Gerte, always thinks about her and would like always to stay with her. When she was in the hospital he was suffering the most. That's very interesting. She could be doing a job for him. For example, Mother married the sister/teacher. Could it be possible that the sister somehow is trying* to separate the mother from her family? At the same time, the daughter is keeping the mother away from her sister, so the father can have a little piece of Mother. The daughter is doing this work for herself and also for the father. She keeps controlling the mother, keeping her busy, not permitting her to visit the sister too often because the sister keeps telling her "You should be more lively, do more things, you are too stuck in the house." The sister is trying to get her out of the house, trying to convince her to do other things. Since the sister is unmarried she probably sends messages like "the two of us together without your family would have a beautiful life." It's possible that Gerte is trying to keep Mother from following her.

GERMAN THERAPIST: We know that the parents have had no sexual life for ten years at least, and probably before that, so what keeps them together? Obviously, Gerte does. She is central to their relationship.

BOSCOLO: This is related to the fact that the mother had a very important marriage with her younger sister. I should have asked a question to the family: Why didn't Mother's sister get married? At a certain point Mother even made a mistake about her sister's age. She said she was twenty-one years old.

CECCHIN: Nearly the same age as Gerte.

BOSCOLO: Exactly. So this couple got married when a marriage already existed between the mother and sister. They got married and then the father did not count very much for the wife because she already had the sister. I could see a kind of relief on the mother's face, a smile, when she said that she has a sister with whom she talks. It is the only moment that she shows any relief from this terrible life she has been leading. The husband tried for years to make contact with the girl but was rejected. He says he tries all the time to get in touch with her, to get in a relationship with her, but the daughter withdraws. She doesn't talk. She gets stuck to the mother. So I think the father's attachment to the daughter is an attempt to have his wife through his daughter. And the daughter reacts by continually going to the mother's side while the father keeps sending messages "Come to me." This looks like what we call a family in schizophrenic transaction, and a plausible hypothesis is not very easy to arrive at. In a family like this you might need two, three sessions really, to get a comprehensive hypothesis. But from what I see, I think that the father is a man who is very attached to home. He's very—

GERMAN THERAPIST: Very bound up.

BOSCOLO: —very bound up and trying to have his daughter. He doesn't care much about the boy. The parents don't fight for the boy, so he is able to have his independence. He has his friends and so on. The parents are not trying to triangulate him too much. But they do try to triangulate the daughter. The mother got stuck with the daughter as a result of the rapport with her own sister. That is one subsystem. Sister, mother, and daughter, they make a family, and father and the boy were left out. Father did not accept this, and over the years he's very attached to the family and he's attached to the daughter. He tries all the time to have a rapport with his daughter. And the daughter says no. Here we can begin to wonder about the problem of incest, at least psychological incest.

CECCHIN: *One of the secrets could be that she cannot get along with men. There is a man who wants to talk to her on the job, so she decides to leave. She became phobic toward men, somehow, at least toward the brother and toward the father. No?*

GERMAN THERAPIST: *There might be some feelings of incest with father or brother, but I was thinking it could not be talked about and that was the unknown secret.*

CECCHIN: *That would bear out this hypothesis. The father is very seductive toward the girl and the girl is trying to put a wall between them—right? She doesn't want to have anything to do with him.*

BOSCOLO: *She is twenty-one years old and the parents say they have not been sleeping together for the past ten years. I wonder when they decided not to sleep together? Of course they give the excuse of Father's smoking. When I asked the question whether, in ten years, either one went to the other's bed, the parents did not say anything. They could have given some information: "Oh, yes, once in a while we make love. Or one goes in the other bed." But they didn't say anything; they kept the matter unclear.*

GERMAN THERAPIST: *I think they felt a little embarrassed. They expressed the feeling that it was indiscreet and embarrassing of the therapist to ask about their night life. They had this kind of shy, embarrassed look.*

BOSCOLO: *I think they did not say anything to avoid defining their own relationship to the children. When the daughter was eleven years old, the parents decided to separate at night. I should have asked whether, after they separated, the sleeplessness of the girl increased or decreased. I suspect it decreased. They also said that for two years, the daughter slept with the mother. I wonder what was going on in that period.*

*I would suspect that the daughter went to sleep with the mother to be out of danger of the father.*

CECCHIN: *So, wait a minute. Now we have two hypotheses to think about. One is that the daughter is trying to keep the mother from becoming completely married to her sister. She is trying to keep her in the home for the father. So she's working for the father, while pretending a tremendous hostility toward the father. Somehow they're all working together to keep the mother in the family. The brother probably would like more from the mother, but he doesn't object when the sister takes all her attention. So all three are trying to keep the mother from going to the sister completely. The other possible hypothesis, as I said, is that the father, having already given up the mother, is trying to get the daughter. So the daughter says "I stay with Mother only. I don't want to have anything to do with men." She stays with Mother all the time to stop the father from getting too close to her. That's another possibility.*

---

CECCHIN: We see how the team is exploring different kinds of alliances, "marriages," triangulations, keeping our minds open to any possibility. Moreover, you can see that the team is not looking for any one "truth," but follows hints here and there, utilizing the impressions as they emerge in the discussion.

For example, Father is very depressed when daughter is not at home, Mother looks happy when she is talking about her sister, Father looks sad when referring to his marriage, Father and Mother look embarrassed when talking about their night life at home. The therapist tries to connect these hints, being especially attentive to the analogic communication. He tries to create a family story which makes sense. Sometimes the therapist entertains two or three hypotheses or stories, both during the session and later on in the team discussion.

BOSCOLO: You said that the team can come up with two or three hypotheses. I think the team in the discussion struggles to come up with one general hypothesis, the so-called systemic hypothesis, and then one or more possible interventions can be created.

If a general systemic hypothesis does not emerge from the discussion, we give up and we try again the following session. Sometimes, in very difficult cases, as with families in schizophrenic transaction, it takes two to three sessions before reaching a consistent systemic hypothesis.

CECCHIN: However, I think there is a danger in aiming at one general hypothesis. The process becomes too rigid. The team should try to reach consensus on a general hypothesis that includes different possibilities, different maps of what has been discussed.

### DISCUSSION BREAK

BOSCOLO: *I see it another way. If the mother loses the daughter, she loses her sister as well, because the pragmatic effect of the illness is to keep all three women attached. The proof is that Mother keeps going to the sister to talk about the daughter's problems.*

CECCHIN: *Yes, but the mother kept saying "my sister tells me that I'm worrying too much about this family." "Let's live together and be happy forever" is the message. You said that the result of Gerte's problem is to keep the mother at home. But the mother, instead, is taking the daughter to find a psychotherapist. This would argue that the result of her illness is to allow Mother and sister to be together.*

GERMAN THERAPIST: *But Gerte doesn't want this.*

CECCHIN: *That's true. Gerte doesn't want this because for her going to therapy is like Mother saying "Leave me alone so I can go with my sister. Instead of me you can have a therapist." When a mother sends a child to therapy the child often thinks "Ah, you want to get rid of me, you want me to find another person to take care of me."*

*So the mother wants to bring the family into therapy so she can get rid of these people to go with her sister. If we follow this idea we can arrive at an intervention, such as: "We think that family therapy is indicated, it's very important that you should come back here for a series of sessions." No more than ten, so as not to scare them.*

BOSCOLO: *The intervention is premature. It is not yet clear what the intervention should be.*

---

BOSCOLO: We can say that hypotheses mostly serve as explanations for team members of what is going on in the family and in the family-therapist relationship. At this point in the discussion, a team member comes up with a hypothesis which satisfies him and proposes an intervention. However, this seems to be premature. The other members do not feel comfortable with the proposal and it is dropped. Again the team members start to find new ideas, new patterns which can bring general consensus.

CECCHIN: The aim of the team is to reach consensus. However, to reach consensus takes time. How much time? If the discussion goes beyond a reasonable time, it becomes uncomfortable, repetitive, and confusing, and must be stopped.

BOSCOLO: In other words, there is an optimum of time during which the team's work is creative and useful. This optimum time, of course, varies with different families and different teams. In simple cases the discussion can be as brief as ten to fifteen minutes. If the team members are experienced and have worked together for a long time, the discussions are shorter.

CECCHIN: The indication that tells us that the team should stop the discussion is when no new ideas, no new patterns are brought up. In the discussion of this case, at times it seems as though the team has reached a dead end, but then the flow picks up again.

## DISCUSSION BREAK

CECCHIN: *You could add that it would be very dangerous to do this now, something like that. You could say that they should wait a few months and explain why.*

BOSCOLO: *This intervention is premature. Gerte is psychotic. According to the re-*

cords, she has been four months in the hospital, she has been on medication for years. She must be in a communicational context in which she has to respond to three or four contradictory injunctions. For instance, the father may have given a message over the years, "I don't have a wife. Please be my wife."

GERMAN THERAPIST: And use his depression to call her to his side. "I am such a helpless soul, please come to me."

BOSCOLO: Yes, "Please come to me," because being depressed he gives the message to the daughter that the mother doesn't lift his depression. So, one message to the daughter, over the years, could be "You are my daughter, but you are my daughter who simultaneously should be my wife." At the same time, the mother could send this message:"You are going to be the child of me and my sister and also of your father. You are our baby." One injunction could be "Please stay with me—my husband is not enough for me."

GERMAN THERAPIST: In other words, "You keep me separate from my husband and give me what my husband doesn't."

BOSCOLO: Yes, and also "By being stuck to me, close to me, you allow me to keep my sister, who doesn't have children. Since she's not married, you help her to be close to me as my sister and to you as a daughter."

GERMAN THERAPIST: You mean that by being a problem, she gives Mother and sister cause to be together? Only by being a problem can she keep the sister in Mother's orbit?

CECCHIN: In fact, they talk about her constantly.

BOSCOLO: If she were closer to her father, this would be no good because she would leave the mother alone with the sister. But if she is with the mother, this is also no good because the father keeps communicating, "Look how sad, how upset I am. I need a daughter." Finally, it is forbidden for her to have a good rapport with the brother because if she had one the parents could not stand to be left out.

CECCHIN: To put it more simply, you could say that she's been working all her life to control her mother. That's why she became crazy the time she left home for a job. Now she stays home and controls the mother. She already succeeded in breaking up the marriage between Father and Mother. Now she has to work to break up the marriage between Mother and sister. If she got a job, then she would have to give up an important family task.

GERMAN THERAPIST: The instrument of control is having secrets which the others should not know or do not know. It was interesting to note that at the moment the mother seemed to have a secret with the brother Gerte got quite upset, which was her strongest reaction in the session.

---

CECCHIN: The team now is beginning to utilize other metaphors—for example, the metaphor of control. The parents complain that Gerte continuously attempts to control the mother. She wants Mother at home, she wants to control the communication between Mother and the other members of the family by forbidding her to tell secrets to them. She also controls the distance between the parents by keeping them together but separate, day and night. For example, during the past ten years Mother and Father have been sleeping in different rooms. Yet for two of those years, Gerte slept with Mother.

BOSCOLO: Another metaphor connected to control is blame. Gerte is blamed by everyone for anything that goes wrong at home. For instance, they blame her for being controlling, but they do not do anything to challenge her control. They just blame her. So, she is controlling, they are blaming. She is black, they are white. Another observation that can be made at this point is that the discussants are not trying to find a hypothesis which links their observations in some logical way; they participate in a flow of talk, producing ideas which at a certain point create "patterns that connect."

CECCHIN: Here you can see that one team member begins to make a connection between control and secrets. This can be considered as an attempt to find a "pattern that connects."

### DISCUSSION BREAK

CECCHIN: *There was another interesting thing. The mother kept saying "I have to stay with her because she is sick now, but I think all the time about my sister." However, at a certain moment she said "My sister is twenty-one years old." So the message for the daughter is "Sometimes my mother thinks about me as if I were her sister. Perhaps I could take the place of her sister." This is a very seductive message.*

BOSCOLO: *A further comment on control: Gerte prevents Mother from talking to the father and to the brother. As a matter of fact, when they are together in the evening, they can't talk. This is to keep them distant, and so this can be in the service of a couple who don't have much together. Another pragmatic effect of her symptoms over the years is to keep her mother closer to her sister because her mother can always talk to the sister in the role of a suffering person who has a daughter who's sick. So she keeps her parents separated and she keeps the mother and sister close.*

---

CECCHIN: Now the discussants go back to the topic of the different possible "marriages" in this family of four, including Mother's sister. They bring forth different family organizations by emphasizing the importance of certain coalitions compared to others; for instance, mother-sister, mother-daughter, father-son, and the many possible triangulations in this group of five people.

BOSCOLO: To sum up, I think we usually utilize three classes of hypotheses.

One class of hypotheses refers to who is with whom in the family: alliances, coalitions, or "marriages."

A second class of hypotheses refers to individual and family premises or myths.

A third class of hypotheses is based on the analysis of the communications in the family and between the family and other systems, including, of course, the therapist. For instance, in this case we try to describe double-bind messages which make the psychotic member's behavior intelligible.

CECCHIN: But we are not looking for an individual double bind, created by one person toward another one. The context created by all the family members results in numerous double binds.

For instance, Gerte does not know whether she is the daughter, the sister, the mother, or the husband. No one specifically gives her this paradoxical injunction, the injunction comes from the context.

BOSCOLO: Another comment: I would like to underline how little interest the discussants have in issues of hierarchy and structure, which are more emphasized in other schools of family therapy.

## DISCUSSION BREAK

GERMAN THERAPIST: *She keeps the parents separated but also united. It is clearly impossible for them to leave each other. If the parents could leave, this would solve the problem, but they cannot.*

CECCHIN: *So we can see that she keeps them together and she keeps them separated. Both. Now, let's get to the intervention because they are already here, in back of the door.*

BOSCOLO: *One more thing. It's about sibling rivalry. Being separated, being split as siblings over the years can be a sign of how heavily the parents split them.*

CECCHIN: *When Karl was born, what happened to the relationship between mother and mother's sister? Perhaps the two women elected Karl as their child instead of the girl. This could be a possibility.*

GERMAN THERAPIST: *He seems to be delegated to fulfill his aspirations. He was studying medicine, he's a good student. He's delegated in a positive way, but not triangulated, so he comes out quite well. This may have caused a lot of jealousy and envy on Gerte's part.*

CECCHIN: *It would be interesting to ask about the relationship between Karl and the aunt. When the aunt comes, she probably talks to the mother and to Karl. He's the child of this marriage, so it gives him a very good position.*

BOSCOLO: *What shall we use as an intervention?*

CECCHIN: *Well, everybody says that they didn't want to come to therapy.*

GERMAN THERAPIST: *I think that nobody wants to come except the mother, and the one who has most control wants to come least, that is, Gerte.*

BOSCOLO: *Gerte.*

CECCHIN: *Because she's afraid that with therapy she will lose control of the situation, and losing control means that the mother would be free from her. That's what the mother is saying, "I think she needs psychotherapy because somebody else will take care of her. I'm tired." Of course she will never accept this.*

CECCHIN: *I would say "This is a very serious situation—"*

GERMAN THERAPIST: *I would praise Gerte very much for not wanting therapy because what would happen if they came in for treatment would be much worse than what's happening now.*

CECCHIN: *For example, an idea would be this: "We think Gerte's resistance to coming to therapy is a very good thing for the moment. You may feel family therapy is indicated. But we think that for the moment it would be a little dangerous, and that Gerte is right. Dangerous for whom? We think it would be dangerous for the father and for the aunt." We could say something mysterious like that. "We think it would be better if you wait for a while. So can you come back in two months? We'll continue to think about it because we're not so sure that you should start therapy. You can also think about it. We'll all think about it. Get in touch with us in two months and we'll discuss the situation or perhaps we can have an appointment in two months and discuss the matter then."*

BOSCOLO: *I suspect that they will react to this intervention by forgetting about it when they go home.*

CECCHIN: *Yes, but they came. They're here today. There is some desire on their part to come.*

GERMAN THERAPIST: *Wouldn't it be helpful if she were also praised for her sacrifice?*

CECCHIN: *Well, we should specify why. To make a sacrifice for what? We should be prepared to explain our reason for saying that.*

*To say that someone is sacrificing in general doesn't have much effect. We should say she is sacrificing for the mother and aunt.*

---

CECCHIN: It is interesting to point out how the team, now, is struggling around two ideas. First, how to find a positive connotation for Gerte's behavior. Second, how to frame the relationship between the family and the therapist. How can the family be praised for not having motivation

324        PART 4

for therapy? Only Mother seems interested in it. The team is struggling
to put together these two elements in a meaningful way.

BOSCOLO: What you are saying relates to the usual attempt by the therapist,
when he is interviewing, and by the team during the discussion, to link
two levels of hypothesis: hypothesis about the family and hypothesis
about the family-therapist relationship.

## DISCUSSION BREAK

BOSCOLO: *We could say that if they come in to therapy now, there is a chance that
Gerte will change, and for the moment we think this would be dangerous for
somebody else. Possibly for Mother and Father or aunt and Father.*

CECCHIN: *We should probably say the father and the aunt. Gerte will be very
surprised.*

BOSCOLO: *Then we could say "We will stop here, but it's very important that you
call back."*

CECCHIN: *It might be better to give them an appointment in two months. They
should come here so you can really discuss the situation to see if it would be
dangerous or not dangerous.*

BOSCOLO: *Another possibility would be to offer therapy while accepting their definition of the relationship they want to have with us. First of all, they don't want
to come as a family. Second, they talk about secrets but want to keep them. So
we could say, for instance, that we think that they did very well to come here.
That we see that there is an indication for therapy—or for some meetings—and
we think that at least two people should come to these meetings. Then we should
say that it's very important that when they come here they discuss what secrets
they want to keep. We should start with a crazy statement.*

GERMAN THERAPIST: *That would work nicely because if only two come, the others
would be left out.*

CECCHIN: *We should have at least two.*

BOSCOLO: *At least two. It will be interesting to see who the mother will try to make
come: the father, the brother, or Gerte.*

CECCHIN: *Or the aunt.*

BOSCOLO: *Or the aunt.*

CECCHIN: *We should say also that the aunt can come.*

BOSCOLO: *It will be interesting to see who turns up. The therapist might say "Next
time I would like to see two more"—this supposing the mother comes—"you
and your sister or you and your husband." But you say only two can come. You
make the rule. They came here with a crazy rule. They came here communicating
that they cannot communicate.*

CECCHIN: *Yes, they also say they cannot come. They come here saying they cannot come.*

BOSCOLO: *Basically they cannot come and they cannot talk. So, you have to accept what they bring, so you accept that at least two have to come, but that they must make the decision on who has to come. You give them a big task, to decide which two should come. Another extremely important task is to have a meeting in the family to decide what secrets they should not tell the therapist. It's very important for the therapist to respect the family's secrets! This is counterparadoxical.*

GERMAN THERAPIST: *That's a good idea, that before they come they should have a family meeting to decide which are the secrets that should under no circumstances be divulged.*

BOSCOLO: *Because the therapist must respect all the secrets.*

CECCHIN: *So they should come here with a list of secrets. So you should say "Family therapy is indicated, but it's very difficult for you to come all together. So at least two of you should come. Any two. It could be mother and daughter, father and daughter, or no daughter.*

CECCHIN: *Karl and Father.*

BOSCOLO: *Or Mother—*

CECCHIN: *Even your aunt if you—*

BOSCOLO: *Mother and your sister.*

CECCHIN: *Just two. We need two.*

BOSCOLO: *And if she comes with sister—*

CECCHIN: *That should be very—*

BOSCOLO: *Yes. Yes.*

GERMAN THERAPIST: *But should they have a family session first and decide who should come?*

CECCHIN: *Yes, and which secrets should not be talked about. They should be prepared to discuss with the therapist which secrets should not be talked about.*

BOSCOLO: *All right.*

---

CECCHIN: This idea of inviting only two of them to the next session probably is related to their difficulty to include a third member at any time in their family organization. Triangles are painful in this family. Any time they are in a threesome, they suffer. This idea seems to have an immediate effect on the team. They like it.

BOSCOLO: For the second time a team member starts to propose an intervention. While the first time the proposal was premature, this time the other team members join to support it. The climate is one of consensus and satisfaction.

CECCHIN: The satisfaction of the team is related not only to the fact that they have reached a consensus on the intervention but also to have found out the double-binding communications which the therapist becomes entangled in. The family messages—we are here, but we are not here; we talk, but we can't talk; we need help, but we don't need help—are matched by an intervention that rescues the therapist from a crazy position.

BOSCOLO: It is probable that with such a family, a therapist is very soon neutralized and gets lost in a communicational labyrinth. In cases like this one, a lone therapist might not be able to free himself from the labyrinth and might need the help of a team or a consultant.

## INTERVENTION

*BOSCOLO: Let me share with you the discussion that I had with Dr. Cecchin about therapy. We think that you did very well to come here and we agree completely with the doctors who sent you here because we strongly believe—and we have had a long experience with this problem—that family therapy is indicated in this situation. However, in the discussion I had with my colleague, we agreed that this may be difficult for you. Father doesn't have much time, and neither does Karl. Gerte did not feel like coming here today. So we took all this into consideration, and we decided that one solution would be for only two persons to come to the next meeting and to any meeting that might be held in the future. At least two should come to each meeting—any two you decide on. So we would like to suggest that before you next come here, you have a family discussion to decide on which two should come to that meeting. You might decide, for instance, that Mother should come with her sister because her sister is important, or that Gerte might be willing and also free to come with Mother or with her aunt or with Karl. Or it could be Father with Mother or Father with his sister-in-law. Or Mother with the sister. Or Karl with Mother or with sister. There are many possible combinations. So, at least two must come. If a third person wants to come, it's all right as long as he's able and willing to come. So we recommend a family gathering just before the meeting to decide who is to come here. The second condition, which is very important, maybe more important than this one, is that during this family discussion to decide, as I said, which two will come to the meeting, you will also make up a list of the secrets that you do not want to have talked about, like today. Because it's very important for the therapist who sees the pair that comes each time for therapy, it is very important that he respects all these secrets, because the therapist doesn't know which secrets must not be discussed. So in this meeting you would have just before coming to the session, you first decide who is to come, and it should be at least two. Second, you should decide what secrets you want not to be revealed to the therapist, and when you come here at the beginning of the meeting, the two who come here must say to the therapist, "These are the secrets that we do not want to have talked about," because it's important that the therapist respect these secrets. Is it understood?*

---

CECCHIN: The structure of this intervention in very simple terms is the following: First, there is a positive connotation of the fact that the family is here. Second, the therapist addresses the double-bind situation created by the family with the message: "We are here, but we are not here." The therapist suggests a solution by inviting to each session only one couple. Third, he suggests a hierarchy of couples starting from the most to the least important.

BOSCOLO: I would include on your list the positive connotation of the referring doctor who sent the family to the clinic. The intervention can be considered a counterparadox in the sense that it matches the relational paradox the family creates with the therapist. As a family they communicate: "We are here, but we are not here; we talk, but we don't talk (we have secrets)." The therapist counterparadox is: the family does not have to come, only two of them have to come. When they come, they must bring a list of secrets, because it is important for the therapist to respect secrets.

CECCHIN: There is a subtle shifting of the problem here. Secrets become a therapist problem, not a family problem. The statement that the therapist has to have a list of secrets he should not talk about discharges the paradoxical situation created by the family and pushes it to an extreme, to the point of absurdity.

## INTERVENTION

GERTE: *The last sentence I did not understand.*

BOSCOLO: *What I was saying is that in this meeting that the whole family will have before coming here—the meeting you will have at home—you will decide who wants to or can come here. It is important that at least two come. As I said before, it could be your mother and you, your aunt and you, or your father and your aunt, and so on, and then you decide. Maybe the first couple that comes can bring a list of all the secrets that all of you decide are not to be revealed here. Understand? So, suppose the next time, Gerte, you can't come because you are not free or because you don't want to come, like today, and Mother and Father or Mother and aunt decide to come, you can tell them all the secrets that you*

*don't want revealed here. Am I clear? The ones that stay home must tell the ones who come here what secrets should be respected. So, for instance, if Mother and aunt or Mother and Karl come, the other ones will say to them "We do not want you to talk to the therapist about this, this, this." The ones who come here will tell the therapist "This is the secret they told us not to reveal." It is very important for the therapist to know this because it's very important that the therapist know the secrets that must not be talked about. All right?*
*[Family speaks in German.]*
BOSCOLO: *You think you understand now, Gerte?*
GERTE: *Yes.*
MOTHER: *Yes.*
BOSCOLO: *You understand?*
MOTHER: *Yes.*
BOSCOLO: *Right. So we can stop here, and I think it will be good if you come back here because we think this is strongly indicated.*
*[Family speaks in German.]*
BOSCOLO: *Thank you very much for the meeting.*
MOTHER: *I thank you too, very much.*
*[Family leaves.]*

———

BOSCOLO: After the therapist says that they should bring a list of secrets that they don't want to have talked about, Gerte—and only Gerte—says "I did not understand." All the other family members nod convincingly, as if they understand clearly. This is fascinating. The only person who can appreciate the "crazy" statement of the therapist is the "crazy member." Neither the parents nor the brother showed any reaction to the fact that bringing the therapist a list of secrets that he should keep will mean that they are no longer secrets.

## Follow-up

Three days after the consultation, the mother called the clinic and complained that the consultants did not give any useful, specific advice on how to deal with her daughter. She said the one who was most disappointed was her son. She then asked if the therapist assigned to them had been behind the one-way mirror during the consultation. The affirmative reply seemed to be appreciated. She asked again for the date of the next appointment but did not say who would come to it.

Mother and daughter came to the next session, which was not very fruitful. They both complained and refused to talk about the secrets. Mother again asked for advice. Gerte was not cooperative. Questioned on who she thought would come to the next appointment, she refused to answer.

The next session was attended by the mother and aunt. The therapist got a lot of interesting information on the important role played by the mother's sister in this family. She was the one who had first noticed that there was something wrong with Gerte. Over the years she kept giving advice to Mother, acting almost like a therapist. The bond between the sisters seemed very strong. The consultants' hypothesis about this being the most important "marriage" in the family was amply confirmed. Later on, there were several other sessions with different members of the family. In the fall of 1981, Gerte started to attend a rehabilitation center on a daily basis. Some time after this, the family terminated treatment.

# REFERENCES

Bateson G. (1979). *Mind and nature.* New York: Dutton.

Bateson, G. (1972). *Steps to an ecology of mind.* New York: Ballantine.

Bogdan, J. (1984). Family organization as an ecology of ideas. *Family Process, 23,* 375–388.

Boszormenyi-Nagy, I., & Sparks, G. (1973). *Invisible loyalties.* New York: Harper & Row.

Campbell, D., & Draper, R. (Eds.). (1985). *Applications of systemic therapy: The Milan method.* New York: Grune & Stratton.

Dell, P. (1982). Beyond homeostasis. *Family Process, 21,* 21–42.

Fisch, R., Weakland, J., & Segal, L. (1982). *The Tactics of change.* San Francisco: Jossey-Bass.

Fruggeri, L., Dotti, D., Ferrari, R., & Matteini, M. (1985). The systemic approach in a mental health service. In D. Campbell & R. Draper (Eds.), *Applications of systemic family therapy: The Milan method* (pp. 137–147). New York: Grune & Stratton.

Goldner, V. (1985). Feminism and family therapy. *Family Process, 24,* 31–47.

Haley, J. (1963). *Strategies of psychotherapy.* New York: Grune & Stratton.

Haley, J. (1976). Development of a theory: A history of a research project. In C. Sluzki & D. Ransom (Eds.), *Double bind: The foundation to the communicational approach to the family* (pp. 59–104). New York: Grune & Stratton.

Haley, J. (1977). *Problem-solving therapy.* San Francisco: Jossey-Bass.

Hoffman, L. (1983). A co-evolutionary framework for systemic family therapy. In J. Hansen & B. Keeney (Eds.), *Diagnosis and assessment in family therapy* (pp. 37–61). Rockville, MD: Aspen Systems Corp.

Hoffman, L. (1986). Beyond power and control: Toward a "second order" family systems therapy. *Family Systems Medicine, 4,* 381–396.

Keeney, B. (1983). *Aesthetics of change.* New York: Guilford Press.

Penn, P. (1985). Feed forward: Future questions, future maps. *Family Process, 24,* 299–311.

Rabkin, R. (1977). *Strategic psychotherapy: Brief and symptomatic treatment.* New York: Basic Books.

Selvini Palazzoli, M. (1980). Why a long interval between sessions. In M. Andolfi & I. Zwerling (Eds.), *Dimensions of family therapy* (pp. 161–169). New York: Guilford Press.

Selvini Palazzoli, M., Boscolo, L., Cecchin, G., & Prata, G. (1980). Hypothesizing-circularity-neutrality. *Family Process, 19,* 73–85.

Selvini Palazzoli, M., Boscolo, L., Cecchin, G., & Prata, G. (1980). The problem of the referring person. *Journal of Marital and Family Therapy, 6,* 3–9.

Selvini Palazzoli, M., Boscolo, L., Cecchin, G., & Prata, G. (1978). *Paradox and counterparadox.* New York: Jason Aronson.

Simon, R. (1987). Palazzoli and the Family Game. *The Family Therapy Networker,* September–October, 17–25.

Sluzki, C. & Ransom, D. (Eds.). (1976). *Double-bind: The foundation of the communicational approach to the family.* New York: Grune & Stratton.

Tomm, K. (1985). Circular interviewing: A multifaceted clinical tool. In D. Campbell & R. Draper (Eds.). *Applications of systemic family therapy: The Milan method* (pp. 33–45). New York: Grune & Stratton.

Von Foerster, H. (1981). *Observing systems.* Seaside, CA: Intersystems.

Von Glasenfeld, E. (1984). An Introduction to radical constructivism. In P. Watzlawick (Ed.), *The invented reality* (pp. 17–40). New York: Norton.

Watzlawick, P., Jackson, D., & Beavin, J. (1967). *Pragmatics of human communication.* New York: Norton.

Watzlawick, P., Weakland, J., & Fisch, R. (1974). *Change: Principles of problem formation and problem resolution.* New York: Norton.

# INDEX

Abuse issues, 179–80; *see also* Incest
Agreement questions, 96
Alliances, *see* Coalitions and alliances
Analogical behavior, 167, 187, 202, 215; co-
alitions revealed by, 114; historical data
and, 164; hypothesis based on, 196; and
questions about future, 124–25
Anorexia nervosa, 184, 186, 188, 191–202,
210, 212–18, 223–28, 232–34, 244, 251
Antipsychiatry movement, 20, 219–20

Blended families, 30–31, 74, 169
Boundary markers, family secrets as, 100
Brain hemispheres, 89

Canceled sessions, 238
Chronic patient, 49, 108, 216, 240, 287
Chronic therapist, 125, 216
Circular intervention, 53
Circularity, 9–11, 270
Circular questioning, 107, 157, 175, 184;
concept behind, 94, 96; development of,
10–11, 58–59; family secrets and, 100; future questions contrasted with, 34–35; hypothesis construction and, 67–68, 94–95;
as intervention, 71, 97; joining and, 153–
54, 195; labeling interrupted by, 29, 44, 53;
neutrality and, 96, 149–50; openings and,
11, 96–97; overly rigid, 195–96; resistance
and, 166; as Socratic method of inquiry,
96, 110; structure of problem system revealed by, 17; techniques of, 95–97; therapeutic jargon avoided in, 161; therapeutic
team functioning and, 32–33

Classification questions, 52, 72, 96, 202, 303
Coalitions and alliances, 43, 126, 318, 329;
analogical behavior as clue to, 114; clarified
in circular questioning, 96; hypotheses
about, 264, 314, 321–22; significance of,
114–15
Coalition theory, 7
Cognitive biologists, 19
Communication system, 43, 96, 326; family
secrets and, 142; hypotheses about, 264,
322; *see also* Double-bind communication
Comparison questions, 255–56
Confidentiality, 180
Consensus-sensitive trait, 249–50
Context, 21–22, 90–91, 153, 174; double, of
family and therapeutic team, 30–33; double
binds in, 322; education bound by, 151;
exploration of, 126; in public agencies, 155;
referring, 117, 154, 183–86, 265; significant
system concept and, 22–24, 107, 184; so-
cietal, 35, 80, 185, 219–21; therapeutic, 83,
151, 184, 212, 219, 221
Control of interview, 177–78, 195–96
Cotherapy, 25, 32, 66–69
Counterparadox, 6–7, 10, 324–28; *see also*
Paradoxical prescription
Countertransference, 13
Crying, 49, 54, 82, 133, 167; as message, 77–
78; as relational event, 113, 136
Cue word, 96, 153
Cybernetic circularity model, 9–10

Data, 96, 163; information vs., 106, 141
Death, 188, 205–6